SIGNING EXACT ENGLISH

SIGNING

EXACT

ENGLISH

revised and enlarged

1972 edition and supplements 1 and 2 in one alphabet

BY
GERILEE GUSTASON
DONNA PFETZING
ESTHER ZAWOLKOW

ILLUSTRATIONS BY
CAROLYN B. NORRIS

MODERN SIGNS PRESS

Library of Congress Catalog No. 75-24651

International Standard Book No. 0-916708-01-2

Signing Exact English is available
from   National Association of the Deaf
814 Thayer Avenue
Silver Spring, Maryland 20910

The publisher welcomes your comments
and suggestions on this and future editions.

Printed in The United States of America

Modern Signs Press wishes to express thanks to all those parents, teachers, and scholars, deaf and hearing, who have offered their time, suggestions, and signs for this and our previous book. Through classes, workshops, and conferences, the aid of too many to mention by name has been invaluable.

ABOUT THE AUTHORS

GERILEE GUSTASON was deafened by spinal meningitis at the age of six. After attending public schools in Nebraska and California, she entered the University of California at Riverside, graduating with a B.A. in English. Three masters' degrees followed, interspersed with teaching English to deaf students at the Virginia School for the Deaf, Gallaudet College, and public day classes in Southern California. A Ph.D. in educational psychology was awarded by the University of Southern California in 1972. She is now Associate Professor of Education at Gallaudet College.

DONNA PFETZING was the mother of a daughter deafened by rubella. After meeting the frustrations of pure oral programs, she became interested in learning the new signs to help her daughter's language development. She was employed as Head Interpreter using the new signs at a junior high school in Southern California and taught several adult education classes to parents and teachers working with young deaf children. She died of bone cancer in March, 1976.

ESTHER ZAWOLKOW, daughter of deaf parents, has known traditional sign language all her life, and has her comprehensive Skills Certificate from the Registry of Interpreters for the Deaf, Inc. She came into contact with the new signs in Southern California and now uses them daily in her work as Head Interpreter for a public day program at the high school level there. She also teaches adult education classes in sign language.

CAROLYN B. NORRIS taught English to the deaf for several years at Gallaudet College before moving to California. Now she does free-lance writing and art work, including publishing sign language primers and other aids for deaf children for Alinda Press. She holds a Ph.D. in English from the University of Maryland. She has also written a novel, Island of Silence, about the deaf.

TABLE OF CONTENTS

Introduction

In January, 1969, a group of deaf individuals, parents of deaf children, children of deaf parents, teachers of the deaf, and interpreters met in southern California to become the first organized venture in Seeing Essential English. From this group developed three published systems: Seeing Essential English by David Anthony, Linguistics of Visual English by Dennis Wampler, and Signing Exact English.

As was pointed out in the winter 1975-75 issue of Gallaudet Today, "the main concern of the original group was the consistent, logical, rational, and practical development of signs to represent as specifically as possible the basic essentials of the English language. This concern sprang from the experience of all present with the poor English skills of many deaf students, and the desire for an easier, more successful way of developing mastery of English in a far greater number of such students". (Gustason, 1975)

The educational retardation of deaf students has been well documented over the years, and has caused deep and widespread concern. In 1965, the Secretary of Health, Education and Welfare's Advisory Committee on Education of the Deaf stated in the Babbidge report that

> the American people have no reason to be satisfied with
> their limited success in educating deaf children and pre-
> paring them for full participation in our society. . . the
> average graduate of a public residential school for the
> deaf ... has an eighth grade education. (Babbidge, 1965)

i

The same committee found the median grade average of 920 students leaving reporting public residential schools in 1963-64 was 6.0; of the 16-year-olds leaving the median was 4.5.

Reading achievement scores and language test scores for the deaf have been uniformly low for at least fifty years, those of older deaf students hovering around the level attained by fourth and fifth grade hearing children, (Wrightstone, Aranow, and Muskowitz, 1963; Office of Demographic Studies, 1969: Goetzinger and Rousey, 1959, Pugh, 1946.) Eighty-eight per cent of 1075 deaf students over the age of 15-½ scored below grade level 4.9 in reading in Wrightstone's 1963 survey, and some thirty per cent of deaf students aged sixteen and older were classified as functionally illiterate by Boatner(1965) and McClure (1966). A 1918 fill-in-the-blanks language test given 1098 deaf students at all grade levels found the average for fourth grade hearing children higher than the average for any grade level of the deaf. (Bintner, 1918).

Yet a number of studies have shown that deaf children have at least average intelligence. (Vernon, 1969). For every study indicating a lower level of intelligence in the deaf than in the hearing (Peterson, 1948; Shirley and Goodenough, 1932; Graham and Shapiro, 1953; Springer, 1938; Zeckel and Kalb, 1939), another study points to average or above average intelligence (MacPherson and Lane, 1932; Bishop, 1936; Scyster, 1936; Myklebust, 1948; Ross, 1953; Goetzinger and Rousey, 1957).

Assuming average intellectual abilities, the academic nonachievement takes on a new dimension, and it is less surprising that little correlation has been found between intelligence and either language or reading scores. (Hart and Rosenstein, 1964).

Language implies communication. It is reasonable to assume that teaching most academic subjects will be extremely difficult, if not impossible, unless some means of communication exists between teacher and student. This communication may be some form of reward or punishment. It may be nonverbal body language---a smile, a frown, a shake of the head. It may be highly technical verbal communication. The deaf are quite accurate at reading nonverbal body language (Fast, 1970), but as noted above, have a great deal of trouble with verbal communication in English.

Language studies of hearing children have brought to light some sobering facts: these children have mastered a great deal of the structure of English, including basic sentence patterns and inflections, by the age of three; their language is fairly stable by age six, and language habits are extremely difficult to modify after the age of puberty. Between two and three years of age, a great jump is made, including the development of prepositions, demonstratives, auxiliaries, articles, conjunctions, possessive and personal pronouns, the past tense suffix, the plural suffix, and the possessive suffix. (Braine, 1963; Brown and Bellugi, 1964; Caxden, 1968; Slobin, 1965; Velten, 1943; Weir, 1962; Penfield, 1964; Hockett, 1950; Labov, 1965; Morkovin, 1963).

Children, in short, learn the language of their environment, be it
Chinese or French or standard English or nonstandard English. Deaf
children, on the other hand, have specific areas of weakness in their
grasp of English. They omit necessary words and use wrong words. These
errors comprise approximately half of their syntax errors (Thompson, 1936;
Myklebust, 1965). They use sentence structures simpler and more rigid
than those of hearing children, those of 17-year-old deaf students compar-
able to those of eight-year-old hearing children (Heider and Heider, 1940).
They learn lexical meanings more easily than structural meanings (Hart
and Rosenstein, 1964), indicating their inability to deduce meaning from
context. No consistent pattern of development is exhibited by deaf
children in the mastery of inflections or structure (Cooper, 1965), and
they use fewer adverbs, auxiliaries, and conjunctions than do hearing
children (Simmons, 1962)

The message is clear. Deaf children must be exposed as young as
possible to English if we want them to learn it well, and since input
must precede output we need to make sure that their perception of the
language is as unclouded as possible.

Since 40 to 60 per cent of the sounds of English look like some other
sound on the lips (Vernon, 1969), it is not surprising that even the best
of speechreaders with a ready command of English have problems (Lowell,
1957-58 and 1969). Speechreading alone is thus rejected as an in-
complete presentation of English. "Young children do not ordinarily
differentiate the parts of what they perceive, especially if the stimuli
are unfamiliar or have no meaning for them. They perceive largely
in terms of context." (Mussen, 1963) Although three-year-old hearing

iv

children, as noted above, are well on their way to the mastery of tenses and function words, as one study has pointed out

> in lipreading...the child does not perceive every word
> in an utterance, but rather, catches the key words, or
> even only the root parts of words (e.g. BOY instead of
> BOYS, WALK instead of WALKED). The words that are
> ignored are words that are not understood, as well as
> the function words (e.g. TO, THE, AT, FOR) that tie the
> communication together. (Hart and Rosenstein, 1964)

Fingerspelling is larger and easier to perceive than speechreading, but there is still a perception difficulty, even for adults. Few would catch the spelling of an unusual proper name the first time it is presented at normal speed. In fingerspelling, as in speechreading, gaps are often filled in through knowledge of the structure of the language. There is also the problem of eye fatigue. To satisfactorily replace the great amount of effortless reception of aural stimuli in the optimum language learning years with either speechreading or fingerspelling requires attention and concentration on the part of the child, and a visual perception of which he may not yet be capable.

Signs present larger, more discrete symbols in communication than either speech or fingerspelling and are thus easier for very young deaf children to pick up. With this advantage in communicating, it is not surprising that deaf children of deaf parents, able to communicate from infancy, enter school more advanced than deaf children of hearing parents, and maintain this advantage throughout school. (Meadow, 1967; Montgomery, 1966; Quigley and Frisina, 1961; Stevenson, 1964; Stuckless and Birch, 1966; Vernon, 1968)

However, American Sign Language is a language in its own right, and this language is not a visual representation of English. (Stokoe, 1970;

1960, 1971; Bergman, 1972; Bellugi and Klima, 1972; Bragg, 1973; Fant, 1971, 1974). Its structure is different from that of English, and the symbols represent concepts rather than English words. A child learning American Sign Language at an early age has communication, but he must still learn English if he wishes to function well in our society, and he must learn it as a different form of communication. Moreover, the difference in structure and symbolism makes ASL a difficult language for many hearing people to master. Since most deaf children have hearing parents whose native language. is English (Office of Demographic Studies, 1971), we suggest that these parents can most comfortably learn to sign English and so expose their child to their own native language, rather than learn ASL and have the child later learn English as a second language. What we would like to see is parents and teachers who treat both American Sign Language and English with respect, who use their own native language (be it ASL or English) with the child, and actively encourage him to learn BOTH.

Our interest in and development of signs for the signing of English has led many concerned individuals to believe that we wish to eliminate Ameslan. This we in no way wish to do. (Gustason, Pfetzing, Zawolkow, 1974) We consider Ameslan a beautiful and expressive language, and are delighted with the increased study it is receiving both by linguists and in classes. We encourage those who work with the adult deaf to learn Ameslan. Our goal is for deaf children to be truly bilingual, at ease in both Ameslan and English. Ideally, we would like to see teachers trained in both who could combine or otherwise utilize the two in and out of the classroom in a variety of ways to enrich the language experiences of the students. We consider Signing Exact English a teaching tool, (both for young children and for older students of English as a second language), a means of manual expression for those who are speaking English, and an introduction to the richness and variety of signs for parents of young deaf children. We would like to see the best of both languages in as many hands as possible.

PRINCIPLES

The most important principle in Signing Exact English is that <u>English should be signed as it is spoken for the deaf child to have a linguistic input that would result in his mastery of English</u>. This means, for instance, that idioms such as "dry up" or "cut it out" will be signed as those exact words, rather than as "quiet" or finish". It also means that inflections must be shown, such as talk<u>s</u>, talk<u>ed</u>, talk<u>ing</u>, govern-<u>ment</u>. A second important principle is that <u>a sign should be translatable to only one English equivalent</u>. Initialized signs contribute a great deal here, providing synonyms such as hurt, pain, ache, and so on. But this principle also means that a common sign needs to be used for such English words as "run", which has a number of different translations in Ameslan. These two principles, an attempt to provide a visual mode of representing English, led to a number of problems and jokes. How did one sign "I <u>saw</u> you yesterday" or "I <u>left</u> home yesterday"? Or right, rite, and write? In an attempt to come to grips with these problems in a sensible way, more principles were developed.

Words are considered in three groups: 1) Basic, 2) Compound, and 3) Complex.

1) BASIC words are words that can have no more taken away and still form a complete word ("girl","talk","the"). For these basic words, the three-point criteria of spelling, sound, and meaning is utilized. If any two of these three factors are the same, the same sign is used. Hence the same sign is used for "run" in "The boys will run, the motor will run, your nose will run," and so on, since spelling and sound were the same and only meaning varies. However, a different sign is used for "wind" in the "wind is blowing, I must wind my watch," since only spelling is the same.

2) COMPLEX words are defined as basic words with the addition of an affix or inflection: "girls","talked". Once such an inflection or affix has been added to a word, the combination is no longer considered a basic word. Accordingly, when the past tense is added to "see" to produce "saw", this is not the same as the basic word for the verb "to saw". An affix is added in signs if it is added in English, regardless of the part of speech. The suffix -s, for instance, is used for both regular plurals ("girls") and the third person singular of verbs ("runs").

3) COMPOUND words are two or more basic words put together, and the source of many jokes and misunderstandings. If the meaning of the words separately is consistent with the meaning of the words together, then and only then are they signed as the component words. Thus "underline" is signed under-line, but "understand", having no relation to the meaning of the words "under" and "stand", is NOT signed under-stand.

When a sign already exists in Ameslan for a given English word, this sign is retained if it is clear and unambiguous, having only one English translation (e.g. "girl","home","know", etc.) As Bornstein (1973) points out, in the original Signing Exact English book, 61% are Ameslan signs, 18% are Ameslan signs modified through the use of initialization or a similar adaptation, and 21% are new signs. In many cases we will in practice use such an unambiguous sign for a compound or complex word (e.g. "careless", "misunderstand","can't") that could, by following the principles outlined above, be signed as its component parts. This is done when ease and economy of movement become possible with no loss of clear, unambiguous English, to maintain as much relation as possible with the existing signs of Ameslan. It is our hope that users will be comfortable with either way of signing

x

a given word, and use the one they prefer while understanding that others may choose the alternate way of signing it.

In the selection of any given sign, the authors have drawn upon existing signs whenever possible in consultation with native signers and professionals working with deaf adults and children, and checked many existing books of signs to determine what, if anything, already exists. The vocabulary in this book is a compilation of the first basic book of Signing Exact English, published in 1972, and the two supplements, published in 1973 and 1975. A few signs differ from those in the first two volumes; the changes that were made were done as a result of extensive use of these signs.

In this book, we are dispensing with the index utilized in the first books in favor of a dictionary-type approach, where all words can be found in alphabetical order. To aid in teaching and learning these signs, groups or families of words are provided. We believe this approach will be the most helpful.

We would like to stress that the rapidly growing interest in signs has resulted in variations in new signs as well as in already existing signs. There have always been, for instance, local variations in signs used for English words such as "early","football","slow". There are now variations in signs used for English words such as "would","could","the". The sign a person uses depends, and should depend, on what is popular usage in his locality.

We would also like to see as many as possible become familiar with the upsurge of books and articles concerning signs, and provide a bibliography here as a starting point.

THE PLEDGE of ALLEGIANCE

I   pledge   allegiance

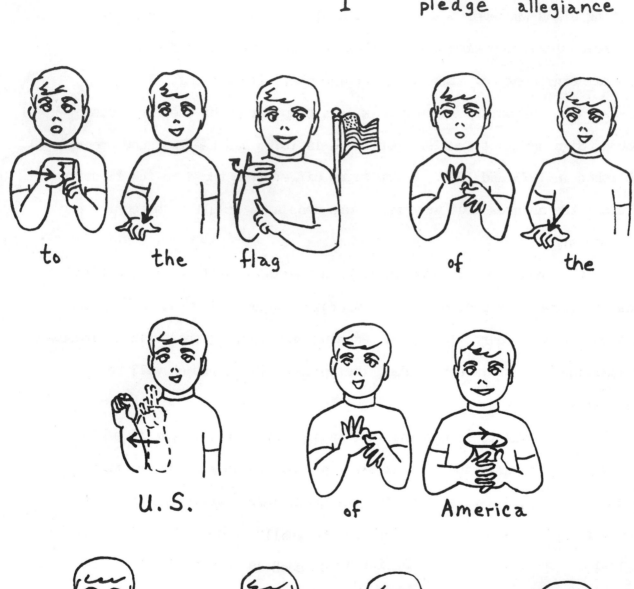

to   the   flag   of   the

U.S.   of   America

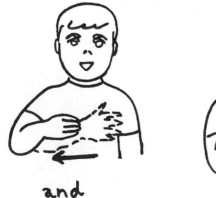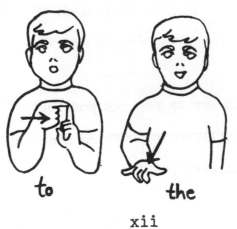

and   to   the   Republic

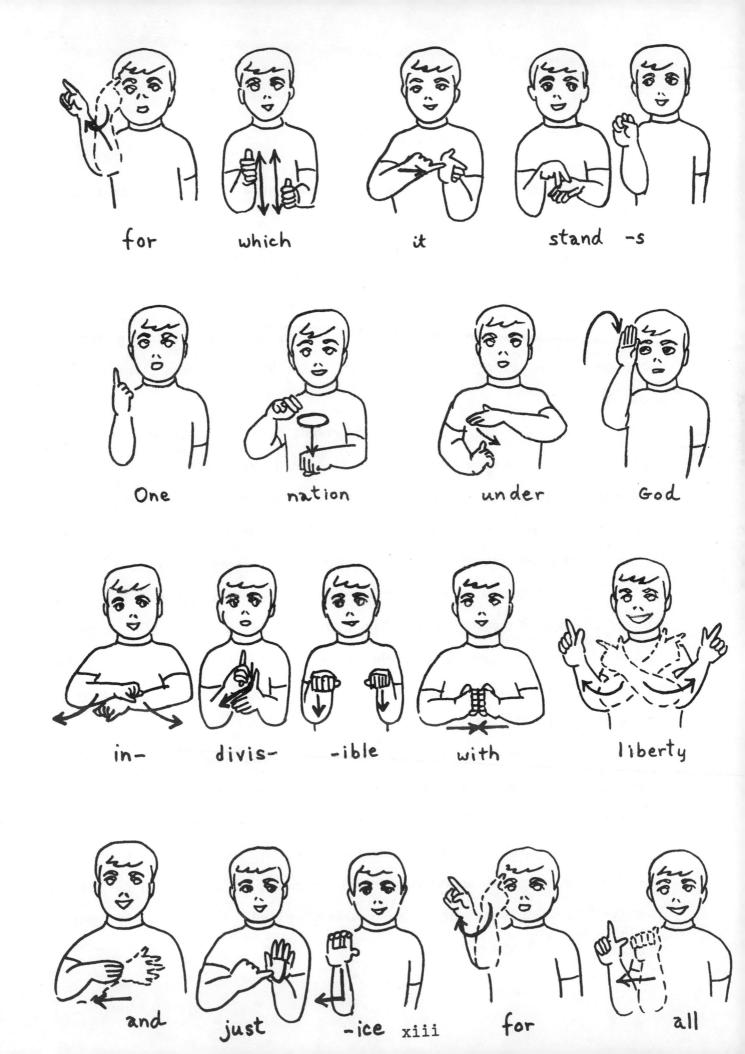

for   which   it   stand -s

One   nation   under   God

in-   divis-   -ible   with   liberty

and   just   -ice xiii   for   all

POINTS TO REMEMBER

Form of hands, position of hands, and movement - if any - are shown in various ways:

1. Arrows show direction and line of movement.
2. Dotted hands represent original positions.
3. Pairs of pictures (1 and 2) show movement too complex for the use of dotted original positions.

Hands are usually in the form of a letter of the alphabet or a number. Modifications are shown, such as "flat O", "bent V", "claw hand", and "bent hand".

Some hand forms are difficult to represent clearly in only one drawing such as those on the alphabet page. It will help you to glance at pictures in the text that use the same form, until you understand and can use that form ("parsnip" and "party" show more P-hands, for example).

Note whether movement is to be repeated. Pay special attention to whether there is touching, brushing, striking or merely an approaching motion. For a right-handed person, usually the right hand is the active hand. "Right" in the directions refers to the right of the person signing - you. Left-handed persons may reverse the hands. Do not, however, make a habit of switching from one hand to the other for movements.

Pictures of the words represented are used, when possible, to aid in understanding why the sign is made as it is (see "hippopotamus","child", "caterpillar"), and we also feel pictures will aid the preschool child.

The affixes and word-endings for tense, person, number and so forth, should not be made with an emphasis equal to that used in the sign for the word itself. Be guided by the practice in spoken English. You do not say "swing -ING", "walk -ED" , or "horse -ES".

Another way to make your signing smooth and clear instead of rigid and arbitrary is to add appropriate expression. In signing pronouns, for instance, if the person referred to is present, sign "he" or "she", "him" or "her" in the person's direction. In showing "fear" of something on your right, do not make the sign toward your left, though in expressing an abstract fear you would follow the directions and do just that.

Some signs can vary somewhat in number of times performed or in the vigor of performance, when you are expressing emotion. A "big" dog is smaller than a "big" dinosaur, for example. "Sympathy" can be more or less intense, as shown by the motion in signing the word.

You must make your own judgement after carefully studying the directions for making each sign. Always speak when you sign, and let facial expressions and body-English aid communication.

THE ALPHABET

From in front of the
speller

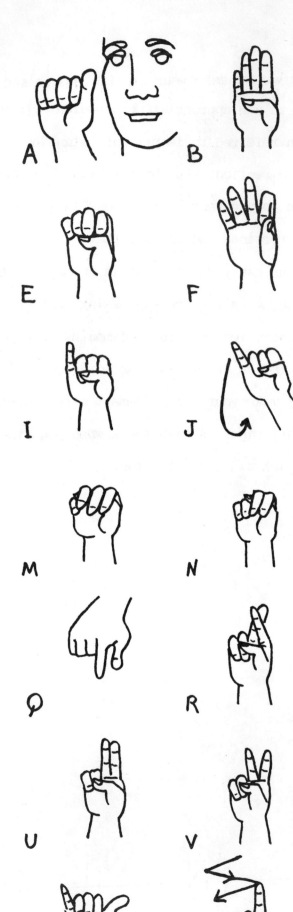

A   B

C   D   E   F

G   H   I   J

K   L   M   N

O   P   Q   R

S   T   U   V

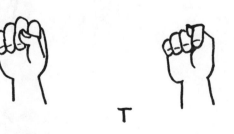
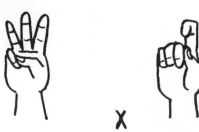

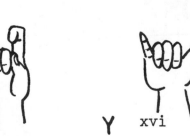
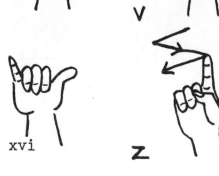

W   X   Y   xvi   Z

HAND SHAPES

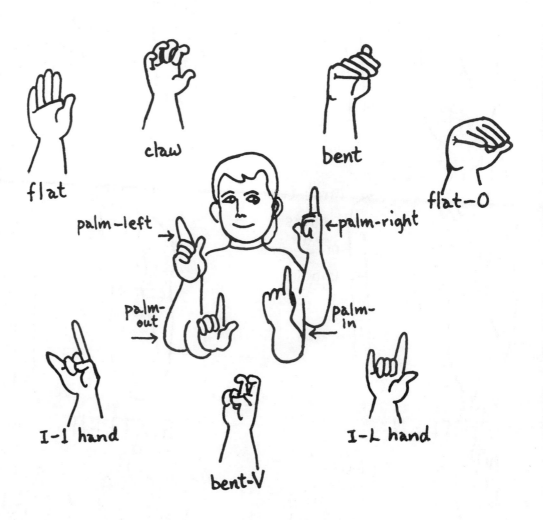

flat

claw

bent

flat-O

palm-left →

← palm-right

palm-out →

← palm-in

I-1 hand

bent-V

I-L hand

NUMBERS

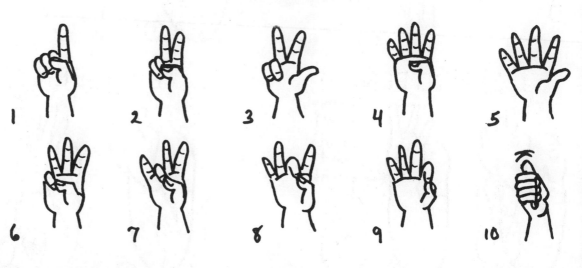

1   2   3   4   5

6   7   8   9   10

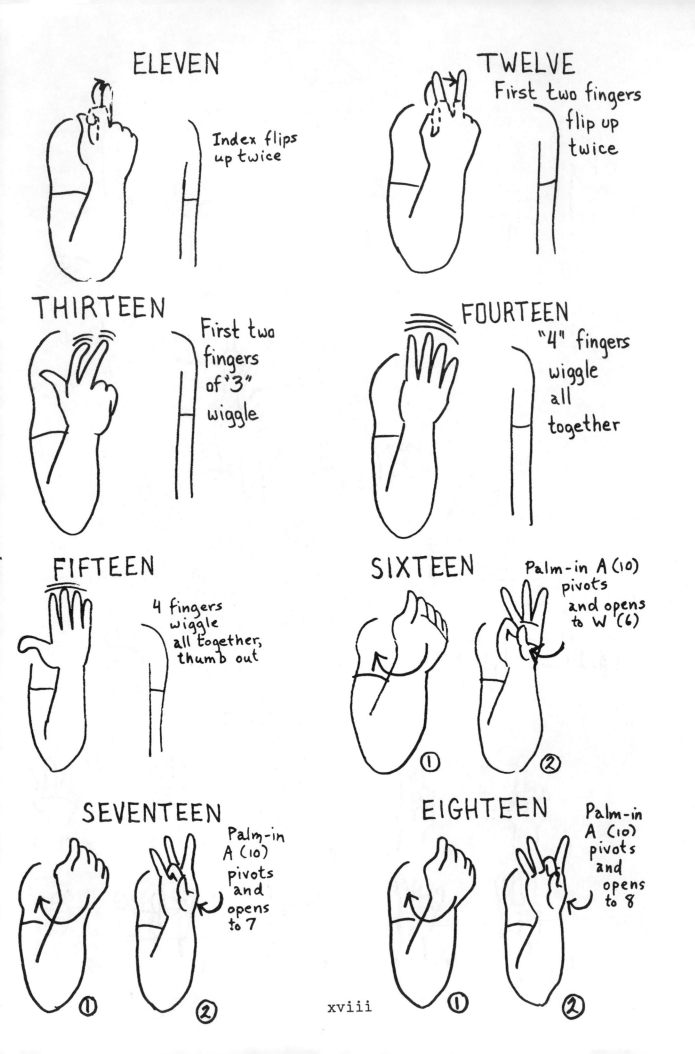

ELEVEN

Index flips up twice

TWELVE
First two fingers flip up twice

THIRTEEN

First two fingers of "3" wiggle

FOURTEEN

"4" fingers wiggle all together

FIFTEEN

4 fingers wiggle all together, thumb out

SIXTEEN

Palm-in A (10) pivots and opens to W (6)

① ②

SEVENTEEN

Palm-in A (10) pivots and opens to 7

① ②

EIGHTEEN

Palm-in A (10) pivots and opens to 8

① ②

NINETEEN

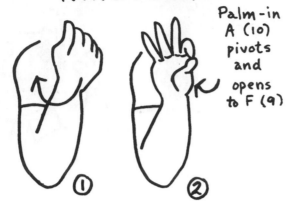

Palm-in
A (10)
pivots
and
opens
to F (9)

TWENTY

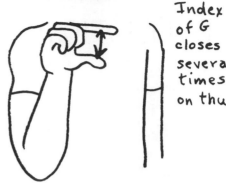

Index
of G
closes
several
times
on thumb

TWENTY-ONE

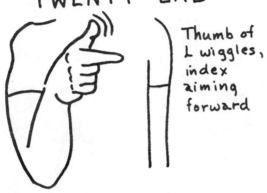

Thumb of
L wiggles,
index
aiming
forward

TWENTY-TWO

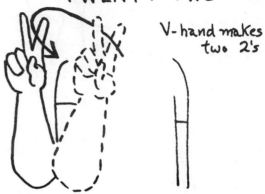

V-hand makes
two 2's

TWENTY-THREE

"L" + 3

TWENTY-FOUR

"L" + 4

TWENTY-FIVE

Middle
two fingers
wiggle
together

26 to 29
are
"L" + 6,7,8, +9   xix

THIRTY

"3" + "0"

40, 50, 60,
70, 80, and
90
all are the
number
plus "0"

CONTRACTIONS

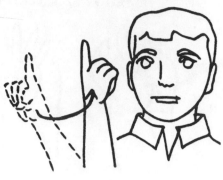

'D
Palm-out
D twists
inward

'LL
Palm-out
L twists
inward

'M
Palm-out
M
twists
inward

N'T
Palm-out
N twists
inward

'RE
Palm-out
R twists
inward

'S
Palm-out
S twists
inward

'VE
Palm-out
V twists
inward

AFFIXES

-AGE

Side of G
slides down
palm

-ANT, -ENT

Side of t slides
down palm

ANTE-

Move A-hand toward body
from left palm

ANTI-

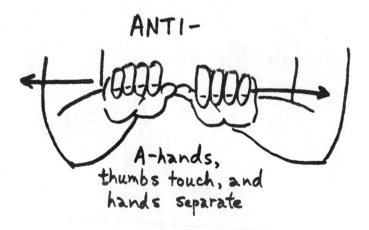

A-hands,
thumbs touch, and
hands separate

-ATE

Drop palm-out
A down, then
move slightly
right

DIS-   D's crossed at wrist
Separate sideways as in "not"

(See
"not")

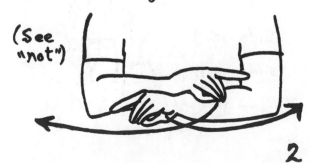

-DOM

D on back of
hand circles
out, left,
and back
along arm
(See "ground")

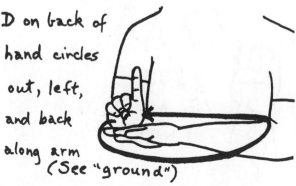

2

-E

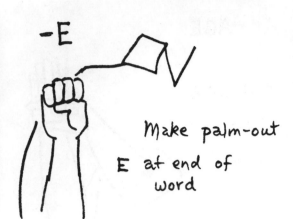

Make palm-out
E at end of
word

-ED AND past tense

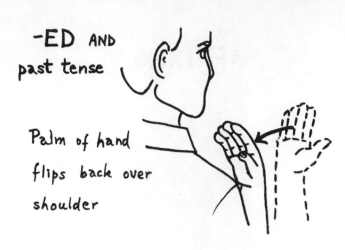

Palm of hand
flips back over
shoulder

-EE

Move E slightly
to the right

-EN and past participle
Flat hands twist to face each other

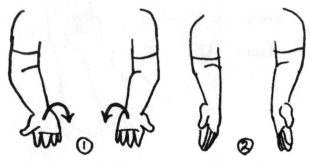

-ENCE, -ANCE

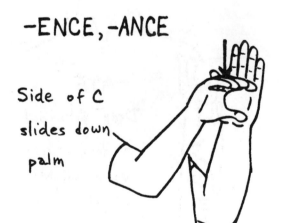

Side of C
slides down
palm

-ER, -AR, -OR

Palm-out R

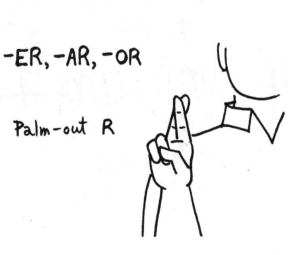

-ESE

E moves down in
a wavy motion

-ESS

Side of S
slides along
jaw forward

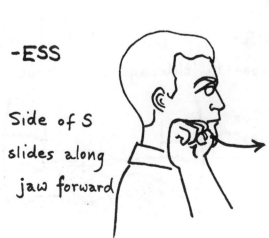

-EST

A-hands together; right moves up

-IC

Palm-out C

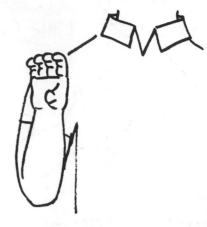

-ICE

Palm-out C moves slightly down, then right

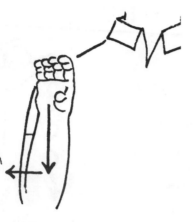

-IFY

F's, resting-right upon left — pivot as in "make"

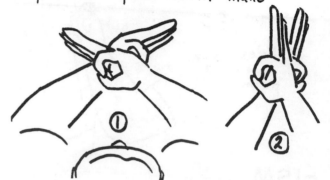

IL-, IM-, IR-, IN-

Palm-down I-hands cross at wrists, separate sideways (See "not")

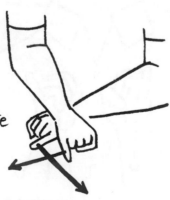

-ILE

Drop L straight down, then move slightly right

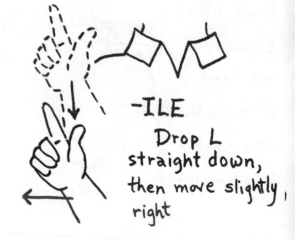

-INE

Drop palm-out N down, then move slightly right

4

-ING

I-hand twists in slight downward arc to right

INTER-

Little finger of **I** weaves among fingers

INTRA-

Little finger of **I** bounces between fingers

-ION, -TION, -SION

Side of S slides down palm

- ISH

I draws wavy downward line

-ISM

Hook little fingers, one hand palm-up, the other palm-down; reverse

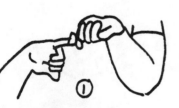
①

②

-IST
Drop I's straight down

(See "person")

-ITE
Drop palm-out T down, then move slightly right

-ITY, -ICITY

Thumbtip of Y slides down palm

-IVE

Palm-out V
shakes
downward

-IZE   I's, resting—right
on left — pivot as in "make"

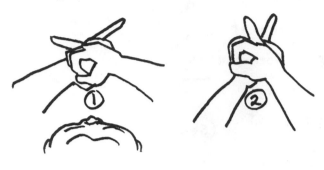

-LY

Palm-out
hand shakes
downward

-MENT

Side of
M slides
down
palm

'NEATH, -NEATH
N circles below palm

Beneath = be + -neath, Underneath = under + -neath
(See "base")

-NESS

Side of N
slides down
palm

-OUS

Palm-out
O
draws
a "U"

PRE-   P moves inward from
palm

(See "fore")

6

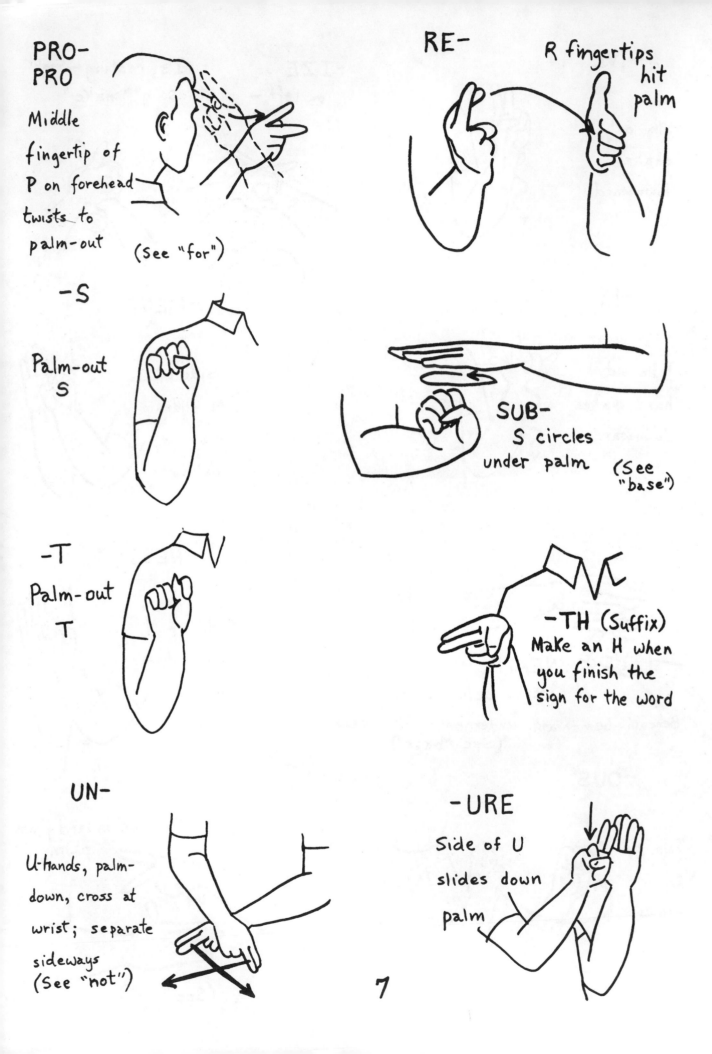

PRO-PRO

Middle fingertip of P on forehead twists to palm-out

(See "for")

RE-

R fingertips hit palm

-S

Palm-out S

SUB-

S circles under palm

(See "base")

-T

Palm-out T

-TH (Suffix)

Make an H when you finish the sign for the word

UN-

U-hands, palm-down, cross at wrist; separate sideways

(See "not")

-URE

Side of U slides down palm

7

YESTER-

Thumbtip
of Y near
chin, then
near ear

-Y

Palm-out
Y shakes
slightly

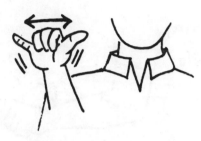

A (article)

Palm-out
A moves
slightly right

ABBREVIATE

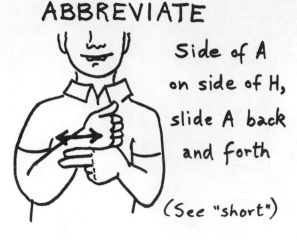

Side of A
on side of H,
slide A back
and forth

(See "short")

ABLE, -ABLE (suffix), -IBLE

Palm-down
A's drop
slightly

ABORT

A-thumb
slides off
back of S

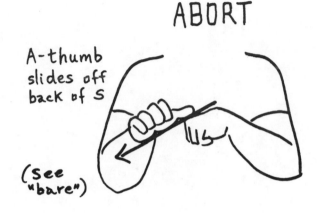

(See
"bare")

ABOUT

Index finger
circles
the tip
of flat-
O hand

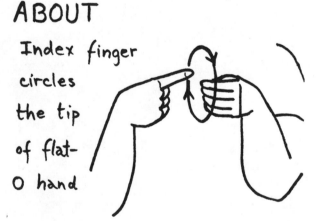

ABOVE

Palm
circles
once
over
head

ABSENT

Right index clips
bent middle finger
of palm-down
hand, right
to left

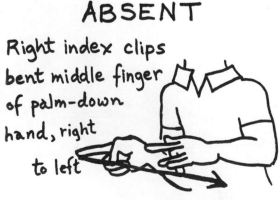

Absence = absent + -ence

ABSTRACT

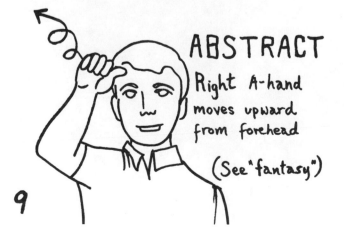

Right A-hand
moves upward
from forehead

(See "fantasy")

9

ACCEPT Palm-down flat hands rise to flat-O's on chest, pointing toward each other

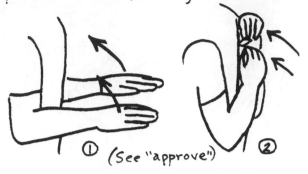

① (See "approve") ②

ACCIDENT Palm-in A's at sides hit knuckles together

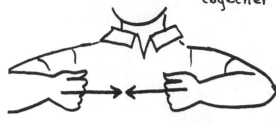

ACCOMPLISH C-hands facing temples twist out and up twice as palm-out C's

(See "success")

ACCUSE

A drops to hit top side of index

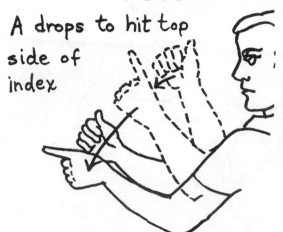

ACHE

Palm-out A's jerk toward each other; repeat
(See "hurt")

ACHIEVE Palm-out, A's twist out and up twice

(See "success")

ACQUAINT

Rest A-thumbs first right on left, then left on right
(See "friend")

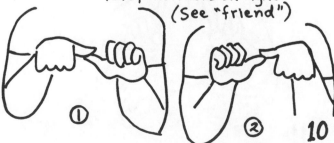

① ② **10**

ACROSS Right palm-left hand arcs across palm-down hand

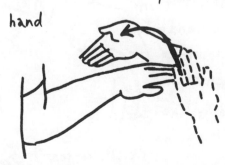

ACT

Thumbs of A-hands brush alternately down chest, hands facing each other

ADAPT
A - palms together, reverse position, right changing to D (See change)

① ②

ADD
Five-hand to flat-O rises to touch little-finger side of palm-in left hand
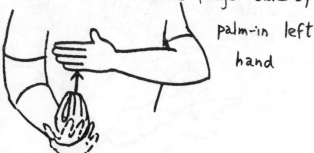

ADDRESS
Palm-in A-hands move up body once

ADJUST
A-palms together, reverse position, right changing to i
(See "change")
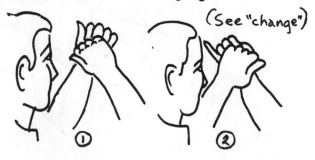
① ②

ADMIRE
A arcs in toward forehead, down and outward
(See "god")

ADMIT
A-hands on chest turn over and out to palm-up open hands
Admission = admit +-tion
(See "confess")

ADOPT
Palm-down 5's up to d's

(See "assume")

11

ADULT

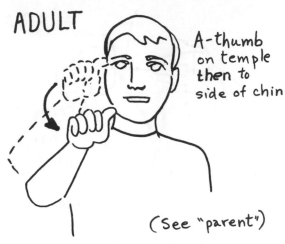

A-thumb on temple then to side of chin

(See "parent")

ADVANCE

Bent hands move up several levels

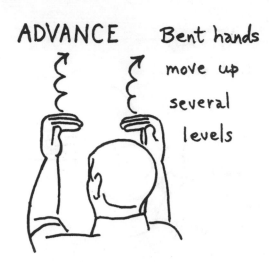

ADVERTISE

Right S in front of left, right moves forward and back, twice

ADVICE ♥

Right flat-O set on back of hand moves forward to palm-down 5

ADVISE

Right flat-O set on back of hand moves forward to palm-down V

(See "advice")

AFFECT

A moves forward off stationary left hand

(See "advice")

AFRAID ♥

Slightly to left, palm-out A's move downward in shaking motion

AFRICA

Palm-left A-hand circles once, sideways in front of nose, then thumb touches nose

African = Africa + -an

12

AFTER

Right palm on back of left hand; twists out to palm-out R

AGAIN

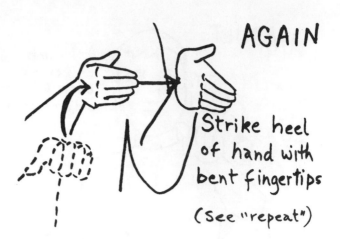

Strike heel of hand with bent fingertips

(See "repeat")

AGAINST

Fingertips of flat hand hit palm at right angles

AGE

A circles, then touches palm

(See "hour")

AGO

Palm-down A twists up and back over shoulder, opening to G

① ②

AGREE

Touch forehead with index finger, then drop to index fingers together

AHEAD

A-hands together; right arcs forward

① ②

AID

Right A pushes left A upward, both palm-in

(See "help")

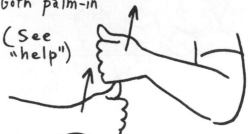

13

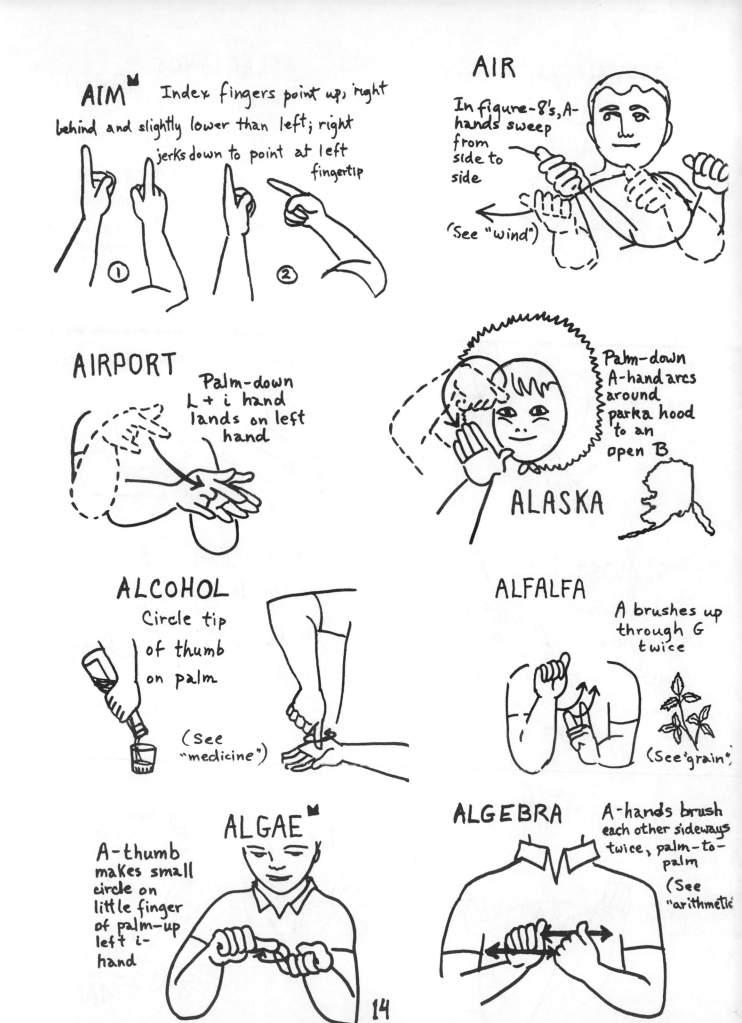

AIM Index fingers point up, right behind and slightly lower than left; right jerks down to point at left fingertip

① ②

AIR In figure-8's, A-hands sweep from side to side

(See "wind")

AIRPORT Palm-down L + i hand lands on left hand

Palm-down A-hand arcs around parka hood to an open B

ALASKA

ALCOHOL Circle tip of thumb on palm

(See "medicine")

ALFALFA A brushes up through G twice

(See "grain")

ALGAE A-thumb makes small circle on little finger of palm-up left i-hand

ALGEBRA A-hands brush each other sideways twice, palm-to-palm

(See "arithmetic")

14

ALL, AL-, -AL (Affixes)

Palm-out A slides right, changing to L

ALLEGIANCE
Palm-in S pushes L up

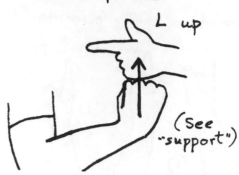

(see "support")

ALLIGATOR

Snap top "jaw" open and closed, heels touching

ALLOW ᴹ Hands point downward, swing upwards, still parallel

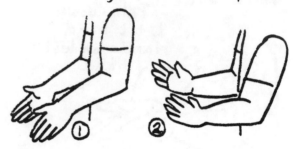

ALMOST
Stroke upwards off back of fingers once

ALONG   Heel of A slides up arm to elbow

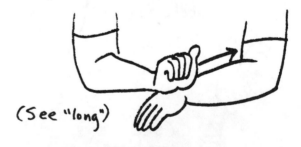

(See "long")

ALPHABET ᴹ

A-hand moves across 5-fingers, changing to B

ALREADY
A-hands swing inward and down; repeat, ending in palm-down 5's

15

ALTAR
Separate and move down A-hands

ALTER
A-palms together, reverse position, right changing to L

(See "change")

ALUMINUM
Hit A-thumb down in arc on index of B-hand

(See "metal")

ALWAYS
Palm-up index, pointing forward, circles clockwise

AM
Thumbtip of A on lips; move forward

AMAZE
Palm-out A-hands circle near eyes flick index and thumb out

(see "fabulous")

AMBITION
Thumbs of A's brush alternately up chest

(reverse of "act")

AMBULANCE
Thumb of A draws cross on left upper arm, across then down

(See "hospital")

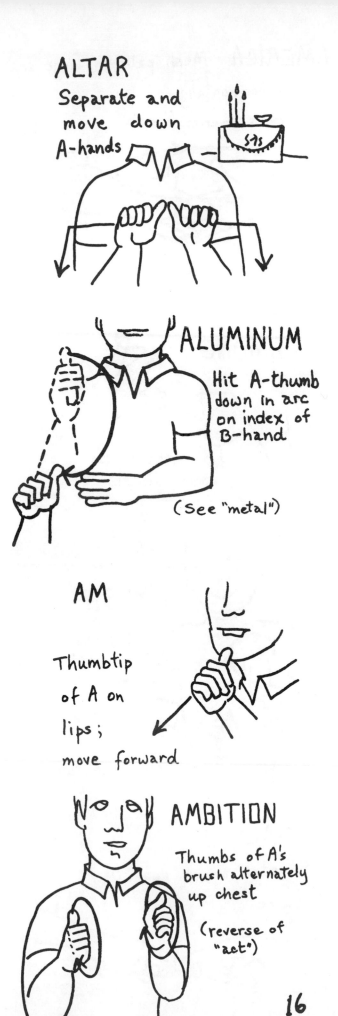

16

AMEND
A-palms together, reverse position, right changing to M

(See "change")

① ②

AMERICA
Mesh palm-in fingers, circle horizontally

American = America + -an

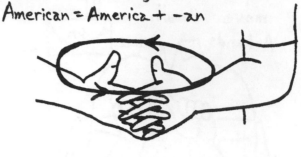

AMESLAN   (AMERICAN SIGN LANG.)
Circle alternately and pull out to L's

①

②

AMONG

Finger weaves among fingers

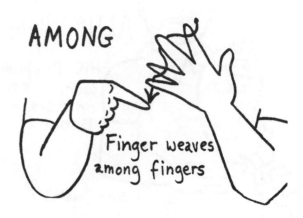

AMOUNT
of hand to fingers as you outline an "amount"

A-thumb on heel side of A on left

(See "pile")

AMUSE

Rub sides of A's in opposing circles on chest and stomach

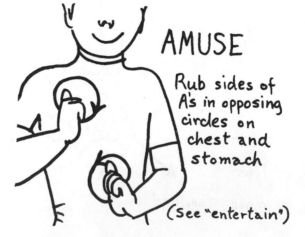

(See "entertain")

AN , -AN (suffix), AN- (prefix)

Palm-up A twists to palm-down

Any = an + -y

ANALYZE
Stretch apart bent-V's twice

17

ANCESTOR

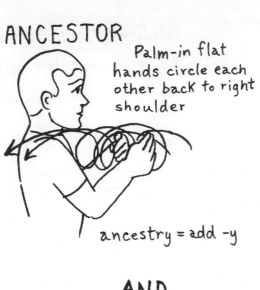

Palm-in flat hands circle each other back to right shoulder

ancestry = add -y

ANCIENT

Left A-thumb supporting right A, move down together in wavy motion

AND

Palm-in, pull 5 to right; close to a flat-O

ANGEL

Fingertips on shoulders swing out

ANGER

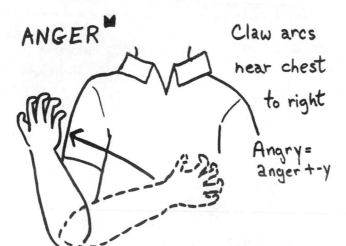

Claw arcs near chest to right

Angry = anger +-y

ANGLE

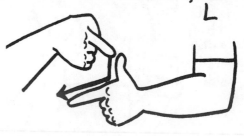

Index finger traces angle of left L

ANIMAL

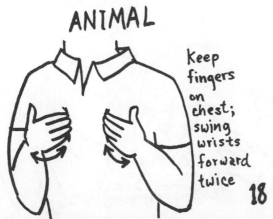

keep fingers on chest; swing wrists forward twice

18

ANNOUNCE

Palm-in index fingers at sides of mouth twist out and sideways to palm-out

(See "proclaim")

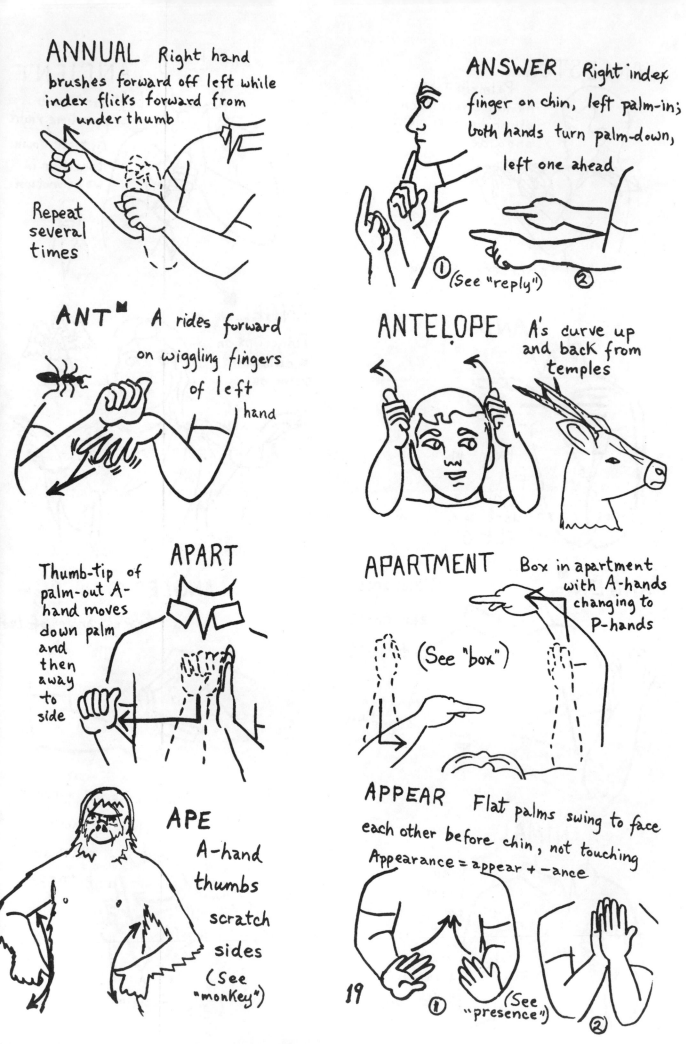

ANNUAL Right hand brushes forward off left while index flicks forward from under thumb

Repeat several times

ANSWER Right index finger on chin, left palm-in; both hands turn palm-down, left one ahead

① (see "reply") ②

ANT A rides forward on wiggling fingers of left hand

ANTELOPE A's curve up and back from temples

APART Thumb-tip of palm-out A-hand moves down palm and then away to side

APARTMENT Box in apartment with A-hands changing to P-hands

(See "box")

APE A-hand thumbs scratch sides (See "monkey")

APPEAR Flat palms swing to face each other before chin, not touching
Appearance = appear + -ance

① ② (See "presence")

19

APPETITE
A-hand moves down chest once
(See "hunger")

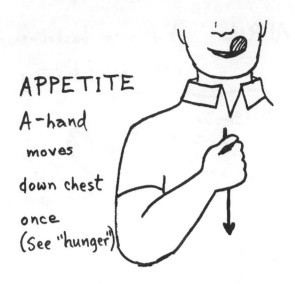

APPLAUSE
Clap several times quickly

applaud= add -d

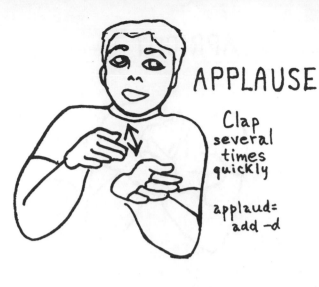

APPLE
Twist X against corner of mouth

APPLY
V falls over left index

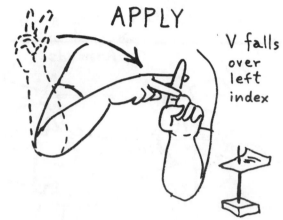

APPOINT
Right A circles over left, then down to wrist
(See "engage")

Appointment= appoint + -ment

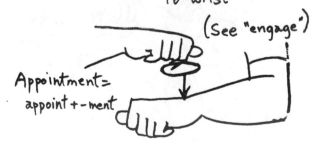

APPRECIATE
A on chest changes to P and circles once on chest

(See "please")

APPROACH
Bent right hand moves in stages toward left palm; does not touch it

APPROVE
5-hands, palm-down, draw back to P's on shoulders

(See "accept")

20

APRICOT

A circles S, touching

APRIL

A traces basket-shape under arm, twisting

(See "basket")

APRON

Outline small apron at waist with A-hands

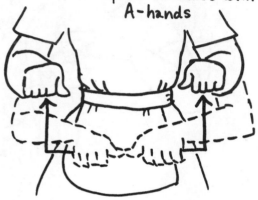

ARCHITECT

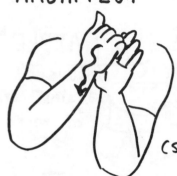

Right A draws down vertical palm, in wavy motion

(See "art")

ARE

R at lips, move forward

AREA

A-thumbs touch, circle in toward chest touch again

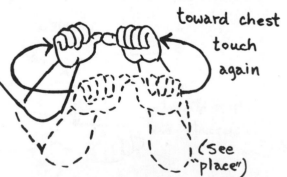

(See "place")

ARGUE

Palm-in index fingers move rapidly up and down from wrists

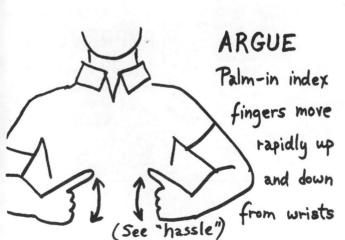

(See "hassle")

ARITHMETIC

Palm-in V's brush past each other sideways several times

21

ARIZONA

Touch chin twice with A-thumb, first on left then on right

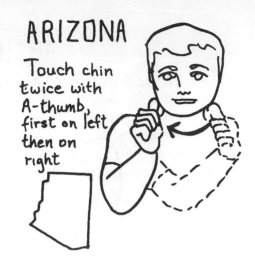

ARM

Pat arm with A

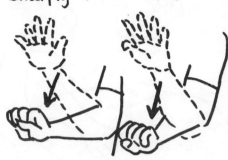

ARRANGE

Parallel palms move right in small vertical arcs

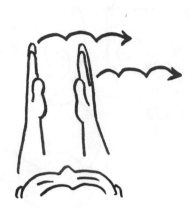

ARREST 5-hands drop outwards, closing sharply to S-hands

ARRIVE

Back of right hand arcs forward and touches left palm (See "reach")

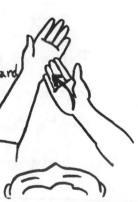

ARROW Pull bowstring back to right V

ART

Fingertip of i draws wavy line on palm

Artist = art + -ist

22

ARTERY

Press side of neck with A-thumb

ARTICHOKE Hold left
S-thumb and peel backward

ARTICLE
Curved index
and thumb
move down
horizontal
left palm

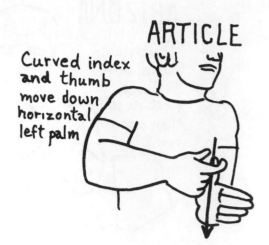

Parallel indexes at right
arc up and then drop,
to the left

AS

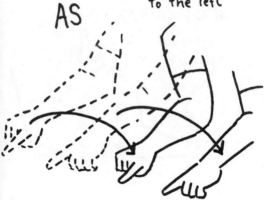

ASHAMED
Palm-out to
palm-in A on
cheek; A opens
fingers brushing
up cheek;
flat hand
falls
forward

ASIA Thumbtip of A at
corner of eye, hand twists
forward slightly

(See "China")

ASK
Palms of hands
together, arc
slightly toward
body
(See
"request")

ASPARAGUS
C-hand grasps
A-hand arm,
slides down

ASSASSIN
Side of A twists diagonally
under left palm

Assassinate = assassin + -ate

(See
"kill")

23

ASSEMBLE

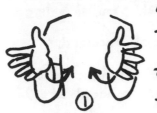

Palm-out 5's approach, close to flat-O's; touch

Assembly = assemble + -y

ASSIGN

Index finger at mouth moves to A on palm

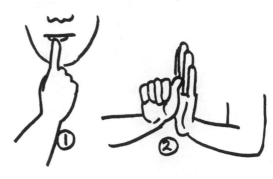

ASSIST

Left L pushes right A upward

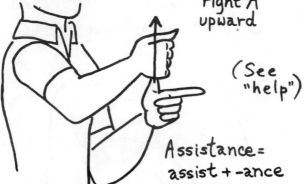

(See "help")

Assistance = assist + -ance

ASSOCIATE

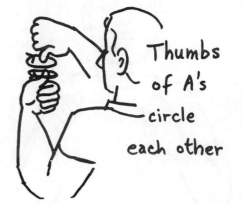

Thumbs of A's circle each other

ASSUME

Palm-down 5's up to S's

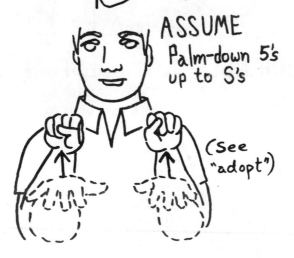

(See "adopt")

AT

Right fingertips approach and touch back of left fingers

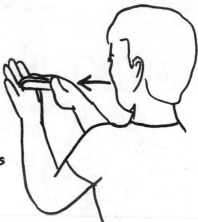

ATLANTA

Thumb of A touches left and then right shoulder

ATTACK

Right claw hand seizes left vertical index finger

24

ATTEMPT

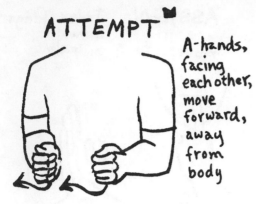

A-hands, facing each other, move forward, away from body

ATTEND Vertical parallel palms drop to point forward

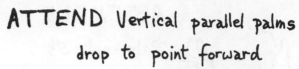

Attention = attend + -tion
(See "concentrate")

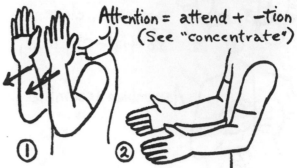

ATTIRE

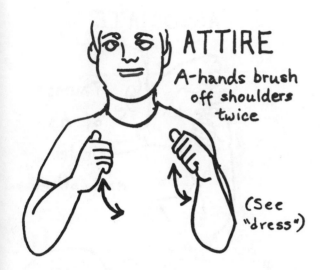

A-hands brush off shoulders twice

(See "dress")

ATTITUDE Right-A hand circles the heart and touches chest

(See "character")

ATTRACT Thumb of right A on palm moves toward left shoulder

(See "belong")

AUDIENCE Parallel claw-hands, palm-down, move forward

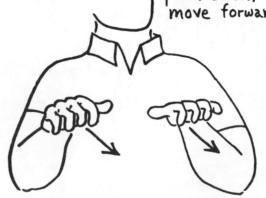

AUGUST

A circles inward twice, touching chest

AUNT

Shake A near jaw

AUSTRALIA   Thumb of
A at temple twists to salute
palm-out

AUTHOR
Palm-down A
writes across
left palm

(See "write")

AUTHORITY   Thumb of
A-hand draws muscle on arm

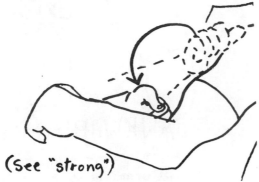

(See "strong")

AUTUMN
A brushes off
left elbow

(See "September")

AVENUE
Palm-down A's
move forward,
zig-zag

(See "boulevard")

AVERAGE
Side of right hand cross-wise on
side of left, rock top slightly
side to side

AVOCADO   Thumb of palm-
down A circles around palm-in
flat O, peeling

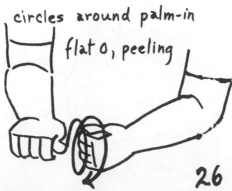

AVOID   Right A, behind
left A, draws wavy motion
back toward
body

(See
evade)

26

AWARD
A's, right above left, arc diagonally forward to left

(See "gift")

AWFUL
8's at temples flick open to 5's

① ②

AXE
Side of palm-down A chops at wrist of vertical left hand

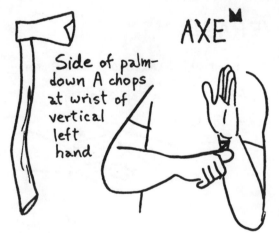

BACHELOR
Arc B-hand from left side of mouth to right side

AWAY
Palm-in hand flips forward and up to palm-down

AWKWARD
3-hands, palm-down, alternately move up and down

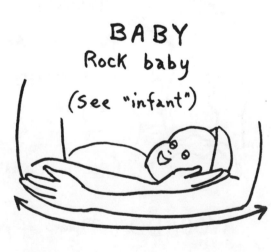

BABY
Rock baby

(See "infant")

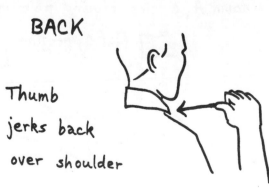

BACK
Thumb jerks back over shoulder

BACON

H fingertips touch and separate, waving first 2 fingers

(See "spaghetti")

BACTERIA

Heel of B circles on finger of palm-up left I

(see "algae")

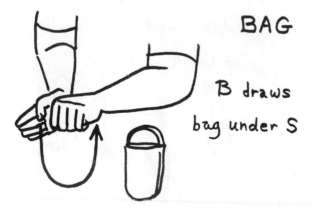

BAD

Twist hand out and throw it down

BADMINTON

Hit bird twice sharply upward to right

BAG

B draws bag under S

BAKE

Right B slides under left hand

(See "roast")

BALANCE

Flat hands rise and fall alternately, palm-down

BALD

Circle middle finger on head

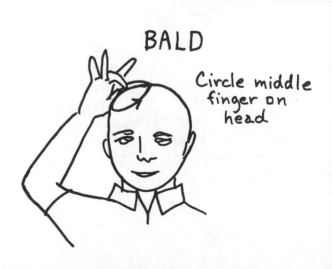

28

BALL
Claw-hands form ball-shape

BALLAD
Right B swings back and forth behind left arm

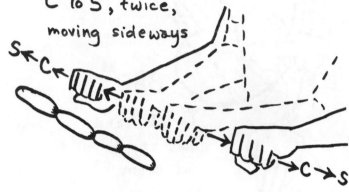

(See "music")

BALLOON
S-hands at mouth open and form ball (like balloon)

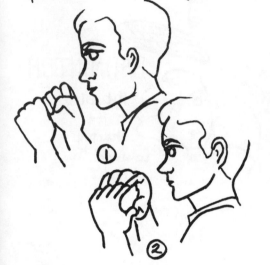

BALONEY
C to S, twice, moving sideways

BANANA   Peel
index finger with thumb-tip twice

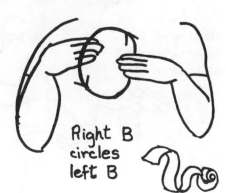

BALTIMORE
Shake B up and down, palm-left

BAND
Palm-out B's together; circle outward to palm-in D's together

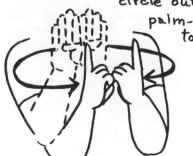

BANDAGE
Right B circles left B

28a

BANG

Hit back of B-hand with S

(See "bump")

BANK

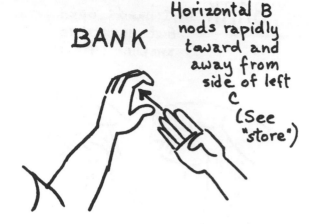

Horizontal B nods rapidly toward and away from side of left C
(See "store")

BANNER

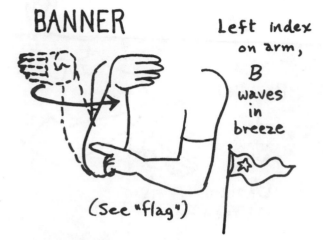

Left index on arm, B waves in breeze

(See "flag")

BANQUET

Flat O-hands circle alternately up to chin

BAPTIZE

A-hands move: to the right, palm-ups left, palm-down, dipping person; return to original position

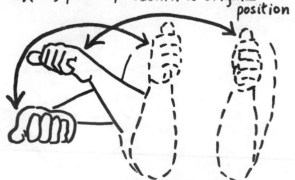

BAR

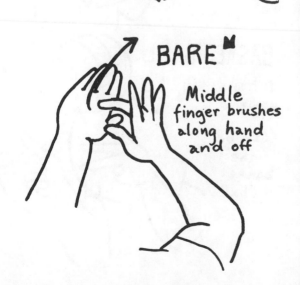

B moves right, off index

BARBER

Clip hair with V

BARE

Middle finger brushes along hand and off

29

BARK
Bent-hands open out one above another. Repeat.

① ②

BARLEY
B brushes up through G twice

(See "grain")

BARN
Palm-out B's outline barn
(See "house")

BASE
B circles under palm
Basic = base + -ic

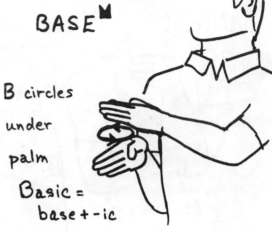

BASEBALL
Swing bat
(Can be signed "base" + "ball")

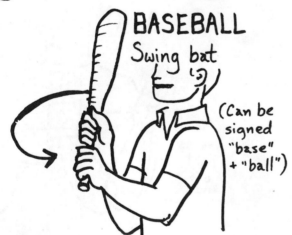

BASKET
Flat hand draws basket under arm

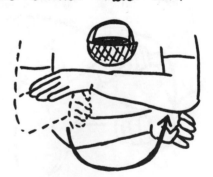

BASKETBALL
3-hands flip ball upward
(Can be signed "basket" + "ball")

BATH
Rub knuckles up and down on chest

Bathe = bath + e

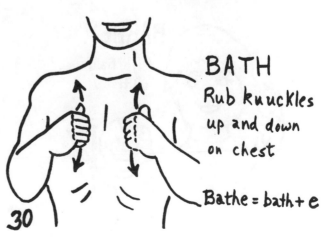

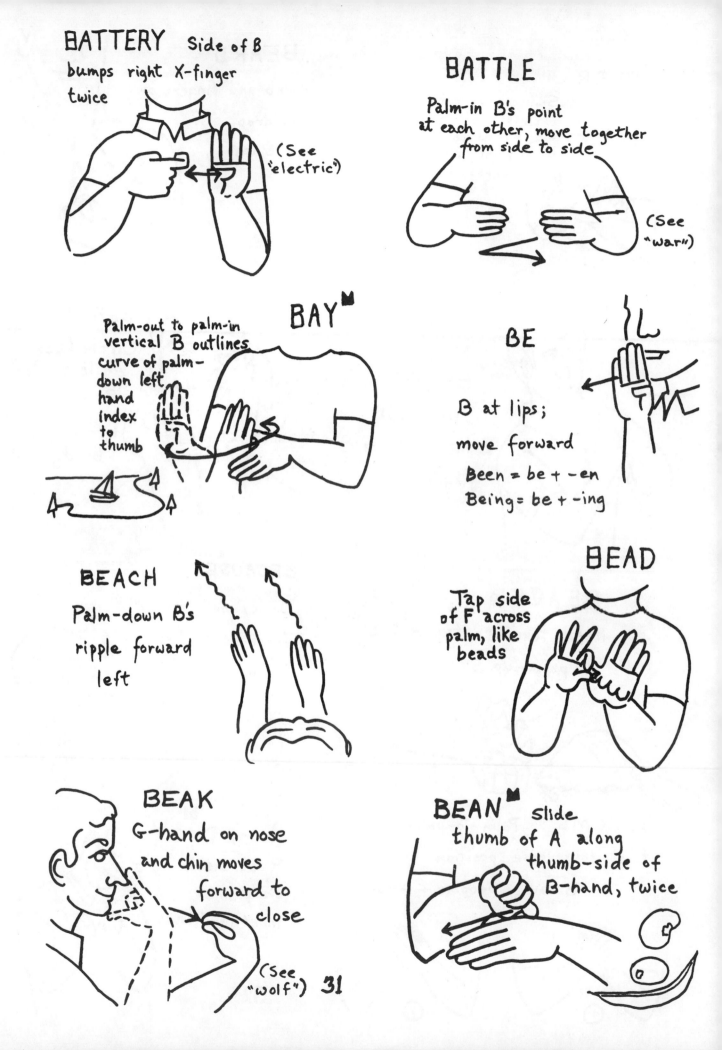

BATTERY Side of B bumps right X-finger twice

(See "electric")

BATTLE

Palm-in B's point at each other, move together from side to side

(See "war")

BAY

Palm-out to palm-in vertical B outlines curve of palm-down left hand index to thumb

BE

B at lips; move forward

Been = be + -en

Being = be + -ing

BEACH

Palm-down B's ripple forward left

BEAD

Tap side of F across palm, like beads

BEAK

G-hand on nose and chin moves forward to close

(See "wolf") **31**

BEAN slide thumb of A along thumb-side of B-hand, twice

BEAR
Swing crossed wrists of claw-hands to the right, still crossed

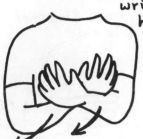

BEARD
Thumb and fingers on chin drop and close

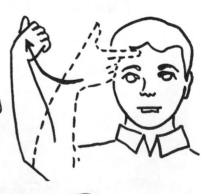

BEAT
Back of right B hits left index finger

BEAUTY
Circle face while closing to O

beautiful = beauty + -ful
(See "face")

BEAVER
Heels together, tap bent-2 on palm-up S

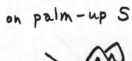

BECAUSE
Index on forehead, lift up and right, closing to A

BECOME
Palm-to-palm hands twist to reverse position

Became = become + -ed

①

②

BED
Rest cheek on palms-together hands

32

BEE
9 to cheek, then brush off bee

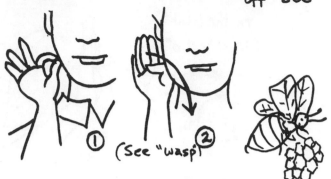

① (See "wasp") ②

BEEF
Right thumb and forefinger grasp side of left B and shake

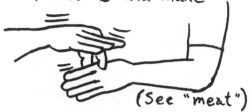

(See "meat")

BEER
Vertical B circles on right cheek

(See "wine")

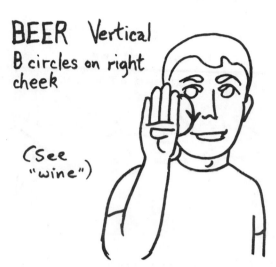

BEET
Slice side of palm-out B with index finger twice

(See "tomato")

BEETLE
B rides forward on wiggling fingers of left hand

(See "ant")

BEG
Palm-up right hand lies on back of left; move both hands toward body while right changes from 5 to claw

BEGIN
Index twists on wrist of B

Began = begin + -ed

Begun = begin + -en

① ② **33**

BEHAVE
Palm-out B's move from side to side

(See "do")

Behavior = behave + -er

BELIEVE
Index finger on forehead; drop to clasp hands

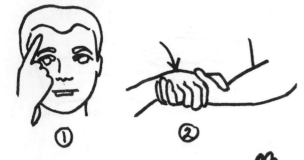

① ②

BELONG

Thumb and finger of right hand hold thumb of left B while moving to left shoulder

(See "attract")

① ②

BENCH

Two fingers sit on side of B-hand

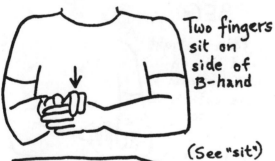

(See "sit")

BENEFIT

"Pin" with 9-hand down shoulder

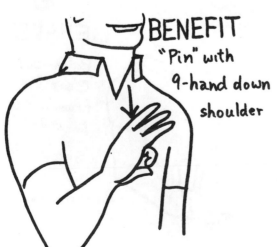

BELL
S hits palm, then shakes to the right
(See "echo")

BELT
H-hands overlap fingertips across beltline, snapping at wrists

BEND

Grasp fingertips and bend inward

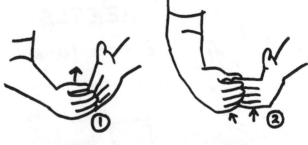

① ②

BERRY

Twist C around i-fingertip

Shake first letter of name of berry by little finger, before signing "berry" e.g., "raspberry" = shake R, sign "berry"

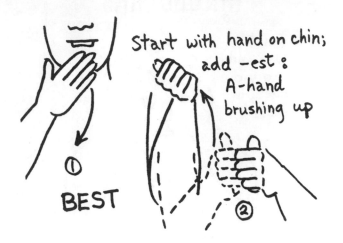

BEST

Start with hand on chin; add -est: A-hand brushing up

① ②

BETTER

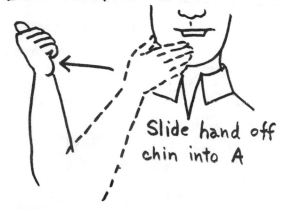

Slide hand off chin into A

BIBLE Prayerful hands drop and open like book

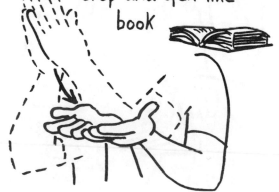

BIG

Palm-out B's arc sideways

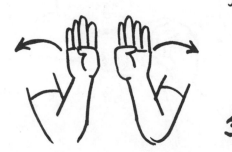

35

BET Palm-up hands, horizontal, right behind left, turn and move forward

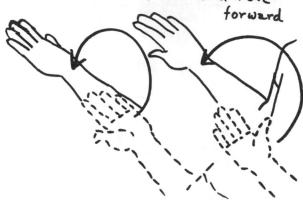

BETWEEN Right hand flutters between fingers

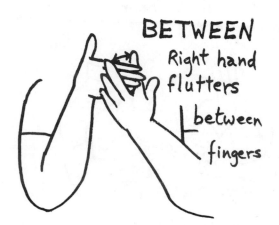

BIBLIOGRAPHY

"Book" moves down, opening repeatedly

BIKE

Pedal palm-down S-hands

BILLION

Heel of right B on heel of left hand; arc B to fingertips as both hands move forward

BINOCULARS

Twist O-hands around eyes, in place

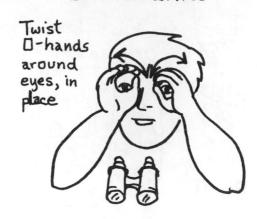

BIOLOGY

Palm-out B's pour alternately

(See "science")

BIRD

At chin close finger on thumb twice

BIRTH

From sides, palm-up hands move forward to rest, right on left

Born = birth + -en

Birthday = birth + day

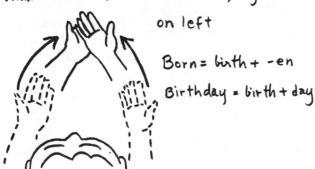

BISCUIT

Thumb and curved index on palm lift slightly, rotate at wrist and touch again

(See "cookie")

BIT

Little finger flips forward from under thumb

BITE

Right hand bites left finger

bit = bite + -ed

BITTER
Index finger of B on chin, twist to palm-in

(See "sour")

BLACK

Palm-down, index moves across forehead right

(See "gray")

BLADE
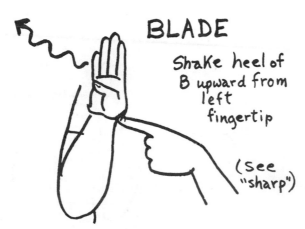

Shake heel of B upward from left fingertip

(See "sharp")

BLAME
A arcs forward, little finger side hitting back of hand

BLANK
Draw a line in the air with the bent middle finger of 5-hand

BLANKET

From in front, arm sweeps across left arm to shoulder near neck (drawing up blanket)

BLEED
Index at chin drops, changing to a palm-in 5 on back of other hand downwards with fluttering fingers

① ②

Bled= bleed + -ed **37**

BLEND
Flat hands draw up to A's with knuckles together

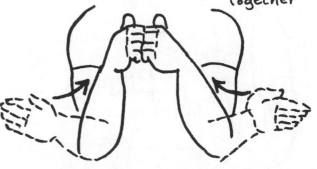

BLESS

Thumbs of A's on chin; move down, opening slowly, to palm-down 5's

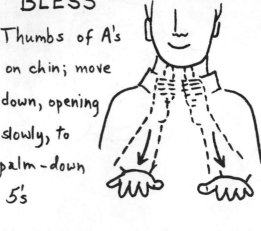

BLIND

Bent-V, palm-in, jerks toward eyes

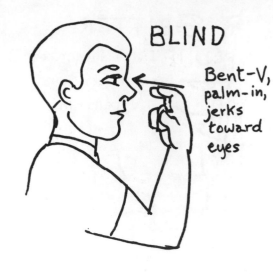

BLINK

Hands stationary, shut and open thumbs and fingers of L's

BLOCK

Tap thumb-tips, palms out

BLOND

B makes a wavy motion down side of hair

Blonde = blond + -e

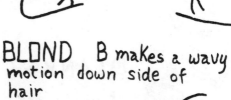
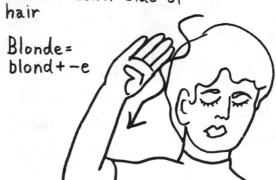

Palm-in 5 touches back of hand, then drops down with fluttering fingers (blood dripping)

BLOOD

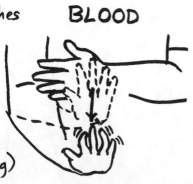

BLOUSE

Palm-out B's on chest move down to waist

(See "coat")

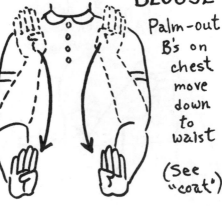

BLOW

Palm-in flat-O at mouth, moves out and opens to palm-in 5; hits side of index finger

① ②

Blew = blow + -ed

38

BLUE
Palm-left B
shakes
from wrist

BLUSH Flat-O
at cheek rises
and opens
to a 5

BOARD
Palm-out
B moves
along
arm
(See "stage")

BOAST
A-thumbs
strike waist
alternately

BOAT
Flat hands
joined at
little finger
sides, move
forward in
wavy up
and down
motion

BODY
Touch
chest
and
then
ribs

BOIL
"Juggle" hands
(alternately)
while fluttering
fingers

BOMB Drop bomb from
under hand, S to 5

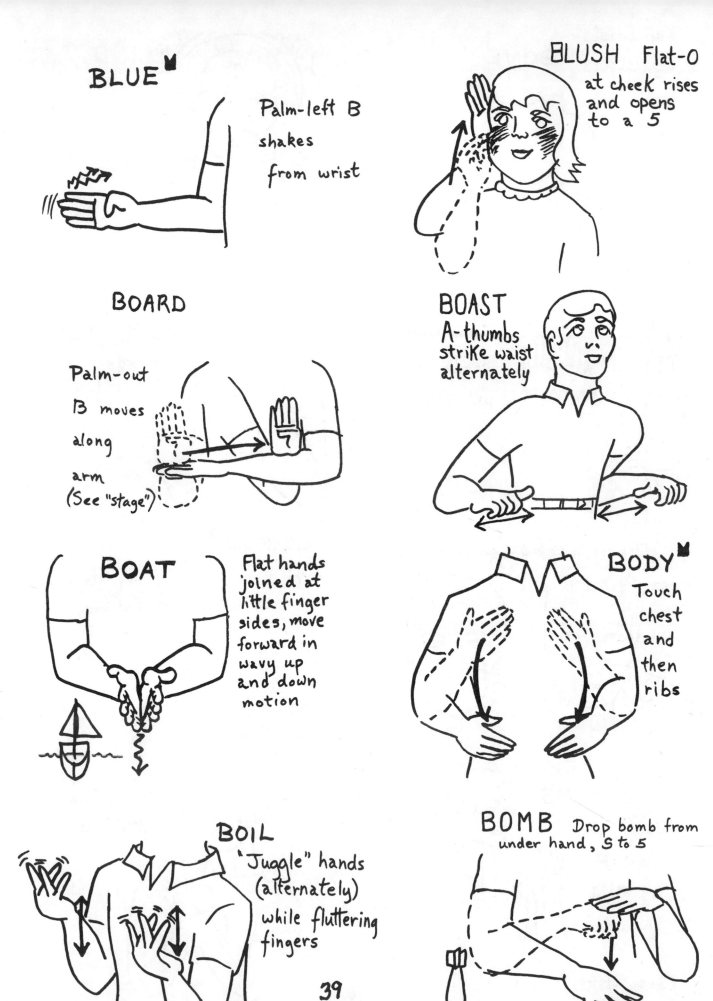

39

Tap wrists
against
each other
twice

BONE

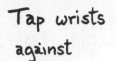

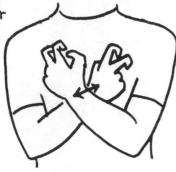

Outline
and tie
on bonnet
with A's

BONNET

BOOK
Palm-to-palm
hands open,
palms up

BOOT

Tap sides of
B-hands
together twice,
palm-out

(See
"shoe")

BORE

Tip of index finger on side of
nose; twist in place

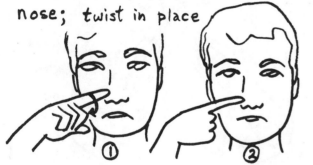

BORROW

Right V on top of left V, both arc
up together toward body

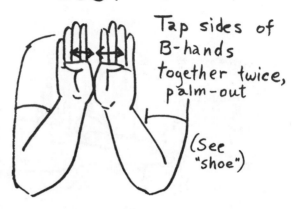

BOSS
Side of
right B
on right
shoulder

(See "office")

BOTH V slides through
C, closing to a U-hand

40

BOTHER
Side of right hand chops into thumb-base of left hand, several times

(See "interrupt")

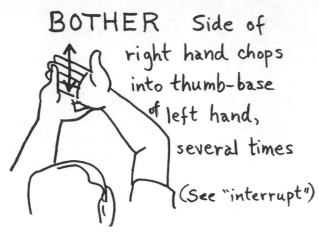

BOTTLE
C on palm closes into S as if outlining a bottle

BOTTOM
Fingertips tap heel of palm—out B

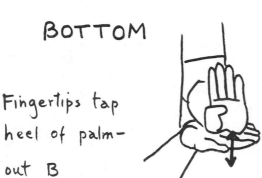

BOULEVARD
2 B's, parallel, move away from body and zag right

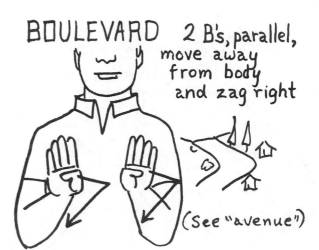

(See "avenue")

BOW
S-hands arc out to V's

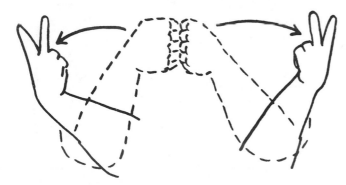

BOW
Bow forward slightly, arm at waist

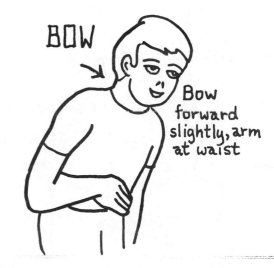

BOWL
Outline bowl with cupped hands

BOWL (verb)
Bowl a ball
Bowling = bowl + -ing

41

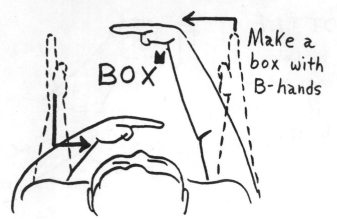

BOX Make a box with B-hands

BOY Touch 4 fingers to thumb several times near temple

BRA L-hands, pointing down, move from mid-chest to sides

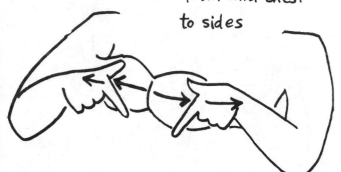

BRACELET G-slides across wrist toward you

BRAG A-thumb strikes waist several times

Flutter fingers slightly across "page" of palm BRAILLE

BRAIN Tap thumb of C on forehead twice

BRANCH

One-hand angles away from base of palm-out B

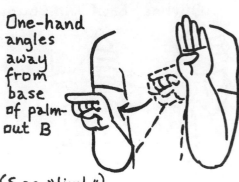

42 (See "limb")

BRASS

Heel of of right B bounces off B

(See "metal")

BRAVE

5's on chest; pull out to S-hands

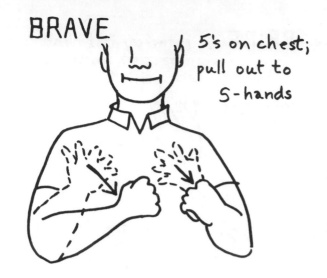

BREAD

Slice back of hand three times with side of right hand

BREAK

Sides of S-hands touch, then separate sharply, twisting to face each other

Broken: break + -en

Broke: break + -ed

BREAKFAST

Rotate B-hand at wrist up to mouth (See "eat")

BREAST

Tap fingertips on each side of chest

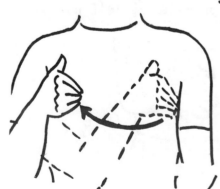

BREATH (NOUN)

Flat hands move together on and off chest

Breathe= breath + -e

(see "sigh")

BREEZE

B-hands swing back and forth, twisting at wrists (as breeze "blows") (See "wind")

BRIBE
Palm-up flat hand passes under left palm toward left

BRICK
Tap back of B on back of S (see "stone")

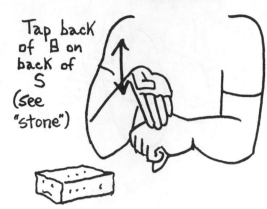

BRIDE
A at jaw drops, opens, goes into clasp of left hand

BRIDGE
FingerTips of V touch palm and arc to touch arm near elbow

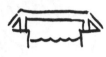

BRIEF
Side of right B slides back and forth on side of left index

(See "short")

BRIGHT
5- hands, palm-out, separate upwards with fluttering fingers

(See "glisten")

BRILLIANT
Bent middle finger shakes up from forehead

BRING
Palm-up hands at left; move back toward body

Brought= bring + -ed

(See "transport")

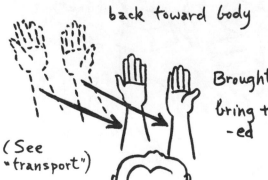

44

BROAD

Heels of B's together, separate forward

BROCCOLI

C-hand grasps B-hand arm, slides down

(See "asparagus")

BROIL
Flutter fingers while circling hand under palm
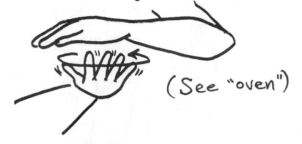
(See "oven")

BROOCH
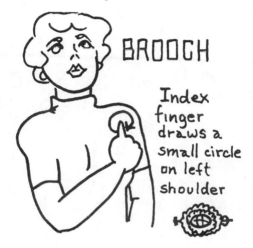
Index finger draws a small circle on left shoulder

BROOK
Parallel B-hands shake forward (like hook-water)

BROOM
Right S on left, sweep to left, repeat

BROTH

Ladle B-hand up to mouth twice (See "soup")

BROTHER
A-hand drops, index fingers together

45

BROWN

Palm-left

B moves down at side of mouth

(See "tan")

BRUSH

Brush top of hand with back of fingers several times

BUBBLE

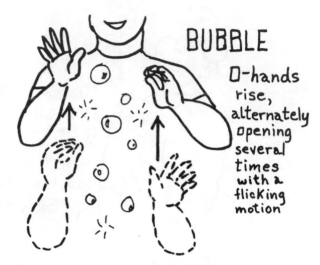

O-hands rise, alternately opening several times with a flicking motion

BUCKET

B-hand points down at side, rises, still pointing down

(See "pail")

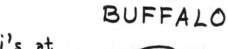

BUCKLE

"Buckle" fingers at waist

BUFFALO

i's at temples

BUFFET

X moves from back of hand, palm-left, along arm   (See "cafeteria")

BUG

Wiggle first two fingers, thumb on nose

46

BUGGY
Palm-out B-hands move straight forward to Y-hands

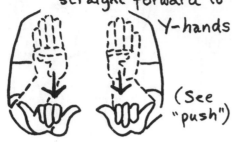

(See "push")

BUILD
Building = build + -ing

Built = build + -ed

Build hands alternately on top of each other, palm-down

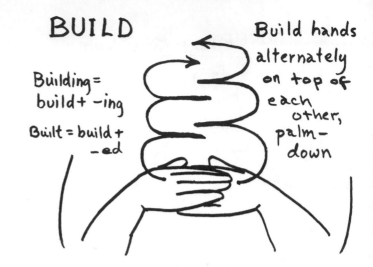

BULB
Heels of B thumbs together, circle out and together again

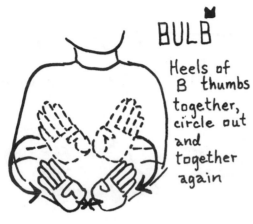

BULL
Y in middle of head

BUMP
From behind, S hits palm

BUNDLE
Quickly rotate right vertical hand around left vertical hand

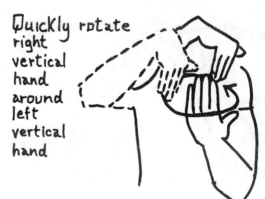

BUNNY
Fingers of B's at temples flop forward and back

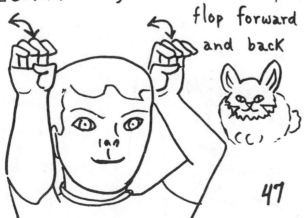

BURN
Right fingers flutter under palm-in horizontal B

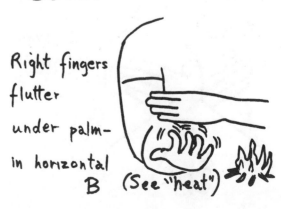

(See "heat")

47

BURY
Palm-down hands arc back toward body

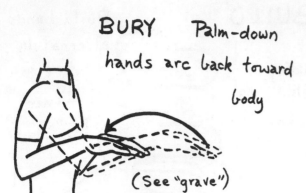

(See "grave")

BUS
Palm-left C behind palm-right B; C moves back

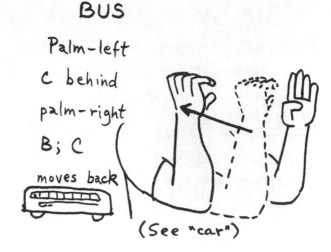

(See "car")

BUSH
Wrist of palm-out B against side of palm-down hand; shake top of B slightly

Bushy = bush + -y

BUSY
Palm-out B arcs from side to side, hitting back of hand

Business = busy + -ness

(See "work")

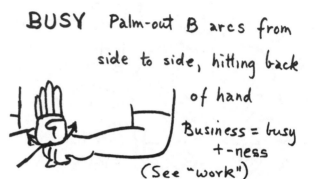

BUT
Palm-out crossed fingers separate

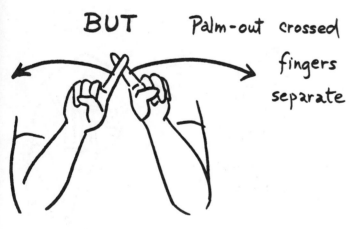

BUTTER

Flick U backwards off heel to N twice

BUTTERFLY
Hook thumbs, flutter hands

BUTTON
9-hand taps its side against chest, high, then lower

48

BUY Palm-up flat-O on palm lifts off, arcs forward

Bought = Buy + -ed

BY
Palm of right hand brushes by side of left hand

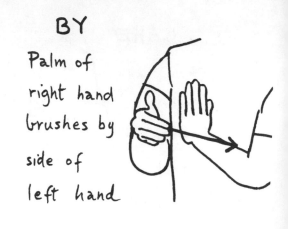

CABBAGE
Hit head with C-heel twice

CABIN Draw roof and sides with palm-out C's

(See "house")

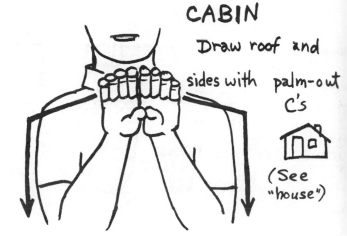

CABLE R moves away from thumb of C in wavy motion

(See "cord")

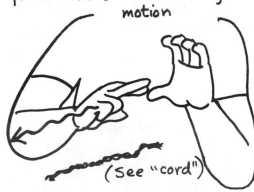

CAFE
Tap C at corner of mouth
(See "restaurant")

CAFETERIA

C on back of hand slides up arm into T
(See "buffet")

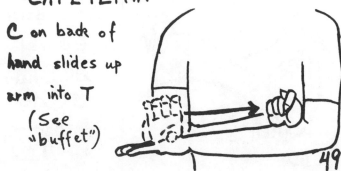

49

CAGE
Palm-in right 4 hits side of left C

(See "jail")

CAKE

Right fingertips bounce on back of left hand

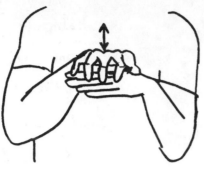

CALCULUS

C's brush past each other at wrists, sideways, repeat

(See "arithmetic")

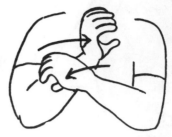

CALENDAR

two

Right C slides up palm-in left hand, over, and down back

CALIFORNIA

Wiggle L-Y hand down to Y from ear

CALF

A's at corners of head, palm in

(For calf of leg, just point.)

CALL

Thumb of right C (palm-left) touches corner of mouth; hand moves short distance forward (see "scream")

CALM

C-hands cross below chin, separate downwards (See "quiet")

CAMEL

Draw back of camel with C-hand

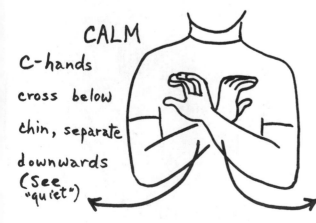

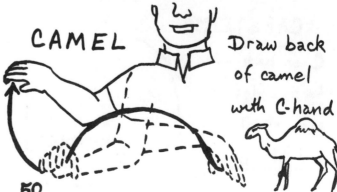

CAMERA

"Click the shutter" with index finger

CAMP

Little and index fingers touch twice

CAN

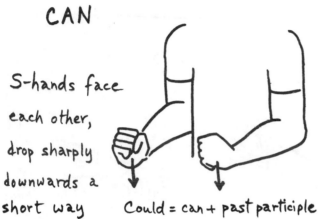

S-hands face each other, drop sharply downwards a short way

Could = can + past participle

CANADA

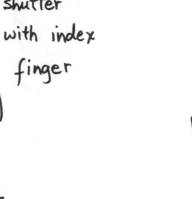

A grasps clothes and taps chest

CANCEL

Index slashes diagonally across palm of left hand

CANCER

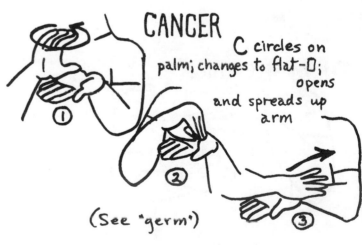

C circles on palm; changes to flat-O; opens and spreads up arm

(See "germ")

CANDLE

Palm of 5 on tip of index finger; flutter fingers

CANDY

Twist hand, index finger on cheek

51

CANNON

Upper hand shoots forward and recoils

CAN'T

Right index strikes down past left index

(May also be signed "can" + "n't")

CANTALOUPE

Thump top of left C with middle finger

(See "melon")

CANYON

Outline canyon with C's

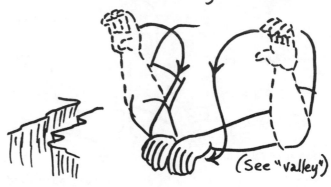

(See "valley")

CAP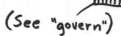

Pat top of C twice

CAPITAL

Tap shoulder with thumb of C twice

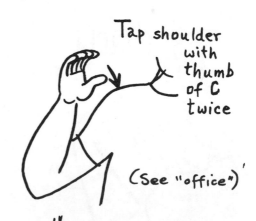

(See "office")

CAPITOL

Pivoting at wrist, C circles near temple, then thumb touches temple

(See "govern")

52

CAPTAIN

Claw-hand taps right shoulder twice

(See "office")

CAPTURE

Claw-hand "attacks" left index, closes, and pulls it back toward right shoulder

CAR

Right C behind left C; right moves backwards

CARE

Right V-hand on left V-hand, circle horizontally

Careful = care + -ful

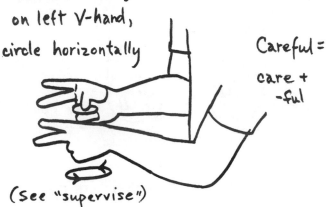

(See "supervise")

CARD

Right C grasps left hand, slides back and forth

CAREER

C slides forward along side of B-hand

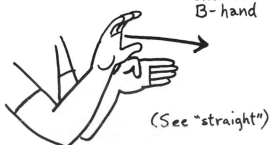

(See "straight")

CARELESS

V arcs past forehead several times

CARNIVAL

Palm-out C arcs down right to palm-out L, moves right

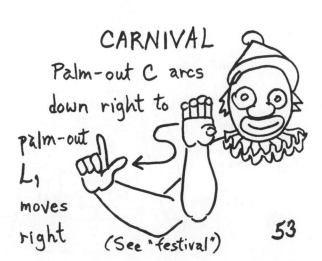

(See "festival")

53

CARPENTRY

S moves forward and back on open palm, like planing; repeat

carpenter = carpentry + -er

CARPET
Drag C across back of left hand

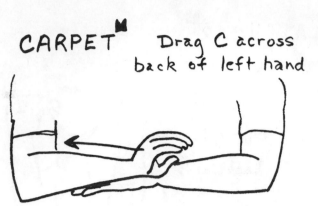

CARROT
Scrape top of C with thumb of A

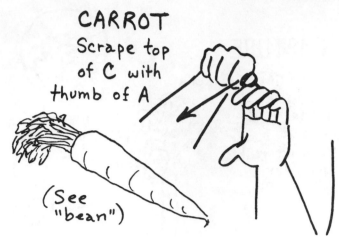

(See "bean")

CARRY
Palms-up, move left in small vertical arcs

CART
Palm-out C-hands move straight forward to T-hands

(See "push")

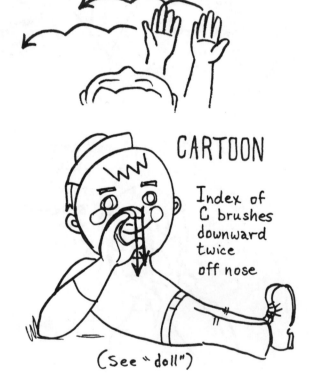

CARTOON
Index of C brushes downward twice off nose

(See "doll")

CASE
Outline box with C's

(See "box")

CASH
C on palm, arc slightly, moving forward
(See "buy")

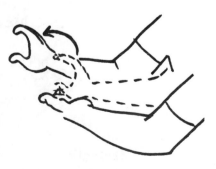

CASTLE
Bent V's build a castle-shape
(See "palace")

54

CAT

Draw out 2 whiskers with 9-hand

CATCH
Palm-out claw above side of other claw; right drops onto left, both close to S's

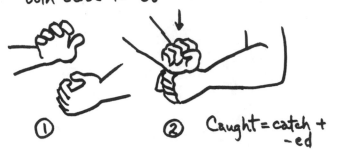

① ② Caught = catch + -ed

CATEGORY
C's make small circles, moving right, 3 times

categorize = add -ize

CATERPILLAR
Pull hand along arm by one alternating with X finger several times

CATHOLIC
Palm-in H fingers make a cross near forehead, vertical, then horizontal

CATTLE
Y-hands, palm-out at temples, curve slightly forward, hands leaving head

CAULIFLOWER
Hit heel of 9 twice on head

(See "cabbage")

CAUSE
Palm-up A's, left ahead of right, drop and open

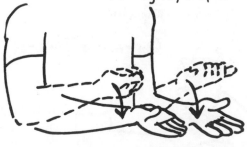

55

CAVE
Little-finger side of right hand hollows out left C, pivoting

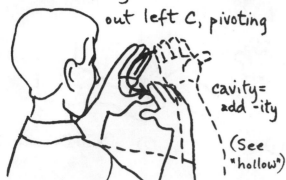

cavity= add -ity

(See "hollow")

CEILING
C-hand slides along underside of arm

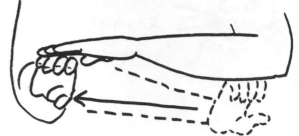

CELEBRATE
A-hands spiral upward toward head

Celebration= celebrate + -tion

CELERY
Right C slides down from wrist to elbow while 5-fingers wiggle

(See "asparagus")

CELL
With index curved, right thumb circles on little finger of i

(See "algae")

CENT
Bring index finger out from forehead

CENTER
C circles over, drops on palm

Central =center + -al

(See "middle")

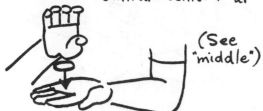

CEREAL
Ladle C-hand up to mouth twice

(See "soup")

56

CERTAIN

Jerk C forward and down from chin

CERTIFY

C-hand inverts and hits flat left hand

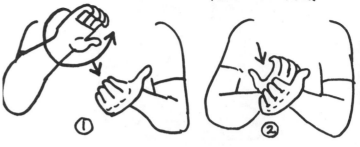

① ②

CHAIN

Link 9-hands, release, reverse, and link again, moving slightly right with each reversal

CHAIR

"Sit" 2 fingers on thumb of left C (See "sit")

CHALK

Thumb of C writes on palm (See "write")

CHALLENGE

A's arc inward, palm-in, but do not meet

CHANCE

Palm-up C's twist to palm-down C's

① ②

(See "happen")

57

CHANGE

Wrists of X touch, stay together; twist to reverse hands

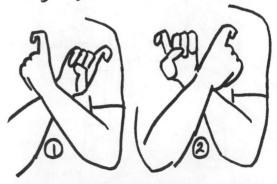

① ②

CHANNEL
Palm-in C's twist to palm-out, moving forward

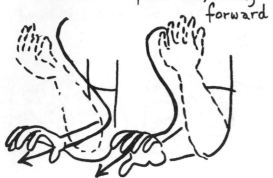

CHAPTER
Thumb and fingertips of C slide down in front of palm

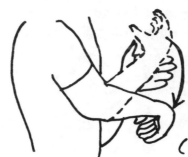

CHARACTER 🦋
C circles clockwise on left chest

CHARGE
Side of palm-out C strikes downward on palm

(See "cost")

CHART
Thumb of C draws wavy line backwards on back of hand

(See "map")

CHASE
Right A behind left A, both move forward and left; right hand circling slightly

CHAT
Hands face each other, open and close, simultaneously and repeatedly

CHATTER
Heels together, right claw fingertips rise and fall quickly on left several times

58

CHEAP Right hand slaps down off left palm

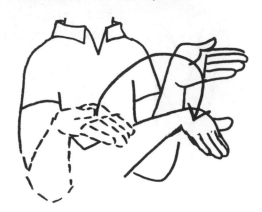

CHEAT Index and little finger out, move from wrist to elbow (putting card in sleeve)

CHECK Index finger makes check mark near palm (see "edit")

CHEEK

Grasp skin of cheek

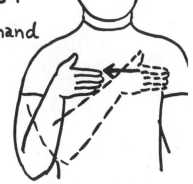

CHEESE Mash — and twist slightly — right heel on left heel

CHEMISTRY Palm-out C's pour alternately. (See "science")

CHERRY

Twist C first around upper V finger, then around lower finger

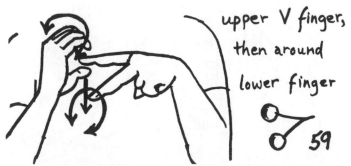

59

CHEST Draw hand across chest

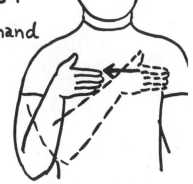

CHEW

Circle top A on palm-up left A

(See "digest")

CHICAGO

C-hand arcs sharply down to right

CHICK

Peck twice with X

Chicken = chick + -en

CHIEF

Thumb of C taps tip of index twice

CHILD

Waist-high flat hand

CHILDREN

Bounce hand to side once

CHILL

C hands face each other; hands shiver slightly

(See "cold")

CHIMNEY

Outline chimney with C's (See "tower")

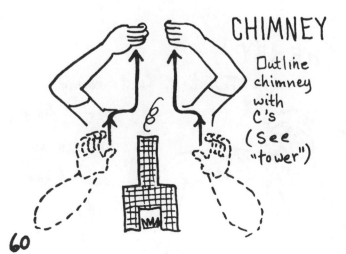

CHINA Index finger at corner

of eye twists slightly forward

Chinese = China + -ese

CHIP

Right C
arcs down
and up, hitting
side of left index
with thumb

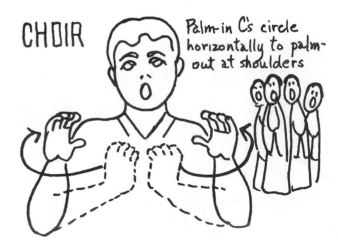

CHIPMUNK

Paws under
chin flap
up and
down

CHOCOLATE

C-thumb traces
a circle twice
on back of hand

CHOICE

Palm-out C
touches
index of V,
moves

back

CHOIR

Palm-in C's circle
horizontally to palm-
out at shoulders

CHOKE

Choke self
with right
hand

CHOOSE   Thumb and finger of

9 pick index and then middle

finger of V

Chose = choose + -ed
Chosen = choose + -en

CHOP

Side of palm-up hand chops at wrist of vertical left hand

(See "axe")

CHORUS

Swing C back and forth inside left flat hand and left arm

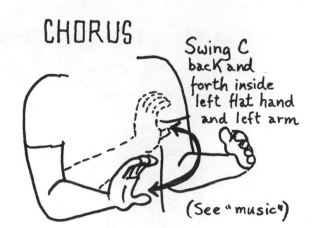

(See "music")

CHRIST

C at left shoulder moves to right side of waist

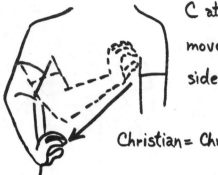

Christian = Christ + -an

CHRISTMAS

Twist C inward

(See "December")

CHURCH

Thumb of palm-out C taps back of S twice

(See "temple")

CIGAR

Wiggle R, hand rests against chin

CIGARETTE

Tap index and little fingers on left index finger

CIRCLE

Draw circle with palm-out index finger

62

CIRCUMSTANCE

C on back of hand, both move in horizontal circle

CIRCUS

V-fingertips touch, separate in 2 side-ways arcs

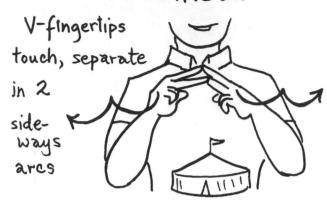

CITY

Tap tip of C twice, both circling (see "town")

CLAM

Palms together, slightly cupped, right opens and closes at little-finger side

CLAP

Vertical hands clap once

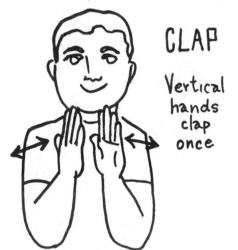

CLASS
Palm-out C-hands circle horizontally to palm-in

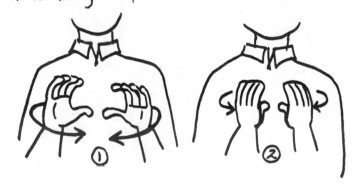

CLAUSE

Palm-out C's separate to L's

CLAW
Claw forward with right hand

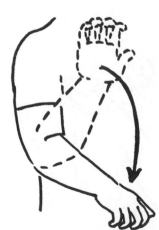

63

CLAY

Squeeze clay, right hand above left

CLEAN

Right palm brushes off left palm once (See "neat")

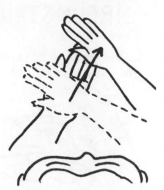

CLEAR

Flat-O's touching, to 5-hands

(See "obvious")

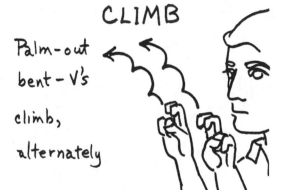

CLEVER

Palm in flicks to palm out, middle finger bent

CLIMB

Palm-out bent-V's climb, alternately

CLIP

Right L clips index

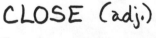

CLOCK

Index circles clockwise in C

CLOSE (adj.)

To your right, side of C approaches back of bent left hand; does not touch it (See "near")

64

CLOSE (verb)
Close hands, sides meet palms down

CLOSET
From beside palm-out B, palm-out C-hand opens toward you, then returns

(see "door")

CLOTH

Rub side of chest with fingertips

Clothe = cloth + -e
Clothes = cloth + -e + -s
Clothing = cloth + -ing

CLOUD
C-hands face each other to left of eyes, move right

CLOWN
Claw-hand shakes slightly in front of nose

CLUB
C's, palms facing, arc out, and touch as palm-in B's

(See "band")

COACH
Right C-hand brushes back and forth on left index finger

(See "practice")

65

COAST
Back of palm-out C moves left along side of hand

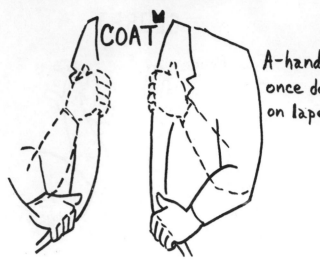

COAT

A-hands once down on lapels

COCOA

Thumb traces circle twice on back of hand (See "chocolate")

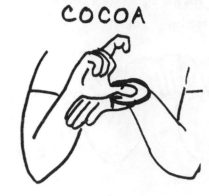

COCONUT

Shake coconut beside ear

COCOON

Palms in, hook thumbs together, close hands on chest

COFFEE

Circle top-S on left-S, in a grinding motion

(See "grind")

COIN

Lay thumb and index of F flat on left palm

COKE

Stick left arm with index of L

COLD

Shake S's as if shivering

COLLAPSE
5-hands fall toward each other, briefly meshing, palm-down, en route

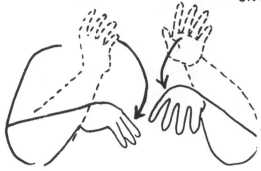

COLLAR
Draw G-fingers across neck to front

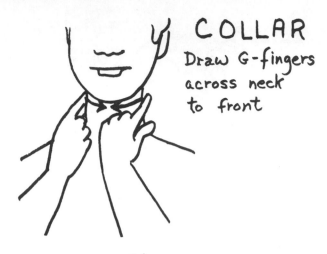

COLLECT
Right hand circles left palm, fingers together and flapping, gathering in money

(See "gather")

COLLEGE
Right hand on left, palm-to-palm. Right rises, circling

COLOR
Flutter fingers in front of chin

COLORADO
Outline big and small mountains with C above left arm

COLT
C at temple nods twice from wrist

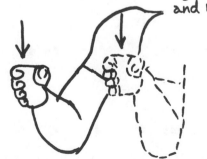

(See "horse")

COLUMN
Palm-out C moves downward, shifts to right and repeats

67

COMB
Claw near side of hair makes a combing motion

COMBINE
5-hands move together, meshing fingers palms-in

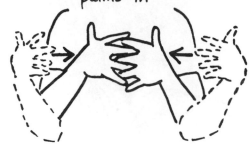

COME
Palm-up index points out; beckons once
Came: come + -ed

COMFORT
Stroke back of left hand down, then back of right hand

① ②

COMIC
C-hands pull up a smile near face (See "smile")

COMMAND
Index at chin twists to palm-out C, arcs forward

(See "order")

COMMENCE
Index fingertip on wrist of palm-out C twists to palm-in
Commencement= commence + -ment
(See "begin")

① ②

COMMERCE
C bounces back and forth on left S

Commercial= add -al

(See "work")

68

COMMITTEE

Claw-hand on left, then right, shoulder

(See "member")

COMMON

C's move in a horizontal circle

(See "standard")

COMMUNICATE

C-hands move alternately to and from chin

Communication= communicate + -tion

(See "talk")

COMMUNITY

Alternate hands in sign for "near", circling in front of you

COMPANY

Interlock thumbs of C and circle horizontally

(See "standard")

COMPARE

Alternately pivot back and forth several times

Comparison = compare + -tion

COMPETE

A's, palms facing, move alternately back and forth

(See "race") **69**

COMPLAIN

Fingertips of claw hit chest twice

Complaint= complain + -t

COMPLETE

Palm-out C slides along side of hand and down at fingertips

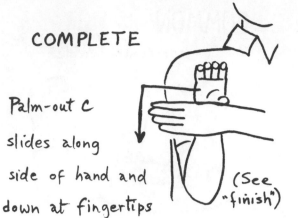

(See "finish")

COMPLEX

Alternating X and 1, hands rise and cross in front of chest

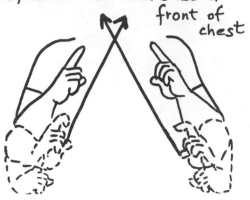

COMPOSE

C-hands face each other at sides, shake C's together to link, right above left

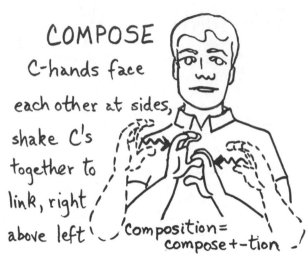

Composition = compose + -tion

COMPUTE

C bounces up arm

CON

Flat right hand approaches, til fingertips hit side of left C

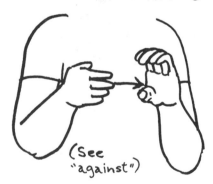

(See "against")

CONCEAL

C moves from chin to under left hand; left pushes down and to left upon right

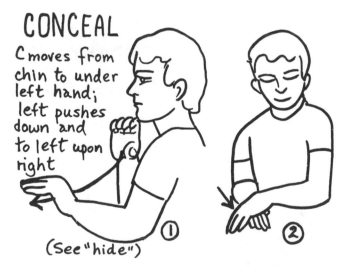

(See "hide")

CONCEDE

Flat hand on chest swings to palm-up

CONCENTRATE

C's at temples move forward a short distance

(See "attend")

70

CONCEPT

Thumb of C on forehead; spiral up and out (see "fantasy")

CONCERN

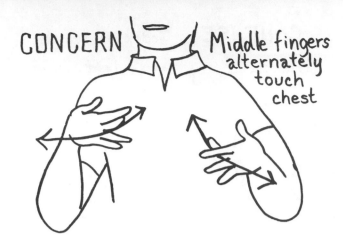

Middle fingers alternately touch chest

CONCRETE

Strike back of C on back of left S

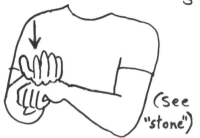

(See "stone")

CONDENSE

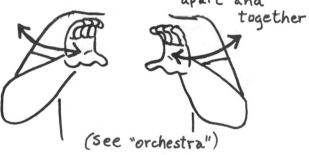

Open hands come together as palm-together S's

CONDITION

Right C-thumb into palm, pull left hand toward body

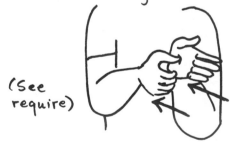

(See require)

CONDUCT

Palm-out C's swing apart and together

(See "orchestra")

CONFESS

C-hands on chest turn over and out to palm-up open hands

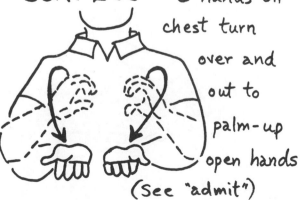

(See "admit")

CONFLICT

Index fingers move forward to hit

71

CONFUSE
Index on temple, then claws, right above left, reverse

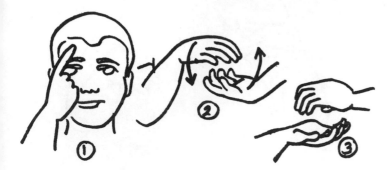

CONGRATULATE
Shake clasped hands near head

CONGRESS
Right C touches left side of chest, then right side

(See "member")

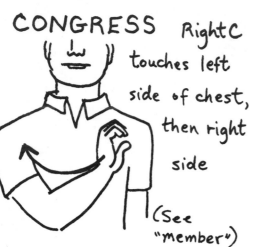

CONSCIENCE
Tap heart with index finger twice
(See "guilt")

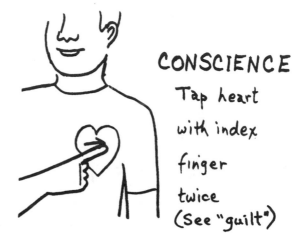

CONSCIOUS
Tap head behind ear with thumb of C

(See "sense")

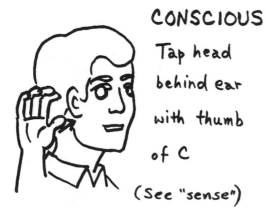

CONSIDER
Index fingers circle alternately in front of face

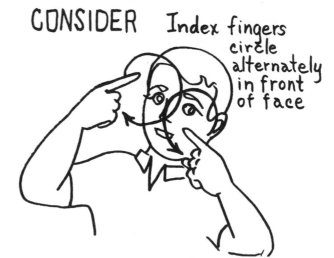

CONSONANT
Palm-out C moves over palm-in 5 fingers of

(See "alphabet")

CONSTANT
C-hands, thumbs touching, move forward
(See "continue")

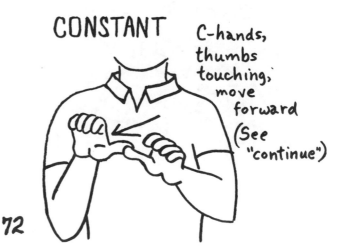

72

CONSTELLATION

Strike side of C upwards off 1-hand, then 1-hand off C, moving upwards

(See "star")

CONSTITUTE

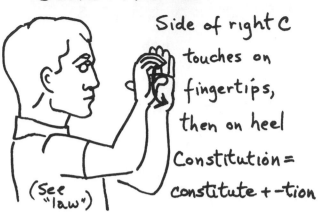

Side of right C touches on fingertips, then on heel

Constitution = constitute + -tion

(See "law")

CONSTRUCT

Build C's alternately on top of each other

(See "build")

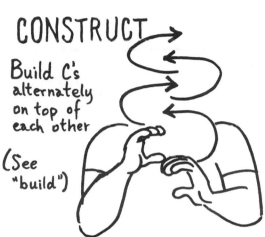

CONTENT (satisfy)

Right C above left on chest, move down together

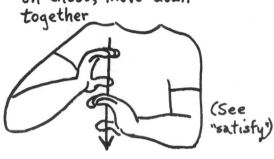

(See "satisfy")

CONTINENT

Palm-out C on back of left hand circles out and back along arm

(See "ground")

CONTINUE

Thumb of right A on thumb of left, both move forward

CONTRIBUTE

F pulls out of pocket, moves forward and opens to palm-down 5

CONTROL

X-hands move forward and back alternately

(See "manage")

73

CONQUER

Right S behind palm-down left S, jerks down at wrist to palm-down, wrist on wrist

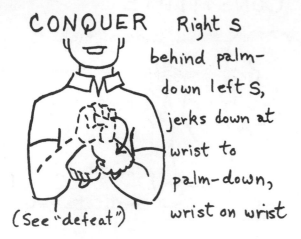

(See "defeat")

CONVERSE

Slightly bent 5-hands face each other, alternately move back and forth (See "talk")

Conversation = converse + -tion

CONVERT

C-wrists together; reverse position (See "change")

CONVINCE

Palm-up hands jerk sharply toward each other

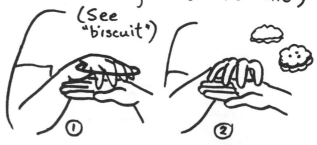

COOKIE

Fingertips touch palm, twist and touch again (cookie-cutter) (See "biscuit")

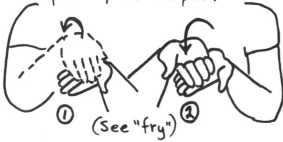

COOK

Flip right from palm-down to palm up on left palm

(See "fry")

COOL

Flutter fingers by side of head

COOPERATE

9's interlock; both circle horizontally

74

COPPER Thumb of C arcs right, hitting side of index

(See "metal")

COPY Palm-down 5 arcs back to flat-O on left palm

CORD ⌄

Wiggle right I-hand down and to side from C

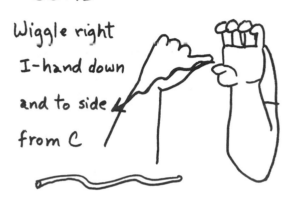

CORN Twist hand inward and out near chin

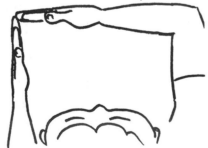

CORNER Flat hands, tap fingertips in corner shape

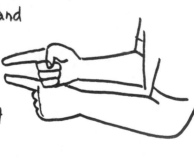

CORRECT Right 1-hand on top of left 1; index fingers at slight angles

CORRESPOND Right hand slightly behind left, index fingers flick from S to G-hands toward each other several times

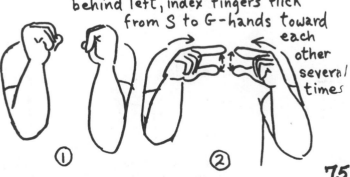

① ②

COST ⌄ Palm-in X, knuckle strikes downward on palm

75

COSTUME

Thumbs of C's brush off chest near shoulders

(See "dress")

COTTON

Pull cotton off left flat-O to right flat-O

COUCH

Sit two fingers on left thumb of C; slide off to right

(See "sit")

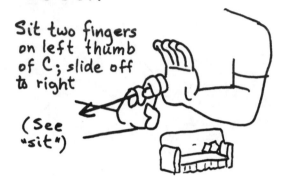

COUGH

Fingertips of claw remain on chest; hand swings up and down

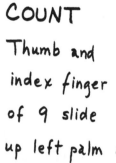

COUNSEL

C on back of hand brushes forward twice

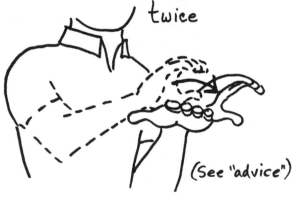

(See "advice")

COUNT

Thumb and index finger of 9 slide up left palm

COUNTRY

Rub palm-in Y in circle near elbow

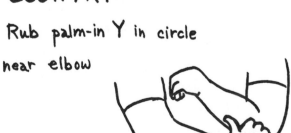

COUNTY

C circles on elbow (See "country")

COUPLE

Thumb and finger of right hand close fingers of C to left thumb

(See "pair")

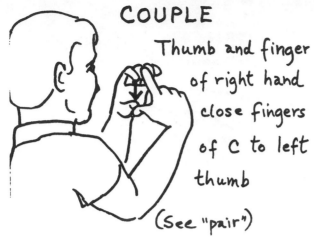

COURAGE

Bent middle finger on heart, then 5-hand moves out to palm-in S

COURSE

Side of C touches fingertips, then heel of hand

(See "lesson")

COURT

C-hands move alternately up and down

(See "balance")

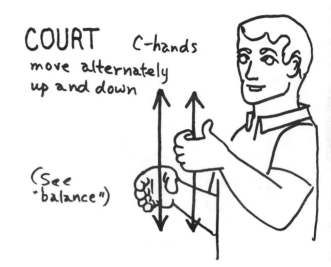

COURTESY

Tap C twice in middle of chest

(See "fine")

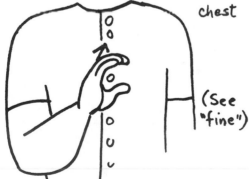

COUSIN

Shake C near ear

(See "aunt")

COVE

Twisting, C outlines curve of palm-down thumb and index

(See "bay")

COVER

Curved palm-up to cover other S-hand

(See "frost")

77

COW
Twist Y-hand down, slightly

CRAB
Move crossed hands forward to right, wiggling fingers

CRACK
Flat hand outlines crack in wall

CRACKER
Side of S taps arm near elbow twice

CRADLE
U in C, rock C

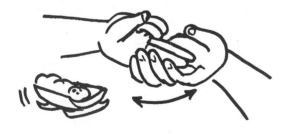

CRASH
Right S hits side of left C

(See "bump")

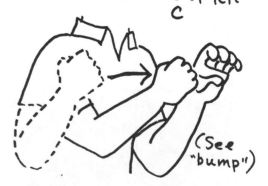

CRAWL
Twist bent V's from "knee to knee" across palm

CRAYON
Index circles on palm

CRAZE
Rotate index near temple

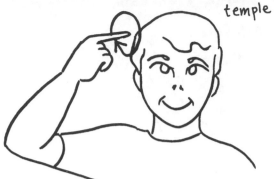

CREAM
C-hand to S-hand across back of left hand

CREATE
Right C on left, twist to palm-in; rest right on left again

Creative = create + -ive

(See "make")

① ②

CREDENTIAL
Tap C-thumbs

(See "license")

CREDIT
Right C resting on left, both move toward body

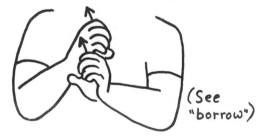

(See "borrow")

CREEP
Fingers creep up arm

Crept = creep + -ed

(See "caterpillar")

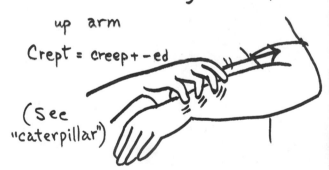

CRIB
Mesh fingers downward

CRICKET
C rides forward on wiggling fingers of left hand

(See "ant")

79

CRIPPLE
Palm-down 1-hands alternately move up and down

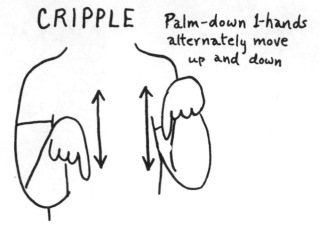

CRITIC
Index makes large X on palm

Critical = critic + -al

Criticize = critic + -ize

(See "discriminate")

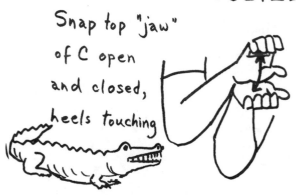

CROCHET
Cross horizontal index fingers; right slides off end of left into X; repeat several times

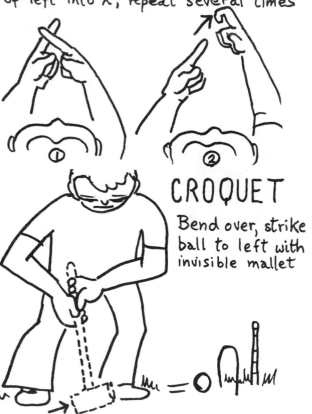

① ②

CROCODILE
Snap top "jaw" of C open and closed, heels touching

CROQUET
Bend over, strike ball to left with invisible mallet

CROSS
Palm-in right index on palm-down left index

(See "hybrid")

CROW
Flat-O opens and closes beak

(See "bird")

① ②

CROWD
S's approach each other, then press outward, lifting shoulders (elbowing through crowd)

① ②

CROWN

C's hold crown above head, put it on

CRUEL

Thumb of C strikes off back of S

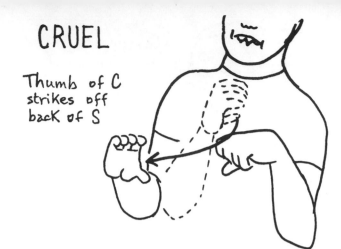

CRY

Drag index fingers alternately down cheeks, marking tear-tracks

CUCUMBER

Index slices past thumb of C several times

(See "tomato")

CULTURE

Right C curves around vertical left index

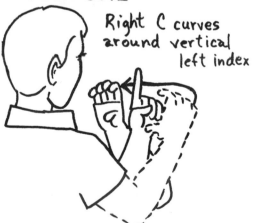

CUP

Set X on palm as if holding cup-handle

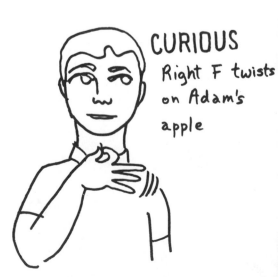

CUPBOARD

Open and close cupboard doors

81

CURIOUS

Right F twists on Adam's apple

CURL

Outline curl from ear down with index

CURRICULUM

Side of C on fingers of upright palm, then side of M on heel

(See "law")

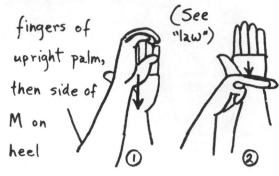

CURSE

Right C from front of mouth strikes side of vertical left index

CURTAIN

C-hands meet, change to 4, and slide down (See "drape")

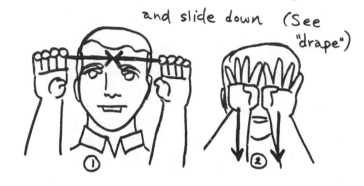

CUSTOM

Wrist of right C on wrist of left, both drop slightly

(See "habit")

CUT

Snip off end of middle fingertip of flat left hand

CYCLE

C's pedal forward alternately

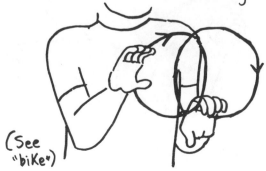

CUTE

Brush chin down with palm-in U to N fingers

(See "sugar")

82

(See "bike")

CYCLONE
Right above left, flat O's rotate around each other, rising to the right

CYMBAL
Strike cymbals together, "holding" them with A's

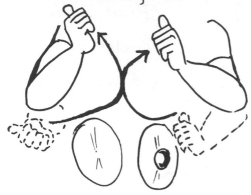

DAD
Tap D at temple

DAMAGE
S strikes side of D-hand; left index bends to X

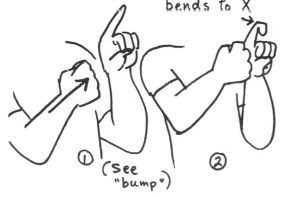

① (see "bump")　②

DANCE   Palm-in
V-fingertips arc from side to side, brushing palm

DANGER
Thumb-side of A arcs up, hitting back of S; repeat

Dangerous = danger + -ous

DARE
D on heart moves sharply forward

DARK
Palm-in hands cross in front of body, going down sideways

83

DARLING

Right D-hand circles on back of left hand over heart

DASH

Move palm-out D toward right a short distance

DATE

Tap D on palm

DAUGHTER

A-hand drops in an arc to palm-up and open on left arm

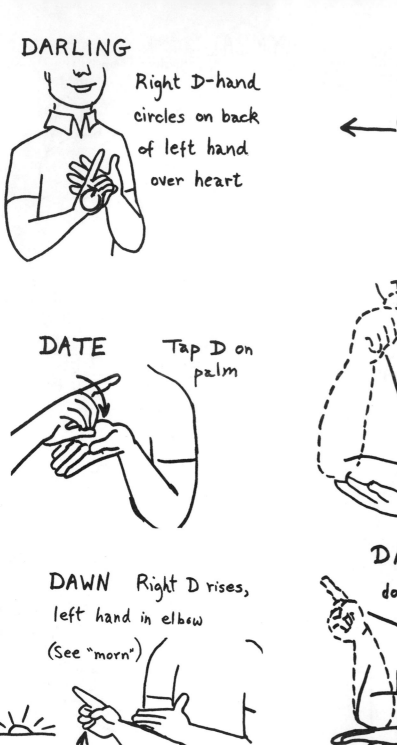

DAWN

Right D rises, left hand in elbow

(See "morn")

DAY

Drop right one-hand down on left arm

Daily = day + -ly

Today = to + day

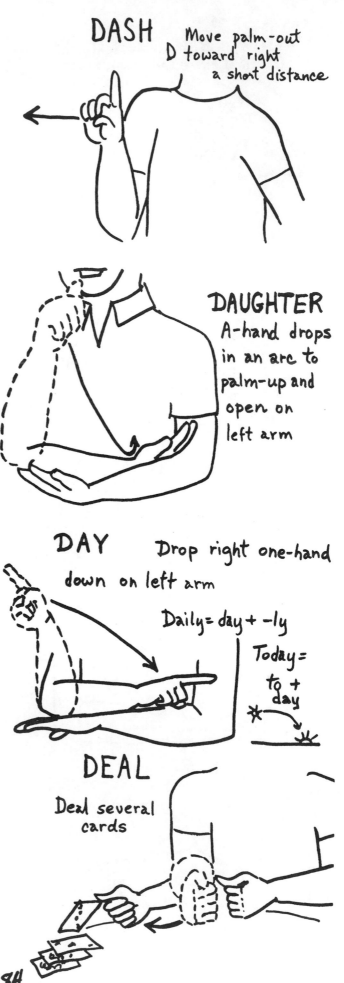

DEAL

Deal several cards

DEAF

Touch ear; sides of palm-down B's touch

①

②

84

DEAR

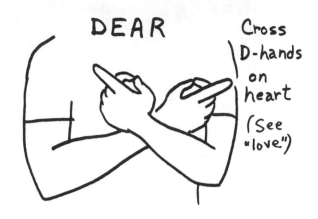

Cross D-hands on heart

(See "love")

DEBATE

Pointing at each other, 1-hands move together back and forth

DEBT

Index finger taps heel of palm-up left hand twice (See "owe")

DECEMBER

Twist D inward

(See "Christmas")

DECIDE

Index on forehead, then both 9's jerk slightly down

Decision = decide + -sion

DECORATE

Palm-out flat O's twist, while putting up decorations

DECREASE

Right H on left, both move slightly down, right twisting off to palm-up twice

(See "reduce")

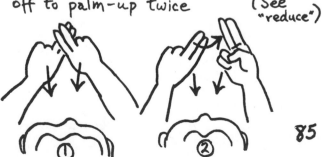

DEEP

Side of index slides down palm-right palm

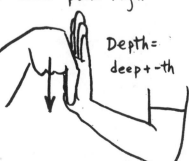

Depth = deep + -th

DEER
Move 5-hands up, to sides

DEFEAT
Right D behind palm-down left S jerks down at wrist to palm-down, wrist on wrist

(See "conquer")

DEFEND
Left D against right D, both move forward, not touching

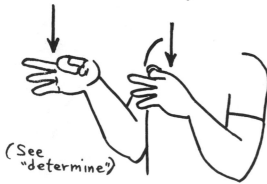

(See "guard")

DEFINE
Touch palm-down D to palm twice, turning between contacts

(See "mean")

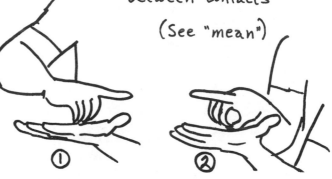

① ②

DEFINITE
Facing each other, horizontal F's jerk down

(See "determine")

DEFLATE
C-thumb, on palm-up fingertips; close C-fingers to thumb

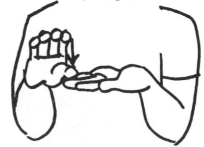

DEFY
Palm-in D swings sharply to palm-out from near shoulder

(See "rebel")

DEGREE
Thumb and fingers of right D move up and down left index finger once

(See "thermometer")

DELICIOUS

Bent middle finger on mouth; twists out and slightly up

DEMAND

Thumb and fingers of D on palm; both arc toward body

(See "require")

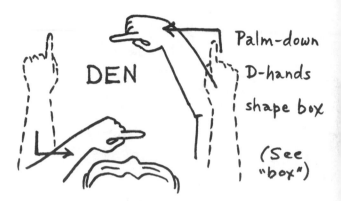

DEMONSTRATE

Index finger touches side of D-wrist; both move forward

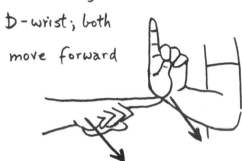

DEN

Palm-down D-hands shape box

(See "box")

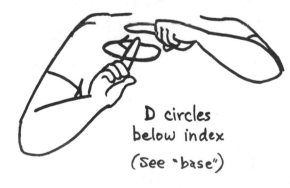

DENMARK

D circles near forehead

DENOMINATOR

D circles below index

(See "base")

DENTIST

Tap D at corner of mouth twice palm-in

DENY

Thumbs of both A-hands under chin, brush forward to palm-out

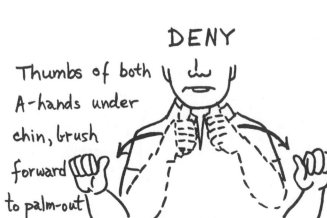

DEPART   Side of
D moves down
palm, then away
to the   side
(See
"apart")

DEPEND
Hang right X on horizontal
left index,
drop slightly
Dependent =
depend + -ent
(See "parasite")

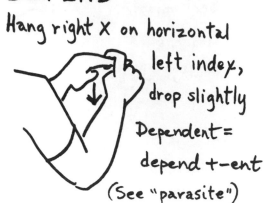

)DEPRESS
Middle finger
slides down
middle of
chest
(Reverse
of "feel")

(See "ill")

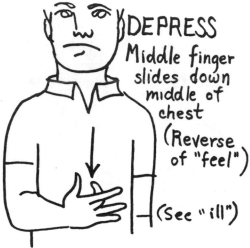

DESCRIBE
D-hands, right behind left,
move hands
alternately
forward
and back
(See "explain")

DESERT   D moves
to right across
forehead

(See "summer")

DESIGN   Palm-down D
draws "S" on
back of S

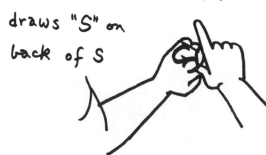

DESIRE

D moves down
chest

(See
"hunger")

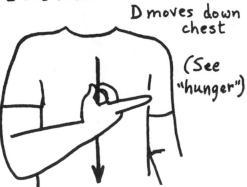

DESK
Bounce D
and elbow
on left
arm   (See "table")

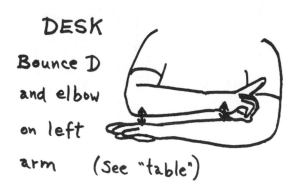

DESSERT

Ladle D-hand up to mouth twice

(See "soup")

DESTROY

Palm-down right hand sweeps back over palm-up left; close left; right closes, then brushes forward, striking left in passing

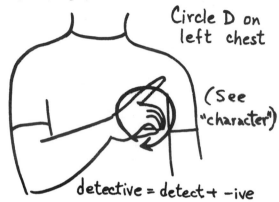

Destruction = destroy + -tion

DETAIN

Right X pulls index of left D backwards

Detention = detain + -tion

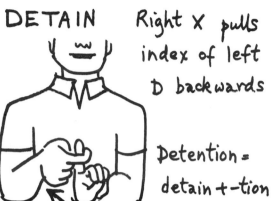

DETECT

Circle D on left chest

(See "character")

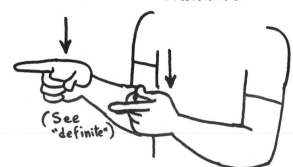

detective = detect + -ive

DETERIORATE

Side of right hand on back of left arm, hops down arm

(See "regress")

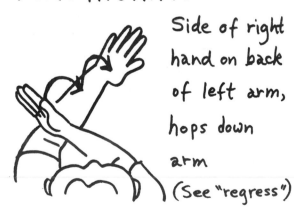

DETERMINE

Horizontal D's jerk downward

(See "definite")

DETROIT

With D hand, arc sharply down to right

(See "chicago")

DEVELOP

Thumb and finger of D slide up palm

(See "tall")

DEVIL

Thumb on temple, wiggle 2-fingers together (See "mischief")

DIAGONAL

Right D moves up to right diagonally

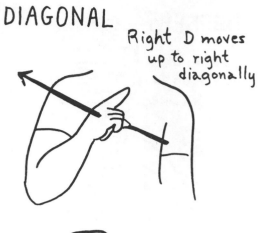

DIALECT

D shakes from lips outward

DIALOGUE

Alternately, D's move from near corners of mouth and back (See "talk")

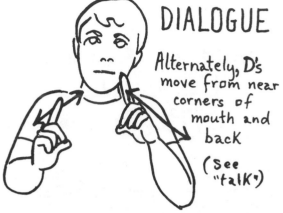

DIAMOND

D rises shaking from left ring-finger

DIAPER

Open and close G-hands at hips (like 2 pins)

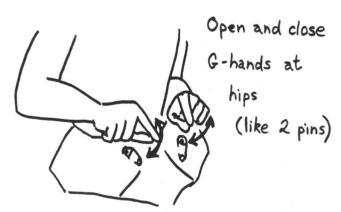

DICTIONARY

Palm-down D arcs down and left, brushing left palm; repeat

(See "encyclopedia")

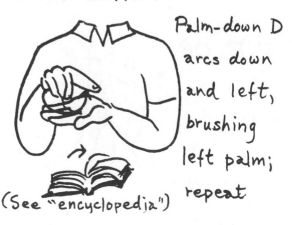

DIE

Turn hands over
Death = die + -th
Dead = die + d
Died = die + -ed

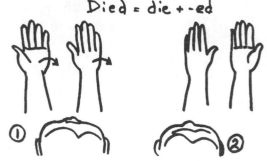

① ②

90

DIET
D's twist inward and down body

(See "slim")

DIFFER
Palm-out crossed fingers separate twice

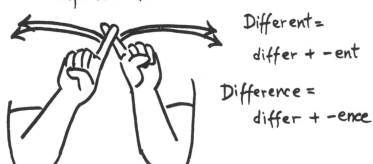

Different = differ + -ent

Difference = differ + -ence

DIFFICULT
Fingers of bent V's brush up and down

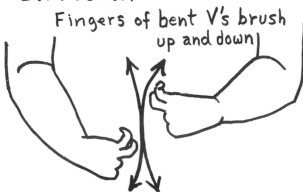

DIGEST
Palm-down D on palm-up D grind on each other alternately

(See "chew")

DIM
Palm-out D's cross in front of face, moving down

(See "dark")

DIME
Tap temple once, shake ten

(See "cent")

DINE
Palm-in D's circle up towards mouth alternately
(see "banquet")
Dining = dine + -ing

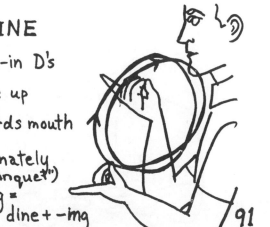

DINNER
D circles in and up near mouth

(See "eat")

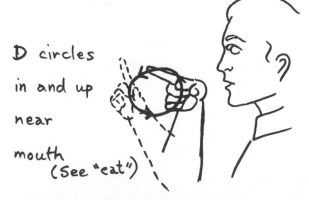

91

DINOSAUR

Arm of flat-O moves along behind left arm

DIPLOMA

F's touching, move outward

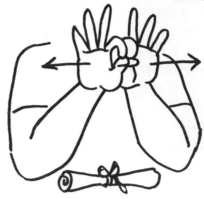

DIRECT

D on index,

D slides forward
(See "straight")

Director = direct + -er
Direction = direct + -tion

DIRT

Wiggle fingers under chin

Dirty = dirt + -y

(See "pig")

DISAGREE

Index at temple moves to tip of left index and then away

DISAPPEAR

Index between fingers of palm-down left hand, then drops down

(See "drown")

DISAPPOINT

1-hand finger rises sharply to chin

DISCOURAGE

Middle fingers slide down chest

92

DISCOVER Palm-down D

moves up across palm

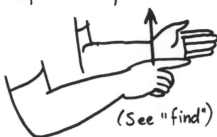

(See "find")

DISCRIMINATE

Make large X on palm
with D

(See "critic")

DISCUSS Palm-in

index taps heel of palm

three times

DISEASE

Palm-in D's
rest on forehead
and stomach

(See "sick")

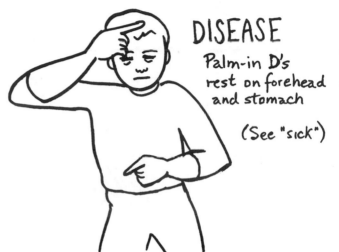

DISGUST

Claw hand
circles on
stomach

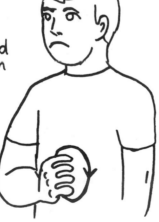

DISH

Outline dish with palms

(See
"plate")

DISSOLVE

Palm-up D's separate, last

3 fingers closing to palm

(See
"melt")

DISTANT

D's touch,
one D moves
forward,
arcing
slightly up

(See "far")

93

DISTORT
Wrists of D's touch crossing, stay together as hands reverse

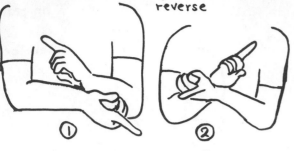

① ②

(See "change")

DISTRIBUTE
Right D curves forward past 5-fingers

(See "populate")

DISTRICT
D-hands, palm-out, circle horizontally out to palm-in   (See "class")

① ②

DITTO
Palm-left D circles by left palm rapidly several times

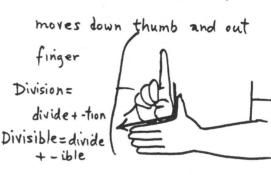

(See "mimeograph")

DIVE
Dive with hands together

DIVIDE
Palm-out D moves down thumb and out finger

Division=
divide + -tion

Divisible=divide
+ -ible

DIVINE
D circles above palm, then slides straight off end of palm

① (See "holy") ②

DIVORCE
D-hands twist to sides

94

DIZZY

Palm-in right claw circles counter-clockwise in front of eyes

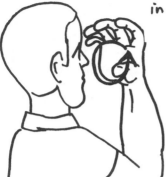

DO ^M

Palm-down C-hands move side-to-side

Does = do + -s
Did = do + -ed
Done = do + -en

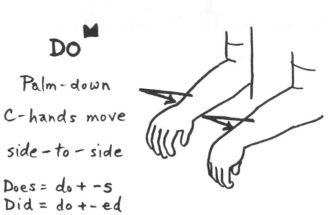

DOCK ^M

D outlines left palm-down arm, starting on outside

DOCTOR ^M

Thumb and finger of D tap pulse of left twice

DOCTRINE

Side of right D touches fingers and then heel of left vertical hand

(See "law")

DOG

Snap fingers of D-hand several times (to call dog)

Hotdog = hot + dog

(See "puppy")

DOLL ^M

Brush right X-finger off tip of nose twice

DOLLAR

Flat-o grasps end of horizontal hand, then slips off; repeat

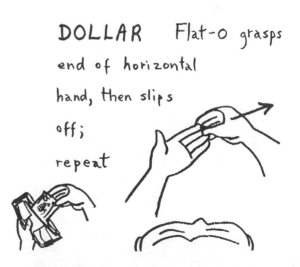

95

DOLPHIN

D makes 2 curves to the left, outside arm

DOMESTIC

D on chin, then on cheek

(See "home")

DOMINO

Two G-hands make the shape of a domino

DONKEY

Fingers together, flap forward

DOOR

Swing right hand open backwards and return

(See "closet")

DORM

D-hand below cheek-pillowing hand

(See "bed")

DOT

Make dot with D forward

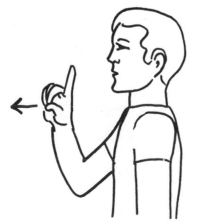

DOUBT

Palm-down S-hands move alternately up and down

(See "balance")

DOUBLE
D on palm arcs up to palm-up

(See "once")

DOUGH

Circle D on back of S
(See "flour")

DOUGHNUT
R's touching, circle downward to palm-up and touching

DOWN
Palm-in hand moves down

DRAGON
Palm-out S's at chin move forward to palm down 5's; fingers fluttering, move forward

DRAIN
D rotates as it falls through C-hand

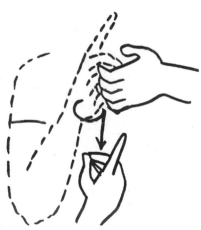

DRAMA
Thumbs and fingers of D's brush down chest alternately

Dramatic= drama+-ic (see "act")

97

DRAPE
D-hands meet, change to 4, and slide down
(See "curtain")

DRAW

With D-hand draw
backwards on palm in wavy line
(see "art")
Drew = draw + -ed   Drawn = draw + -en

DRAWER
Draw D-hands toward body

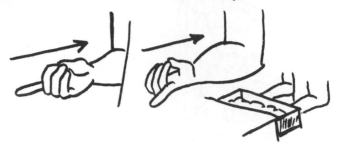

DREAM
Palm-in 1 on
forehead, move up to
right, alternating
X and 1

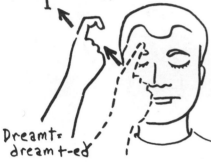

Dreamt=
dream+-ed

DRESS

Thumbs of
5-hands
brush down
chest twice,
palm-in

DRIFT

D drifts forward
left on back
of hand

DRILL

D brushes
back and
forth on
side of
index

(See "practice")

DRINK

Thumb on chin, drink
from C

Drank = drink +
-ed

Drunk = drink +
-en

DRIVE

S-hands
grasp
invisible wheel,
then
steer

Drove =
drive +
-ed
(see
"tractor")

98

DROP
Flat-o drops and opens

DROWN

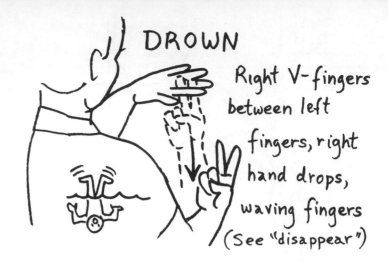

Right V-fingers between left fingers, right hand drops, waving fingers (See "disappear")

DRUG

D circles on palm

(See "medicine")

DRUM

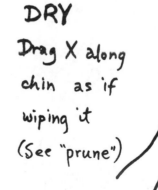

Drum alternately with both A hands

DRUNK (noun) (adj.)

A-hand with thumb extended swings past mouth, palm out

DRY

Drag X along chin as if wiping it

(See "prune")

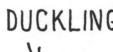

DUCK

Close two fingers on thumb twice

(See "bird")

DUCKLING

Two fingers open and close on thumb

DULL

Side of X pulls back across fingertips of D

(see "stale")

DUMB

Hit forehead with palm-in A

DUMP

Dump D off palm; left palm-up to palm-down

① ②

DURING

Indexes near right shoulder, arc down and out

Durable = add -able   (See "while")

DUST

Back of palm-up D circles on back of palm-down S

DUTY

Right D taps back of left wrist twice

(See "obligate")

DWARF

Palm-down D shows height of dwarf

(See "child")

DYE

Parallel palm-down 9-hands move down and up several times

100

(See "rinse")

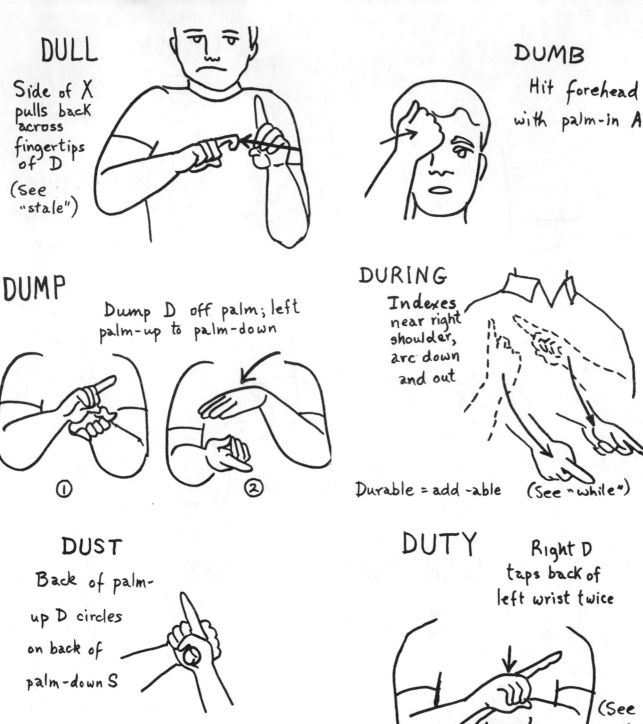

EACH
Thumb of right A rubs down side of left index once

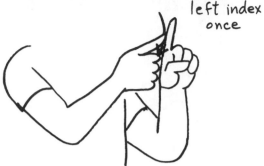

EAGER
Palm-to-palm E-hands rub back and forth on each other (See "enthuse")

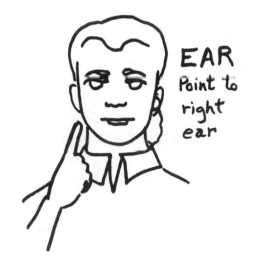

EAGLE
X on nose, pointing forward

EAR
Point to right ear

EARLY
S on back of hand slides inward, opening to 5

① ②

EARN
C closes to S, moving across palm toward you

EARRING
Clip earring on right ear with thumb and index

101

EARTH
Thumb and middle finger hold sides of S; right hand shakes, side-to-side

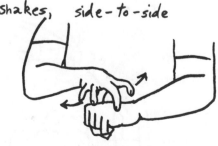

EASE

Stroke upwards on back of bent left fingers, circling up and out several times

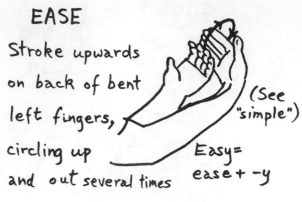

(See "simple")

Easy = ease + -y

EAST

Palm-out E moves right

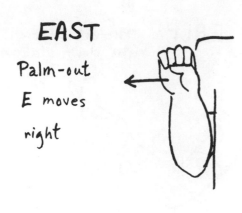

EASTER

Palm-to palm E-hands separate, shaking

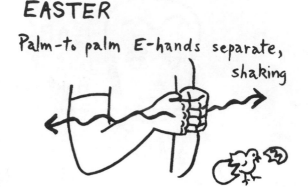

EAT

A circles in and up near mouth, spooning food in

Ate = eat + ed

ECHO

Side of E hits left palm, shakes to right, "bouncing off"

(See "bell")

ECOLOGY

Palm-up E on back of left hand circles out and back to elbow, and along arm

(See "ground")

ECONOMY

Palm-up E taps left palm twice

Economic = economy + -ic

(See "money")

EDGE

E moves around edge of palm-down hand

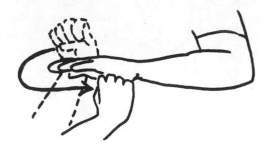

EDIT

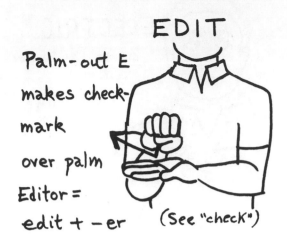

Palm-out E makes check-mark over palm
Editor = edit + -er

(See "check")

EDUCATE

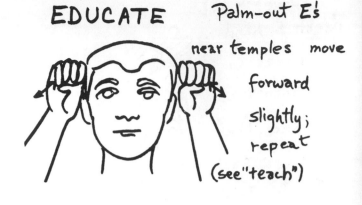

Palm-out E's near temples move forward slightly; repeat
(see "teach")

EFFECT

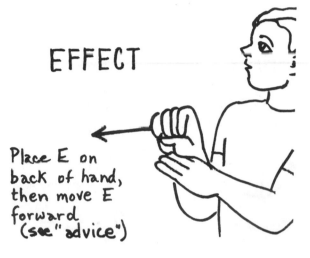

Place E on back of hand, then move E forward
(see "advice")

EFFORT

Palm-out E's move forward with slight arc

(See "attempt")

EGG

Break one H on the other H

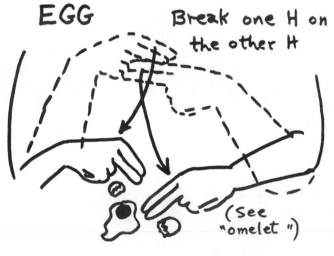

(See "omelet")

EGYPT

X on forehead, palm out

EITHER

Palm-out E off thumb, then off fingertip
(see "then")

103

ELBOW

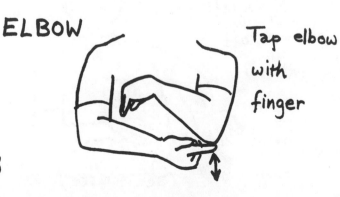

Tap elbow with finger

ELECT

Right 5-hand moves to touch 9 at left index, then moves back

Election = elect + -ion

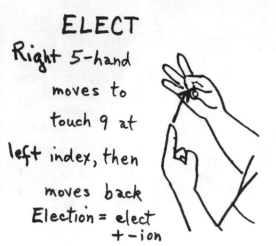

ELECTRIC

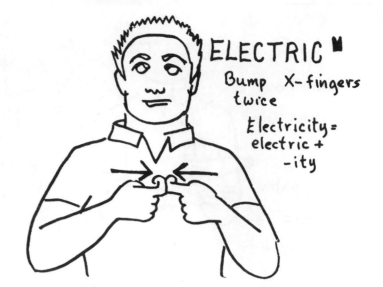

Bump X-fingers twice

Electricity = electric + -ity

ELEMENT

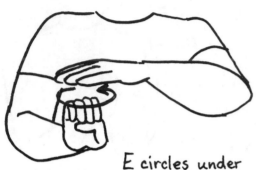

E circles under palm

(See "base")

ELEPHANT

From nose, trace elephant's trunk

ELEVATE

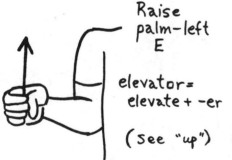

Raise palm-left E

elevator = elevate + -er

(see "up")

ELF

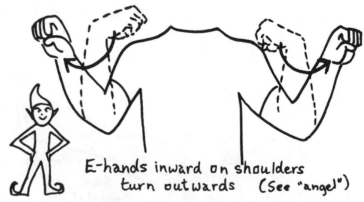

E-hands inward on shoulders turn outwards   (See "angel")

ELIMINATE

E on left palm, arc off to throw open hand down

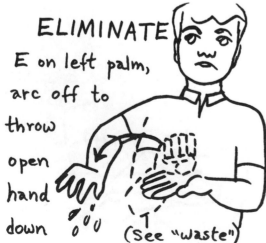

(See "waste")

ELK

E's move up and out from temples (see "deer")

104

ELSE

Palm-down E twists over to palm-up

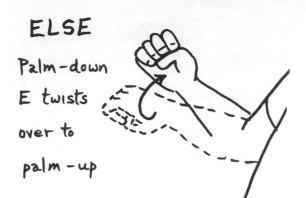

EMBARRASS

Flutter fingers as hands move up past cheeks

EMBROIDER

9 sews up and down between fingers of palm-down hand

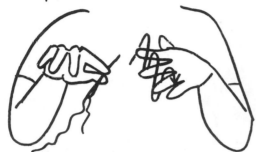

EMBRYO

Left C covers right E

EMOTION

E brushes once up chest

(See "feel")

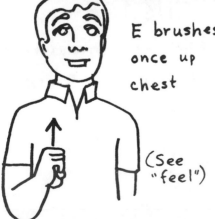

EMPHASIS

Open thumb of A on left palm, both move forward, A twisting to palm-in

Emphasize = emphasis + -ize

EMPLOY

Palm-out E arcs side-to-side hitting back of S

Employee = employ + -ee
Employer = employ + -er
Employment = employ + -ment
(See "work")

EMPTY

E brushes along back of hand and off

(See "bare")

105

ENCOURAGE

Flat hands push (someone) forward; repeat

(See "motive")

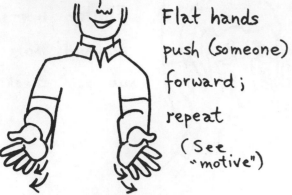

ENCYCLOPEDIA

Palm-down E arcs down and left, brushing left palm; repeat

(See "dictionary")

END

Palm-out E slides along side of hand and down fingertips (see "finish")

ENEMY

Pull index away from palm-out E

(See "oppose")

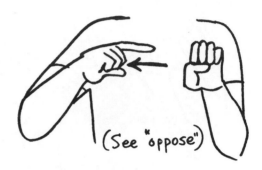

ENERGY

E-hand draws muscle

(See "strong")

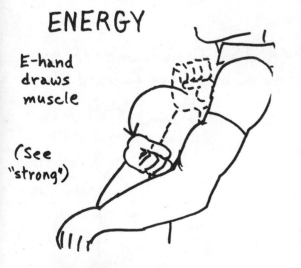

ENGAGE

Palm-out E circles once horizontally over S and drops on back of S

(See "appoint")

ENGINE

Right S behind left, hands move piston-like alternately up and down

Engineer = engine + -ee + -er
(See "motor")

ENGLAND

Right pulls left toward body

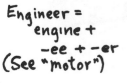

ENGLISH
Right pulls left toward body,

and
add
-ish

① ②

ENJOY
Palm-in E brushes up chest repeat (See "happy")

ENOUGH
Right palm brushes twice across left S

ENTER
Right palm-down flat-hand arcs out under horizontal palm

Entrance = enter + -ance

ENTERTAIN
Circle E's in opposite directions on chest (See "amuse")

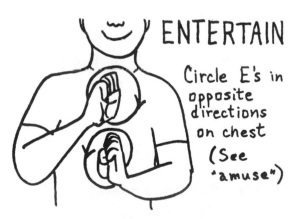

ENTHUSE
Rub palms together

Enthusiastic = enthuse + -ic
Enthusiasm = enthuse + -ism

(See "eager")

ENTIRE
Circle E horizontally from palm-down to end palm-up on left palm

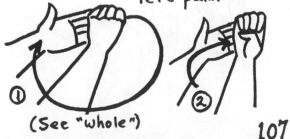
① ②
(See "whole")

107

ENVELOPE
Pass hand in front of mouth and insert in left hand

ENVIRONMENT
Right E curves around vertical left index

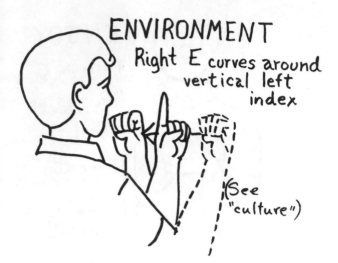

(See "culture")

ENVY
Palm-out E at side of mouth twists to palm-in (see "jealous")

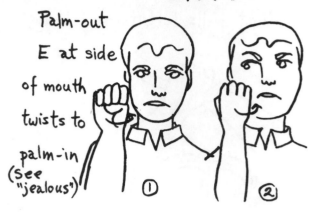

① ②

EPISCOPAL
With right index, outline full sleeve under left horizontal arm

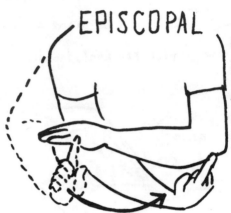

EQUAL
Bent hands tap fingertips twice

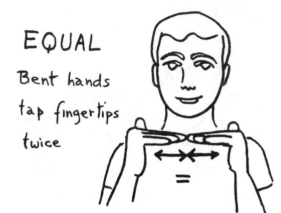

EQUATOR
Right E circles palm-in S, from palm-out to palm-in position

EQUIP
Skip palm-up E to the right twice

Equipment = equip + -ment (See "thing")

ERASE
E rubs back and forth on palm. Eraser = erase + -er

ERROR
Hit chin lightly twice with side of E

108

ESCALATE
E on side of index; both move forward and up

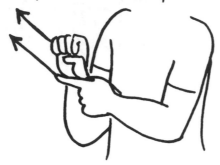

ESCAPE
Index finger between fingers of left; "escapes" sharply to side

ESKIMO
E-hands outline parka hood

ESPECIALLY
Palm-out E on tip of middle finger of palm-in 5, both move up

ESSAY
Right E moves down across palm in wavy motion

(See "read")

ESSENCE
E's, palm-up to palm-down in vertical circle

(See "important")

essential = add -al

ESTABLISH
Twist A-hand to palm-left and bring down on back of hand (See "found")

ESTIMATE
Palm-left E arcs in front of forehead (see "guess")

109

EUROPE E faces
temple, circles vertically

EVADE Right E wiggles
back from A

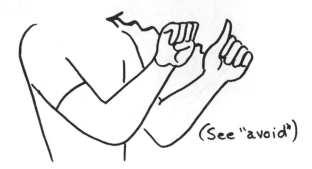

(See "avoid")

EVALUATE Palm-to-palm E's
move alternately up and down

(See "balance")

EVAPORATE

E shakes
up out
of C

EVE
Flat right hand sets over left
to a level position

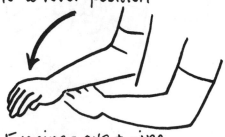

Evening = eve + -ing

EVEN E-fingertips touch, and then
N-fingertips

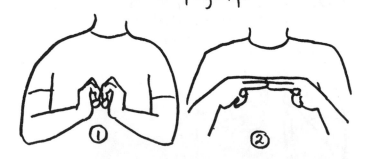

① ②

EVENT
Palm-up E's twist
to palm-down (see
"happen")

① ②

EVER
Palm-out
E circles

Every = ever
+ -y

(See
"circle")

EVERY

Thumbtip of right A slides down thumb of left A twice

EVIDENT

Palm-up E falls on palm

evidence = evident + -ence

EVIL

Palm-in E at mouth twists to palm-out, moves sharply to palm-down

(See "bad")

EVOLVE

Wrists of E's touch, crossing, and stay together as hands reverse

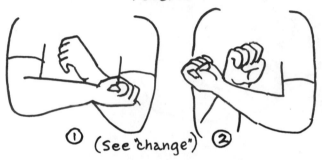

① (see "change") ②

EXACT ∎

Right X circles and drops on palm-up left X

EXAGGERATE

Right S in front of left; right S shakes forward

(see "propaganda")

EXAM

Index faces palm, moves downward, alternating index and X

Examine = exam + -ine

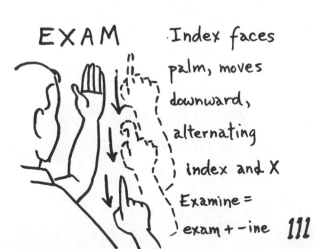

111

EXAMPLE

Index fingertip on wrist of palm-out E; both move forward (see "demonstrate")

EXCEED

Bent right on bent left hand; right swings upward in a forward arc

EXCEL

X holds side of hand, jerks away forward

(See "expert")

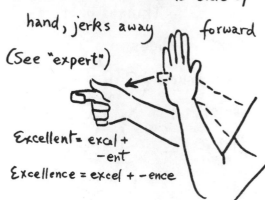

Excellent = excal + -ent

Excellence = excel + -ence

EXCEPT

9 grasps index finger of palm-in hand and pulls up left hand

EXCHANGE

X-hands, right in front of left, arc vertically to change places

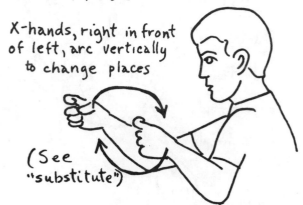

(See "substitute")

EXCITE

Brush upward on chest with middle fingers alternately

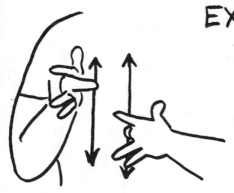

EXCUSE

Right fingertips brush off left fingertips several times

(See "pardon")

EXERCISE

S's move up and down above shoulders

EXIST

Palm-in E's move upwards on body (See "address")

112

EXIT
Right E rises toward body from under left palm

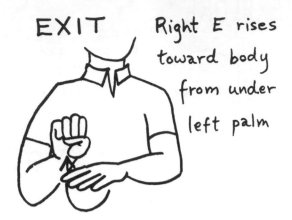

EXPAND
S-palms together, separate vertically, opening

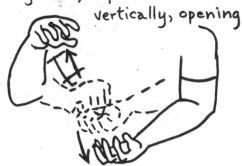

EXPECT
Index at temple, then hands face each other and bend quickly, right behind left

EXPENSE
Palm-up flat-O on palm rises, throws (money) down, and opens to 5

Expensive = expense + -ive

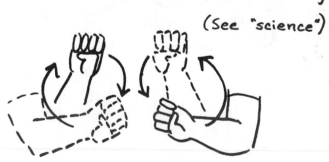

EXPERIENCE
Palm facing head, 5 on temple closes into flat-O; repeat

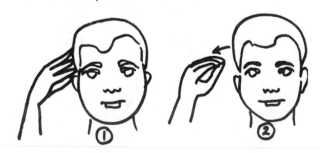

EXPERIMENT
Palm-out E's pour "chemicals" alternately

(See "science")

EXPERT
Grasp side of hand, slide off forward into A

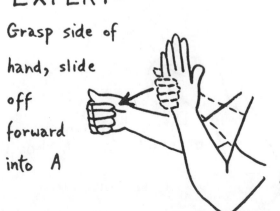

113

EXPLAIN
9-hands, right behind left, move alternately forward and back

(see "describe")

EXPLODE

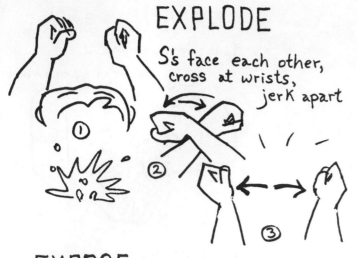

S's face each other, cross at wrists, jerk apart

EXPLORE

Palm-out E at eye moves down and out across left palm

(See "inspect")

EXPOSE

E's, palm-down together, open outwards

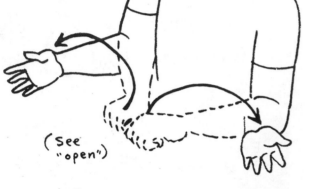

(See "open")

EXPRESS

E's facing each other near chin, left ahead of right, move forward together in slight arc

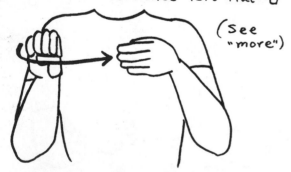

EXTRA

Palm-out right E moves toward and touches left flat-O

(See "more")

EYE

Point to right eye

FABLE

Right F-hand shakes away from stationary left F

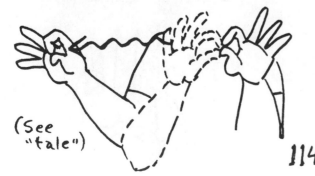

(See "tale")

FABRIC

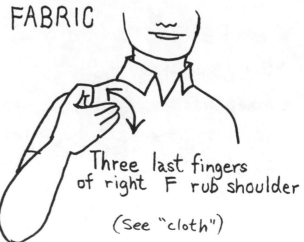

Three last fingers of right F rub shoulder

(See "cloth")

114

FABULOUS
Palm-out F's near temples make small outward circles, then flat hands palm-out push forward slightly

① ②

FACE
Circle face with index finger

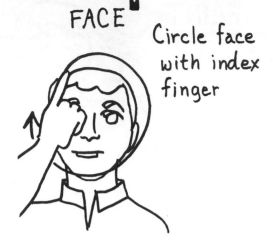

FACT
Fingers of 9 at chin;

move

forward

(See "certain")

FACTOR
Side of F arcs across palm

(See "some")

FACTORY
Palm-out 9-hands tou outline roof and sides

(See "house")

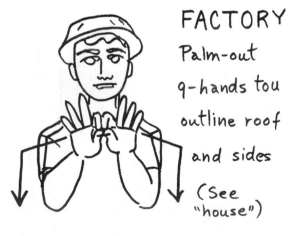

FACULTY
F-hand at left, then right shoulder

(See "member")

FADE
F's fall, gradually close to palm-up A's

(See "melt")

115

FAIL
Back of V slides forward across palm

Failure = fail +-ure

FAINT

Palm-down, A's drop from temples to 5's

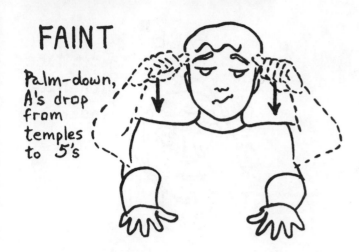

FAIR

Tap chin with middle finger of F

FAIRY   Fingers of 9's on shoulders, twist to point out

(See "angel")   (Wings)

FAITH

Touch forehead and sign "trust" with S on S at shoulder level

FAKE

Fingers of F brush past mouth

(See "false")

FALL

Palm-down V on elbow, twists over and out to palm-up

Fell= fall +-ed
Fallen= fall +-en

FALSE

Index brushes past mouth

FAME   Index fingers at corners of mouth spiral up and out

Famous= fame +-ous

116

FAMILIAR

Tap forehead with fingertips of palm-in F
(see "think")

FAMILY

F-hands touch first index, and then circle outward to touch little fingers

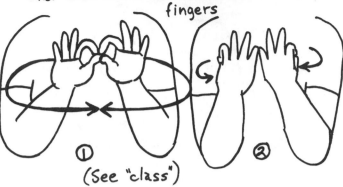

① ②

(See "class")

FAN

4-hand fans face

FANCY

Thumb of palm-left 5 brushes upward on chest several times

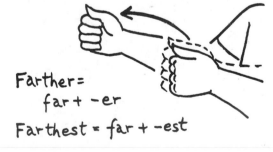

FANTASY

4 off temple loops forward right
fantastic = fantasy + -ic

FAR

A-hands together, right arcs forward

Farther = far + -er

Farthest = far + -est

FARM

Right thumb is drawn across the chin

farmer = farm + -er

(See "ranch")

117

FASCINATE

5's before face draw out to A-hands

① ②

FASHION

Index and little finger out, hand nods down, arcs, and nods to left

FAST

Indexes point forward, right ahead, jerk back into X's

Fasten= fast + -en

(See "speed")

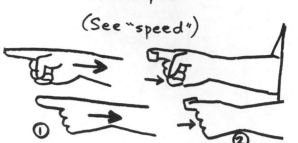

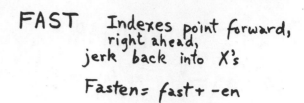

FAT

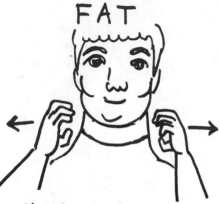

Claw-hands face the neck, move out to sides

FATE

F's flip over (See "happen")

Fatal= fate + -al

FATHER

Thumb of 5 on forehead

FAUCET

Turn faucet twice, to the right

FAULT

Palm-in, fingertips of F on right shoulder

FAVOR

Fingertips of right B-hand move up and down toward left index finger several times

FEAR
Palm-out F's shake downward slightly to left

(See "afraid")

FEAST
F's move alternately to and from mouth

① ② (See "banquet")

FEATHER
F-hand arcs up from back of head

FEBRUARY
9's draw heart over own heart

(See "heart")

FEDERAL
F circles once near temple, then touches temple with middle finger

(See "govern")

FEE
Middle fingertip of F brushes down across left palm

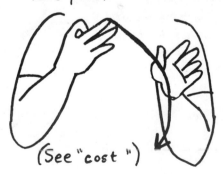

(See "cost")

FEED

Flat O's hand food from mouth, left hand ahead of right.

Fed = feed + -ed

119

FEEL
Brush chest upwards with middle finger

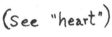

Felt = feel + -ed

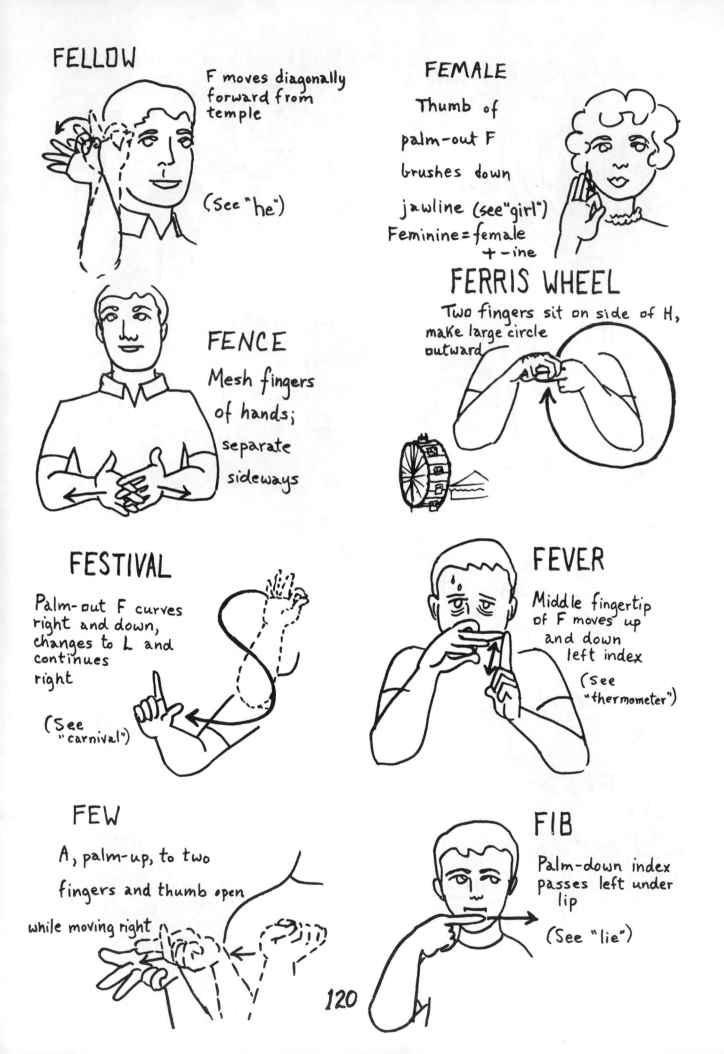

FELLOW

F moves diagonally forward from temple

(See "he")

FEMALE

Thumb of palm-out F brushes down jawline (see "girl")

Feminine = female + -ine

FENCE

Mesh fingers of hands; separate sideways

FERRIS WHEEL

Two fingers sit on side of H, make large circle outward

FESTIVAL

Palm-out F curves right and down, changes to L and continues right

(See "carnival")

FEVER

Middle fingertip of F moves up and down left index

(See "thermometer")

FEW

A, palm-up, to two fingers and thumb open while moving right

FIB

Palm-down index passes left under lip

(See "lie")

120

FICTION Middle finger of F on temple circles up to right (See "fantasy")

FIELD F on back of hand, circle out, back to elbow, along arm to hand (see "ground")

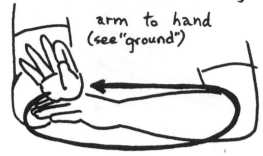

FIG

Finger and thumb of F on S; goes around S (See "apricot")

FIGHT S-hands face each other, jerk to cross at wrists; repeat

Fought = fight + -ed

① ②

FIGURE

Palms of 9's brush sideways twice (see "arithmetic")

FILE

Push side of F-hand toward wrist along each finger

FILL Palm-down flat hand rises inside palm-right left C

FILM Heel of 9-hand stays on side of left, fingers of 9 move side-to-side slightly

(See "movie")

FILTH

Open hand sharply from S to 5 under chin

FINAL

The right F-hand moves down past the little finger of the left i-hand

Finally = final + -ly

FINANCE

Palm-up right F taps left palm twice

Financial = finance + -al

(See "money")

FIND

9-hand pulls up past palm of left hand

Found = find + -ed

(See "discover")

FINE

Tap chest with 5-thumb

FINGER

Rub back of index finger with fingertip

FINISH

Palm-out F hand slides along side of hand and down fingertips

FINLAND

9 circles near forehead (see "Denmark")

122

FIRE   Palm-up bent 5's move
upward, fluttering fingers

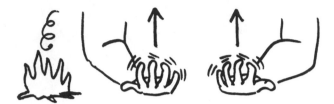

FIRST   Index hits
thumb back
toward
body
once

FISH
Flutter hand forward
like swimming

(See "tuna")

FIT
Palm-out
right 9
moves down to
touch thumbtips
with palm-up
left 9

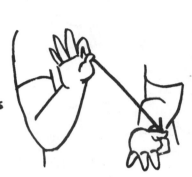

FIX   Thumbs of 9's together; left is
stationary, right twists down from wrist
(See
"repair")

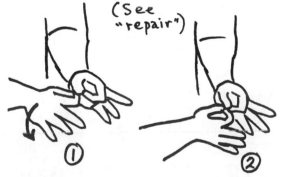

① ②

FLAG
Flat hand
waves
in
breeze,
index
on arm

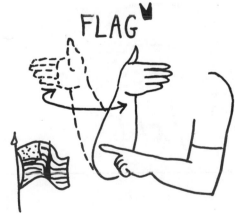

FLAKE   Palm-up F arcs downward,
striking side of index
in passing

FLAME
Palm-in 9
moves up,
fluttering
fingers

(See "chip")   123

FLAP
Hang right hand over index and flap up and down

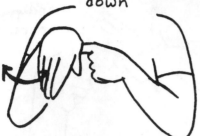

FLAPJACK
F slides forward and flips over

(See "pancake")

FLARE
O opens to 5 and rises, fingers fluttering, from wrist against left index

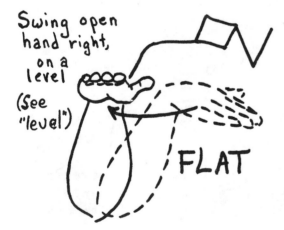

— (See "torch")

FLASH
Right O-hand snaps open to 5, wrist against left index; Repeat several times

① ②

FLAT
Swing open hand right, on a level (See "level")

FLATTER
Right hand "paints" left index finger

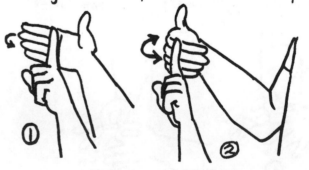

① ②

FLAVOR
Palm-in, middle finger of F taps chin

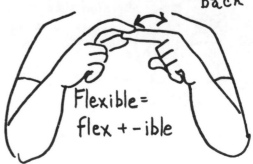

FLEX
Seize left index finger and flex forward and back

Flexible = flex + -ible

124

FLIRT

Flat 5-hands, thumbs together, wiggle fingers like a girl's lashes

FLOAT

Right F, palm-up on back of left flat hand; float forward together

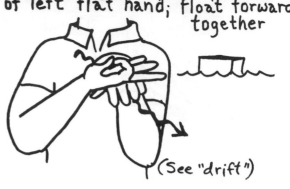

(See "drift")

FLOOD

Palm-down 5-hands point to each other; rise, fluttering fingers

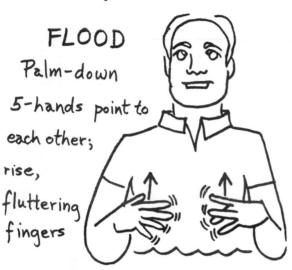

FLOOR

Flat hands separate

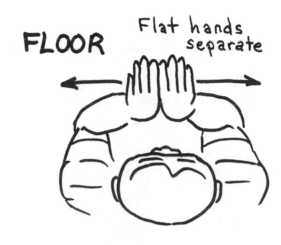

FLOUR

9 circles on back of S-hand

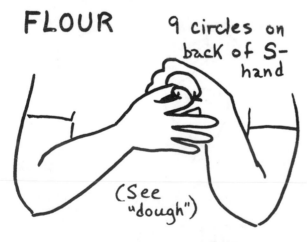

(See "dough")

FLOW

Right behind left, fingers flutter, hands flow forward left

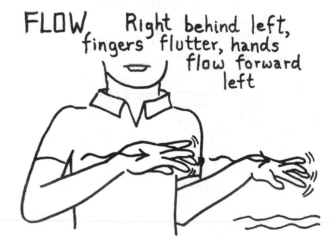

FLOWER

Flat-O at right of nose, then at left

FLUID

Right F moves downward from lips with wavy motion

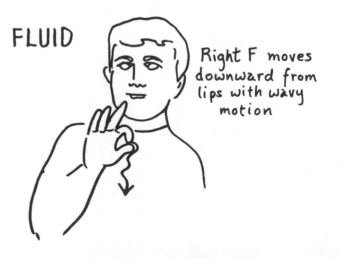

125

FLUNK

Thumb-and-finger side of F hits left palm sharply

(see "forbid")

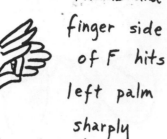

FLUTE

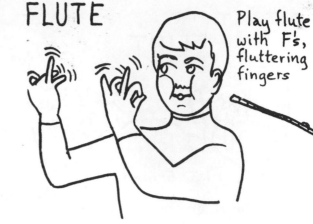

Play flute with F's, fluttering fingers

FLY

Bent hands at shoulders, flap fingers like wings

Flew = fly + -ed
Flown = fly + -en

Flight = fly + t

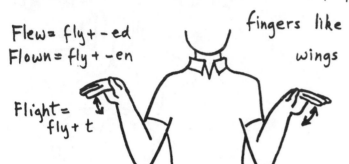

FOAM

Spiral F-hand up from palm

FOE

1-hand moves sharply away from stationary left F. (See "oppose")

FOG

From sides, arc up and cross palm-in F's at wrists, near face

(see "dark")

FOLD, -FOLD (Suffix)

① ②

Palm-to-palm, keep fingertips together and roll hands back-to-back
Folder = fold + -er

FOLK

F-palms face each other, circle alternately up and down forwards

(See "people")

126

FOLLOW

Right A follows left A, both move forward and left

FOND

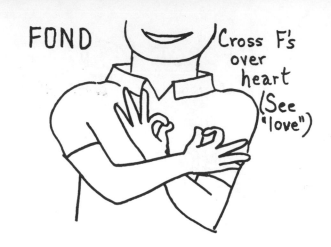

Cross F's over heart (See "love")

FOOD

Palm-in flat-o nods toward mouth (Putting food in)

FOOL

Palm-left F arcs in front of eyes

Foolish = fool +-ish (See "strange")

FOOT

F-hand moves down, past flat wrist

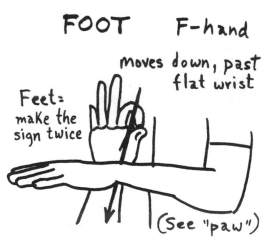

Feet: make the sign twice

(See "paw")

FOOTBALL

Mesh fingers of 5-hands several times

(Can be "foot" + "ball")

FOR

Index on forehead twists to palm-out

(See "pro")

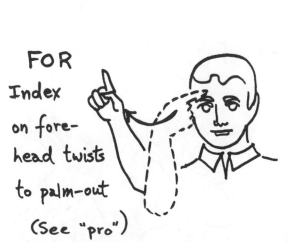

FORBID

Side of vertical 1-hand strikes left palm

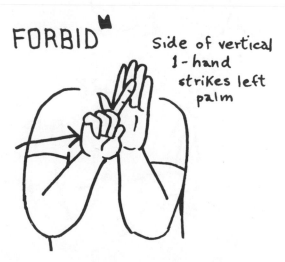

127

FORCE

Thumb of palm-left C at shoulder; move sharply forward

FORE

Bent right hand behind bent left; right moves back

(See "pre")

Before = be + fore

FOREIGN

Fingers of 9 rub arm in circles near elbow

(See "country")

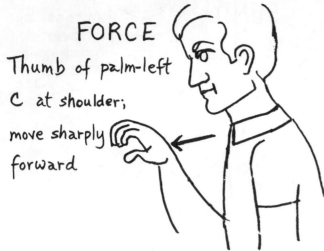

FOREST

Elbow of F on back of hand, shake F slightly

(See "tree")

FORGET

Palm-in hand on forehead; wipe off to right, to palm-in A

Forgot = forget + -ed

Forgotten = forget + -en

FORGIVE

Flat hands brush off each other; right off left, turn over, then left off right

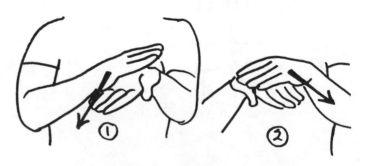

FORK

Stab palm with "tines" of W

FORM

Outline form with palm-out F-thumbs

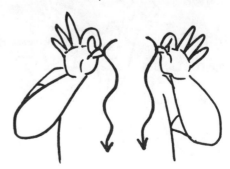

128

FORMULA
Side of right F on left fingers, then on heel

(See "law")

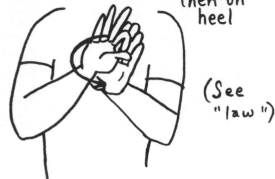

FORTUNE
Palm-up F on left palm, swing up over palm, inverting

(See "rich")

FOUND
Palm-down F twists, and side of F falls on back of hand

(See "establish")

Foundation = found + -tion

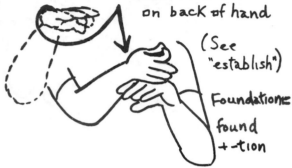

FOUNTAIN
F rises behind S, fingers fluttering, and "flows" down other side

① ②

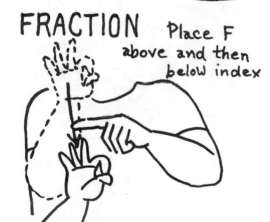

FOX
Nose in center of F, twist F around nose, wrist stationary

FRACTION
Place F above and then below index

FRAGILE
Three fingers of F do push-ups on palm

(See "weak")

129

FRAGRANT
Palm-in F circles vertically near nose

Fragrance = fragrant + -ance

(See "smell")

FRAME

F-hands form a square

FRANCE

9 twists outward   French = France + -h

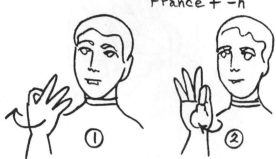

① ②

FRANK

Side of F on palm; move F straight forward

(See "honest")

FRANKFURTER

Pull out of F alternately S and C

(see "baloney")

C ← S

FRECKLE

Spot left cheek with thumb & fingertip of 9

(See "measles")

Palm-in F's crossed at wrists,

separate and twist to palm-out

FREE

② ①

FREEZE

Draw back hands to claws

Froze = freeze + -ed

Frozen = freeze + -en

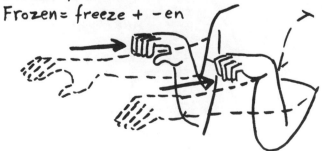

FRESH

Back of F-hand slides left across palm, arcing up

(See "new")

130

FRESHMAN
Point to right 5's third finger with index

FRIEND
Hook index fingers, first right over left then left over right

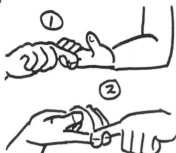

FRIDAY
Palm-out F-hand circles slightly

FRIGHT
Palm-in F's jerk toward each other

Frighten = fright + -en   (see "scare")

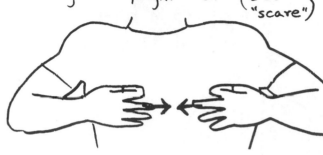

FROG
Flick fingers out twice from S under chin

FROM
Back of palm-in X touches palm-out index, then moves toward body

FRONT
Palm-in hand arcs downward in front of face

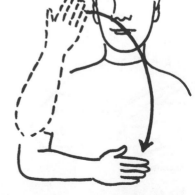

FROST
Smooth 3-fingers of F up and over back of S-hand

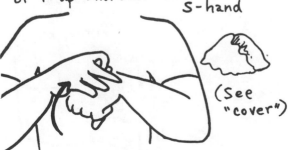

(see "cover")

FROWN
Indexes above eyes drop to point downwards over eyes

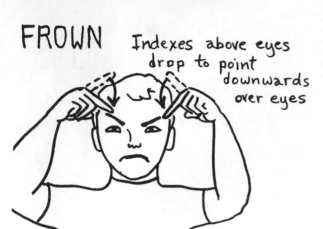

FRUIT
Finger- and thumbtip of F on cheek; twist (see "apple")

FRUSTRATE
Flat hand flips up in front of face

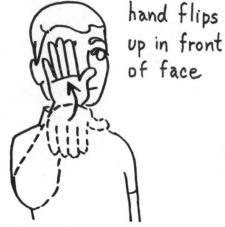

FRY
Flip F on palm, palm-down to palm-up

(See "cook")

FULL, -FUL (suffix)
Palm-down hand

brushes

inward

across side

of left S

(See "mature")

FUN
Palm-in U on nose strokes downward to palm-in N (see "doll")
Funny = fun + -y

FUNCTION
Palm-out F arcs, side-to-side, hitting back of S

(See "work")

FUNDAMENTAL
Circle F below palm

(See "base")

132

FUNERAL

Palm-out right V behind left; move forward in slightly down and up motion twice

FUNGUS
Circle heel of F-thumb on little fingertip of palm-up left i

(See "algae")

FUR

Slide F-hand up arm and over shoulder (See "wool")

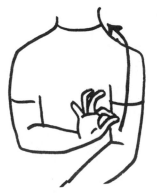

FURNISH
F-hand, palm-up, skips twice to the right

Furniture = furnish + -ure

(see "thing")

FURY

F jerks up right chest

(See "anger")

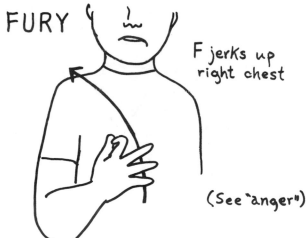

FUSS
Tap palm-in F on chest sharply (See "complain")

FUTURE

Palm-left F near side of head, arc forward

(See "will")

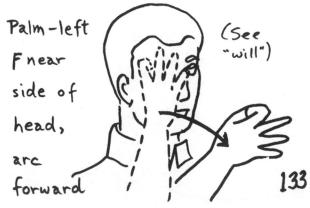

133

GAIN
Right palm-up H swings over to hit top of left G

(See "increase")

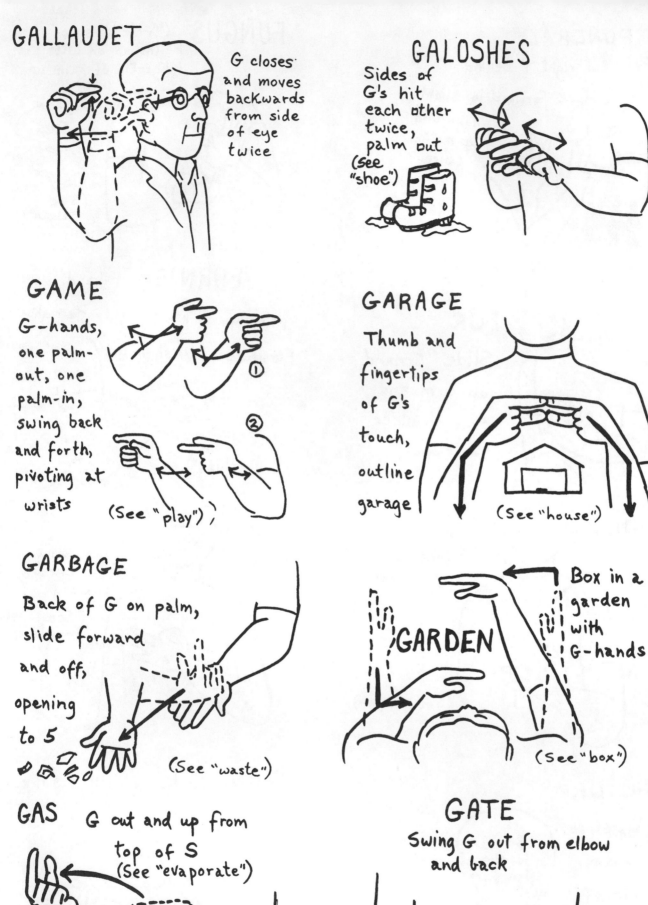

GALLAUDET

G closes and moves backwards from side of eye twice

GALOSHES

Sides of G's hit each other twice, palm out (See "shoe")

GAME

G-hands, one palm-out, one palm-in, swing back and forth, pivoting at wrists

① ②

(See "play")

GARAGE

Thumb and fingertips of G's touch, outline garage

(See "house")

GARBAGE

Back of G on palm, slide forward and off, opening to 5

(See "waste")

GARDEN

Box in a garden with G-hands

(See "box")

GAS

G out and up from top of S
(See "evaporate")

GATE

Swing G out from elbow and back

134

GATHER
Starting at sides, flat hands flap forward to meet, palm-in

(See "collect")

GAY
Sides of G-hands brush upwards on sides of chest; repeat

GEESE
Sign for "goose" works down to wrist, opening and closing

GENDER
G at temple, then at jaw

(See "parent")

GENERAL
Palms of G-hands touch; then separate forward

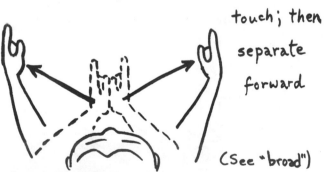

(See "broad")

GENERATE
Palms facing each other, G's circle each other forward from right shoulder

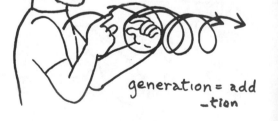

generation = add -tion

GENTLE
G-hands cross under chin, separate downward

(see "quiet")

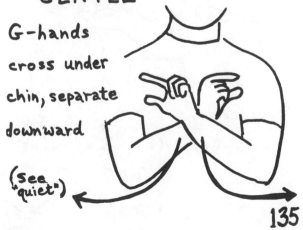

135

GENTLEMAN
A-thumb on temple to chest

(Can be signed "gentle" + "man")

GENTLEMEN

A-thumb on temple drops to 5 on chest

(Can be signed "gentle" + "men")

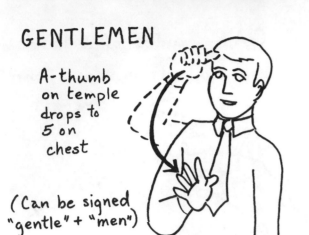

GEOGRAPHY

Right G on left, then circle each other vertically once

(See "world")

GEOMETRY

Little finger side of palm-in right G hits thumb and finger of left G twice

(See "arithmetic")

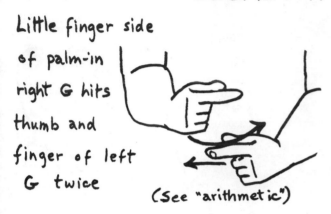

GERBIL

Brush G off nose-tip twice

(See "mouse")

GERM
G circles on palm, flat-O opens over palm and spreads up arm

(See "cancer")

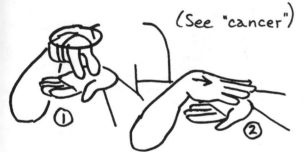

GERMAN   S-hands cross

at wrists, open to 5's

Germany = German + -y

GET Right open hand above left, draw toward body, closing to S-hands
(See "receive")

Got = get + -ed
Gotten = get + -en

GHOST

Palms face each other, right rises, left drops, close to flat O

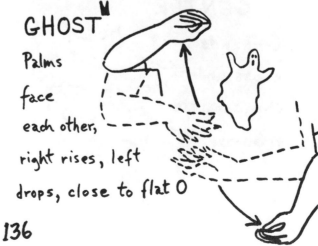

136

GIANT
G's move out from shoulders in big arcs

GIFT
G's point up, left ahead of right, drop to left to level position

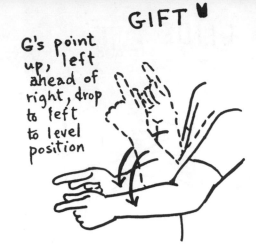

GINGER
Right G above left, tap twice

GIRAFFE
C-hand traces up neck

GIVE
Palm-in flat-O's near body turn outwards to palm-up

Gave = give + -ed

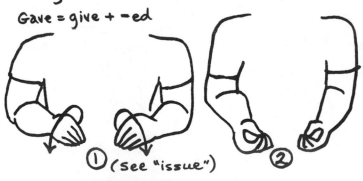

① (see "issue") ②

GIRL
Thumb of A-hand moves down jawline

GLAD
G-hand brushes chest upward twice

(See "happy")

137

GLASS
Drop G from temple to palm

Glasses = glass + -s

GLIDE
G glides forward on back of hand

(See "drift")

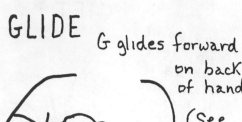

GLISTEN
G's move up and out with wavy motion

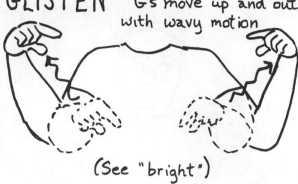

(See "bright")

GLOBE
2 G's separate, outline globe and touch again (see "bulb")

GLORY
Palm of 5 on palm, right lifts off, shaking

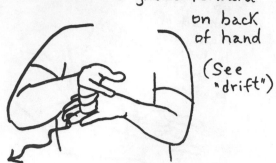

GLOVE
Draw on invisible gloves

Gloves = glove + -s

①   ②

GLOW
G-thumb and finger on back of hand rise up and off, shaking

(See "shine")

GLUE
G-hand twists to palm-down; sweeps across palm

(See "paste")

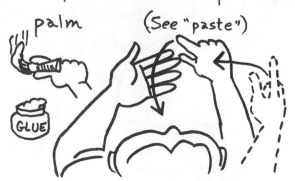

GO
G-hands face each other, roll out to point forward

Went = go + -ed

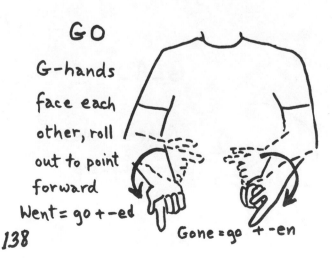

Gone = go + -en

138

GOAL Right index behind left G, turns down to point at G

(See "aim")

GOAT Palm-in fist on chin moves to forehead, where two fingers flick out

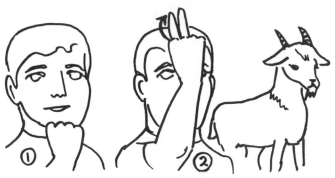

GOBBLE Palm-in G circles toward mouth; repeat (see "eat")

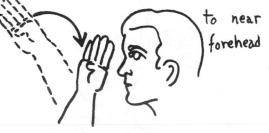

GOBLIN G's pull away from each other vertically and close

(See "ghost")

GOD Palm-left B arcs down from above to near forehead

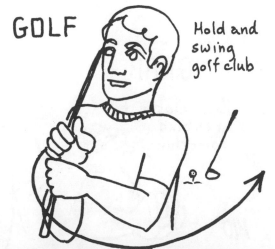

GOLD G at ear shakes downward to right Golden = gold +-en

(See "California")

GOLF Hold and swing golf club

GOOD Palm-in fingers on chin drop to palm of left hand

139

GOOSE   First two fingers open and close on thumb

GOPHER   Tips of G's tap under chin

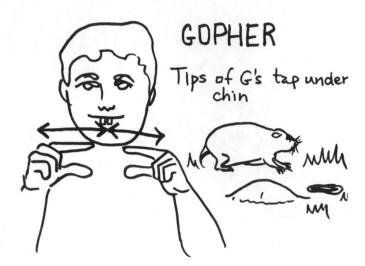

GORILLA
G-hands' thumbs scratch sides (see "monkey")

GOSPEL   Little-finger side of G-hand brushes up palm

GOVERN   Circle X-hand near temple, then touch
Governor = govern + -er
Government = govern + -ment

GOSSIP   G-hands face each other near chin, circle outwards, horizontally with indexes and thumbs opening and closing

GOWN

Brush thumbtips down off chest twice

(See "dress")

GRAB

Hand closes to S, grabbing something

140

GRACE

G from heart glides off palm and forward

GRADE

G circles over and drops on left palm

GRAIN

G brushes up G twice

GRADUATE

G on palm circles up

(See "college")

GRAMMAR

G-hands separate, shaking slightly

(See "sentence")

GRAND

G-hands face each other, twist apart to (See "big") palm-out D's

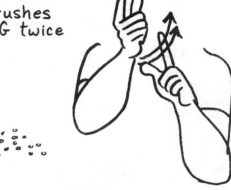

GRANDFATHER

From temple 5 makes two arcs, palm-left, diagonally right

(See "grand" + "father")

GRANDMOTHER

Palm-left 5 makes two arcs diagonally to right from chin

(Can be signed "grand" + "mother")

GRAPE Hop right hand fingers across back of left hand (See "raisin")

GRAPH Draw a cross on palm with G

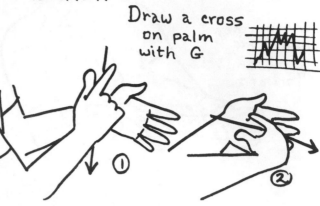

GRASS Fingers of palm-up right claw move up through fingers of left claw several times

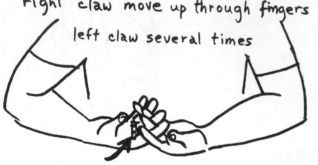

GRAVE Palm-down G-hands arc toward body, ending palm-out

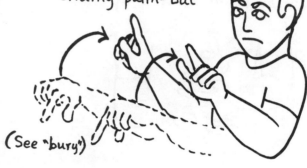

(See "bury")

GRAVEL Back of G taps of S

(See "stone")

GRAVY Right 9-hand slides off lower edge of left; repeat

(See "oil")

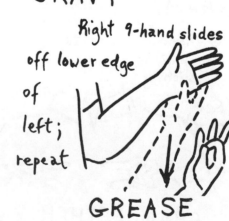

GREASE

GRAY (GREY) Side of G moves right across forehead

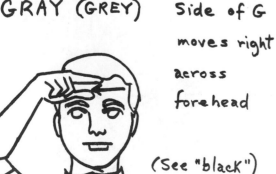

(See "black")

Flick U-fingers back into N off heel of G-hand

see "butter")

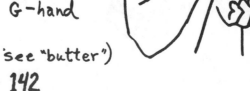

142

GREAT

G-hands face each other, arc apart

(See "big")

GREECE

G arcs down inward near nose

Greek = Greece + -k

GREEN

Palm-left G shakes

(See "blue")

GREMLIN

G's on shoulders swing off

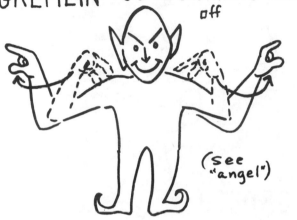

(see "angel")

GRIEF

Middle right finger touches heart; C's close to S's, twist (wet handkerchief) in opposite directions

① ②

GRILL

Circle G under palm

(See "oven")

GRIM

G-hands at sides of mouth drop slightly

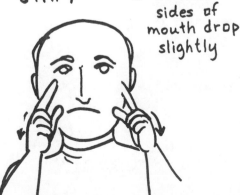

GRIN

G-hands twist upwards near corners of mouth

(See "smile")

GRIND

Circle G on S in grinding motion

Ground = grind + -ed

(See "coffee")

GRIPE

Tap two fingers of G on chest sharply

(See "complain")

GROAN

G-hand at throat shakes up and out under chin

(See "moan")

GROCER

Back of right G nods toward and away from side of left C

Grocery = grocer + -y

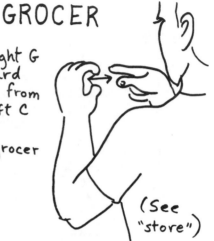

(See "store")

GROUCH

Outline half of sour mouth with G

GROUND (noun)

G on back of left hand circles out and back, along arm

GROUP

G-hands circle from palm-out to palm-in horizontally

(See "class")

GROW

Right flat-o "grows" through left C, to a palm-in 5

Grew = grow + -ed

Grown = grow + -en

Growth = grow + -th

144

GUARANTEE

Index from mouth to rest against left hand as G

(See "promise")

GUARD

Left G against right G, both move forward, not touching

GUESS

Right hand arcs past eyes, closing to S

(See "estimate")

GUIDE

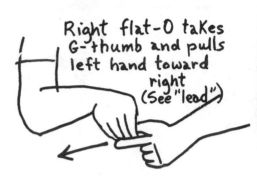

Right flat-O takes G-thumb and pulls left hand toward right
(See "lead")

GUILT

Tap G on left chest twice

Guilty = guilt + -y

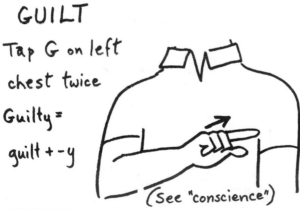

(See "conscience")

GUINEA PIG

G under chin + "pig"

GUITAR

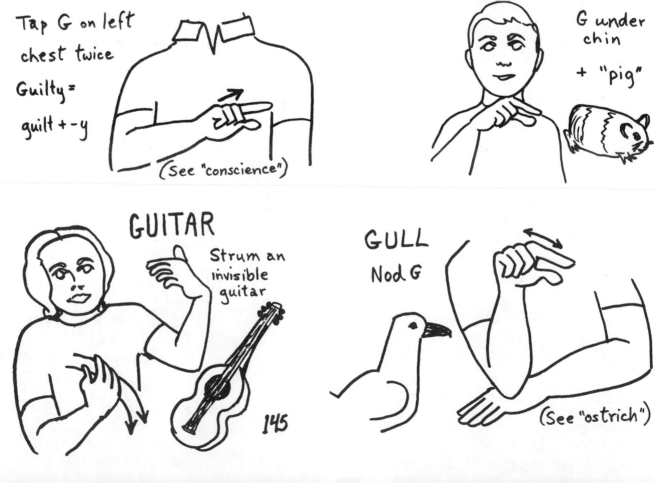

Strum an invisible guitar

145

GULL

Nod G

(See "ostrich")

GUM
Fingertips of V stay on cheek; bend and straighten them

GUN
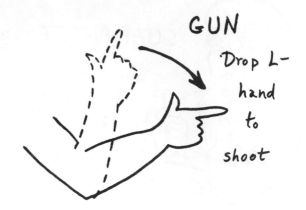
Drop L-hand to shoot

GUY

G from temple forward slightly right

(See "he")

GYM
Hit thumbs of palm-in A's upward on shoulders

GYMNASTIC
U-hand twists around left index

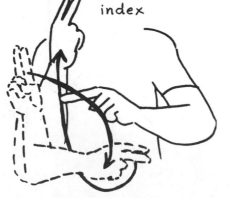

HABIT
Wrist of right S on wrist of left S, drop both slightly

(See "custom")

HAIL
H beats on back of left hand as both fall diagonally left down

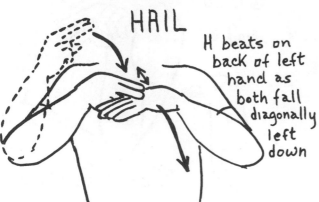

HAIR
Hold hair with F-hand

146

HALF

Palm-in 1

drops to

palm-in 2

(½)

HALL

Parallel
U-hands
move
forward
not touching

HALLOWEEN

Palm-in U's before eyes move around to sides

(See "mask")

HALO

Index fingers and thumbs outline halo above head

HALT

Side of right H falls on palm

(See "stop")

HAM

Thumb and finger of 9 pinch side of H-hand and shake hand slightly

(See "meat")

HAMBURGER

Clasp hands, right on left, separate, then left on right (Make a patty)

147

HAMMER

Hammer with A-hand

HAMSTER

Tip of palm-in flat-H brushes side of nose downward twice

(See "mouse")

HAND

Draw H-finger across back of hand

HANDKERCHIEF

H at nose — thumb extended — pulls away, and thumb and 2 fingers meet; repeat

HANDLE

Alternately H's move to right and left (like reins)

(See "manage")

HANDSOME

Circle face with H-hand

(See "face")

HANG (a picture)

Hook right X on side of left H

HANG (a man)

Thumb of palm-out Y on neck, move upward

Hanged = hang + -ed

HAPPEN

Palm-up index fingers twist to palm-down

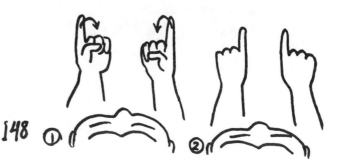

148 ① ②

HAPPY

Brush middle of chest upward twice

HARBOR Palm-out

vertical H outlines curve of palm-down left hand's index and thumb, ending palm-in

(See "bay")

HARD

Bent-V hits bent-V

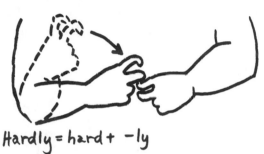

Hardly = hard + -ly

HARE

Wiggle fingers together, in and out

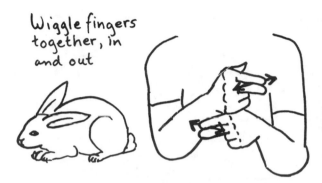

HARM

H arcs up, striking side of S

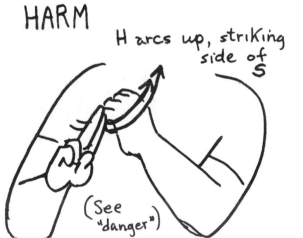

(See "danger")

HARMONICA

Palm-in flat O's move harmonica back and forth in front of mouth

HARP

Fluttering fingers draw 5-hand toward you past left palm

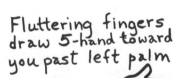

HARVEST

Palm-left curved index slices to and across left S

149

HASSLE
Palm-in H's point at each other, jerk up and down

(See "argue")

HAT
Pat head twice

HATCH
H's together; turn over and out to palm-up

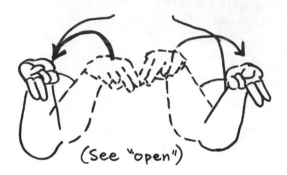

(See "open")

HATCHET
Side of palm-up H chops at wrist of vertical left hand

(See "axe")

HATE
Parallel 8's snap open to 5's

① ②

HAUNT
H's pull away from each other

(See "ghost")

HAVE
Fingertips of slightly bent hands approach and touch chest

Has = have + -s
Had = have + -ed

HAWAII
Hands do hula motion to the left

150

HAY

H brushes up G twice

(See "grain")

HE

E at forehead moves forward and slightly right

HEALTH

Palm-in H's touch chest, then body

(See "body")

HEAD

Touch temple, then jaw

HEAR

H-hand rises to ear

Heard = hear + -ed
(See "sound")

HEART

Draw heart with index fingers — over heart

♡

HEAT

Palm-up, right fingers flutter under left H

(See "burn")

HEAVEN

Right flat hand passes under left and up (entering heaven)

① ②

(See "paradise")

151

HEAVY
Slightly bent palms-up drop slightly, twice

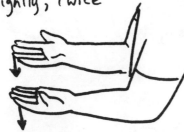

HEEL
Tap heel of hand with right L-thumb, twice

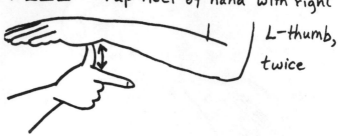

HELICOPTER
Palm of bent-5 on index fingertip, shake 5-hand

HELLO
Flat hand, fingertips at forehead moves right and forward

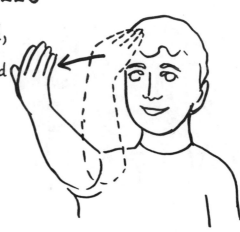

HELMET
Put on helmet with claw-hands

HELP
Palm lifts bottom of S

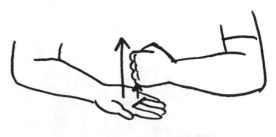

HEN
S's on chest, flap elbows twice

HER
Palm-out R slides down jawline, forward

Hers = her + -s (see "girl")

152

HERD
Palm-out U-hands circle horizontally to palm-in (See "class")

HERE
Palm-up hands circle horizontally in, apart, out, together

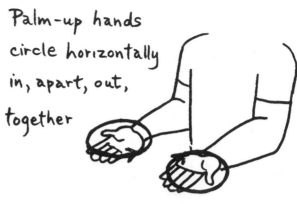

HEREDITY
Palms facing each other, H's circle each other forward from right shoulder

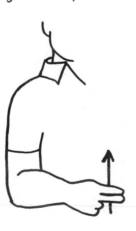

(See generate)

HIDE
A at chin moves down under bent hand

Hid = hide + -ed
Hidden = hide + -en

HIGH
Palm-in H moves upward (See "up")

Height = high + -t

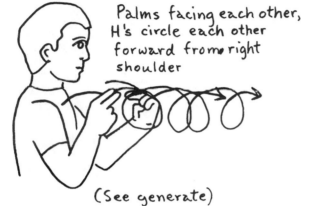

HIKE
Walk palm-down H's forward, alternately (See "walk")

HILL
Palm-down hand draws hill

HIM
M at forehead moves forward and slightly right (See "he")

153

HIND
A-hands together; right arcs sideways behind left

Behind = be + hind

HIP
Pat right hip

HIPPOPOTAMUS
Snap Y's open and closed, wrists together

HIRE
Palm-up, extended H moves in to near body

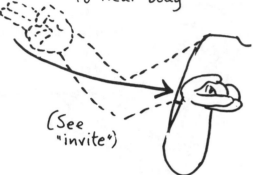

(See "invite")

HIS
S at forehead moves forward and slightly right
(See "he")

HISTORY
H circles forward from right shoulder

HIT
H slightly behind index, moves forward to hit index finger

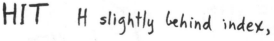

(See "beat")

HOLD
Right claw-hand seizes left index finger

154

HOLE

Side of S on palm opens to C

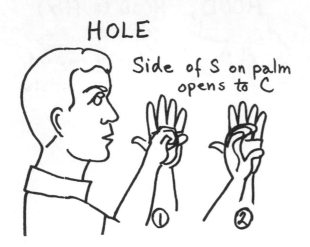

① ②

HOLIDAY

Palm-in H's tap sides of chest twice while thumbs touch chest

(See "leisure")

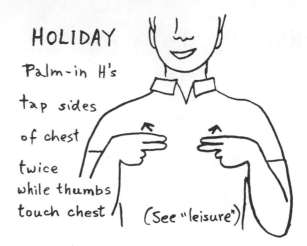

HOLLAND

Thumb of Y at mouth, arc out

HOLLOW
Palm-up H carves out left C, ending palm-down

(See "cave")

HOLY

Right H circles above palm and off

HOME

Flat-o fingertips touch below lip, then flat palm on cheek

(See "domestic")

HONEST

Middle fingertip of palm-left H slides forward on left palm-up hand

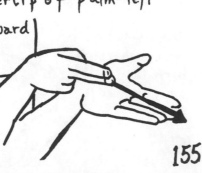

HONEY

Rub chin in circle with H

(See "sweet")

155

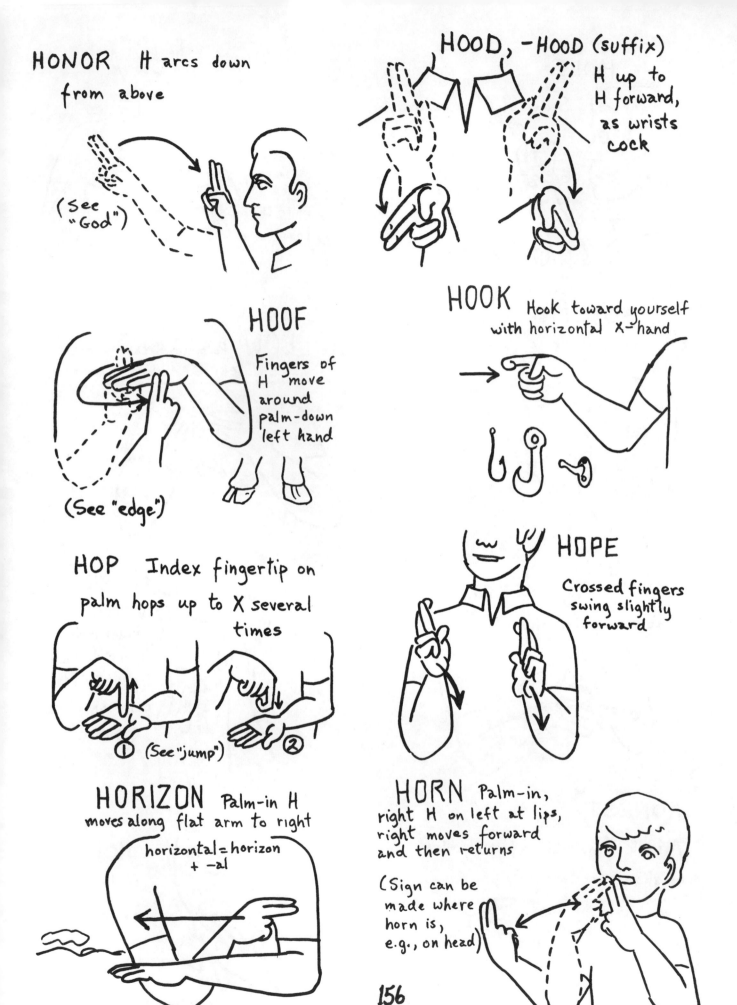

HONOR H arcs down from above

(See "God")

HOOD, -HOOD (suffix) H up to H forward, as wrists cock

HOOF Fingers of H move around palm-down left hand

(See "edge")

HOOK Hook toward yourself with horizontal X-hand

HOP Index fingertip on palm hops up to X several times

① (See "jump") ②

HOPE Crossed fingers swing slightly forward

HORIZON Palm-in H moves along flat arm to right

horizontal = horizon + -al

HORN Palm-in, right H on left at lips, right moves forward and then returns

(Sign can be made where horn is, e.g., on head)

156

HORROR
H-hands shake down toward body

Horrible= horror + -ible

(See "afraid")

HORSE
Flap H-fingers forward together twice

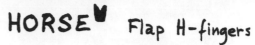

HOSE

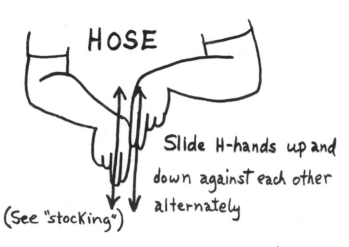

Slide H-hands up and down against each other alternately

(See "stocking")

HOSPITAL
H draws cross on upper left arm ✚

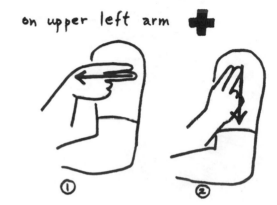

① ②

HOT
Palm-in claw at mouth twists downward and to side

① ②

HOTEL
Rest cheek on back of left hand; H under palm

(See " bed ")

HOUR
Palm-left H touches left palm, circles forward once, touches again

157

HOUSE
Outline roof and sides with flat palms

HOW
Roll hands from inward up to outward

HUG
Hug self with H's

HULA
Do hula on each side

HUMAN   H-hands
face each other, move down

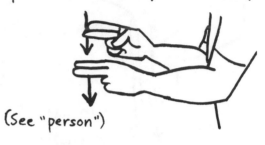

(See "person")

HUMBLE
Right B-hand, palm-left, moves down under left flat hand

HUMID   H-hand moves
right across forehead

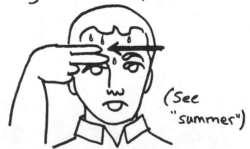

(See "summer")

HUNDRED
Fingers pull inward to palm-out C

HUNGER
C strokes once down chest

Hungry = hunger + -y

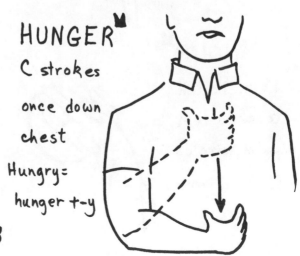

158

HUNT

Thumbs up, drop H-hands, to shoot twice, left a bit ahead of right

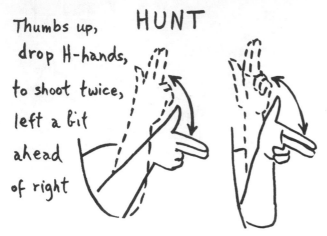

HURRICANE

H's rotate around each other, rising to right

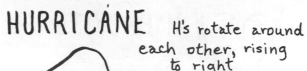

(See "cyclone")

HURRY

Parallel H-hands shake forward

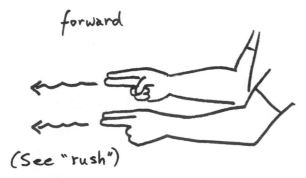

(See "rush")

HURT

Palm-in index fingers jerk toward each other twice

HUSBAND

A at temple to clasped C-hands

HUT

Draw hut with H-hands

(See "house")

HYBRID

H's move toward each other and cross

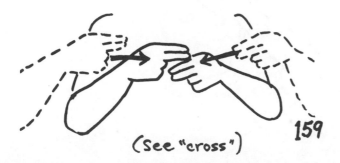

(See "cross")

159

HYMN

Palm-left H swings from side-to-side behind palm-in left hand

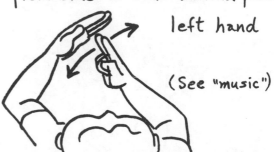

(See "music")

HYPOCRITE

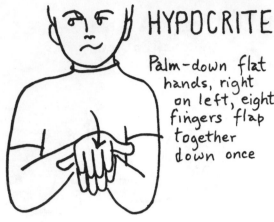

Palm-down flat hands, right on left, eight fingers flap together down once

I

I-hand touches chest

ICE

W on chin moves forward, fingers bending (contract-ing)

ICE CREAM

Right S circles inward at mouth

(Can be "ice" + "cream")

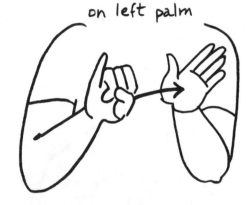

IDEA

From side of forehead, palm-in I moves up and out

IDENTIFY

Strike side of I on left palm

IDIOM

Palm-out i's together, separate to bent-V's that twist slightly down

(See "quote")

IDIOT

Circle thumb-side of I-hand on right forehead

160

IDLE

Thumbs resting on side of chest, wiggle fingers

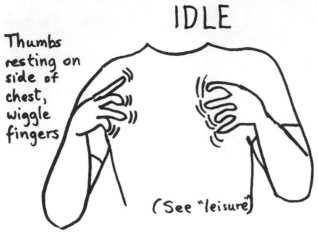

(See "leisure")

IF

F-hand; two middle fingers move up and down several times

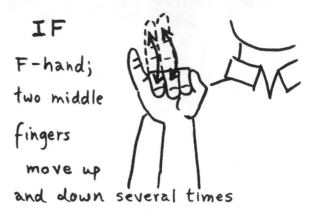

IGNORE

Index of 4 on nose, flip hand down and to left

ILL

Brush little finger of I-hand down chest

(See "depress")

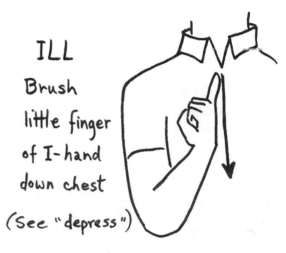

ILLUSTRATE

From eye, side of I-hand moves to palm

(See "picture")

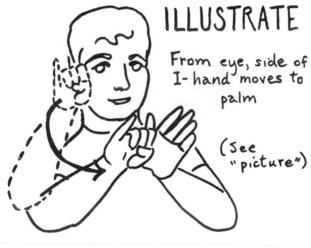

IMAGE

Palms facing each other, I's outline shape downward

(See "form")

IMAGINE

Palm-in I's on forehead, alternately circle up and out

Imagination = imagine + -tion

IMMEDIATE

Slightly drop palm-up Y-shapes (See "now")

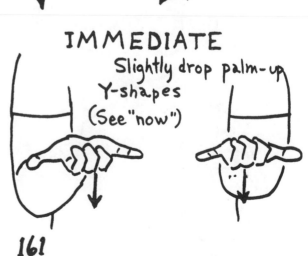

161

IMPORTANT

F's, palm-up to palm-down in vertical circle

Importance = add -ance

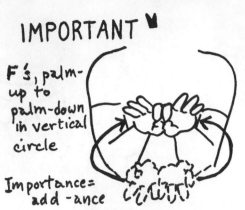

IMPROVE Side of right hand on back of left, hops up arm

INCH Palm-left I moves down on index finger

INCLUDE Palm-out i circles, goes into grasp of left hand

(See "involve")

IMPRESS Open thumb of A on palm, move back toward body

(See "require")

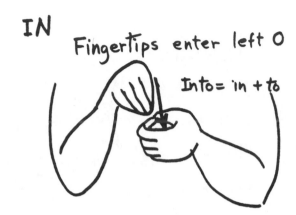

IN Fingertips enter left O

Into = in + to

INCIDENT Palm-up I's twist to palm-down

(See "happen")

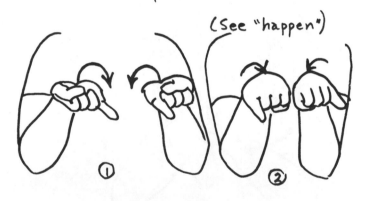

① ②

INCREASE Palm-up H twists up and over onto palm-down H

(See "gain")

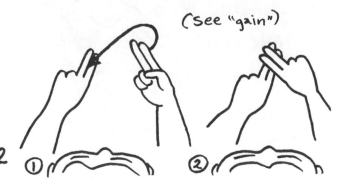

162 ① ②

INDIAN

F from corner of mouth to ear draws on warpaint

INDICATE

I against left palm, both arc forward together

(See "show")

INDIVIDUAL

i-hands face each other, move downwards, first at right, then at left

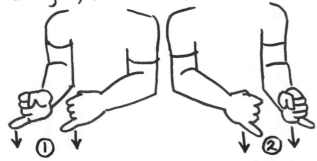

INDUSTRY

Palm-out i arcs side-to-side, hitting back of left S

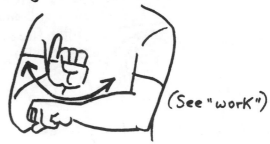

(See "work")

Rock arms as if holding infant

INFANT

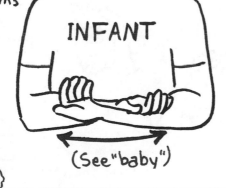

(See "baby")

INFERIOR

I-hand rotates under palm

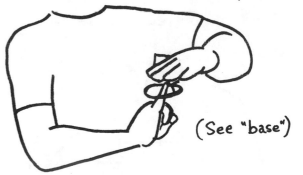

(See "base")

INFIRMARY

Draw cross on shoulder with little I-finger

(See "hospital")

INFLATE

Flat-0 on palm opens (inflates) to C

163

INFLUENCE
Flat-O on back of left hand opens to 5 and then moves in an outward arc (Spreading influence)

(See "advice")

INFORM
Flat-O at forehead moves forward and down, opening to palm-up

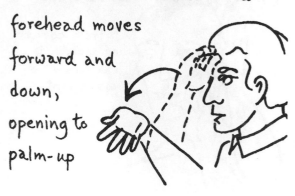

INHERIT
I-hands roll forward from right shoulder, little fingers circling each other

(See "generate")

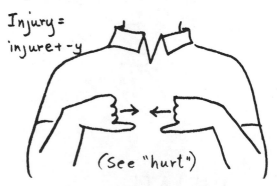

INITIATE
Index on wrist of palm-out I, twist index

Initial = initiate + -al

(See "begin")

① ②

INJURE
Palm-in I-hands jerk toward each other twice

Injury = injure + -y

(See "hurt")

INNOCENT
I-fingers cross near mouth, palm-in swing out, twisting

(See "naïve")

INSECT
I rides forward on wiggling fingers

(See "ant")

INSIST
Tip of i on palm, both arc toward body

(See "require")

INSPECT

Index at eye, then brushes forward off palm twice

INSPIRE

S's on chest slide up, opening to 5's

INSTANT

I-hand rests against left palm, turns forward from palm-out to palm-down

(See "minute")

INSTITUTE

Side of right I taps on index-side of left I

INSTRUCT

I-hands at forehead jerk slightly forward twice together

(See "teach")

INSULT

Index finger, pointing forward, moves out and up (jab)

INSURE

Shake palm-out I

Insurance = insure + -ance

165

INTEGRATE

S-hands arc toward each other, meshing fingers

INTELLECT

Side of index on forehead, slide up and forward

Intelligence = intellect + -ence

Intelligent = intellect + -ent

(See "invent")

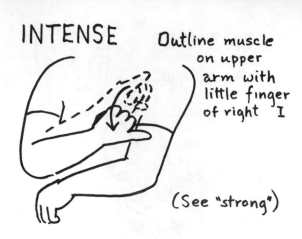

INTENSE

Outline muscle on upper arm with little finger of right I

(See "strong")

INTEREST

Palm-in 5's on chest move out to 8's

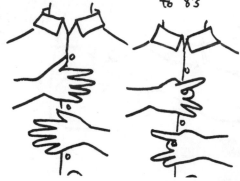

INTERMEDIATE

Circle I over palm, then touch tip to midpalm

(See "middle")

INTERPRET

9's, thumb-on-thumb, one palm-up and one palm-down, then reverse; repeat

① ②

INTERRUPT

Side of i-hand chops into thumb-joint of left hand several times

(See "bother")

INTERVAL

Right flat hand arcs over thumb and jerks toward finger-gaps

INTERVIEW

I's move to and from face alternately

(See "talk")

166

INTRIGUE

I moves from chin to under left hand

(See "hide")

INTRODUCE Palm-up H's swing to point at each other

Introduction = introduce + -tion

(See "prologue")

INVENT

Index of 4 on forehead; arc up and out

(See "intellect")

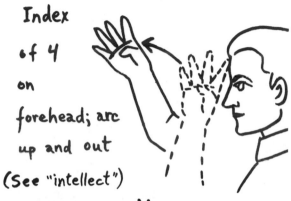

INVESTIGATE   V at eye, then V brushes forward on palm twice

(See "inspect")

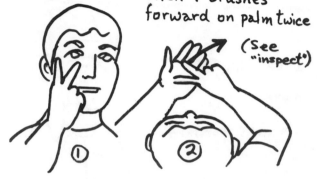

INVITE

Palm-up right hand sweeps horizontally toward body

INVOLVE   Palm-down right hand circles horizontally, goes into grasp of left flat-o

(See "include")

IRELAND

Bent V circles over, then drops on back of left hand

IRON   Palm-in I arcs right, hitting side of index

(See "metal")

167

IRRIGATE

I at mouth, side then slides across palm and to side, palm-up

IRRITATE

Palm-in I jerks up body

(See "anger")

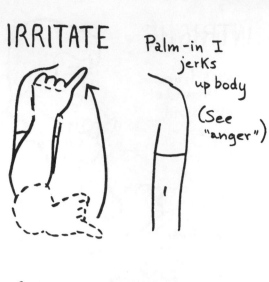

IS

I on chin moves straight forward

I's face each other, circle horizontally toward body and touch

ISLAND

(See "place")

ISOLATE

Palm-out I-hands touch, separate sideways

(See "separate")

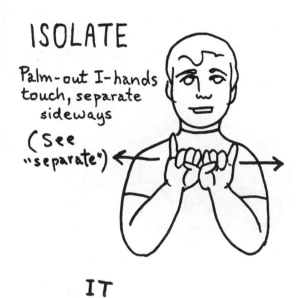

ISSUE

I's, palm-down to palm-up, arc outwards

(See "give")

IT

Tip of I touches palm of left hand

Its = it + -s
It's = it + 's

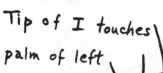

ITALY

Little finger makes cross near forehead

Italian = Italy + -an

ITCH

Scratch arm

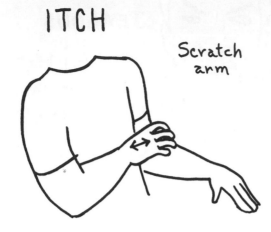

ITEM

Palm-up I-hand arcs once to right (See "thing")

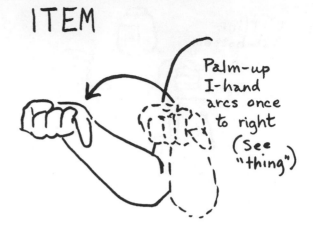

JACKET

Palm-in I-fingertips draw lapels on chest

(See "coat")

JACK O' LANTERN

Make J + O + L above back of S (See "melon")

① ② ③

JAIL

Palm-in V-hands, right behind left; right hits left

JAM

Flick I off palm inwards twice

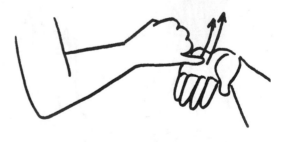

JANUARY

Little I-finger brushes off thumb of left hand

(See "first")

169

JAPAN

Little fingertip at corner of eye, hand twists slightly forward (See "China")

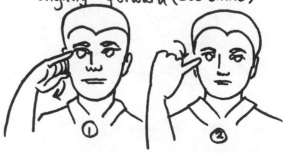

① ②

Outline jar-bottom with I fingers

JAR

JEALOUS
Draw a j near corner of mouth (See "envy")

Jealousy = jealous + -y (See "envy")

JEANS
Little fingers inwards, make J's at waist

JELL
Jiggle claw over palm

Jelly = jell + -y
Jello = jell + -o

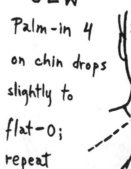

JESUS Bent right middle finger touches palm; reverse

(nails in hands of Jesus)

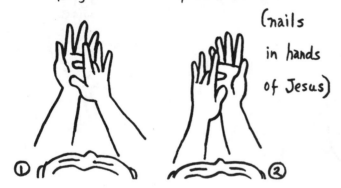

① ②

JEW
Palm-in 4 on chin drops slightly to flat-0; repeat

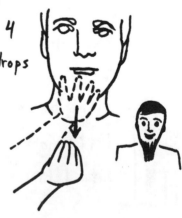

JEWEL
i-finger shakes off ring-finger

Jewelry = jewel + R + Y

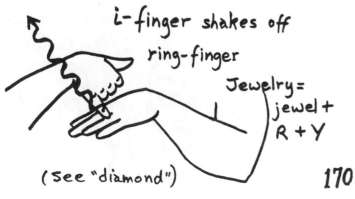

(See "diamond")

JOB Side of little finger arcs once from right to left, hitting back of S

(See "work")

170

JOIN H-fingertips are into side of O

Joint = join + -t

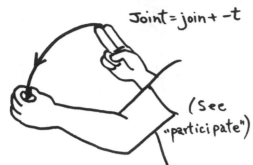

(See "participate")

JOKE Palm-in H-hands cross before face; repeat

① ②

JOURNAL Little finger of I brushes off edge of flat hand twice

(See "magazine")

JOY Brush fingertip of palm-in I up chest twice (See "happy")

JUDGE Parallel 9-hands move alternately up and down

(See "balance")

JUICE Thumb-side of Y cuts down back of S

JULY Palm-in little finger brushes straight across forehead (See "summer")

JUMP V-fingertips on left palm, jump up with bent fingers and down again

(See "hop")

① ② ③

171

JUNE I traces J around fingertips

JUNGLE Draw J, elbow resting on back of hand, repeat

(See "tree")

JUNIOR Touch left index with right index

(See "freshman")

JUNK Back of palm-up I brushes off left palm, twists to palm-out, then throws (junk) down to 5

(See "waste")

JUST

I-fingertip draws "J" on palm of left hand

Justice = just + -ice

JUVENILE Brush J-hands upward twice off chest

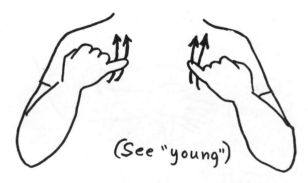

(See "young")

KANGAROO

Body stationary, hop bent hands forward

(Australian sign)

KEEP Tap right K on left K, twice

Kept = keep + -ed

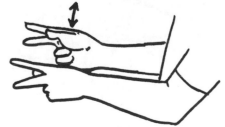

172

KERCHIEF

Outline and tie kerchief on with K's

(see "bonnet")

KETCHUP CATSUP

Shake side of K downward, like a bottle

KEY

Twist thumbtip and finger of X on palm

KICK

Side of right hand rises from below to strike side of left hand sharply

KID

Shake K-hand in front of nose

KIDNAP

Pull back K sharply to A near shoulder

KILL

Side of index twists under left palm

KIND

Right K on left, then circle vertically around each other

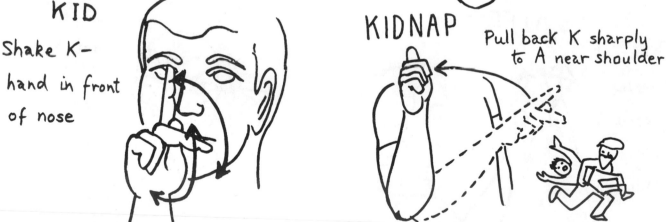

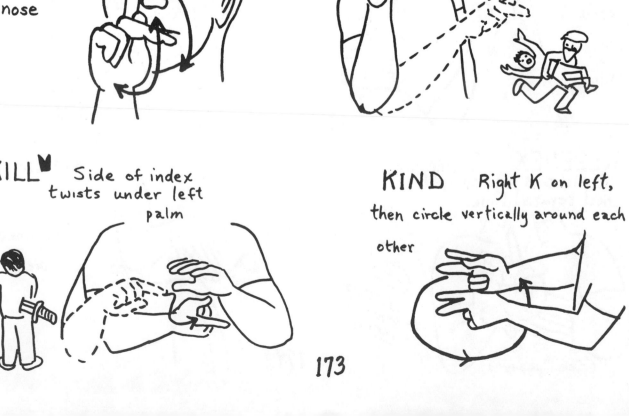

KINDERGARTEN
K circles under left palm

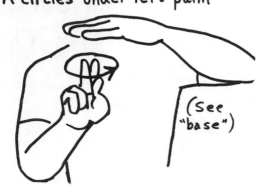

(See "base")

KING
Right K on left shoulder, then right side of body

(See "Christ")

KISS
Touch below lips and on cheek

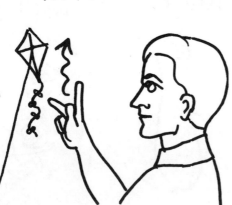

Palm-down K-hands form box-shape

KITCHEN

(See "box")

KITE
Palm-out K moves upward in wavy motion

KITTEN
Right K moves out from mouth
(See "cat")

KLEENEX
Strike heel of right K across left heel several times

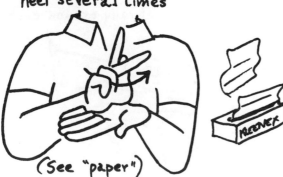

(See "paper")

KNEE
Tap knee twice

174

KNEEL   First two fingers kneel on left palm

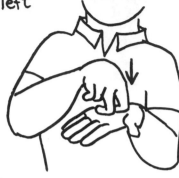

KNIFE
Flick H off H twice

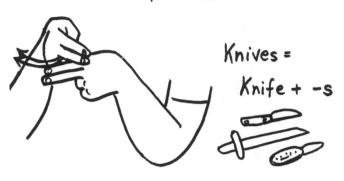

Knives = Knife + -s

KNIT

Cross horizontal index fingers; separate to X's; repeat several times

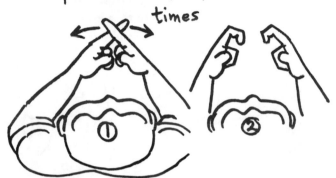

KNOCK

Knock with right S-hand

KNOT   Right A circles thumb of left A and jerks back to tie knot

KNOW

Fingers of palm-in hand hit forehead lightly, twice (see "think")

Knew = know + -ed
Known = know + -en
Knowledge = know + age

KOREA

Middle fingertip of K at corner of eye; hand twists slightly forward (See "China")

LABOR   Palm-out L arcs side-to-side, hitting back of S-hand

(See "work")

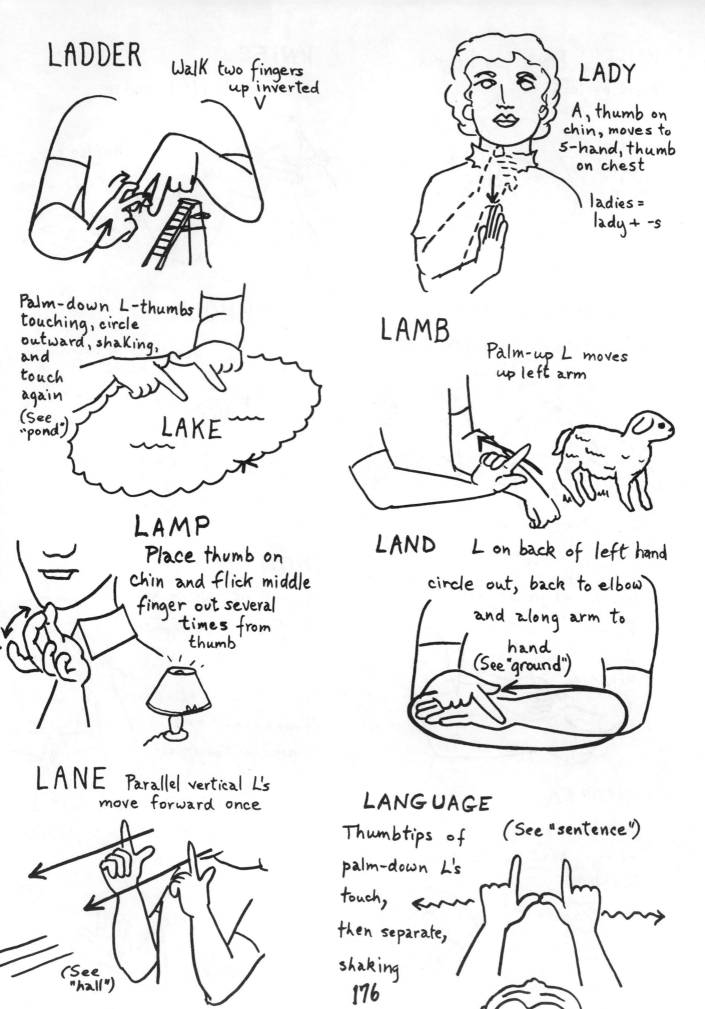

LADDER
Walk two fingers up inverted V

LADY
A, thumb on chin, moves to 5-hand, thumb on chest

ladies = lady + -s

Palm-down L-thumbs touching, circle outward, shaking, and touch again (See "pond")

LAKE

LAMB
Palm-up L moves up left arm

LAMP
Place thumb on chin and flick middle finger out several times from thumb

LAND
L on back of left hand circle out, back to elbow and along arm to hand (See "ground")

LANE
Parallel vertical L's move forward once

(See "hall")

LANGUAGE
Thumbtips of palm-down L's touch, then separate, shaking

(See "sentence")

176

LAP
Arc L forward twice, knuckles hitting palm

(See "slip")

LARD

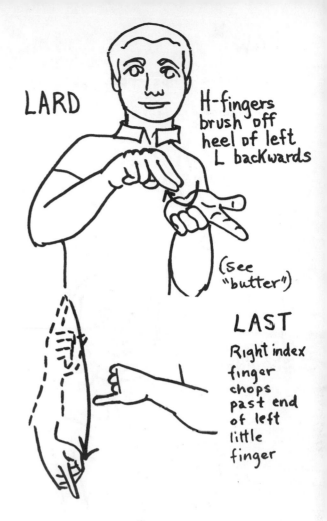

H-fingers brush off heel of left L backwards

(See "butter")

LARGE
L hands face each other, arc apart

(See "big")

LAST

Right index finger chops past end of left little finger

LATITUDE
Thumb of right L slides around palm-in S

(See "equator")

LATE
Thumbtip of palm-out L on left palm, twist to palm-down

Later = late + -er

① ②

(See "minute")

LAUGH

Index fingers of L's brush up and outward at corners of mouth several times

(See "smile")

LAUNDER

L-knuckles circle on left palm

(See "wash")

177

LAW

L on fingertips, then on heel

Lawyer = law + -er

LAY

Set back of 2 on back of hand

Laid = lay + -ed

LAZY

L on shoulder

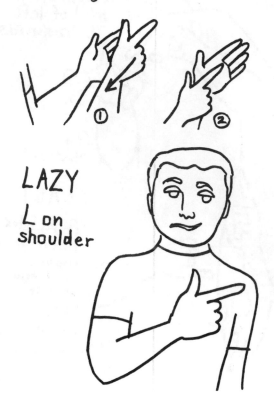

LEAD Grasp tip of hand and pull right, leading hand

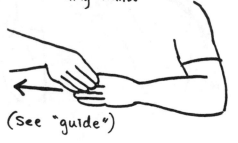

(See "guide")

LEAD (metal)

Heel of L strikes off index

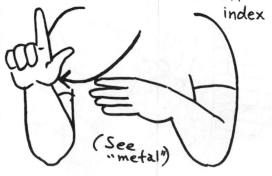

(See "metal")

LEAF Wrist of 5 on index; wave 5 side-to-side

Leaves = leaf + -s

LEAGUE Thumbtips together, L's circle out and touch little fingers

(See "class")

LEAK 4-hand "leaks" down from left S, fingers fluttering

LEAP
Inverted V jumps up and bends, then leaps forward off palm

① ②

LEARN
Open palm-down right fingers on palm-up hand, move to right flat O at forehead

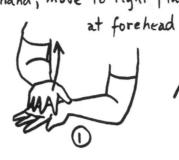

① ②

LEATHER
L brushes down across back of palm-in left hand

LEAVE
Palm-down 5's at right draw back, closing to O's

Left = leave + -ed

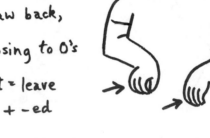

① ②

LECTURE
Palm facing side of head, shake hand slightly and quickly back and forth from wrist

LEFT
Palm-out right L moves left

LEG
Pat thigh

179

LEGEND
L's circle each other forward from right shoulder

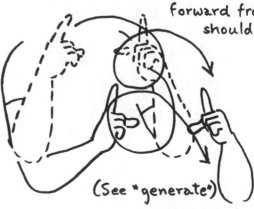

(See "generate")

LEGISLATE
Thumb of L touches left, then right side of chest

Legislature = legislate + -ure

(See "member")

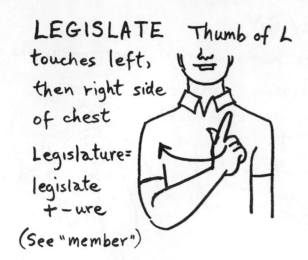

LEISURE
Poke L-thumbs into sides of chest

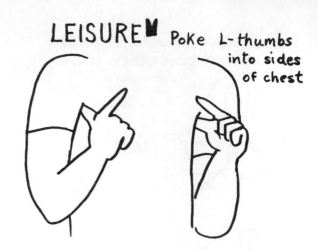

LEMON
Tap chin with L-thumb

LEND
Right V on left V, arc forward

Lent = lend + -ed

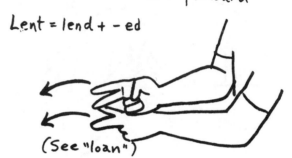

(See "loan")

LEOPARD
Move L's to side twice (See "cat")

LEPRECHAUN
L's at shoulders swing out

(See "angel")

LESS, -LESS (suffix)
Right bent hand under left bent hand; drop right downward

Least = less + -est

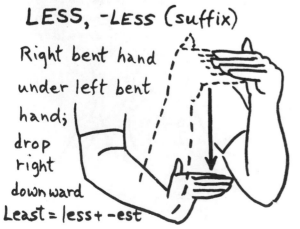

LESSON
Side of bent hand on fingertips, then on heel

180

LET L-hands face each other, pointing down; swing to point forward (See "allow")

LETTER A-thumb at mouth to touch palm-up index finger

① ②

LETTUCE Hit heel of L upwards on head **twice**

(See "cabbage")

LEVEL L, palm-down, moves to right

(See "flat")

LIBERTY Palm-in L's, crossed at wrists,

② separate and twist to palm-out (breaking bonds)

(See "free")

①

LIBRARY Palm-out L makes a small circle twice

LICENSE L-thumbs tap twice

(See "credential")

LICK Right hand flaps up against left palm; repeat several times

181

LID

Palm-down L drops
on side of left

S

(See "cap")

LIE (to tell a...) Side of palm-down
B moves left across chin

Lied =
lie + -ed

Liar =
lie + -er

(See "fib")

LIE (recline) Back of
V on palm; slide toward body

Lay = lie + -ed
Lain = lie + -en

LIFE   Palm-in 9-hands

move up

body

(See "address")

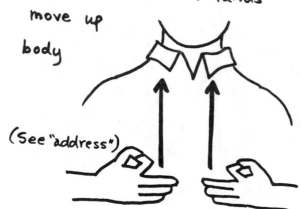

LIFT   L's face each other,
twist in and up to lift, palms up

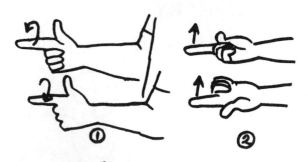

① ②

LIGHT   Palm-in 0-hands

touch,
spring
up, and
open to
palm-in
5-hands

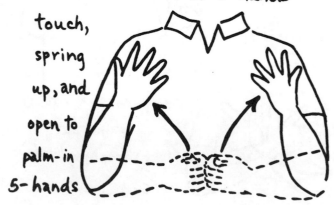

LIGHTNING

Draw a large
Z rapidly with
index finger

LIKE, -LIKE (suffix)

Palm-in L on
chest moves
forward,
closing
thumb and
182 finger

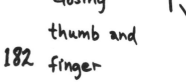

LIMB

One-hand angles away from touching thumb of palm out left L

(See "branch")

LIME

Thumb edge of L cuts down back of S

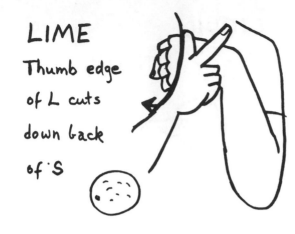

LIMIT Bent hands, right above left, pivot to point at each other

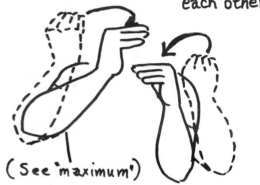

(See "maximum")

LINCOLN

Tap temple with right L thumb

LINE

Palm-out L slides along and off side of left index (See "bar")

LINOLEUM

Drag L across back of hand (See "carpet")

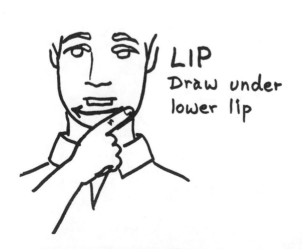

LION Claw hand combs backward with a shaking motion over mane

LIP

Draw under lower lip

183

LIQUID

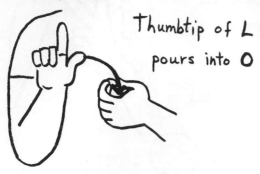

Thumbtip of L pours into O

LIQUOR

Index and little fingers out, right taps left hand

(See "whiskey")

LIST

Bent right hand moves down left palm and arm

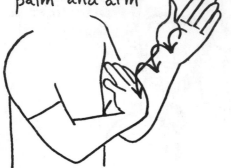

LISTEN

Thumb of palm-out L points to ear

(See "sound")

LITTER

Palm-in L behind left palm swings under and out to palm-out

LITTLE

L-hands face each other, jerk slightly toward each other; repeat (See "small")

LIVE

Palm-in L-hands move up body

(See "address")

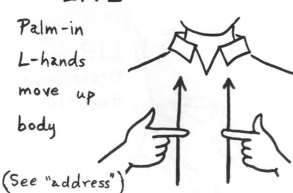

LIZARD

Slide L-hand up palm while index finger moves from X to straight several times

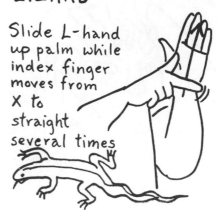

184

LOAD
Palm-up L flips to palm-down on left palm-down

LOAN
Right index on left index, arc forward

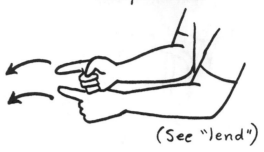

(See "lend")

LOBSTER
Move forward and to right, V's scissoring

(See "crab")

LOCAL
L circles left index

(See "culture")

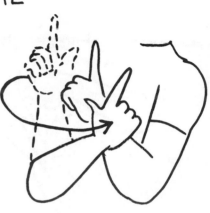

LOCK
Palm-down S-hands, right over left; right twists to palm-up, drops on wrist. Locker = lock + -er

 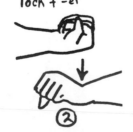

LODGE
Palms down, right L on left L thumbs, right lifts off and drops down

(See "stay")

LOGIC
L circles on forehead (See "reason")

LOLLIPOP
Lick index of L twice

(See "ice cream")

185

LONE Palm-out L twists to palm-in, moves forward

Alone = a + lone

Lonely = lone + -ly

LONESOME Move index finger down chin once

LONG Finger slides up arm

(See "along")

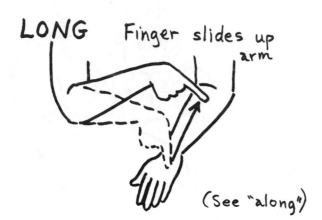

LONGITUDE L thumb draws arc near left S, outlining longitude

LOOK Thumb of L at eye; move forward

(See "see")

LOOSE Claw on S, shake loose claw

LORD L from left shoulder to right hip

(See "Christ")

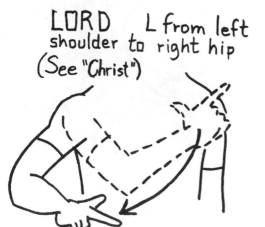

LOSE Palm-up flat-O's point to each other, drop to palm-down open hands

Lost = lose + -ed

186

LOT
Palm-down L-hands touch thumbtips, circle toward body, and touch again

(See "place")

LOTION
L shakes into palm

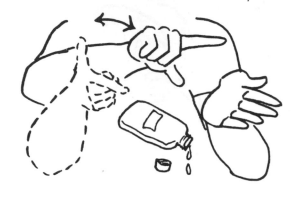

LOUD
Right index at ear opens to 5 and shakes down to right

LOUSE
Throw 3 off nose

Lousy = louse + -y

(See "rot")

LOVE
Cross S-hands on heart

LOW
Palm-left L drops slightly

Below = be + low

(See "down")

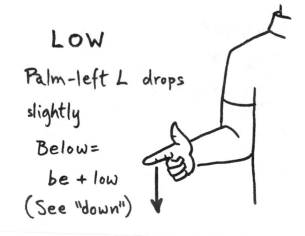

LUCK
Palm-up L's turn to palm-down

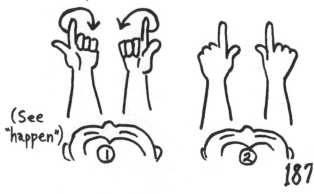

(See "happen")

① ②

187

LUMBER
Shake right L-hand while resting elbow on left hand

(See "tree")

LUMP

Thumb of right L on back of left S arcs to heel of L

LUNCH

Thumb of L circles in and up near mouth (See "eat")

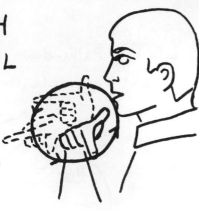

LUTHERAN

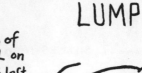

Tap L-thumb twice on palm-right palm

LYRIC

Right L swings back and forth behind left arm

(See "music")

MACARONI

Shake M's to sides (See "spaghetti)

MACHINE

Mesh bent fingers like gear-teeth and shake up and down

MAD

5-hand in front of face contracts to claw

188

MAGAZINE

Thumb and finger of palm-up 9 grasp side of flat hand and slide forward and off (See "journal")

MAGIC Right hand behind left at eye-level, palm-down; flutter fingers

MAGNET Palm-down M's meet at index tips

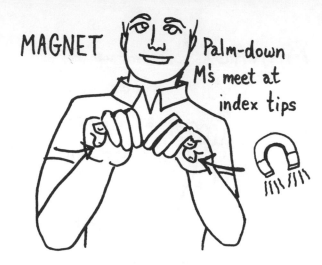

MAIL

Palm-down M brushes down elbow

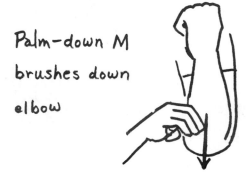

MAIN M-hands touch each other, are up to touch sides; palm-up to palm-down

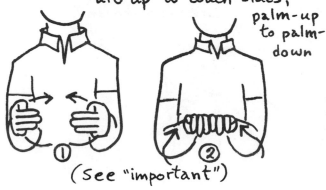

(See "important")

MAJOR
Right M on left M; right moves forward

(See "straight")

MAKE
Touch right S on left S, twist to palm-in and touch again

Made = make + -ed

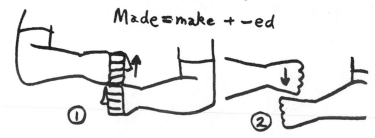

MALE
Palm-down flat M slides right across forehead

Masculine = male + -ine

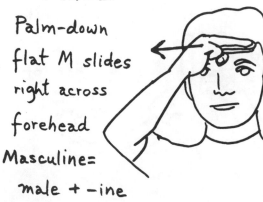

MAN

A on temple, then measure height with bent hand

189

MANAGE

Palm-up A-hands move alternately forward and back, diagonally

MANNER
Palm-down M's move side to side (See "do")

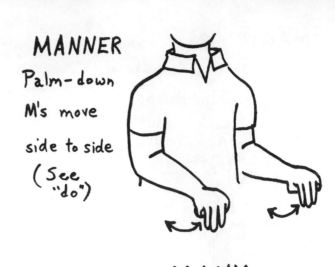

MANUSCRIPT
Write forward on palm-up left with M

(See "write")

MANY
Palm-up S's spring open into 5's; repeat

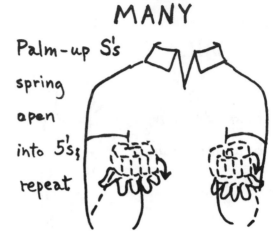

MAP
Draw wavy line with M on back of left hand

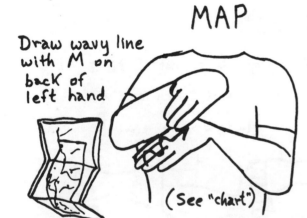

(See "chart")

MARBLE
M's rotate, in small circle, one above the other

MARCH
Swing hands sharply out and up twice, right behind left

(See "parade")

MARGARINE
Flick U back to N off heel of open M, twice

(See "butter")

MARGIN

Index finger bent, side of thumb slides down outside of palm-in left hand

MARK

Jerk thumb and fingertip toward palm

MARKET

Right M-fingertips move rapidly towards and away from side of left C

(See "store")

MARRY

Clasp C-hands right on left

Marriage = marry + -age

MARSHMALLOW

M-hand taps top of horizontal index, then bottom

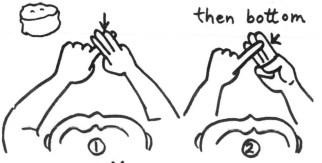

① ②

MARVEL

Palm-out M's make small circle, jerk slightly forward to 5's

marvelous = marvel + -ous (See "fabulous")

MASK

Palm-in M's before eyes circle back to sides

191

MAST

M, palm-down, slides up vertical left arm

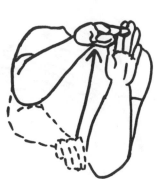

MASTER

M-fingertips on shoulders pivot to palm-out and drop

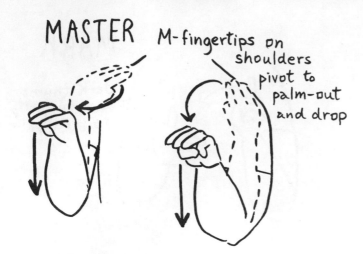

MAT

Drag M across back of hand

(See "carpet")

MATCH

Palm-in M's; tip of right arcs down, striking tip of left

MATE

Both hands' M-fingers rest, first right on left, then left on right

① ② (See "friend")

MATERIAL

Palm-up M arcs twice to the right

(See "thing")

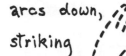

MATH

Brush little finger side of palm-in right M on index finger of palm-in left M, twice

(See "arithmetic")

MATTER

Open M's alternately slap back and forth

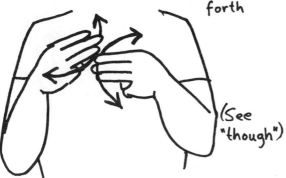

(See "though")

MATURE

Right M strikes off side of palm-in S

(See "full")

192

MAXIMUM
M-hands, palm-in, twist to face each other, right above left (See "limit")

MAY
Palm-up hands move alternately up and down

Might = may + -en (past participle)
Maybe = may + be (See "balance")

MAYONNAISE
Fingers of palm-down right M brush (See "butter") brush heel of left palm toward body twice

MAYOR
Circle M by forehead and then touch

(See "govern")

ME
Index points to and touches chest

MEADOW
From back of hand, M circles off left forearm (See "ground")

MEAL
Ladle M-hand up to mouth twice

(See "soup")

MEAN
Touch M to palm twice, turning between contacts

② meant = mean + ed

193

MEASLES

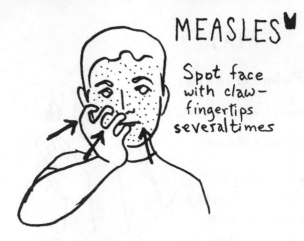

Spot face with claw-fingertips several times

MEASURE

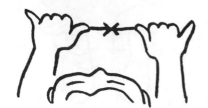

Palm-down Y's tap thumbtips twice

MEAT

Pinch flesh and shake hands

MECHANIC

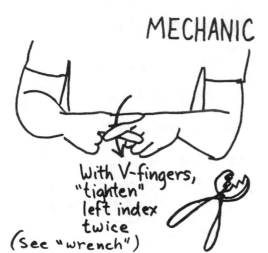

With V-fingers, "tighten" left index twice
(See "wrench")

MEDIC

Place M on pulse and tap

(See "doctor")

MEDICINE

Bent middle finger rubs tip in circle on palm

MEDIUM

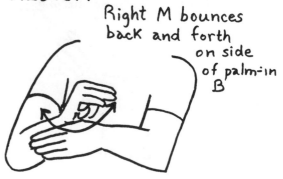

Right M bounces back and forth on side of palm-in B

MEET

One-hands meet

Met-meet+-ed

194

MELON
Snap middle finger on back of S (as if testing ripeness)

MELT
Palm-up flat-O's separate, changing to palm-up A's

(See "dissolve")

MEMBER
M-fingers touch left shoulder, then right

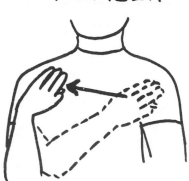

MEMORIZE
Palm-in 5, middle finger on forehead, move forward and down, closing to S

MEMORY
A-thumb on forehead, twist at wrist

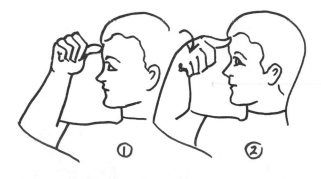

① ②

MEN
A on temple, then measure two heights with bent hand

MENSTRUATE
Tap flat of A against cheek twice

195

MENTION
Index at mouth drops to touch palm-up left hand

① ②

(See "report")

MENU

M-fingertips move down palm twice (as if scanning menu)

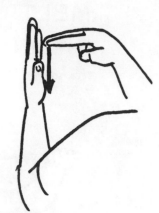

MERRY

Side of M brushes up chest twice

(See "happy")

MESS

M, right above left, reverse

METAL

Palm-in M arcs right, hitting side of index

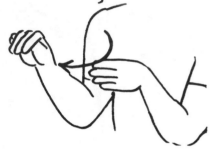

METER

Fingertips of right M slide up and down index finger

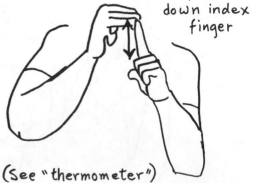

(See "thermometer")

METHOD

Palm-down M's move forward, right, return; then forward left

(See "system")

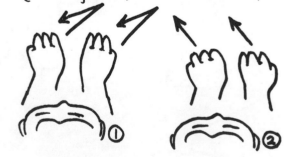

MEXICO

Index on shoulder drops to palm-up X

Mexican = Mexico + -an

MICE

Brush past nosetip twice with both index fingers alternately

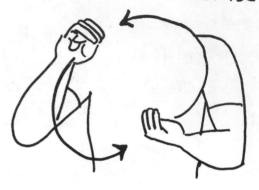

(See "rodent")

196

MICROSCOPE

Focus microscope with two S's, right on left

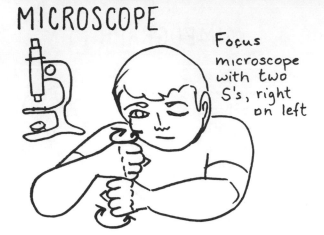

MID

M falls on left palm

MIDDLE

Right M circles once over left palm, then touches mid-palm

MIDGET

Palm-down M pats head of midget twice

(See "child")

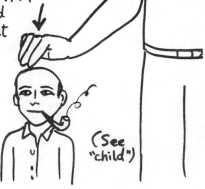

MIGHT (Power)

M-fingertips draw muscle

(See "strong")

MILE

M brushes up arm; two motions

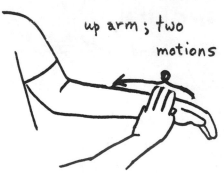

MILK

Squeeze S-hand in a milking-motion

197

MILLION

Fingertips of M hit heel, then fingers, of left hand while both hands move forward

(See "billion")

MILWAUKEE

Index finger moves left twice under lip

MIMEOGRAPH

Side of S circles near left palm rapidly several times

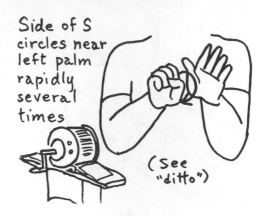

(See "ditto")

MIND

Tips of M tap temple

(See "think")

MINE (noun)

X picks at left vertical palm several times

MINIMUM

Right M over left M, right hand moves down toward left hand

MINISTER

Palm-out M near head jerks slightly forward twice

(See "lecture")

MINOR

M moves out from under palm-right flat hand

MINUS

Side of right index finger horizontally on left palm-out hand

(See "forbid")

198

MINUTE

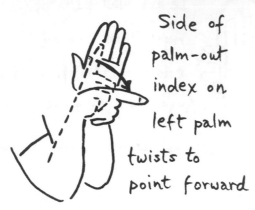

Side of palm-out index on left palm twists to point forward

MIRROR

Pivot hand slightly towards face

MIS- (prefix)

Palm-down M's, crossed at wrists, separate (See "not")

MISCHIEF

Thumb on temple, wiggle index

Mischievous = mischief + -ous

(See "devil")

MISS

Right hand passes left index and changes to S

MISS (title)

Fingertips of M on cheek twist out-ward (See "girl")

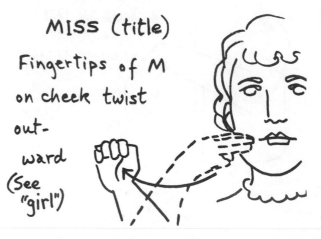

MISTAKE

Right Y on chin, then left Y

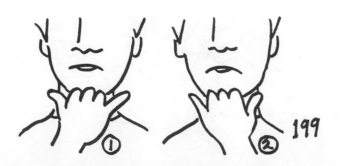

199

MISTER

Finger-tips of M on temple twist to palm-out R (See "he")

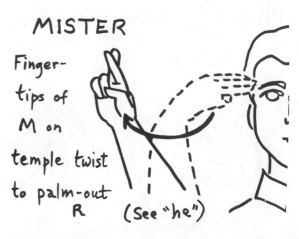

MISUNDERSTAND
Palm-out V on temple, reverse to palm-in

MITT
Draw flat palm of right hand around edge of left from index finger to little finger

Mitten = mitt + -en

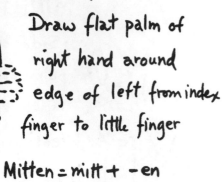

MIX
Circle claw-hands, right above left, alternating in the same direction

MOAN
M at throat shakes up and out under chin

(See "groan")

MODEL
Tip of index on palm-up left, make horizontal circle together

MODERN
Back of M brushes down, along left palm and up

(See "new")

MODIFY
M-hands, palm to palm, reverse positions; repeat, slightly to right (See "change")

MOLASSES
Index finger brushes across chin and flicks forward, wiping

200

MOLE

Hands rest against cheeks and "dig," flapping

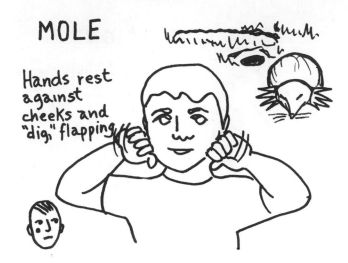

MOM

Tap M near chin

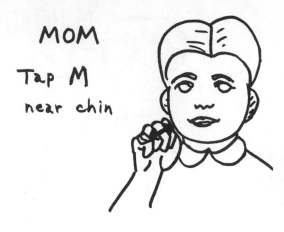

MOMENT

Side of M on palm, twist in 2 motions to point downward

(See "minute")

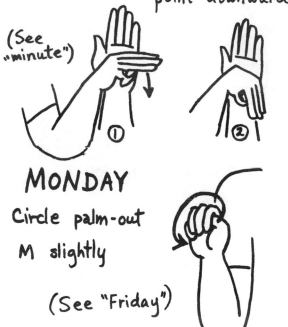

MOMENTUM

Wrist of right M pushes left index forward

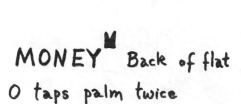

MONDAY

Circle palm-out M slightly

(See "Friday")

MONEY

Back of flat O taps palm twice

MONKEY

Scratch sides upwards

MONSTER

Raise claw-hands to sides of head

MONTANA

Palms out, outline state with M's

MONTH

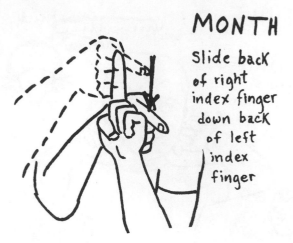

Slide back of right index finger down back of left index finger

MOOD

M-fingers move up chest once

(See "feel")

MOON

Tap thumb of C at side of eye twice

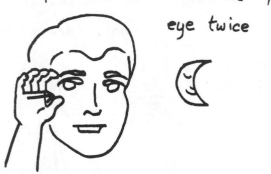

MOOSE

Flat hands move up and out from temples

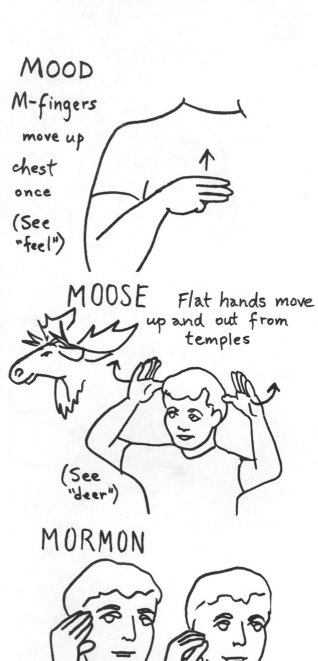

(See "deer")

MORE
Flat O's bounce tips together twice

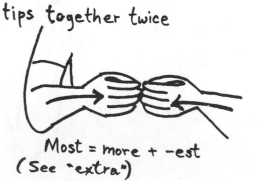

Most = more + -est
(See "extra")

MORMON

Close right hand on cheekbone to flat O; repeat

① ②

MORN

Right hand rises

Morning = Morn + -ing

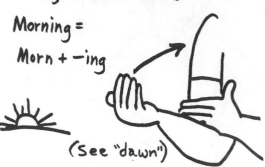

(See "dawn")

202

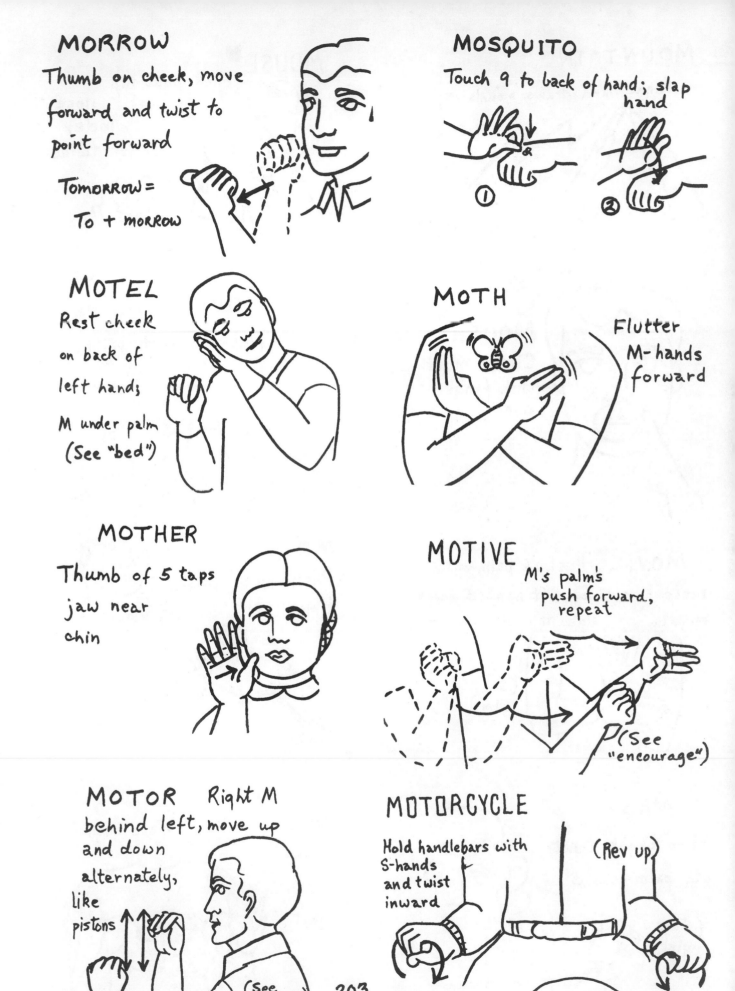

MORROW

Thumb on cheek, move forward and twist to point forward

TOMORROW = To + MORROW

MOSQUITO

Touch 9 to back of hand; slap hand

① ②

MOTEL

Rest cheek on back of left hand; M under palm (See "bed")

MOTH

Flutter M-hands forward

MOTHER

Thumb of 5 taps jaw near chin

MOTIVE

M's palm's push forward, repeat

(See "encourage")

MOTOR

Right M behind left, move up and down alternately, like pistons

(See "engine")

203

MOTORCYCLE

Hold handlebars with S-hands and twist inward

(Rev up)

MOUNTAIN

Right hand draws mountaintops; left stays still

MOUSE ⌄

Flick past tip of nose with index finger twice

MOUTH ⌄

Circle mouth with finger once

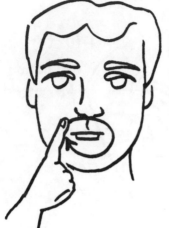

MOVE   Palm-down flat-O's arc to right

(See "transfer")

MOVIE   Heel of palm-out 5 rests on side of left hand; 5 moves slightly, side-to-side

(See "film")

MOW
Push mower several times

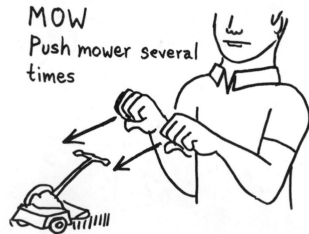

MRS.

M on cheek twists to palm-out S

(See "girl")

MUCH ⌄   hands face each other, arc apart

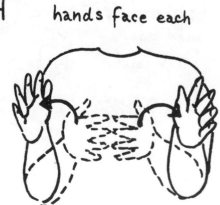

204

MUD

Flap M from under chin

(See "pig")

MUFF

Palms-in, right flat hand moves behind left as if into muff

MULE

Thumb on temple, flap flat hand forward twice

(See "horse")

MULTIPLY

Back of palm-in V brushes sideways across left palm

MURDER

Side of M twists diagonally under left palm

(See "kill")

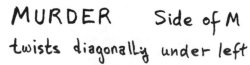

MUMPS

Tap claw-hands on sides of neck twice

MUSEUM

Draw house with M's

(See "house")

MUSCLE

Index finger pokes muscle twice

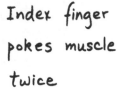

205

MUSHROOM

M-fingertips circle on back of R, palm-down

MUSIC

FingerTips pointing toward palm, flat hand arcs side-to-side behind palm

MUST

Palm-down X jerks sharply downward once

(See "necessary")

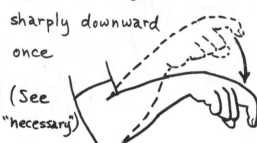

MUSTACHE

G's on upper lip move sideways to A's

MUSTARD

M-fingertips circle several times on palm

MY

Place palm on chest

Mine = my + -en

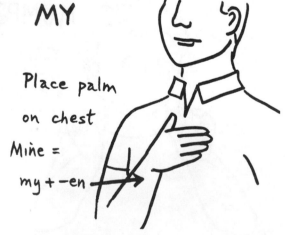

MYSTERY

M moves down from chin to under left hand

(See "hide")

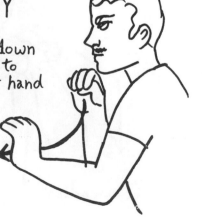

MYTH

Right M arcs twice off forehead

(See "fantasy")

NAG

N-fingertips peck vertical index twice

(See "peck")
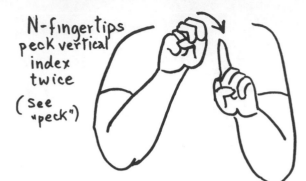

NAIL

Tap nail with fingertip
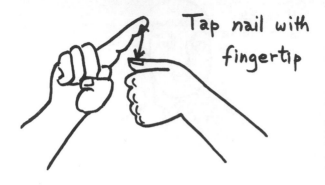

NAIVE
Cross palm-in H-fingers before chin, open outwards to palm-out

(See "innocent")
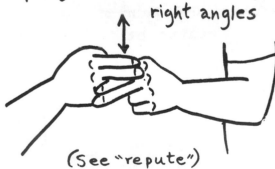

NAKED
N-hand brushes off back of left A-hand

(See "bare")
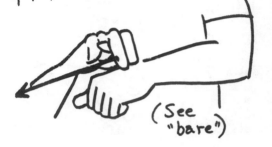

NAME
Tap right H on left H twice, at right angles

(See "repute")

NAP
N moves down in front of face, head on hand

(See "bed")

NAPKIN
Palm-in A brushes off chin several times

NARROW
Hands converge forward to touch fingertips
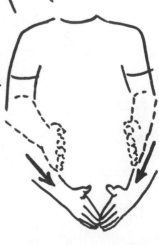

NASTY
N jerks out twice from under chin

NATION
N circles over, then drops on back of S

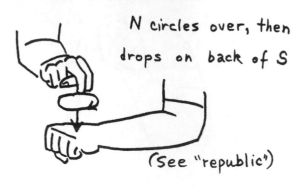

(See "republic")

NATURE
Back of A against palm; A twists down and out under left hand to palm-down A

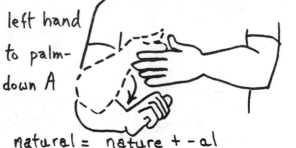

natural = nature + -al

NAUGHTY
N facing mouth swings outward and drops
(See "bad")

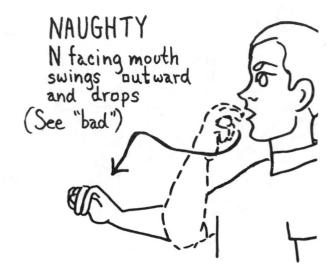

NAVY
B-hands move from left to right sides of waist (buttoning pants)

NEAR
Move palm of right hand nearer back of left hand

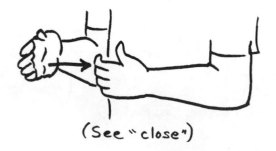

(See "close")

NEAT
Heel of N slides across palm

(See "clean")

NECESSARY
Palm-down N jerks down sharply once
(See "must")

NECK 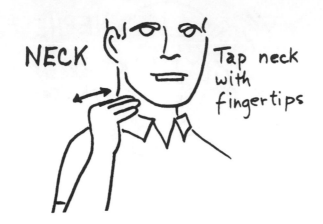 Tap neck with fingertips

NECKLACE 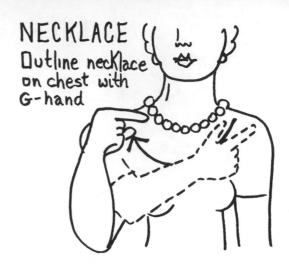 Outline necklace on chest with G-hand

NECTARINE 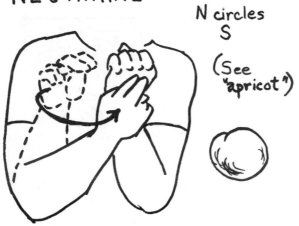 N circles S

(See "apricot")

NEED 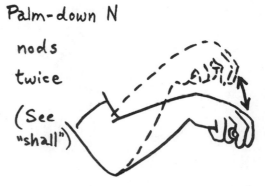 Palm-down N nods twice

(See "shall")

NEGATIVE 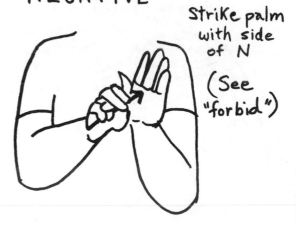 Strike palm with side of N

(See "forbid")

NEEDLE  Thread fingertip with 9-hand

NEGRO  N on nose; twist slightly

NEIGHBOR Rest H-fingers first right on left, then left on right

(See "friend")

NEITHER

N swings off L thumb, then E off fingertip (See "then")

NEPHEW

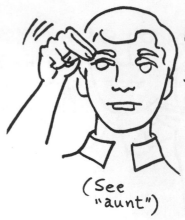

Shake N near temple

(See "aunt")

NERVE

N wiggles up arm

(tracing nerve)

NERVOUS

Shake palm-down 5's

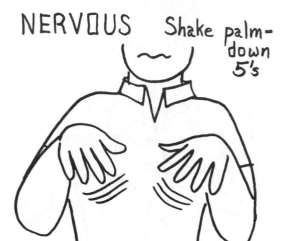

NEST

N's, touching, palms up, swing upward to face each other

(See "jar")

NET

Right 4 on left, draw "U" shape

(See " r")

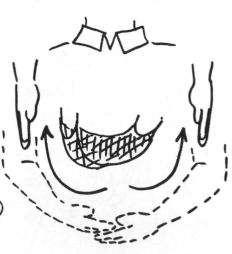

NEUTER

N at temple and at jaw

Neutral = neuter + -al

(See "parent")

NEVER

Open hand in vertical question-mark movement with the tip

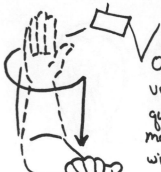

210

NEW
Palm-up right hand arcs down, brushes across palm, and arcs up slightly

News = new + S

Newspaper = news + s + paper

NEW ORLEANS
O brushes off palm twice

NEW YORK
Y slides off palm, little-finger side first

N.Y.

NEXT
Back hand jumps to front

① ②

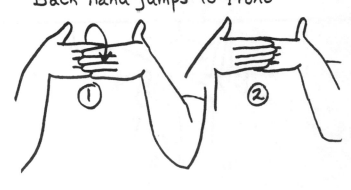

NIBBLE
Thumb + N nibbles index several times

NICE
Fingers of N slide along side of hand

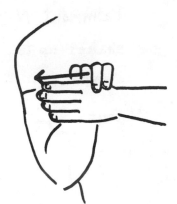

NICKEL
Tap temple once, open to palm-in 5 (See "cent")

① ② 211

NIECE
Shake N near jaw (See "aunt")

NIGHT

Drop bent hand over edge of left

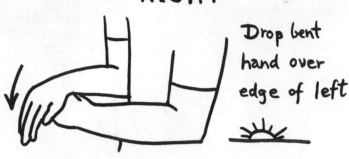

NIP

Thumb and 2 fingers nip index finger

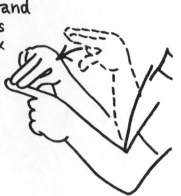

NO

First two fingers close onto thumb

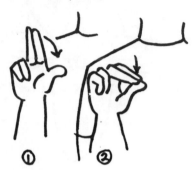

① ②

NOBLE

Palm-in N circles, then touches left shoulder
(See "character")

NOISE

Palm-out N shakes up to ear

Noisy = noise + -y

(See "sound")

NONE

Palm-out O moves right

NOODLE

Shake N's to sides
(See "spaghetti")

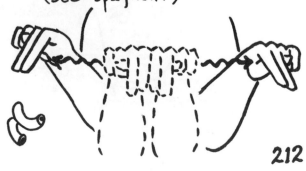

NOON

Right vertical arm on back of left hand

Afternoon = After + noon

212

NOR
N off L-thumb; O off fingertip of index

(See "then")

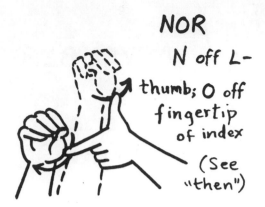

NORM
N-hands tap together twice

Normal= norm +-al

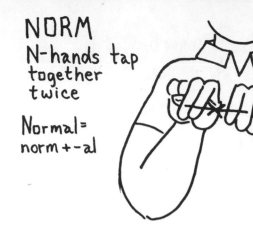

NORTH
Palm-out N moves up

(See "up")

NORWAY
N circles near forehead

Norwegian= Norway + -an

(See "Denmark")

NOSE
Point to nose

NOT
Palm-down hands cross at wrists, separate sideways

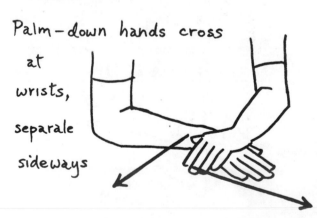

NOTE
Palm-in H at eye twists out down to touch palm

Notice = note +-ice

(See "recognize")

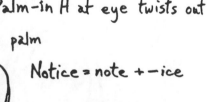

NOTHING
Palm-out O moves right, opening sharply

213

NOUN
Fingertips of N tap side of H index

Pronoun = pro- + noun

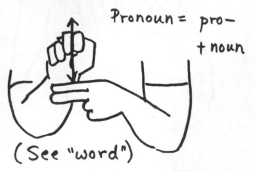

(See "word")

NOVEMBER
Shake N down in 3 steps (3 syllables)

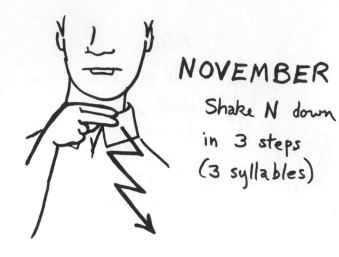

NOW
Slightly drop palm-up bent hands

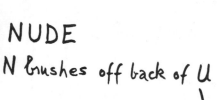

(See "immediate")

NUCLEUS
N circles and drops on left palm
(See "middle")

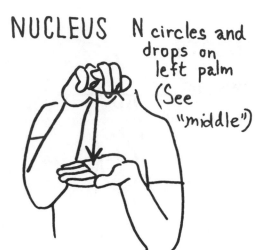

NUDE
N brushes off back of U

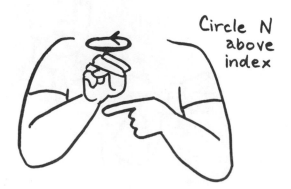

(See "bare")

NUMBER
Flat O-tips touch, one palm up, one palm down; reverse; repeat

Numeral = number + -al

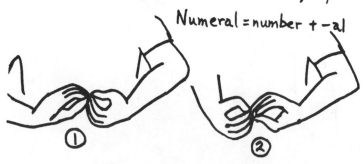

① ②

NUMERATOR
Circle N above index

NUN
N circles over face

214

NURSE

Tap pulse
with N
fingertips twice

Nursery = nurse +
   -er + -y

(See "doctor")

NUT

Flip thumb
out from
under teeth

OAT

O brushes
up G
twice
(See
"grain")

OATH

Index at chin, to
palm-out O against
left
horizontal
wrist

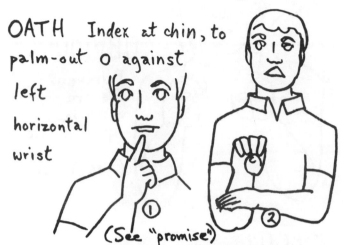

(See "promise")

OBEY

Flat O's, left near
forehead, right near
chin, both drop down
and open

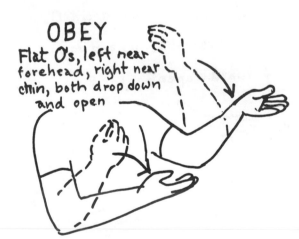

OBJECT
(noun)

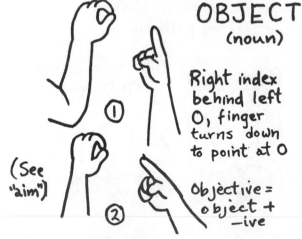

Right index
behind left
O, finger
turns down
to point at O

(See
"aim")

Objective =
object +
   -ive

OBJECT
(verb)

Side of O hits
chest twice

Objection =
object +
-tion

(See "complain")

OBLIGATE

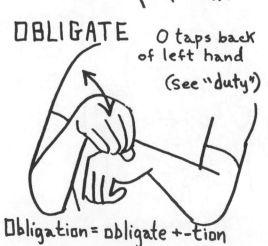

O taps back
of left hand

(See "duty")

Obligation = obligate +-tion

215

OBSERVE

O's circle alternately before face

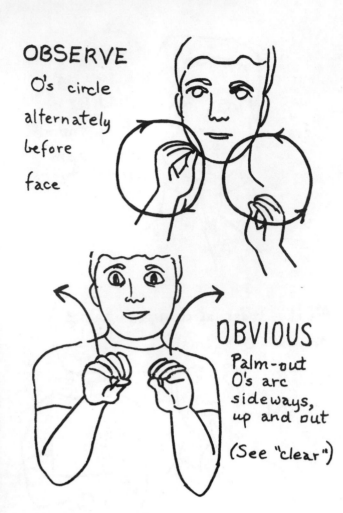

OBSTACLE

Side of right flat hand strikes thumb side of palm-down hand

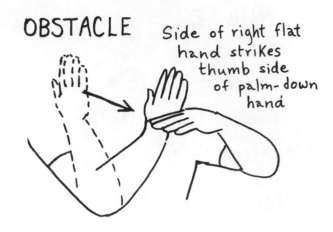

OBVIOUS

Palm-out O's arc sideways, up and out

(See "clear")

OCCUPY

Strike left wrist with palm-out O

OCCUR

Palm-up O's twist to palm-down

(See "happen")

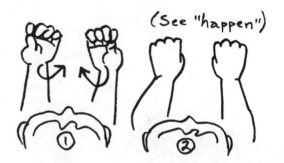

OCEAN

Palm-down O's move wave-like up and down forward, opening to 5's

(See "sea")

OCTOBER

O's before eyes, circle back to sides

(See "mask")

OCTOPUS

O sits on 5-hand, 5 doing "push-ups"

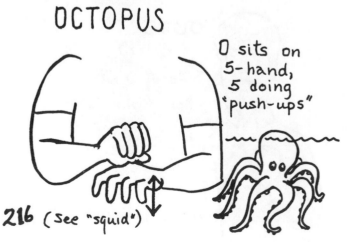

216 (See "squid")

ODD
Right palm-left O arcs in front of nose to palm-down O (See "strange")

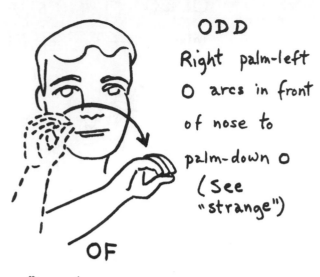

ODOR
O-hand brushes upward at nose

(See "smell")

OF
Open hands approach and link thumbs and index fingers of 9's

OFF
Right palm on back of left hand; lift off

OFFER
Palm-up, parallel O's arc forward

(See "suggest")

OFFICE
Tap shoulder with O

Officer = office + -er

OFTEN
Tap heel and then left fingertips with bent right fingertips (see "frequent")

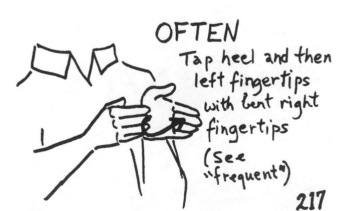

OIL
Pinch O with index finger and thumb of 9; slide off and shut

(See "gravy")

217

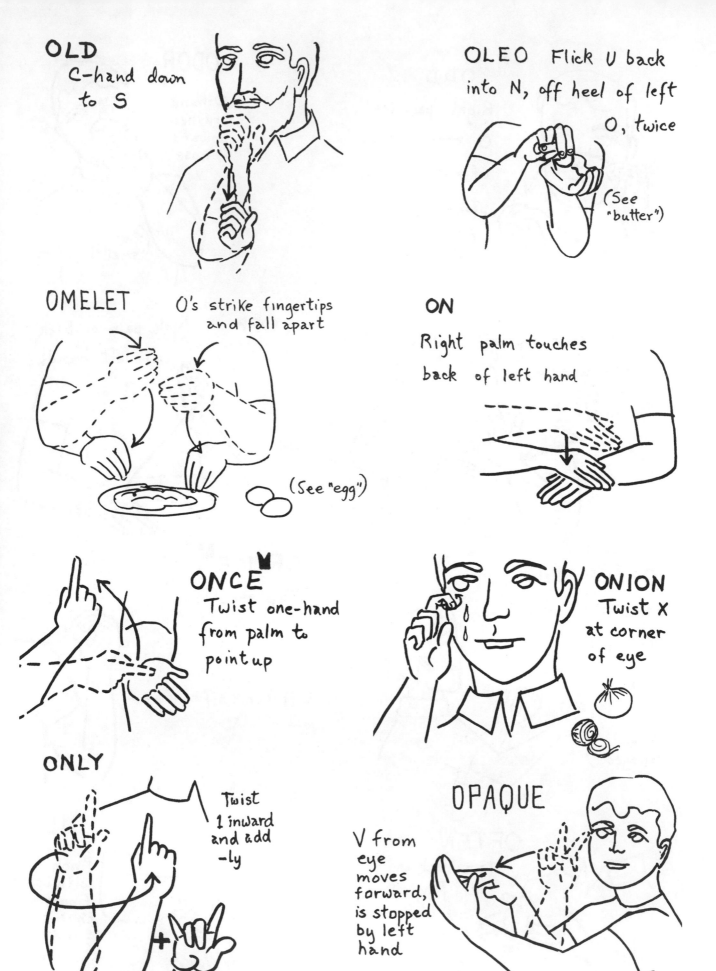

OLD
C-hand down
to S

OLEO Flick U back
into N, off heel of left
O, twice

(See
"butter")

OMELET O's strike fingertips
and fall apart

(See "egg")

ON
Right palm touches
back of left hand

ONCE
Twist one-hand
from palm to
point up

ONION
Twist X
at corner
of eye

ONLY

Twist
1 inward
and add
-ly

+

OPAQUE

V from
eye
moves
forward,
is stopped
by left
hand

218

OPEN

Palms down and sides touching, twist hands apart to sides, palms facing up

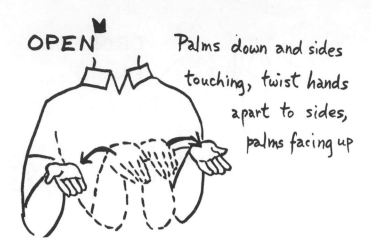

OPERA

O arcs out twice from mouth

(See "sing")

OPERATE

Palm-out O arcs side-to-side, hitting back of S

(See "work")

OPINION

O circles on forehead

(See "reason")

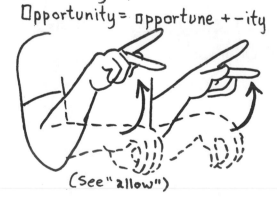

OPPORTUNE

O's change to P's, arcing upward

Opportunity = opportune + -ity

(See "allow")

OPPOSE

Indexes point at each other; hands jerk apart

Opposite = oppose + -ite

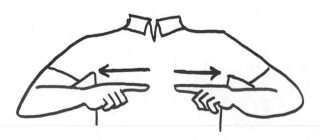

OR

Palm-out O off thumb, then off fingertip

(See "then")

219

ORAL

O circles before mouth

(See "mouth")

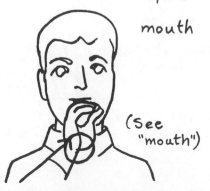

ORANGE
Squeeze S in front of chin

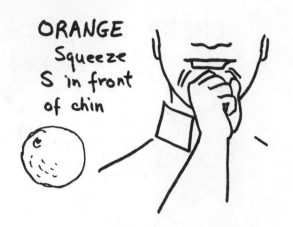

ORCHARD
Elbow of palm-out O on back of hand, twist back and forth

(See "tree")

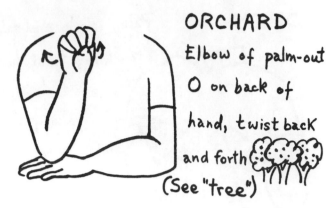

ORCHESTRA
O's swing apart, then together, twice

(Conducting the orchestra)

(See "conduct")

ORDER
Index on chin twists to palm-out, jerks to point forward, slightly bent

(See "command")

ORGANIZE
Palm-out O-hands circle horizontally to palm-in

(See "class")

ORIGIN
Right index fingertip touches wrist of palm-out left O, then twists to palm-in

Original = origin + -al, Originate = origin + -ate

(See "begin")

ORPHAN
O at temple, then at jaw

(See "parent")

OSTRICH
Nod O-hand

(See "gull")

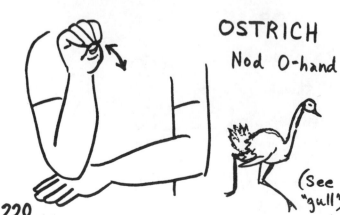

OTHER

Palm-down A-hand twists over to palm-up

Another= an + other

OUGHT

Palm-out O twists to palm-in

(See "seem")

OUNCE

Rock O on index finger of H-hand

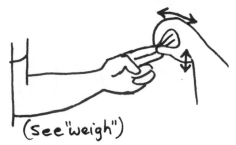

(See "weigh")

OUR

O on right side of chest, circles to left side

Ours = our + -s

OUT

Hand leaves left O

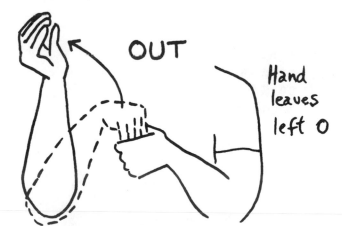

OVAL O circles behind left C

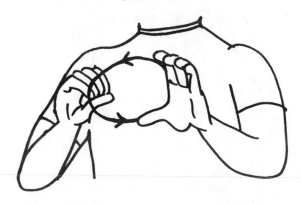

OVEN

O circles under palm

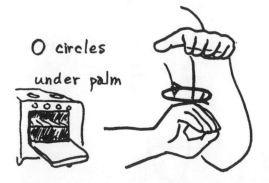

OVER, OVER- (prefix)

Palm-down right hand circles over back of left

221

OVERALLS

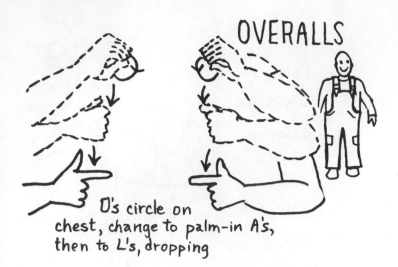

O's circle on chest, change to palm-in A's, then to L's, dropping

OWE

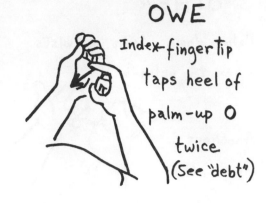

Index-finger tip taps heel of palm-up O twice (See "debt")

OWL

C's at eyes

OWN

C-hands approach each other and link O-hands

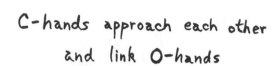

OYSTER

Right hand cups over left O; flaps up and down

PACK

Flat O's alternately pack circularly

PAGE   P turns page on palm

(See "recipe")

① ②

222

PAIL

P-hand, at side, rises

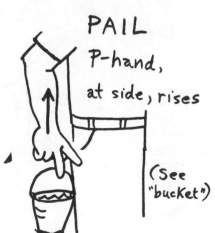

(See "bucket")

PAIN P-hands point at each other, jerk toward each other; repeat

(See "hurt")

PAINT Right open hand fingertips brush back and forth across palm of left

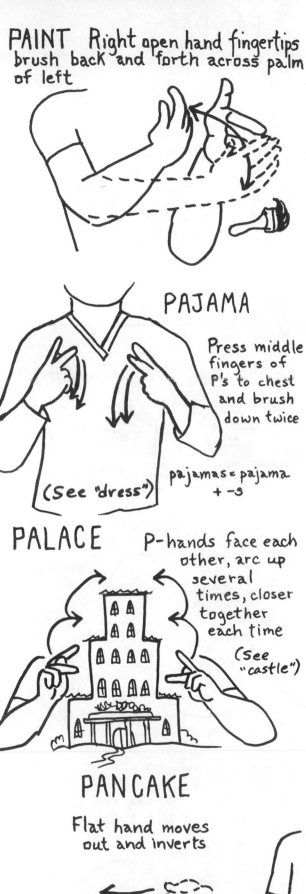

PAIR Thumb and finger of right hand close

P-fingers together

(See "couple")

PAJAMA

Press middle fingers of P's to chest and brush down twice

(See "dress")

pajamas = pajama + -s

PAL Brush chin with thumb of L-hand

PALACE P-hands face each other, arc up several times, closer together each time

(See "castle")

PAN Outline pan-rim and handle with middle P-finger

PANCAKE

Flat hand moves out and inverts

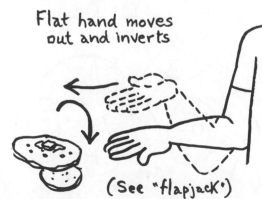

(See "flapjack")

223

PANDA

Palm-in P circles eye

PANT Tap P's at waist twice

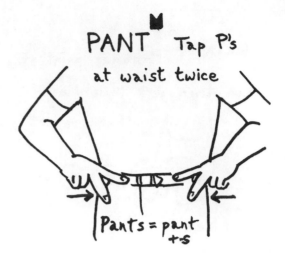

Pants = pant +s

PANTHER

Move 3-hands to side twice

(See "cat")

PAPER

With palm-down right heel, hit palm-up left heel outward and slightly left twice

PARACHUTE

Palm-up O under open hand, swing together downwards

PARADE

P's left behind right, palm down, jerk away from body in parallel jerks

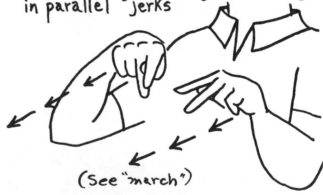

(See "march")

PARADISE

Right P passes under and around left P above head; P's separate

(See "heaven") ① ②

PARAGRAPH

Thumb and fingertips of C tap left palm twice

PARALLEL

Palm-down indexes move forward

(See "hall")

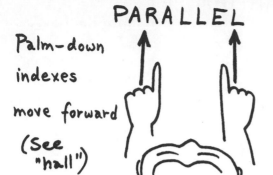

PARANOID

P-hand stationary, middle finger flexes and scratches temple twice

(See "suspect")

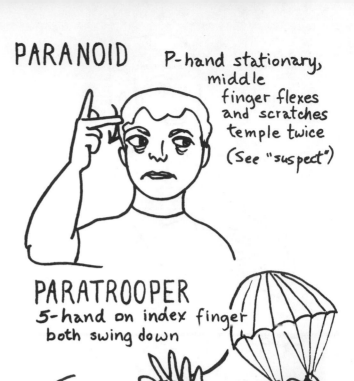

PARASITE

Right index rests on left index; both drop slightly

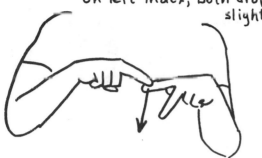

(See "depend")

PARATROOPER

5-hand on index finger both swing down

PARDON

Middle P-fingertip brushes off left fingertips several times

(See "excuse")

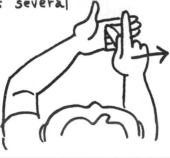

PARE

Brush back of right H inward off back of left H as if paring

PARENT

Touch middle fingertip of P-hand to temple, then to jaw

PARENTHESIS

P's draw parentheses

225

PARK

Palm-left
3 set
on palm

PARLIAMENT

Middle finger
of P touches
left, then right,
shoulder

(See "member")

PARSNIP

Slice side of p with
finger twice

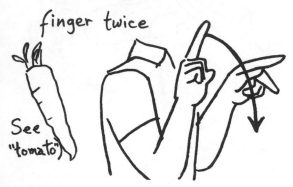

See
"tomato"

PART

Middle
fingertip of P
draws arc on
palm-up
left hand
(See "some")

PARTICIPATE

Middle finger of P
arcs into
O

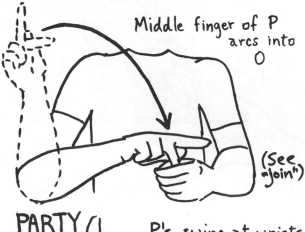

(See
"join")

PARTNER

K-hands first right on left,
then left on right

① (See "friend") ②

PARTY

P's swing at wrists
from side to side
rapidly
L (See
"play")

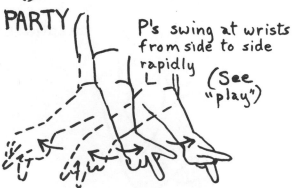

PASS

Right
A-
hand
passes
left A

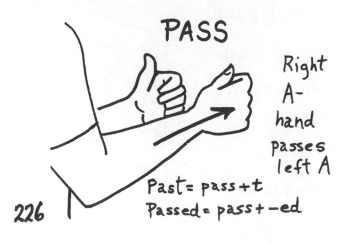

Past= pass + t
Passed= pass + -ed

226

PASSENGER

Two fingers sit on thumb of C, both hands move forward

PASTE

Palm-up H turns to palm-down; fingers sweep across left palm

(See "glue")

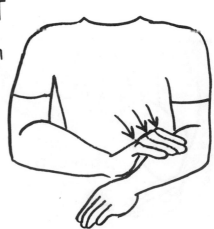

PASTRAMI

Right palm slices thumb of P twice

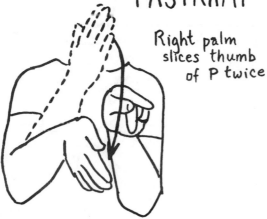

PAT

Pat arm several times

PATH

Palm-down P's move forward, weaving slightly side-to-side (See "way")

PATIENT

Side of A moves down chin once

Patience = patient +-ence

(See "lonesome")

PATIO
Outline patio horizontally with P outside (palm-down) left hand and wrist from arm to fingers

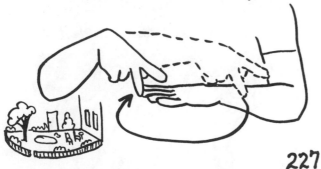

227

PAUSE

Palm-down P behind palm-up left hand; flutter left fingers

(See "wait")

PAW

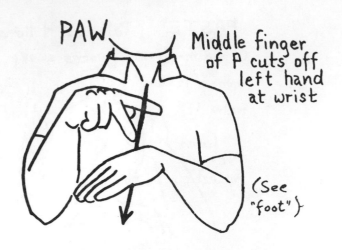

Middle finger of P cuts off left hand at wrist

(See "foot")

PAY

Middle finger of P on palm; flip up and out

Paid = pay + -ed

PEA

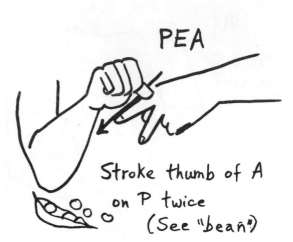

Stroke thumb of A on P twice (See "bean")

PEACE

P-hands cross below chin; separate downwards

(See "quiet")

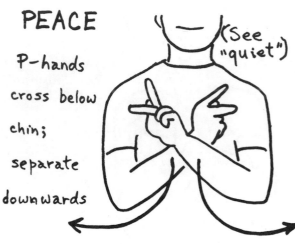

PEACH

Stroke cheek, 5 to flat-O twice

PEACOCK

Right elbow on back of left hand, palm-down P rises and opens to 5 (like tail)

PEANUT

P index and then thumb of A jerk from under teeth

(see "nut")

PEAR

Right hand grasps left flat-O; slides off into flat-O; changes to index and touches left fingers

PEBBLE

Palm-up P taps back of S

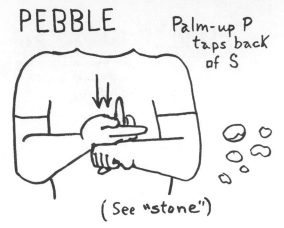

(See "stone")

PECK

Peck at index finger (See "nag")

PEEK

Peek through P-fingers

PEEL

P middle finger, twisting outward, slides down back of S hand and fingers

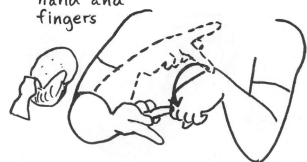

PEN

Middle fingertip of P writes on palm (See "write")

PENCIL

Thumb and index finger at mouth, then write on palm

(See "write")

PENGUIN

Inside of wrists on hips, hands bent back, tilt body from side to side

229

PENNANT

P waves in breeze, left index on arm

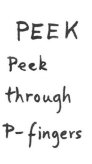

(See "flag")

PENNY Tap temple once, then shake P slightly

(See "cent")

PEOPLE Palm-out P's circle alternately up and down forward

PEPPER

Thumb-side of 9-hand sprinkles palm

PERCENT

O moves diagonally up to right then down

%

PERCH

Perch fingers on left P-index

(See "sit")

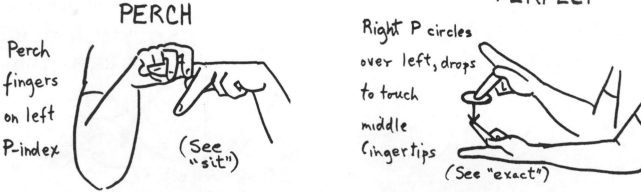

PERFECT

Right P circles over left, drops to touch middle fingertips

(See "exact")

PERFORM

P's, palm out, with backs brushing alternately down on chest

(See "act")

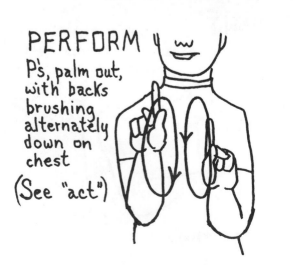

230

PERFUME

9-hand at side of neck tips bottle onto neck

PERHAPS

Palm-down
P pivots
several
times to
side to
side

PERIOD

P circles forward

once near palm,

then touches
palm

(See "hour")

PERISCOPE

X rises outside forearm
and moves
slowly
toward
elbow

PERMANENT

Middle finger
of right P on left,
both move forward

(See
"continue")

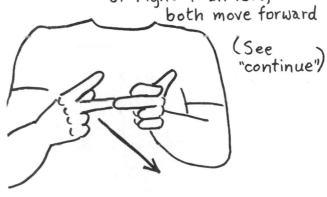

PERMIT

Palm-down P's twist to
palm-out
(See "allow")
Permission = permit + -tion

PERSECUTE

Right X hits off top of left X,
then left X off right X

① ②

PERSON

Palm-down P's move

straight down

PERSONALITY

P circles on left
shoulder

(May be signed
"person" + -al
+ -ity)

(See
"character")

231

PERSPECTIVE

Swing P from eye in arc halfway to left P

PEST

P rides on wiggling fingers

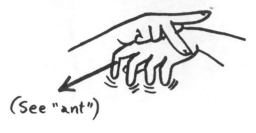

(See "ant")

PET

Pet back of hand

(See "tame")

PHILADELPHIA

P arcs sharply down to right

(See "chicago")

PHILOSOPHY

Right P moves up and down near forehead

(See "wise")

PHONE

Thumb of Y near ear, little finger near mouth

PHOTO

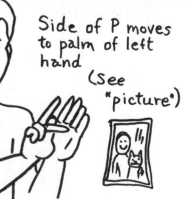

Side of P moves to palm of left hand

(See "picture")

PHOTOGRAPH

Left hand palm-out, right P arcs back against palm

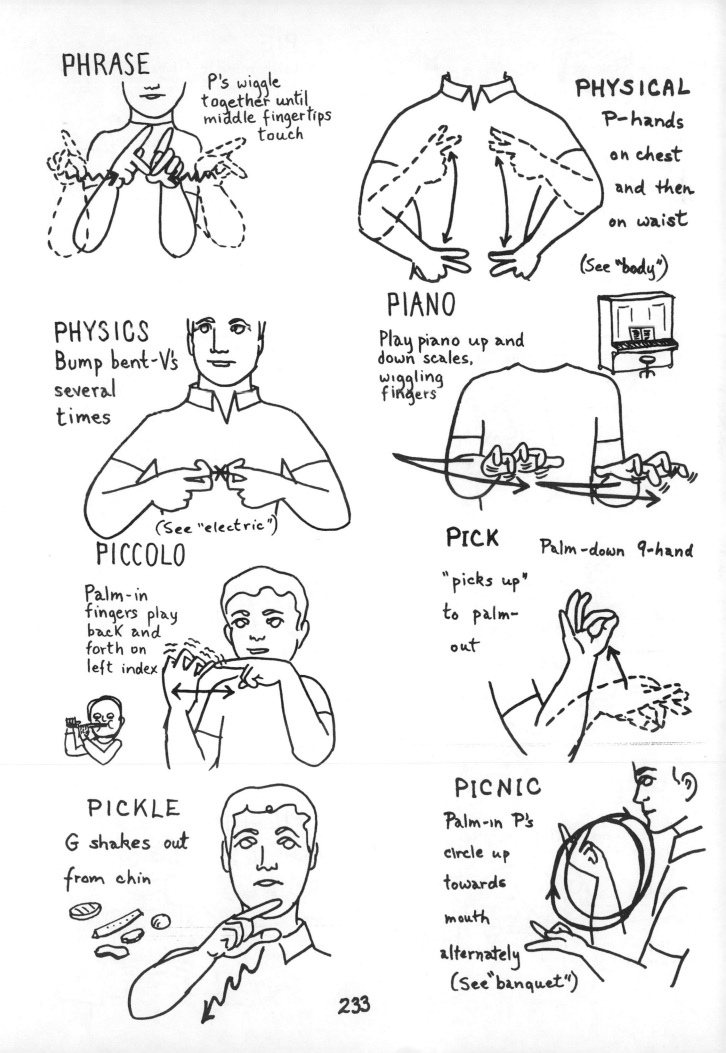

PHRASE

P's wiggle together until middle fingertips touch

PHYSICAL

P-hands on chest and then on waist

(See "body")

PIANO

Play piano up and down scales, wiggling fingers

PHYSICS

Bump bent-V's several times

(See "electric")

PICCOLO

Palm-in fingers play back and forth on left index

PICK   Palm-down 9-hand

"picks up" to palm-out

PICKLE

G shakes out from chin

PICNIC

Palm-in P's circle up towards mouth alternately

(See "banquet")

233

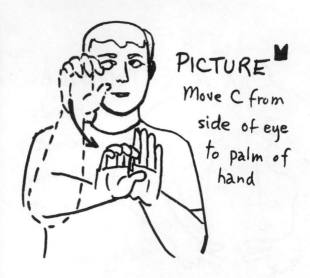

PICTURE

Move C from side of eye to palm of hand

PIE

With middle finger of P draw an X on the palm

PIECE

Middle finger of P arcs down, hitting side of Index

(See "chip")

PIER

P circles hand and arm starting at outside

(See "dock")

PIG

Flap hand under chin, fingers together

PIGEON

Close index finger of P to middle finger twice

(See "bird")

PILE

Flat hand outlines a pile in your palm

(See "amount")

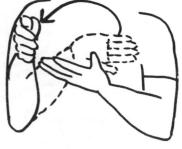

PILGRIM

Middle fingertips of P's on chest move to side, then up on chest

234

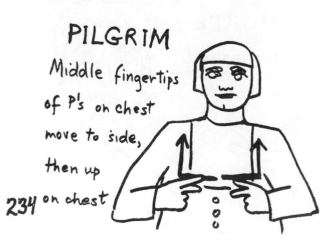

PILL

Flick thumb and finger toward mouth (popping pill in)

(See "vitamin")

PILLOW

Pat underside of invisible pillow

(See "bed")

PIMPLE

Hand moves around face, index finger flicking repeatedly off thumb

(See "measles")

PIN

"Stick" two invisible pins in right shoulder with 9-hand

PINAFORE

4's at sides of chest curve down body

(ruffles on pinafore)

PINCH

Thumb slips past tip of index while resting on back of left

(takes a pinch)

PINEAPPLE

Twist middle finger of P at corner of mouth

(See "apple")

PINGPONG

Right wrist swings A from side to side (holding paddle)

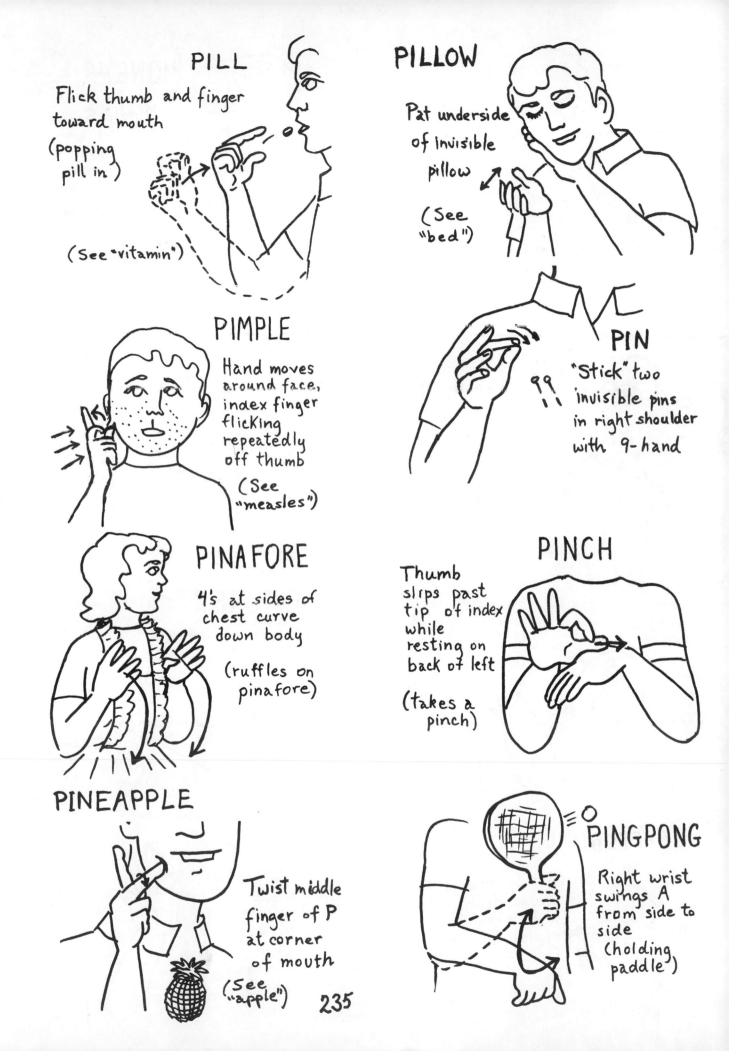

235

PINK

Brush middle finger of P down chin twice

(See "red")

PIONEER

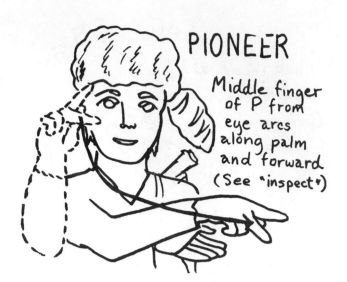

Middle finger of P from eye arcs along palm and forward

(See "inspect")

PIPE

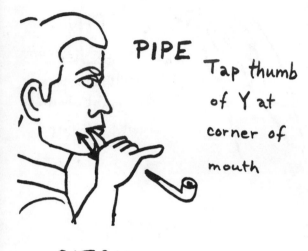

Tap thumb of Y at corner of mouth

PIRATE

Cover right eye

PITCH

P throws forward from near shoulder

(See "throw")

PITCHER

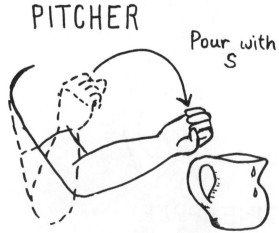

Pour with S

PITTSBURGH

Brush 9 index and thumb down right chest rapidly several times

PITY

Right middle finger strokes the air, hand arcing up and down

236

PIXIE 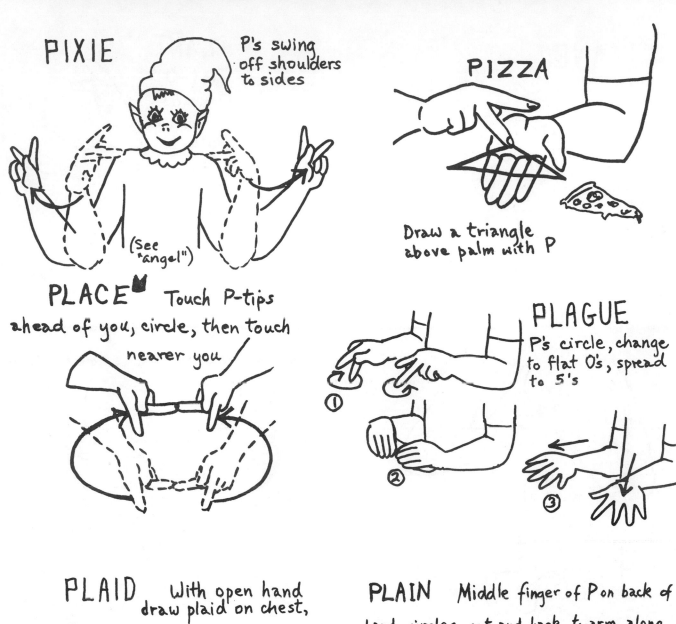 P's swing off shoulders to sides

(See "angel")

PIZZA

Draw a triangle above palm with P

PLACE Touch P-tips ahead of you, circle, then touch nearer you

PLAGUE P's circle, change to flat O's, spread to 5's

① ② ③

PLAID With open hand draw plaid on chest,

palm across; back, down

PLAIN Middle finger of P on back of hand, circles out and back to arm, along arm to hand

(See "ground")

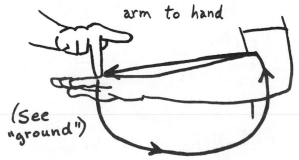

PLAN

Parallel palms move right smoothly

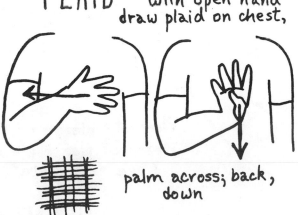

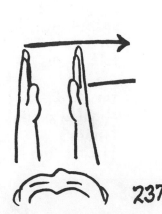

PLANE Palm-down

L + i on palm, move right hand forward slightly

Airplane = air + plane

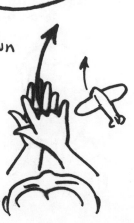

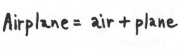

PLANET

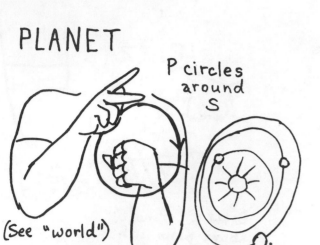

P circles around S

(See "world")

PLANT

Flat-O, through C, "grows" like a plant into P

(see "grow")

(See "grow")

PLASTIC

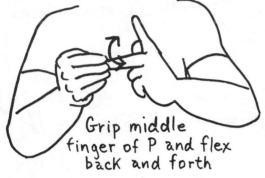

Grip middle finger of P and flex back and forth

Hands swing to right, twisting, then back again

PLAY

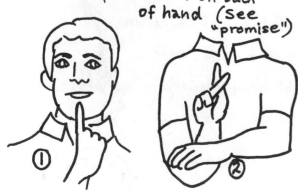

PLATE

Middle fingers touch; outline plate with palms, touch thumbs

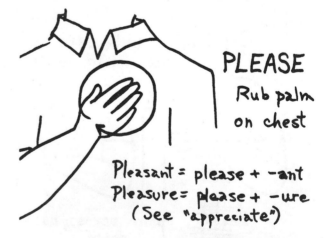

(See "dish")

PLEASE

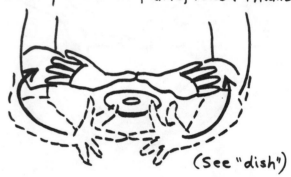

Rub palm on chest

Pleasant = please + -ant
Pleasure = please + -ure
(See "appreciate")

PLEDGE

Index at chin to palm-out P on back of hand (see "promise")

PLENTY

Fingers of palm-down 5 on top of left S, move off and forward, slightly down, fingers fluttering

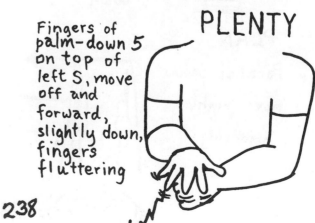

238

PLIERS

Use invisible pliers to "tighten" left index

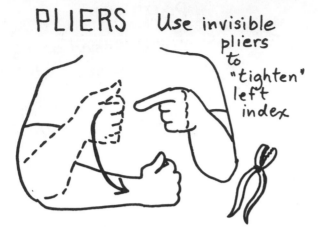

PLOW

Palm-left side of flat hand along palm slides forward to palm-up

PLUM

Middle finger of P slices around left S-hand

(See "apricot")

PLURAL

Point middle fingertip of P at three things in succession moving right

PLUS

Index fingers form plus sign

PNEUMONIA

Fingertips of bent hands rub up and down on chest

POCKET

Right hand slides into left C wherever pocket is located

POEM

P arcs behind palm, ending in palm-out M

(See "music")

POET
Parcs behind palm,
ending in palm-out T

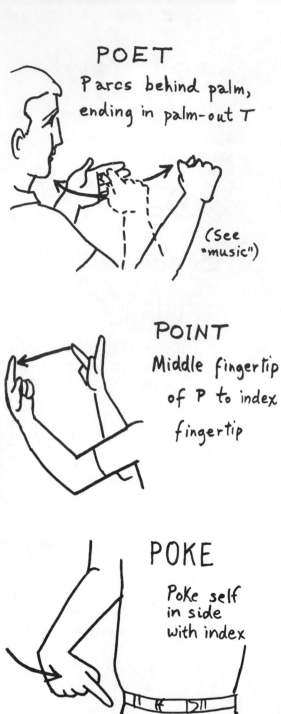

(See "music")

POETRY
Parcs behind palm,
ending in palm-out Y

(See "music")

POINT
Middle fingertip
of P to index
fingertip

POISON
Cross P's
under chin,
palm-out

(See "skull")

POKE
Poke self
in side
with index

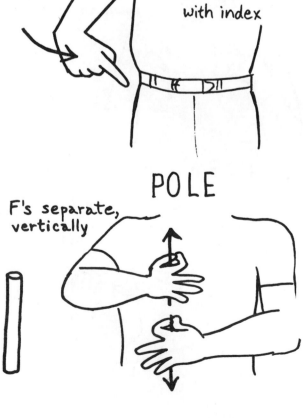

POLAND
A-thumb
flicks off
nose-tip
twice

Polish = Poland
+ -ish

POLE
F's separate,
vertically

POLICE
Thumb and
index finger
show badge

240

POLISH (verb)

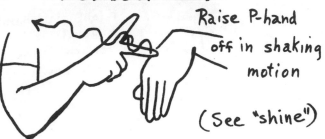

Raise P-hand off in shaking motion

(See "shine")

POLITE

Tap side of P on chest twice

(See "fine")

POLITIC

P circles once near temple, then touches temple

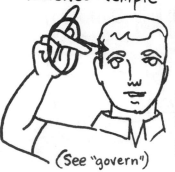

Politics = politic + -s

Politician = politic + -ar

Political = politic + -al

(See "govern")

Middle fingers of P's touch, shake forward in a circle, touch again

(See "lake")

POND

PONY

Pat temple nods twice from wrist.

(See "horse")

POOL

Back of P arcs down to right across palm and up again

POOR

Grasp elbow, close to flat-O, repeat

POP

Put 9 inside of S, then slap S

① ②

241

POPSICLE

Stroke down chin with V fingertips twice

(See "ice cream")

POPULAR

Right claw-hand moves to left vertical index and touches side of left index

POPULATE

Middle fingertip of P brushes across 5-fingers of left hand

Population = populate + -tion

(See "distribute")

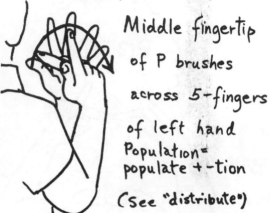

PORCH

Outline front of porch with P's

PORK

Thumb and finger of 9 grasp side of P and shake

(See "meat")

PORPOISE

Make 2 curves left with P along arm

(See "dolphin")

POSITIVE

Index at chin drops to hit left index

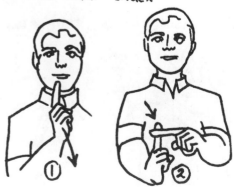

POSSIBLE

Middle fingertips of P's on chest drop to palm-down A's

242

POST, POST- (Prefix)

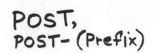

P moves from back of hand straight forward

POSTPONE

F's arc forward

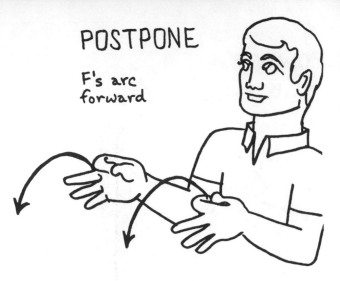

POT

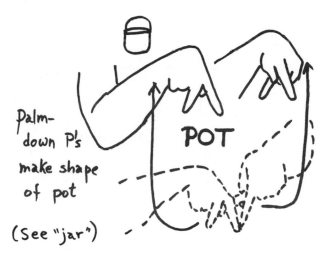

Palm-down P's make shape of pot

(See "jar")

POTATO

Tap 2 bent fingers on back of S

POUCH

H draws pouch under palm-down S

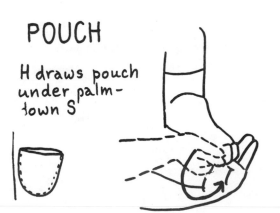

POUND

Rock middle finger of P on index of horizontal H-hand

(See "weigh")

POUR   A lifts and "pours" into side of left C

POUT

P's beside mouth pull down

(See "grim")

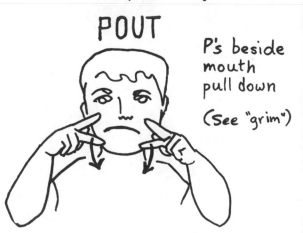

243

POWDER

Shake c-hand to sprinkle

POWER

Middle finger of P draws muscle

(See "strong")

POX

Make spots on face with middle finger of P

(See "measles")

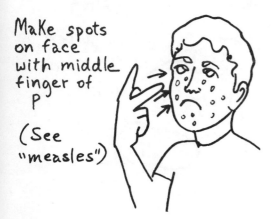

PRACTICE

Palm-down A brushes back and forth on index

PRAISE

Flat hand on chin, then clap hands

PREACH

Palm-out 9 jerks slightly forward twice (See "lecture")

PRAY

Palms together, hands move slightly up and down before face

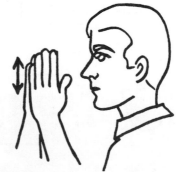

PRECIPITATE

P's move down in small jerks

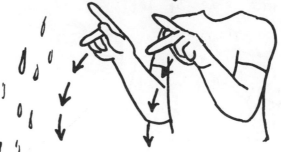

244

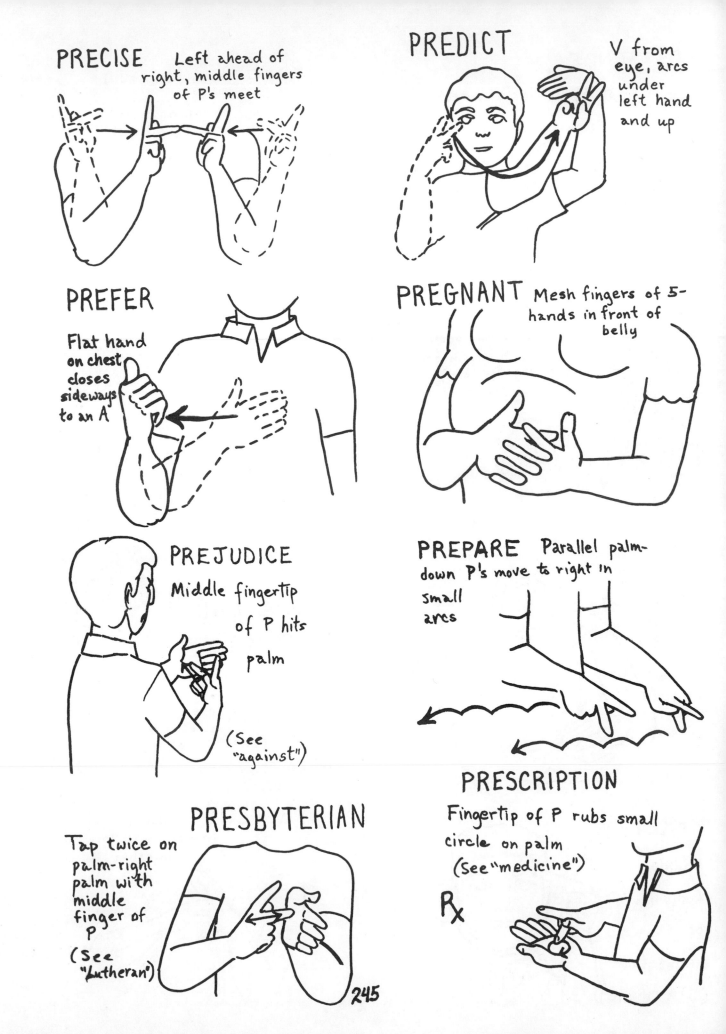

PRECISE   Left ahead of right, middle fingers of P's meet

PREDICT   V from eye, arcs under left hand and up

PREFER   Flat hand on chest closes sideways to an A

PREGNANT   Mesh fingers of 5-hands in front of belly

PREJUDICE   Middle fingertip of P hits palm

(See "against")

PREPARE   Parallel palm-down P's move to right in small arcs

PRESBYTERIAN   Tap twice on palm-right palm with middle finger of P

(See "Lutheran")

PRESCRIPTION   Fingertip of P rubs small circle on palm (See "medicine")

Rx

245

PRESENCE

P's swing up to face each other before chin, not touching

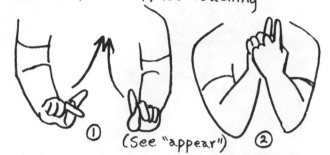

① (See "appear") ②

PRESENT (noun, adj.)

Palms facing nearly up drop slightly P-hands

PRESENT

(verb) P's left behind right, with forefingers pointing forward, arc forward

(See "suggest")

PRESIDENT

Palm-out C's at temples rise to sides, closing to S's

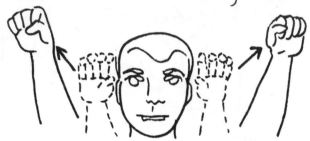

PRESS

Press palms together, right hand on top

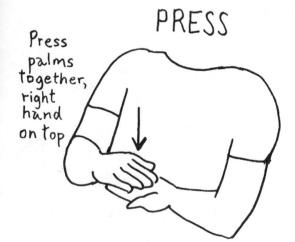

PRETEND

Side of P brushes across chin twice (See "false")

PRETTY

Middle fingertip of P circles face (See "face")

PREVENT

Crossed flat hands move forward together

246

PRICE
Middle fingertip of P strikes downward on palm

(See "cost")

PRIDE
Draw P middle finger up chest

(See "feel")

PRIEST
Side of G-hand slides across neck

PRIMARY
P circles under palm (See "base")

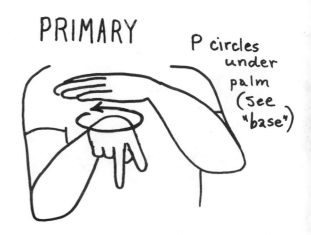

PRINCE
Middle P fingertip touches left shoulder, then right side of body

Princess = prince + -ess

(See "Christ")

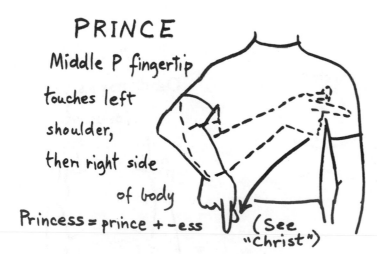

PRINCIPAL
Right P circles over, drops on back of left S

PRINCIPLE
Side of P on left fingers, then on heel

(See "law")

247

PRINT
Open and close G on left palm

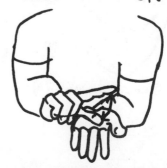

PRIOR
Middle finger of P taps extended thumb of A twice

(See "first")

PRISON
Right behind left 5; right hits left

(See "jail")

PRIZE
X-hands, palms facing, right ahead of left, drop to your right

(See "gift")

PROBLEM
Knuckles hit, separate; right bent-V rotates forward, left rotates back; knuckles hit again

PROCLAIM
P's from corners of mouth swing out

(See "announce")

PROBABLE
P-hands face each other, raise and lower alternately

Probably = probable + -ly
(See "balance")

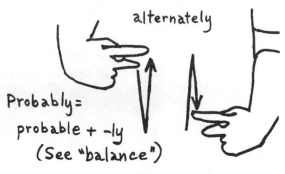

PROCEED
Bent hands move forward

PRODUCE
Right P on left, twist hands to palm-in

Product = produce + -t
(See "make")

248

PROFESS
Middle fingertip of P slides forward on side of left hand

Profession = profess + -ion

Professor = profess + -er

(See "straight")

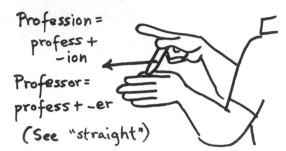

PROFIT
Side of 9 on body near waist, slide down

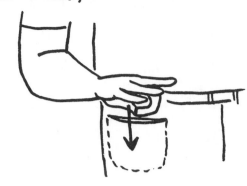

PROHIBIT
Strike side of P against left palm

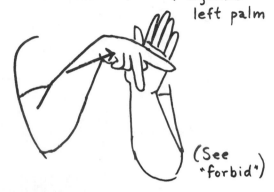

(See "forbid")

PROGRESS
Put bent hands one in front of the other several times while moving forward

PROGRAM
Middle fingertip of right P moves down palm-in left hand, then down back of stationary left hand

(See "project")

PROJECT (verb)
Flat-O against left palm, moves forward and opens

Projector = project + -er

PROJECT (noun)
P moves down palm, then I arcs down back of hand

(See "program")

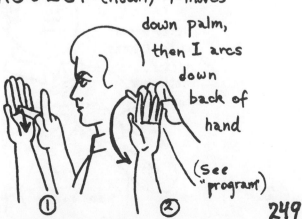

PROLOGUE
P's swing inward to touch middle fingertips

(See "introduce")

249

PROMISE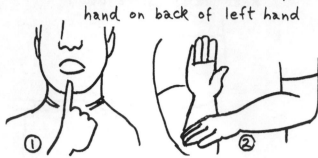

Index on chin, to heel of hand on back of left hand

① ②

PROMOTE

Bent hands, facing each other, arc up once

PRONOUNCE   Palm-down P

(pointing left) circles out from mouth

Pronunciation = pronounce + -tion

PROOF   Back of hand, behind palm-out 9, moves forward to touch it

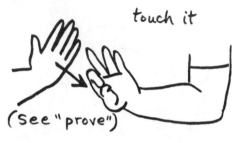

(See "prove")

PROPAGANDA

Right P in front of left S; P shakes forward

(See "exaggerate")

PROPHECY

P from eye arcs under left P and up

PROSE   Middle finger of right P moves in wavy motion down across palm

(see "read")

PROTECT

Defend self with P near left P; both move forward

(see "guard")

250

PROTESTANT

Tap bent V knuckles twice on palm-right left palm

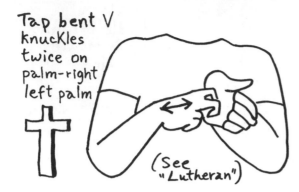

(See "Lutheran")

PROUD

Draw right A-thumb up chest, palm-right

(See "feel")

PROVE

Back of right hand, behind palm-out V, moves forward to touch it

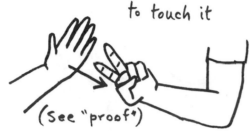

(See "proof")

PROVIDE

P rises out of pocket and twists forward to palm up

PRUNE

Draw P across chin, index crooking

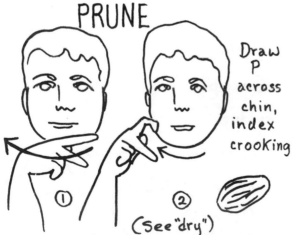

① ②

(See "dry")

PSYCHIATRY

Middle finger of right P taps left S-wrist

(See "doctor")

Psychiatrist= psychiatry + -ist

PSYCHOLOGY

Flat right hand chops into left thumb joint from behind twice

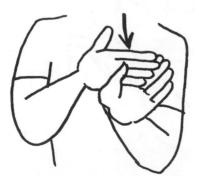

PUBLIC

(See "broad")

P's move out and forward

251

PUBLICITY

Right P in front of left S; right pushes forward, like a trombone, repeat rapidly

PUDDING

Ladle P-hand up to mouth twice

(See "soup")

PUDDLE

Outline puddle in wavy circle on back of left hand

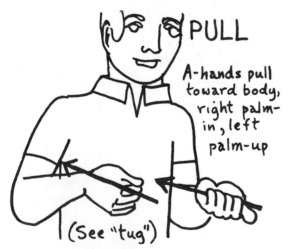

PUFF

P at mouth out to F

PULL

A-hands pull toward body, right palm-in, left palm-up

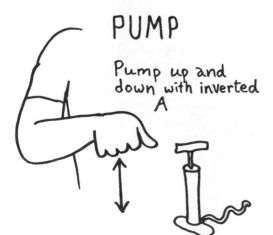

(See "tug")

PULSE

Grasp pulse, thumb on bottom

(See "doctor")

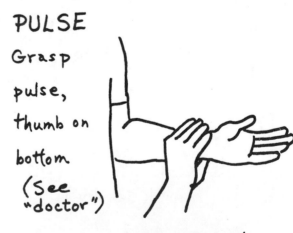

PUMPKIN

Tap middle finger of P on back of S (See "melon")

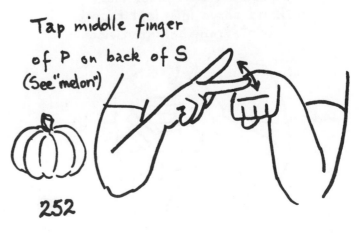

PUMP

Pump up and down with inverted A

252

PUNCH

P slightly behind index, moves forward to hit index with middle finger
(See "beat")

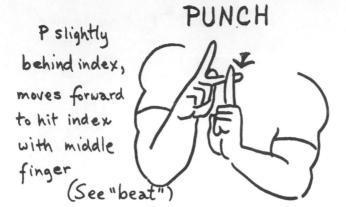

PUNISH

Index finger strikes down on elbow

PUPIL

P brushes off palm twice

PUPPY

Right P-thumb is rubbed by first two fingers

(See "dog")

PURCHASE

Right palm-in P moves forward off left palm

(See "buy")

PURE

P circles over left palm, then wipes off left palm

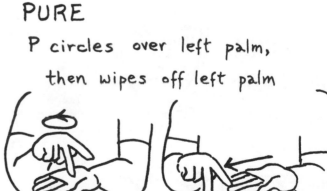

① ② (See "holy")

PURPLE

Palm-down P shakes slightly to right

(See "blue")

253

PURPOSE

P on palm, twist to right and touch again
(See "mean")

①   ②

PURSE P draws bag under arm

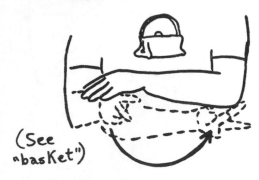

(See "basket")

PUSH Flat hands push forward

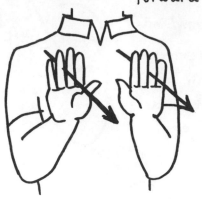

PUT Flat-O moves forward to put something down

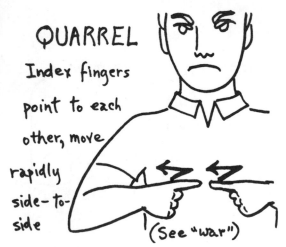

PUZZLE Index finger jerks back to an X on forehead

QUARREL Index fingers point to each other, move rapidly side-to-side

(See "war")

QUARTER Index at temple, move L out slightly, flutter last 3 fingers together in palm-in 25

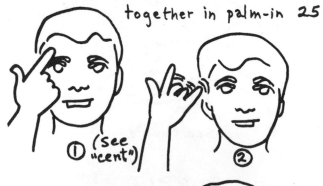

① (See "cent") ②

QUEEN Right Q on left shoulder, then on right side of body (See "Christ")

QUEER Right palm-left G arcs in front of nose to palm-down (See "strange")

254

QUESTION
Flick a question-mark 1 to X to 1 with right hand

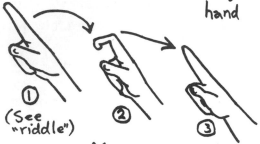

① ② ③

(See "riddle")

QUICK
Thumb inside right fist; snaps out

① ②

QUIET
Flat hands cross under chin and separate downwards

QUIT
H-fingertips start in O; pull out and up (See "resign")

QUITE
Q's move on a curve to the side (See "much")

QUIZ
Draw question marks with both fingers

QUOTE
Bent V's twist slightly, outlining quotation marks

" "

RABBI
R-hands outline prayer-shawl around neck

255

RABBIT

Wiggle palm-in U-fingers backward together

RACE

R-palms face each other; move alternately forward and back

(See "compete")

RACCOON

Outline bottom of mask with R's

RADIO

R rises from side to ear, shaking slightly

(See "sound")

RADISH

R shakes down from fingertips of flat O

RAG

Rub R-fingertips on chest near shoulder

(See "cloth")

RAGE

Palm-in R near stomach jerks up to near shoulder

(See "anger")

256

RAIN

Drop palm-down claw hands sharply twice

RAISE

Palm-up hands rise

RAISIN

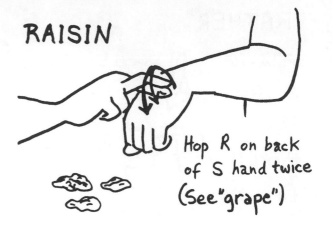

Hop R on back of S hand twice (See "grape")

RAKE

Rake with claw-hand several times

RAM

R's circle back like horns from temples

RANCH

Extended thumb of R moves under chin left to right

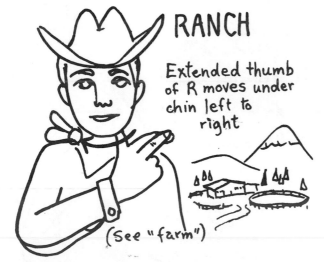

(See "farm")

RANGE

R circles over left arm

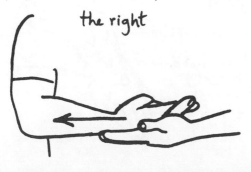

(See "ground")

RARE

Slide the back of right R off left palm, toward the right

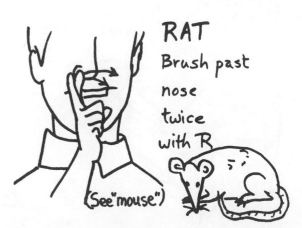

RAT

Brush past nose twice with R

(See "mouse")

257

RATHER

Palm-out
R off
thumb,
then off
fingertip

(See "then")

RATTLE

Shake
R

RAW

Brush R arcing across palm

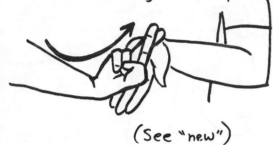

(See "new")

RAZOR

Flick R
off cheek
twice

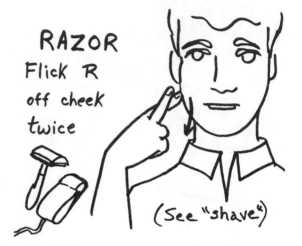

(See "shave")

REACH

Back of R
approaches
and touches
left palm

(See "arrive")

READ

Left palm in; right
palm-down V
fingertips move down
past palm in wavy motion
Read (past tense) = read + -ed
(See "essay")

READY

R-hands, palm-
out, move to the
right

REAL

Fingertips of R
slide down palm-
up left hand
(See "honest")
Really = real
+ -ly

258

REALIZE

R on forehead moves up and forward, remaining palm-in

(See "understand")

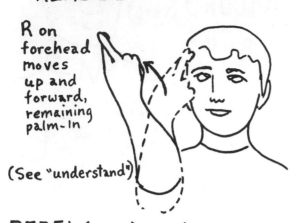

REASON

Circle R-fingertips near temple

REBEL (verb)

Palm-in S turns to palm-out S

Rebellious = rebel + -ous

(See "defy")

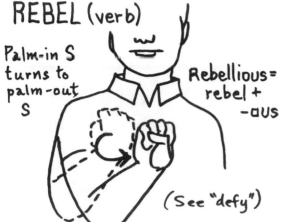

RECEIVE

Right R on left, pull toward body, closing to S's

(See "get")

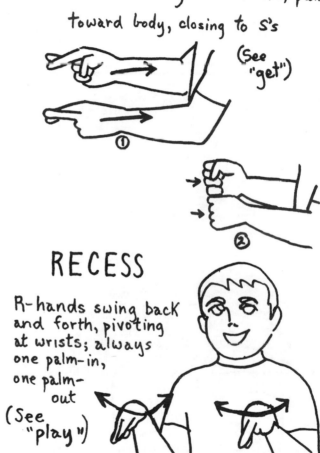

RECENT

Side of X-hand on cheek; wiggle finger

RECESS

R-hands swing back and forth, pivoting at wrists; always one palm-in, one palm-out

(See "play")

RECIPE

Palm-up R on palm flips to palm-down

(See "page")

259

RECOGNIZE

R at eye drops to palm of left hand

(See "note")

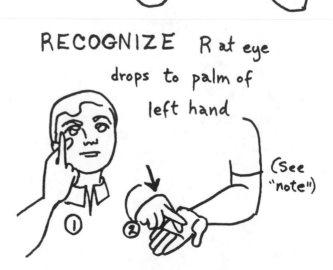

RECOMMEND

R's, palm-up, move forward and slightly up (See "suggest")

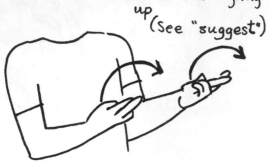

RECORD (verb)

Write with R-fingers across left palm

(See "write")

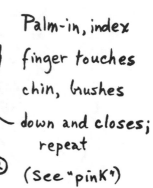

RECORD

Tip of R circles above, drops on palm

RED

Palm-in, index finger touches chin, brushes down and closes; repeat (See "pink")

①   ②

REDUCE

Right flat hand descends in stages to above left

REEL

Circle R around S

(See "spool")

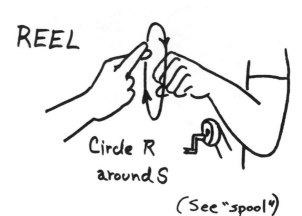

REFLECT

Palm-out R hits palm and reflects back, palm-in

REFLEX

Tap R on wrist of limp hand (causes a reflex up-flip)

REFRIGERATE
Move R's back and forth toward each other in shivering motion

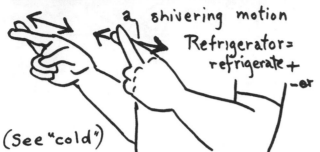

Refrigerator= refrigerate + -er

(See "cold")

REFUSE
S-hand jerks back toward shoulder

REGISTER
Right R-fingertips hop backwards twice along palm

REGRESS
Right R moves down in hopping motion

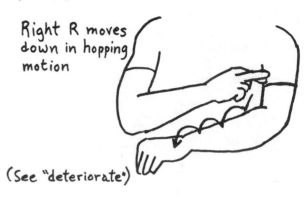

(See "deteriorate")

REGRET
Right R circles on chest

(See "sorry")

REGULAR
Bounce right index on left while moving forward

REHABILITATE
R on left palm; both rise

(See "help")

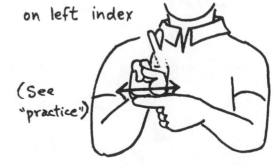

261

REHEARSE
Heel of R brushes back and forth on left index

(See "practice")

REIGN

R's move alternately forward and back, forward left, then forward right

(See "manage")

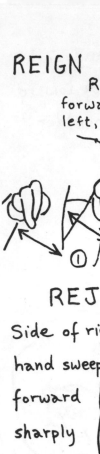

REINDEER   Thumbs of

R's on temples, move up and out

(See "deer")

REJECT

Side of right hand sweeps forward sharply off left palm

(See "rid")

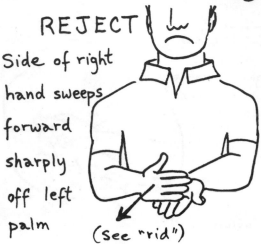

RELATE   Rest R-fingers

first right on left, then left on right

Relative = relate + -ive
Relation = relate + -tion

① (See "friend")   ②

RELAX

Rest crossed R's on chest

RELIEVE

Right R above left R on chest, both move down

(See "satisfy")

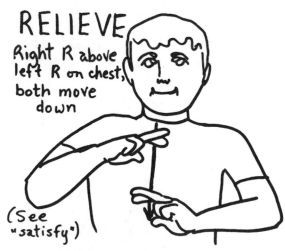

RELIGION

R on heart arcs down and forward

Religious = add -ous

REMAIN

Right R-fingers on left R; both move forward

262   (See "continue")

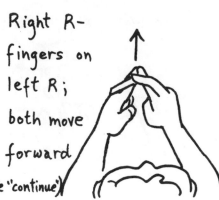

REMEMBER   Thumb of A on forehead; drops to touch left A-thumb

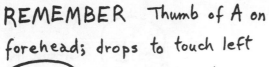

REMIND   Tap forehead twice with right R-fingers   (See "think")

REMOVE   R-fingertips on left palm, arc off to throw open hand down

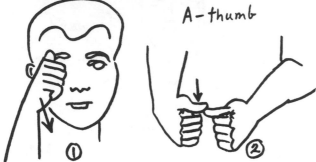

(See "waste")

RENT   R on R, arc back toward body

(See "borrow")

REPAIR   R-tips touch; twist in opposite directions

(See "fix")

REPEAT   R turns over and strikes palm; repeat

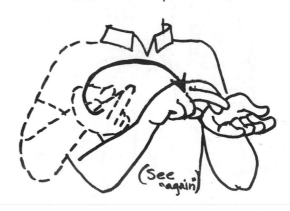

(See "again")

REPLY   Index finger near lips, left R palm in; both hands turn palm-down left one ahead

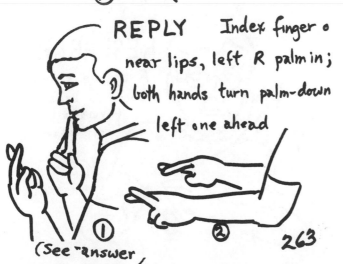

(See "answer")

263

REPORT   R on lip moves to palm

(See "mention")

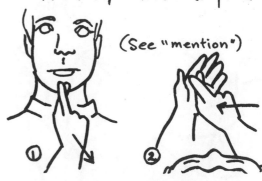

REPRESENT
Tip of R on palm, move both forward

Representative = represent + -ive

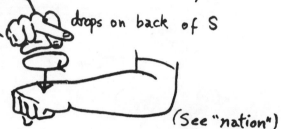

(See "show")

REPTILE
Circle R forward from chin

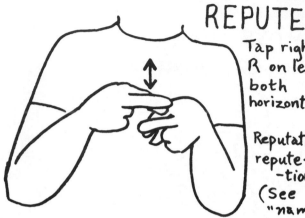

(See "snake")

REPUBLIC
R circles over, then drops on back of S

(See "nation")

REPUTE
Tap right R on left, both horizontal

Reputation = repute + -tion

(See "name")

REQUEST
R's touching, pull toward self

(See "ask")

REQUIRE
Tip of X on palm, both arc together toward body

RESCUE
Separate palm-in crossed R's to sides, twisting to palm-out
(See "free")

264

RESEARCH
R at eye swings down to brush forward twice off palm

(See "inspect")

RESENT

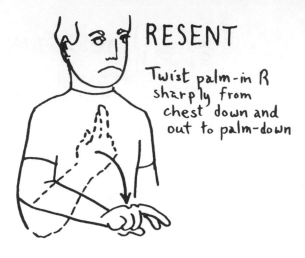

Twist palm-in R sharply from chest down and out to palm-down

RESERVE

R-fingertips tap back of A-hand
Reservation = reserve + -tion

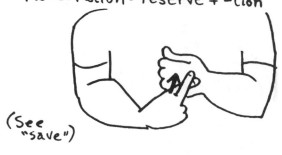

(See "save")

RESIDE

R's slide up body

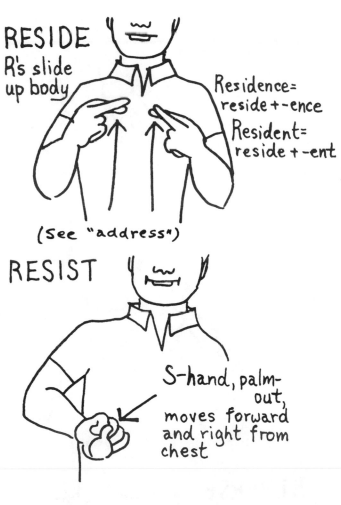

Residence = reside + -ence
Resident = reside + -ent

(See "address")

RESIST

S-hand, palm-out, moves forward and right from chest

RESIGN

R-fingertips arc back out of O

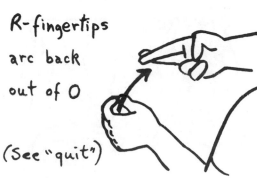

(See "quit")

RESPECT

R arcs in and down near forehead

(See "god")

RESPONSIBLE

Both R-hands on right shoulder

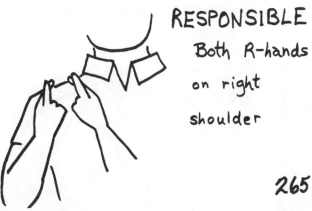

REST

Right R behind left; both move slightly down

RESTAURANT

Tap R at right corner of mouth, then at left corner

(See "cafe")

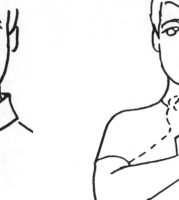

RESTRAIN

Right claw to S at neck

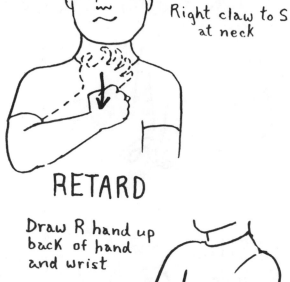

RESULT

Palm-up R's

twist to palm-down

① ②

(See "happen")

RETARD

Draw R hand up back of hand and wrist

(See "slow")

RETURN

R's point at each other, circle alternately toward body

REVEAL

Palm-down R's open outward

(See "open")

REVENGE

X-hands hit each other sharply and separate

266

REVERSE

R-hands, palm-to-palm, reverse position

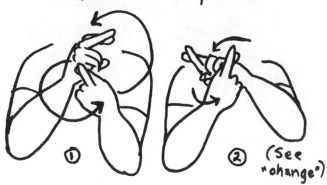

① ② (See "change")

REVISE
R-hands, palm-to-palm, reverse positions quickly twice

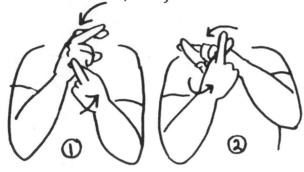

REVOLVE
R's move right, revolving around each other

REWARD
Vertical R's, left slightly behind right, arc forward, remaining vertical

(See "gift")

RHINOCEROS
C-hand up to S

RHUBARB
Right C slides from wrist to elbow of left R

(See "asparagus")

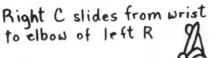

RHYME
R-fingertips touch thumb and middle and little fingertips (alternate rhyming-lines)

RHYTHM
Palm-down R swings side-to-side behind palm

(See "music")

267

RIBBON
Wiggle right i-hand out and slightly downward

(See "cord")

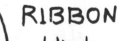

RICE

Ladle R-hand up to mouth twice

(See "soup")

RICH

Palm-up flat-O on palm turns over and opens above palm to daw (as if spilling coins)

① ②

RID

Side of R sweeps forward sharply off left palm

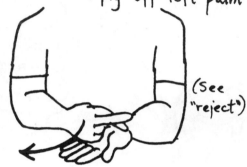

(See "reject")

RIDDLE

Draw question mark with R

(See "question")

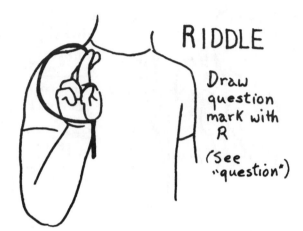

RIDE

First two fingers straddle left hand; arc both forward

RIDICULE

Jerk hands diagonally left twice, index and little fingers out

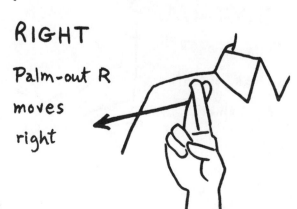

RIFLE

Hold rifle pointing left

RIGHT

Palm-out R moves right

RING
Index finger of R-hand from ring finger shakes outward

Rang = ring + _ed   Rung = ring + -en
                           (See "diamond")

RINSE
Inverted R's rise and fall simultaneously twice

(See "dye")

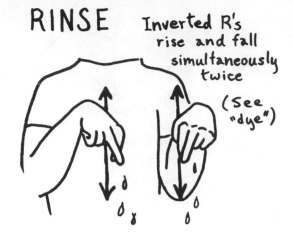

RIPE
R-hand on R-hand

RISE
Palm-up R rises

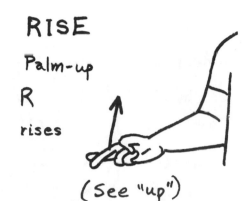

(See "up")

RIVER
Palm-down R's ripple forward to left up and down (See "brook")

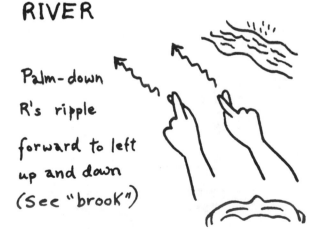

ROACH
R rides forward on wiggling fingers of left hand

(See "ant")

ROAD
Palm-down R's move forward, weaving slightly side-to-side

(See "way")

ROAR
R's face each other, right above left at chin, move outward separating, with wavy motions

269

ROAST
Slide R
under palm

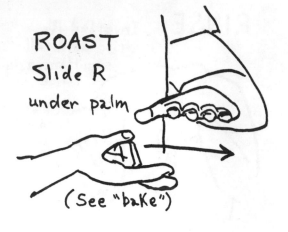

(See "bake")

ROB
R slides along under arm, from elbow to wrist

(See "steal")

ROBE
Palm-in
R-hands
arc
inward
on chest
(See "coat")

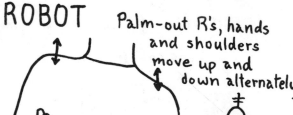

ROBIN
R-fingers open
and close on
thumb by mouth

(See "bird")

ROBOT
Palm-out R's, hands
and shoulders
move up and
down alternately

ROCK
Rap back of
R on back of
S twice
(see
"stone")

ROCKET
Side of R
on palm,
R moves
upward

270

RODENT
Brush
past tip
of nose
twice alternately
with both
R's
(See "mice")

ROLL

Roll R-hands over and forward to palm-over

ROOF

R's outline roof

ROOM

Palm-down R-hands box in a room (see "box")

ROOST

Roost 2 fingers on left R

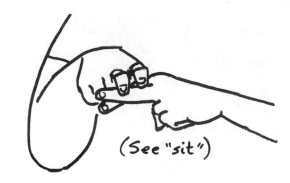

(See "sit")

ROOSTER

Thumb of 3 on forehead

ROOT

Flat-O "grows" down through C to a 5

ROPE

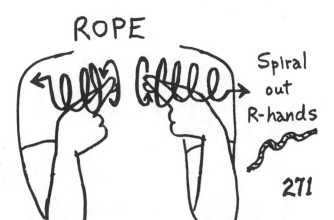

Spiral out R-hands

271

ROSE

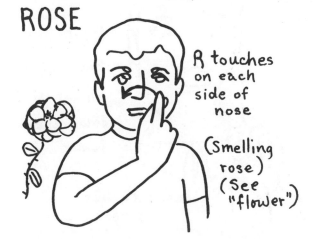

R touches on each side of nose

(Smelling rose) (See "flower")

ROT
Thumb of R flings off nose to the left

(See "louse")

ROTATE
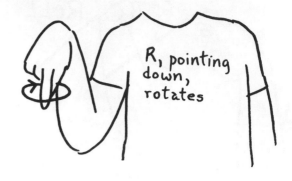

R, pointing down, rotates

ROUGH
Fingertips of right claw on left palm, move claw sharply forward and off

ROUND
Palm-out R circles once

Around = a + round

(See "circle")

ROW
Palm-out R slides along and off side of index

(See "bar")

RUB
Rub A on back of arm

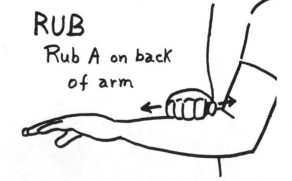

RUBBER
Side of X finger slides down cheek twice

Rubbers = rubber + -s

RUBELLA

Spot face with R-fingers in three positions

(See "measles")

272

RUDE
R on chin;
twists to
palm-out
and throw
down

(See "bad")

RUG
Drag R
across back
of hand

(See "carpet")

RUIN   Right X on left;
right X (only) moves sharply
forward and down

RULE   Side
of R on fingers,
then
heel
of
left
palm

(See "law")

RUMOR
R-fingertips touch
near chin, circle
horizontally,
shaking, to
touch
again

RUN   Palm-down L thumbtips
touch; hands
move forward,
index fingers
flicking in and
out rapidly
Ran = run + -ed

RUSH
Parallel R-hands shake
forward

(See "hurry")

273

RUSSIA
Horizontal
5-hands
tap waist
twice

RYE

R brushes up through G twice

(See "grain")

SABBATH

F-hands sets past horizontal left arm

SAD

Pull hands down in front of face

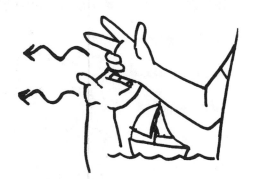

SAFE

Fingertips of 9 tap back of S

(See "save")

SAIL

Side of 3 on flat palm; both hands move forward in slight up and down motion

SAINT

Palm-down S circles above palm, then slides off end of palm

(See "holy")

SALAD

Toss salad with V's

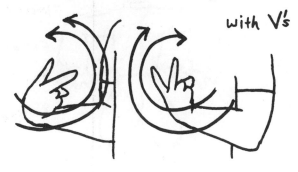

SALAMI

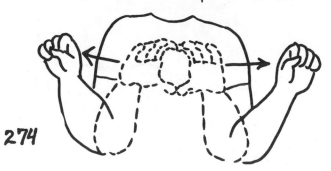

Palm-out C's separate to S's

274

SALE
Flat-O, palm-down above left palm, flips up at wrist several times

SALT
Tap fingers alternately on left Z

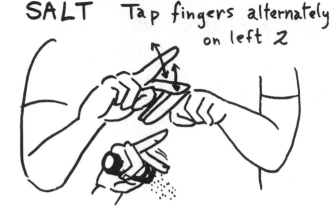

SALUTE
B at forehead, palm-out

(See "scout")

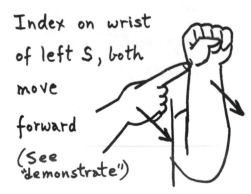

SAME
Palm-down index fingers tap sides together

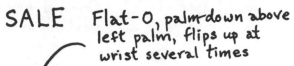

SAND
Rub thumbs back and forth across backs of fingers

SAMPLE
Index on wrist of left S, both move forward

(See "demonstrate")

SANDWICH
Insert filling-hand from side between thumb and fingers

SANDAL
Hook index finger in V, then draw it back across hand

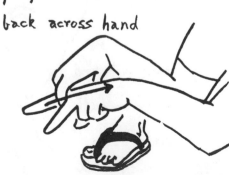

SANTA CLAUS

Palm-in C at chin curves down to touch chest

SATISFY

Open B-hands, resting on chest, both move downward

(See "content")

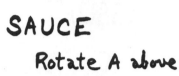

SATURDAY

Palm-out S-hand circles slightly

(See "Friday")

SAUCE

Rotate A above palm as if pouring

Saucer = sauce + -er

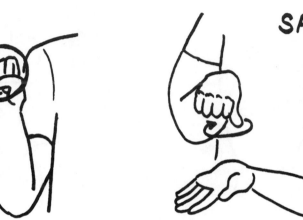

SAUSAGE

Open and close fingers of G to outline sausages

(See "baloney")

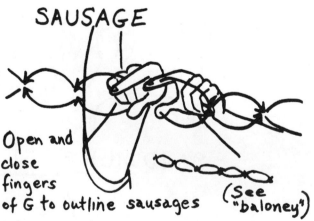

SAVE

Fingers of V tap back of S

SAW

Saw edge of right hand on back of left

SAY

Index circles up and outward near mouth

Said = say + -ed

276

SCARE S-hands, palm-in, move toward each other, opening to palm-in 5's (See "fright")

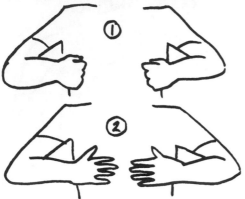

SCARF Draw scarf around neck and tie at side, finishing in flat O's

(See "bonnet")

SCATTER Flat-O tips together; open to palm-down 5's that separate, fluttering fingers

SCHEDULE Right 4 behind left; right drops

SCHIZOPHRENIC

Palm-in, bent hand outlines crack down midline

SCHOOL clap hands twice

SCIENCE A-hands alternately pour

SCISSOR Scissor forward

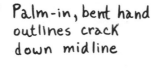

Scissors = scissor + -s

277

SCOLD

Shake index finger at someone

SCORE

Check off 2-fingertips with thumb and index

SCORPION

X rides forward on wiggling claw

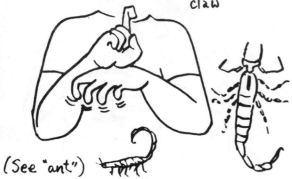

(See "ant")

SCOT

4 fingers

draw a cross on upper arm
Scotland = Scot + land
Scotch = Scot + h

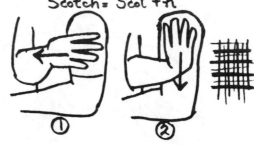

SCOUT

Salute with three fingers

(See "salute")

SCRATCH

Claw scratches palm

SCREAM

Palm-in claw shakes up and to side from chin, rapidly

SCREEN

Palms-in, right vertical 4 falls inside left horizontal 4

278

SCREW

Twist index finger in middle of palm

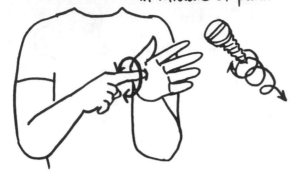

SCREWDRIVER

Twist H-fingers in palm of left hand

SCULPT

Sculpt with extended thumb of A on palm
sculpture=sculpt +ure

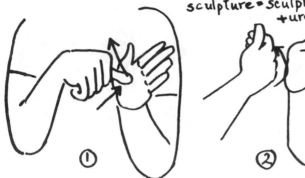

① ②

SEA

Palm-down S's sweep up and down forward, opening to 5's   (See "ocean")

SEAL

Right on left, close top hand on left, twice

SEARCH

Right C-hand makes several circles in front of the eyes

SEASON

Palm-out S moves downward in wavy motion

(See "weather") 279

SEAT

Sit 2 fingers on side of left S-hand

(See "sit")

SECOND
Palm-down 2 twists
to palm-up
(See "third")

SECRET
Tap lip
with A-thumb
twice

SECRETARY
H takes
pencil from
ear and
writes
across palm
(See "write")

SEE
V from eye
outward
saw = see + -ed
seen = see + -en

(See "look")

SEED
Thumb of flat-O
rubs fingers,
hand moving
right
(sowing seeds)

SEEM
Pivot at wrist
to palm in

(See "ought")

SELECT
Heel of S
rests on
left index
finger,
then pulls
back toward
chest;
left is
stationary

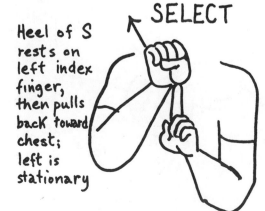

SELF
Thumb-up A moves
forward
selves = self
+s

Note: Use
for all -self's
except oneself, in
which A turns to
palm-right and touches
own chest

280

SELFISH

Palm-down V's pull back to bent V's

SELL

Palm-down flat-O's flip up at wrist twice   Sold = sell + -ed

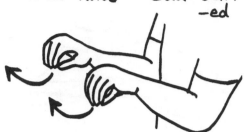

SEMESTER

Side of S circles once on left palm

(See "hour")

SENATE

S on left shoulder, then on right

(See "member")

SEND

Right fingertips on back of palm-down left flip forward to palm-down

sent = send + -ed

SENIOR

Bounce palm of right 5 on vertical thumb of left 5

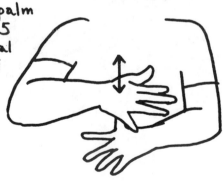

SENSE

Tap twice behind ear with bent middle finger

Sensible = sense + -able

Sensitive = sense + -ive

(See "conscious")

281

SENTENCE

Palm-to-palm 9-hands separate, shaking

SEPARATE

Backs of bent hands together;
separate hands

(See "isolate")

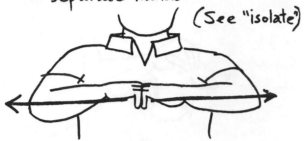

SEPTEMBER

Palm-down S
brushes down
elbow twice

(See "autumn")

SEQUENCE
Index of palm-down
L between left thumb and index, turn
to palm-up between index and middle
fingers

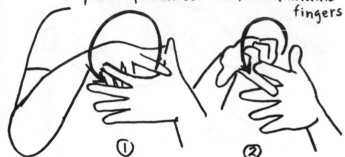

SERGEANT

3 draws
chevron on
shoulder

SERIES

Right index on
palm-in vertical
index,
right index
dots off to
right; left
is stationary

SERIOUS

S-hand moves
forward from
chin

(See
"certain")

SERVE

Palms-up, move
hands alternately
to and from body

Servant = serve
+ -ant

Service = serve
+ -ice

SET
Set A
on back
of hand

282

SETTLE

Palm-down S's circle and drop to palm-down 5's

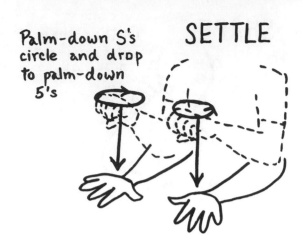

SEVERAL

A moves to open palm, one finger at a time

SEW

Sew left thumb and fingertip of 9 with right 9

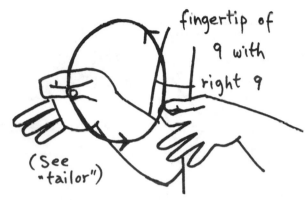

(See "tailor")

SEX

X at temple, then on jaw

(See "parent")

SHADE

Bring both S-hands down and cross at wrists

Shadow = shade + w

(See "dark")

SHAKE

Shake S

SHALL

Palm-down X nods several times

Should= shall + -en (past participle)

(See "need")

283

SHAME

Brush hand up cheek over and out

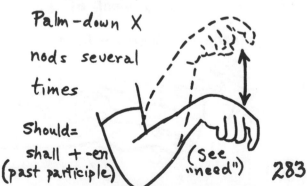

SHAMPOO
Washing motion with hands

SHAPE
Outline shape with palm-out A thumbs

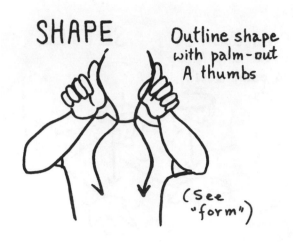

(See "form")

SHARE Side of right hand arcs from side to side hitting side of left thumb

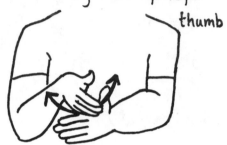

SHARK
Fingertips between third and fourth fingers — swim forward

SHARP
Shake upwards from touching fingertips

Sharpen = sharp + -en

(See "blade")

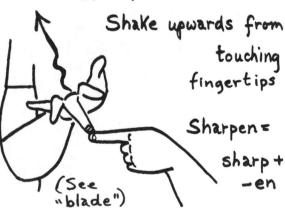

SHAVE
Draw Y along cheek twice
(See "razor")

SHE
Palm-out E slides along jawline and forward
(See "girl")

SHEEP   Clip wool off arm

Shepherd = sheep + herd

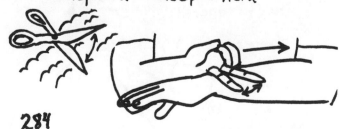

284

SHEET

Right arm bends in and up, over left hand near chest (drawing up sheet)

SHELF
Fingertips of bent hands touch at eye-level, then separate

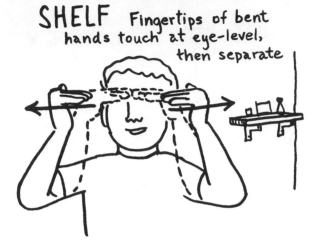

SHHH

Shush against index

SHINE

Raise hand off, shaking

SHIP, -SHIP (suffix)

Palm-out S on left palm, both move forward

SHIRT

Palm-out S-hands on chest, arc inward, downward

(See "coat")

SHOCK

Touch forehead, then drop hands into claws, palm-down

SHOE

Bump together S-hands twice
Shoes= shoe + -s

SHOOT Jerk back to X

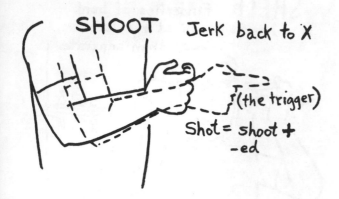

(the trigger)

Shot = shoot + -ed

SHOP Back of S on palm; S arcs away from body

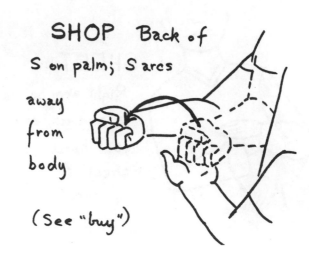

(See "buy")

SHORE

Fluttering fingers of palm-down 5 sweep, wave-like, onto and back from left palm-down hand (See "tide")

SHORT

Rub side of right H on side of left

Shorten = short + -en

SHOULDER

Pat opposite shoulder

SHOUT

C before chin jerks up and forward-right (See "scream")

SHOVEL

Back of right hand slides forward in palm of left, and flips up

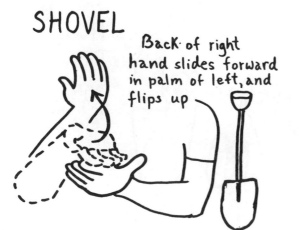

SHOW

Index on palm; both move forward

SHOWER
Jerk hand toward and away from head, fingers remaining curved

SHRIMP
Move to front and right, wiggling 2 little fingers

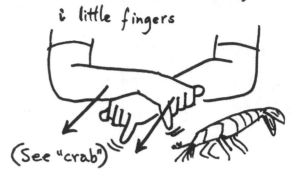

(See "crab")

SHUT

Right hand drops once on side of left B

SHY
Bent hand, palm-in, moves up cheek

SICK

Middle fingers touch forehead and stomach

(See "disease")

SIDE
Palm-in right hand brushes down past side of palm-down left hand

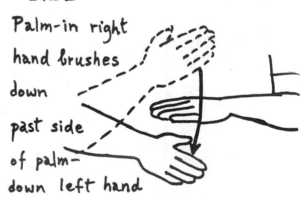

SIGH
Both hands in S, on chest, right above left, move out and in again

(See "breath")

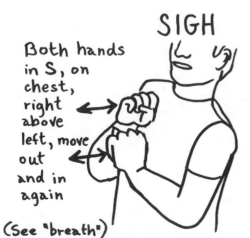

SIGHT
S-hands before eyes, left before right, separate sideways, opening to C's

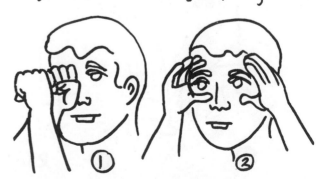

① ②

287

SIGN

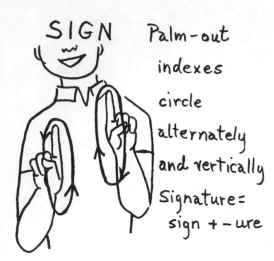

Palm-out indexes circle alternately and vertically

Signature = sign + -ure

SILENCE

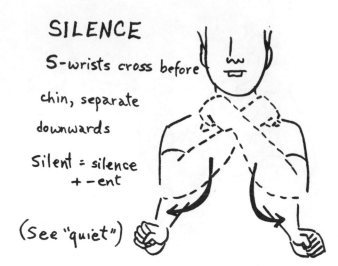

S-wrists cross before chin, separate downwards

Silent = silence + -ent

(See "quiet")

SILLY

Y-hand shakes in front of eyes

SILVER

S at ear shakes down right

(See "California")

SIMILAR

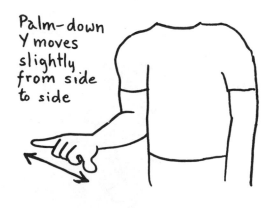

Palm-down Y moves slightly from side to side

SIMPLE

S brushes up back of bent-hand fingers twice

(See "ease")

SIMULTANEOUS

Touch wrist, then separate to palm-down Y's

① ② 288

SIN

Index fingers spiral down sideways

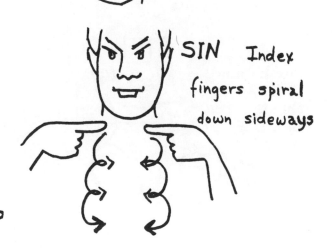

SINCE

Palm-in indexes on right shoulder, are up and out to point forward

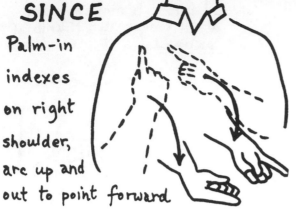

SING Palm-out H

from corner of mouth forward and out, slightly to the side

Sang= sing+-ed

Sung = sing+ -en

(See "opera")

SINGLE

Right index, palm-right, circles slightly (horizontal circle) in front of chest

SINK

Drop 3 off palm downward

Sank = sink+-ed
sunk = sink+-en

SIR S at temple goes forward right to palm-out R

(See "he")

SIREN

Flat-O repeatedly opens and closes as it revolves within left C

SISTER

A-hand drops to index fingers together

① ②

SIT

Sit 2 fingers on left U

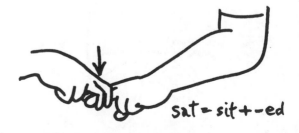

sat = sit+-ed

SITUATE
Palm-out S-hands touch, circle horizontally toward body, touch again

Situation=
situate
+ -tion
(See "place")

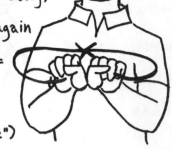

SIZE
S moves from little finger to thumb of palm-down Y

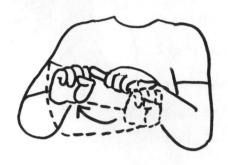

SKATE
Palm-up V's, bent, swing forward left, then forward right

SKELETON
Scratch away from center twice

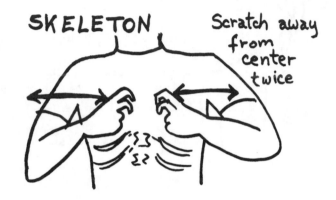

SKI

Palm-up X's arc forward

SKILL
Grasp side of left S; slide off forward into A

(see "expert")

SKIN
Pinch skin on back of hand

SKIRT
Thumbs of 5-hands brush down and out from waist

290

SKULL

Cross wrists below neck

(See "poison")

SKUNK

K moves back across middle of head

SKY

Palm-down at left arcs to palm-up at right

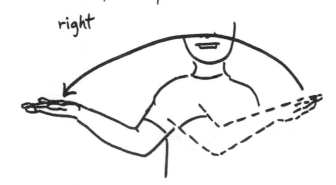

SKYSCRAPER

1-hands alternately move up and down, moving hands to right

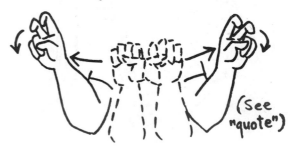

SLACK

Tap waist with S-hands

Slacks = slack + -s

(See "pant")

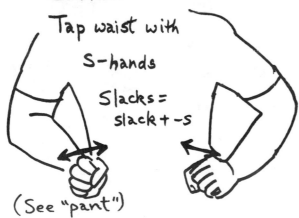

SLANG

S's together, palm-out, separate to bent-V's that twist slightly down (" ")

(See "quote")

SLED

Back of bent-V on left palm; both arc forward

(See "toboggan")

SLAVE

Wrist of right S on wrist of left S, both arc to side (wrists tied)

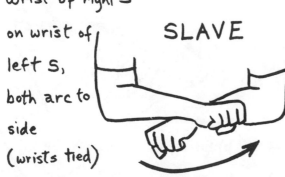

291

SLEEVE

C-hand moves from elbow to grip wrist

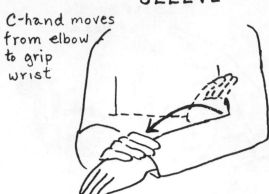

SLEEP

Before face, 5-hand drops to flat-0

Slept = sleep + -ed

SLEIGH

1-hands circle forward to open palm-up hands that pull back

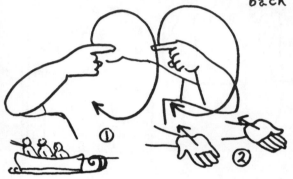

SLICE

Slice side of S with palm

SLIDE

Right palm-down slides down and over back of left hand

SLIM

Before body, palms facing each other hands curve in and down (See "diet")

SLIP

Arc out hand along palm

(See "lap")

SLIPPER

Slide right hand, palm-down, in and out of palm of C

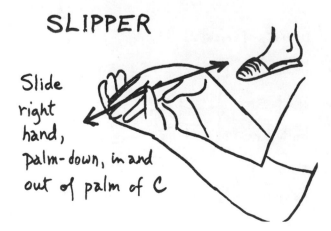

SLOP
Thumb under chin, 5-hand moves to right under chin, fingers fluttering

SLOPE
S-hand outlines slope up and to right

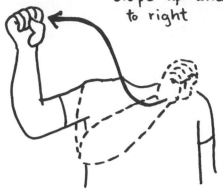

SLOW
Palms down, right hand moves slowly up back of horizontal left hand

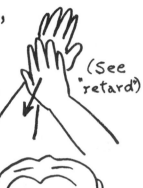

(See "retard")

SLUG
S moves along left arm, palm-up

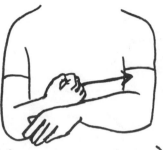

(See "caterpillar")

SMALL
Palms face each other, jerk slightly toward each other; repeat

SMART
Palm-in, bent middle finger on forehead; snaps off and twists to palm-out

SMELL
Palm-in hand near chin rises past nose with the "fumes"

SMILE
Lift corners of mouth with index-finger side of hands

293

SMOKE

V moves forward from corner of mouth

SMOOTH

Right palm-up flat-O behind left, both move toward left, closing to palm-up A's

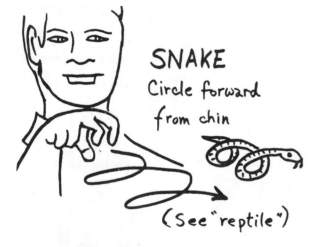

SNACK

Snap fingers of D to G at mouth.

SNAIL

Heel of bent V slides up forearm

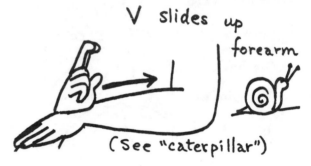

(See "caterpillar")

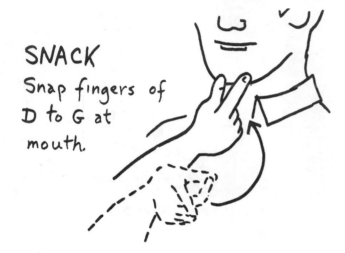

SNAKE

Circle forward from chin

(See "reptile")

SNEAK

X sneaks around S to peek at little finger of left hand

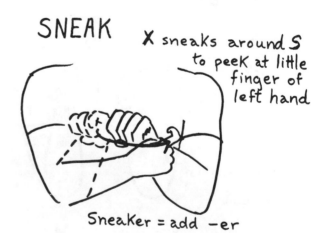

Sneaker = add —er

SNEEZE

Place index-finger under nose; jerk head back and forward slightly

SNIP

First two fingers snip corner of first knuckle off S, palms down (See "cut")

294

SNOB

Index finger on nose tilts head back, little finger out

SNOW

Drop hands slowly, palm down, fluttering fingers

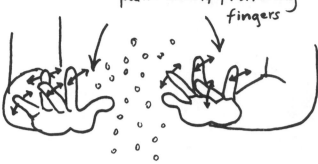

SO

Right S moves sharply down, striking side of left S in passing

Also = al- + so

SOAP

Flick fingers back, off left palm, twice

SOCIAL

Right S curves around vertical left index

Society = social + -ity

(See "culture")

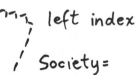

SOCK

Hit S forward along side of index finger

Socks = sock + -s

SODA

Flutter fingers up from S, palm-down

SOFA

First two fingers sit on middle finger of 9

(See "sit")

SOFT

Palm-up open hands drop slightly, closing to flat-O's; repeat

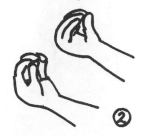

① ②

SOIL

Rotate thumb on balls of fingers

SOLAR

Right S behind left, palms out; right circles around left to palm-in (See "equator")

SOLDER

Index, thumb extended, circles near left S

SOLDIER

A's tap over heart twice (holding gun)

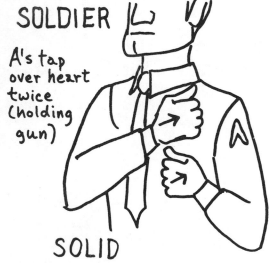

SOLE

Slide index finger back and forth under horizontal palm

SOLID

Right A knocks on left palm

296

SOME; SOME-, -SOME (affixes)

Side of right hand draws arc across left palm

SOMERSAULT

S somersaults twice off palm, twisting

(See "tumble")

SON

Right hand drops in an arc to palm-up on palm-up left arm

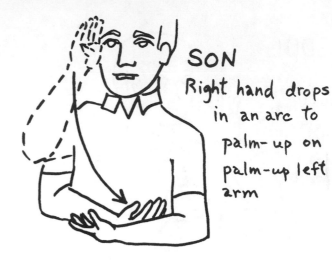

SONG

S arcs from side-to-side behind palm

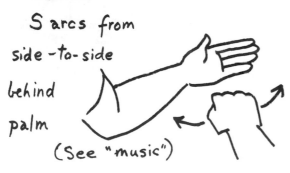

(See "music")

SOON

Side of palm-out S on palm, twist to palm-down

(See "minute")

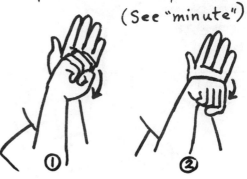

① ②

SOPHISTICATE

Thumb of 3 brushes off chin twice

Sophistication = sophisticate + -tion

SOPHOMORE

Touch middle finger of 5 with index

(See "freshman")

SORE

S twists on chin

297

SORRY

A circles on chest

Sorrow = sorry + w

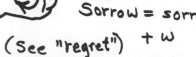

(See "regret")

SOUL

F rises, shaking, from flat-O near heart

SOUND

Palm-out 5 moves to ear, closing to flat O

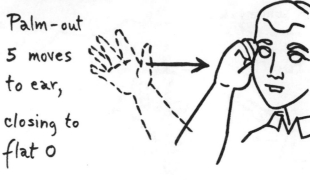

SOUP

Ladle H-hand from palm to mouth twice

(see Spoon)

SOUR

Index finger on chin, twist to palm-in

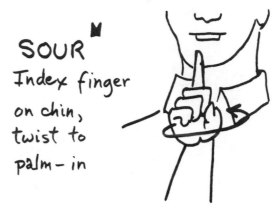

SOUTH

Palm-out S moves down

(See "down")

SPACE

S arcs in front of face

SPAGHETTI

Separate i's with shaking movement

SPAIN

Index fingers on shoulders drop to interlocking X's (fastening cape)

Spanish= Spain + -ish

298

SPEAK

Palm-left 4 at chin
moves forward,
fluttering
fingers;
repeat

Spoke = speak + -ed
Spoken = speak + -en

SPECIAL

9 pulls upward middle
finger of palm-in
5

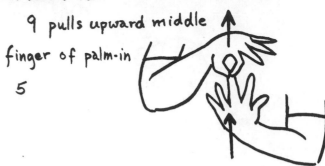

SPECIFIC   Tip of 1-hand

circles, then jerks toward
left vertical index

specify = add
-fy

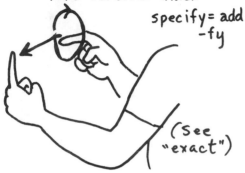

(See
"exact")

SPEECH

Bent-V circles
in front of mouth

(See "mouth")

SPEED   Left S ahead of

right index, jerk both toward
body, closing index to X

(See "fast")

SPELL   Palm-down

hand moves right, fingers
waving
alternately

SPEND   Back of flat-O on

palm slides off, closing to A

Spent =
spend +
-ed

SPIDER

Interlock little fingers and wiggle forward

299

SPILL
C-hand tips forward off left palm

(Spill glass)

SPINACH
Heels together, S-hands open

① ②

SPINSTER
Arc S-hand from left side of mouth to right side

(See "bachelor")

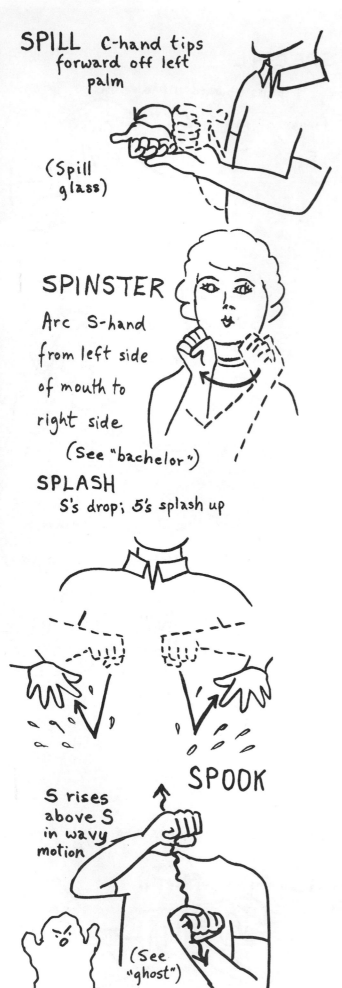

SPLASH
S's drop; 5's splash up

SPIRIT
Right F and left separate up and down in wavy motion

(See "ghost")

SPLIT
At right angles, side of right hand on side of left, separate sideways and down

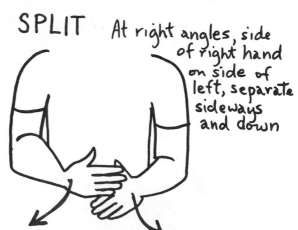

SPOOK
S rises above S in wavy motion

(See "ghost")

SPOOL
Circle fingertip around side of S-hand

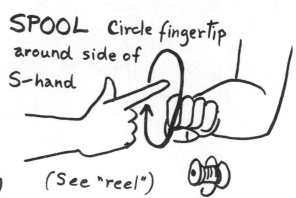

(See "reel")

300

SPOON

Spoon up from palm with H

SPORT

S-hands swing side-to-side (See "play")

SPREAD

Spread O to 5 on palm

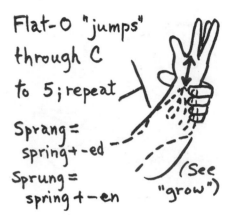

SPRING

Flat-O "jumps" through C to 5; repeat

Sprang = spring + -ed

Sprung = spring + -en

(See "grow")

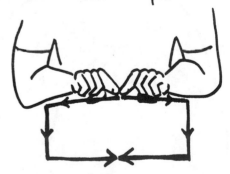

SPRINKLE

Palm-down 5 circles horizontally, fluttering fingers

SQUARE

Indexes draw a square

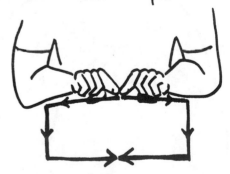

SQUASH

Twist upper palm on other palm (squashing)

301

SQUEEZE

Squeeze from claw to S

SQUID
S sits on 5; 5-hand does push-ups

(See "octopus")

SQUIRREL
Tap bent fingertips together twice, heels together

STAGE
Heel of S slides across arm

(See "board")

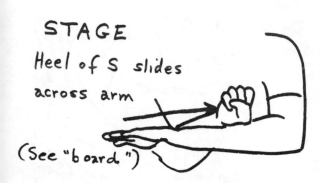

STAIR
Right palm describes stair-steps

STALE
X draws across thumb-side of S

(See "dull")

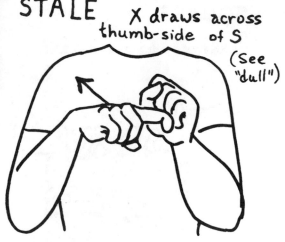

STAMP
Hit palm with side of fist of S

STAND
V-fingertips stand on palm

Stood =

stand+-ed

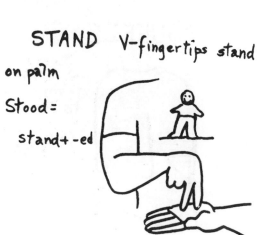

STANDARD
Palm-down Y's move in circle horizontally together

STAR
Side of right index finger strikes other hand upward, then left strikes right one upward

(See "constellation")

STARE
Both V-hands, palm down, near eyes, right behind left, move forward slightly

START
Index fingertip on wrist of left S; twist

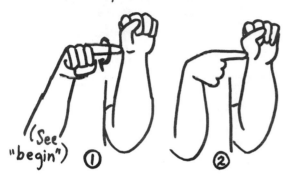

(See "begin") ① ②

STATE
S on left fingers arcs to heel

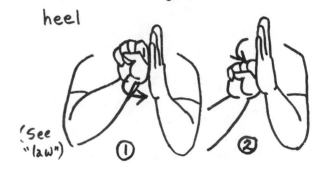

(See "law") ① ②

STATION
Palm-out 5's touch, outline roof and sides

(See "house")

STAY
Palm-down Y thumbs together; right arcs slightly down to right

(See "lodge")

① ②

STEAD, -stead- (affix)
Side of S hits heel of left hand

Steady = stead-+-y

Instead = in- + -stead

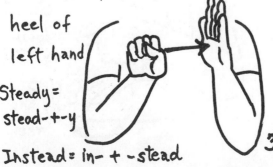

303

STEAK
Pinch thumb knuckle of S and shake both hands

(See "meat")

STEAL Bent-V

pulls to right from
left elbow

Stole = steal + -ed
Stolen = steal + -en

(See "rob")

STEAM Spiral W upwards from chin

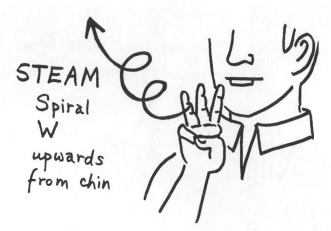

STEEL Palm-in S arcs right, hitting side of index

(See "metal")

STEP Palms down; one steps forward

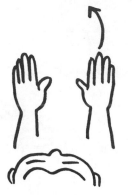

STEREO S's wiggle to ears from sides

STETHOSCOPE Grip at ears, drop to meet on chest, then right hand touches chest at left and right

STICK Palm-to-palm G's

close on each other

Sticky = stick + -y

Stuck = stick + -ed

STILL Swing down Y-hand and then up

304

STIMULUS Flick index of right S repeatedly toward left S

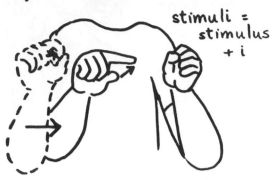

stimuli = stimulus + i

STING   Hit S sharply with index finger

Stung = sting + -ed

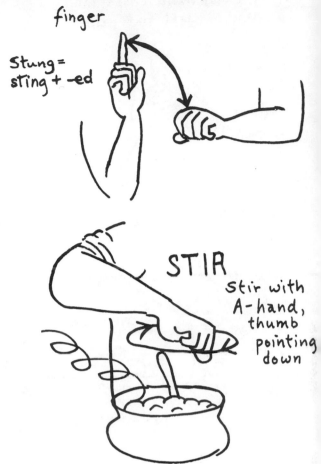

STINK

Pinch nose

STIR

stir with A-hand, thumb pointing down

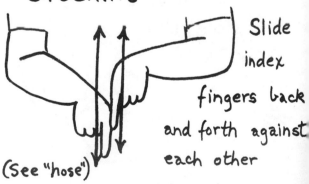

STITCH

Tap X-fingertip forward on palm

STOCKING

Slide index fingers back and forth against each other

(See "hose")

STONE

Back of S raps back of S twice

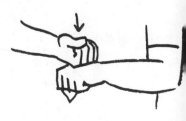

STOMACH

Pat stomach

305

STOP
Side of right flat hand chops into left flat palm

(See "halt")

STORE
Flat-O behind left C, nod rapidly toward and away from side of C

Storage = store + -age

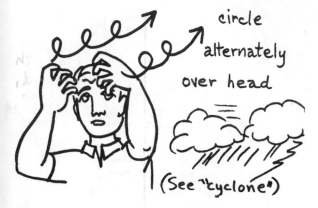

STORM
Claw hands circle alternately over head

(See "cyclone")

STORY
Open 9-hands approach, close, and separate several times

STOVE
Turn on 2 burners of the stove - along arm

STRAIGHT
Side of right B slides forward on side of left B

STRANGE
Right palm-left C arcs in front of nose to palm-down C

STRAW
S brushes up through G twice (See "grain")

306

STREAM

Palm-down S's ripple forward left up and down

(See "brook")

STREET Palms in, right slightly before left, hands sweep left

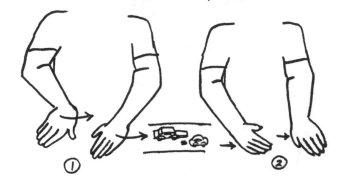

① ②

STRETCH   Pull apart S's

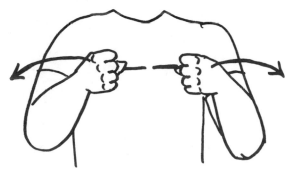

STRICT

Palm-left bent-V hits bridge of nose lightly

STRIKE

S-hand strikes side of left ndex

(See "beat")

STRING

I-finger-tip shakes out and down from left S

(See "cord")

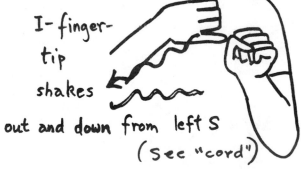

STRIP G's together, pull to sides and close

307

STRIPE

4-hand slides across chest to the right

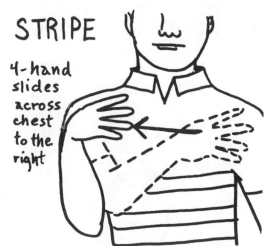

STRONG

Index finger draws muscle

Strength = strong + -th

STRUCTURE

S's build alternately upward on each other (see "build")

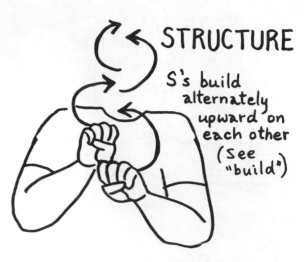

STRUGGLE

S's rock back and forth toward each other

(See "war")

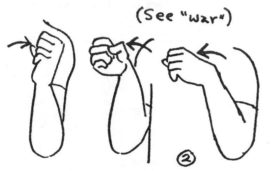

① ②

STUBBORN

Right fingers together, flap forward (donkey-like)

(See "horse")

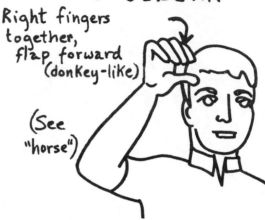

STUDY

Wiggle fingers above palm

Student = study + -ent

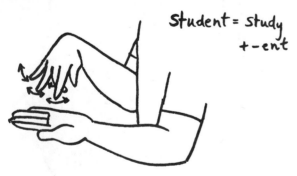

STUFF

Right palm-down S makes stuffing motion through left C

STUPID

Back of V hits forehead

SUBJECT

Side of right S on left fingers, then on left heel

(See "lesson")

SUBMARINE
3-hand glides under left palm

SUBSCRIBE
L-hand moves back toward body, closing to A; repeat

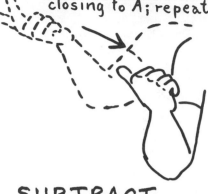

SUBTRACT
Fingertips of C scratch left palm downwards to S

SUBSTITUTE
9 hands right in front of left, arc vertically to change places

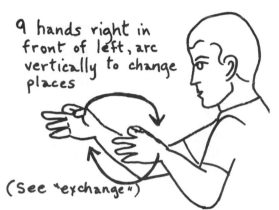

(See "exchange")

SUCCESS
Index fingers at temples twist out + up to sides, twisting twice

SUCCEED
Index fingers at temples twist out to sides and up

(See "success")

SUCH
Palm-down S-hands together, arc up and apart
(See "much")

SUCK
Draw flat hands inward sharply to rest on each other

SUCKER

Pull an invisible sucker in and out of mouth

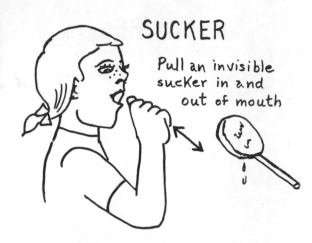

SUDDEN Thumbs flip out from under index fingers

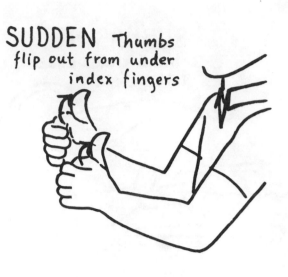

SUFFER

Thumb of A on chin, twist several times

SUGAR

Brush fingertips downward off chin twice

(See "cute")

SUGGEST

Palm-up hands arc up and forward

SUIT

Y-hands face each other, thumbs on chest, then arc down to little fingertips on body

SUMMARY

5-hands face each other, approach, close to right S on left S

Summarize = summary + -ize

SUMMER

Palm-down X is dragged across forehead (wiping sweat)

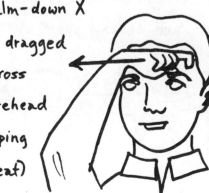

310

SUN
C at temple
and up to
side

SUNDAY
Palm-out
hands circle
outward

SUPER, SUPER- (Prefix)
S circles
over hand

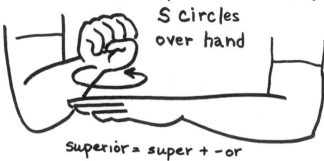

Superior = super + -or

SUPERVISE
Right S on
side of left V, both circle
horizontally

supervision=
supervise +
-tion

(See "care")

SUPPER
Circle
middle
finger of P
forward
near
mouth

(See "eat")

SUPPORT
Support side of left
S on top of
right S;
push up

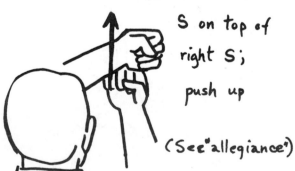

(See "allegiance")

SUPPOSE
I-hand
at temple moves out in
two arcs

SURE
Index finger at
chin arcs up
and forward
(See "certain")

SURPRISE

S-hands, facing each other near eyes, snap open to L-hands

SURRENDER

Palm-down A's open and swing up to 5's

SURROUND

Horizontal 5-hand circles vertical index and closes to flat-O

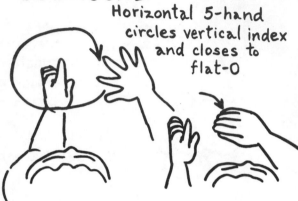

SURVIVE

S-hands, palm-down, slide up chest

(See "address")

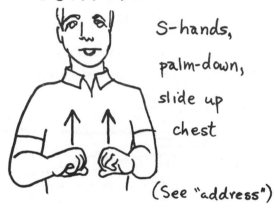

SUSPECT

Scratch temple twice

Suspicion = suspect + -tion
(See "paranoid")

SUSPEND

Right X hooks on horizontal left index and both move upward

Suspension = suspend + -ion

SWAN

Draw arm back to S-shape

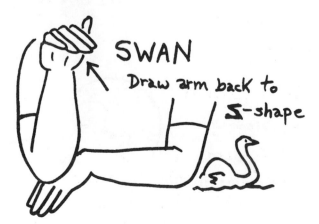

SWEAT

Palm-down 4 moves left over forehead, fluttering fingers

312

SWEATER

S-hands
pull sweater
down,

over

head

SWEDE   S circles

near forehead
Sweden = Swede + -n
Swedish =
Swede +
-ish

(See "Denmark")

SWEEP

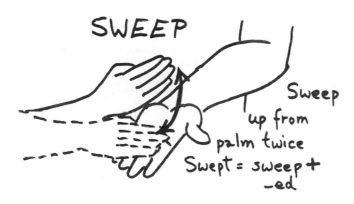

Sweep
up from
palm twice
Swept = sweep +
-ed

SWEET

Rub chin

circularly

(See
"honey")

SWEETHEART

Knuckles together, thumbs
wiggle toward each other

(Can be
"sweet"
+ "heart")

SWIM   Palms down, breast-
stroke
forward

Swam = swim + -ed

Swum = swim + -en

SWING

Bent-V sits on index

and swings forward

and back

Swung =
swing + -en

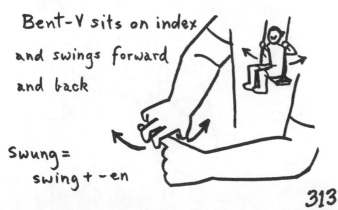

SYLLABLE   Thumb and
index finger close to each other
brush tip of
index several
times

313

SYMBOL

Right S on palm, both move forward together

(See "show")

SYRUP

I-little finger brushes side of mouth

SYSTEM

S-hands move forward-left, back, then forward-right

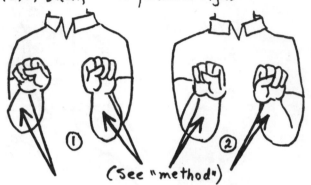

(See "method")

TABLE

Right palm and elbow bounce on left arm

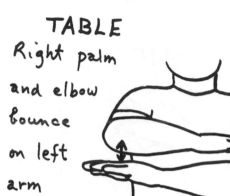

(See "desk")

TAIL

Rest wrist on left finger and wag hand

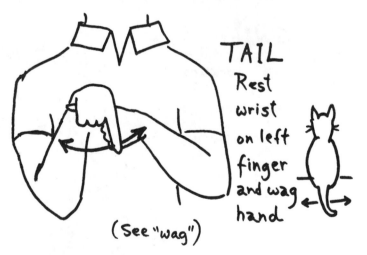

(See "wag")

TAILOR

Right 9-hand sews near left T

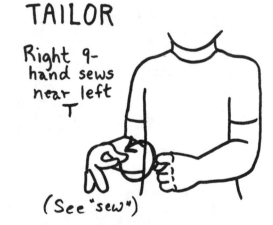

(See "sew")

TAKE

5-hand draws back toward body, closing to S

Took = take + -ed
Taken = take + -en

TALE

Right F shakes away from left T to the right

(See "fable")

TALK

Index fingers move alternately to and from lips

TALL   1 index finger slides up palm

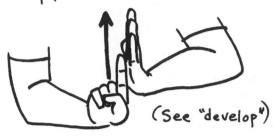

(See "develop")

TAME

Pet back of T-hand

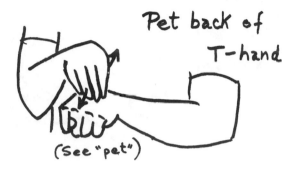

(See "pet")

TAN

Palm-left T moves down on cheek

(See "brown")

TANGERINE

T circles S

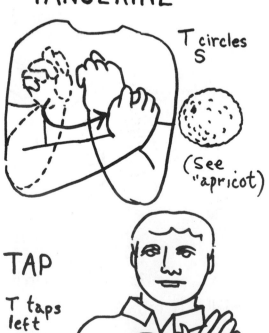

(See "apricot)

TANTRUM

Palm-in T's near stomach jerk up

TAP

T taps left palm

TAPE   U-fingers brush across backs of left fingers

315

TARDY

Right T pivots forward on left vertical palm

(See "minute")

TARGET

Right index behind left T; index jerks down to point at T

(See "aim")

① ②

TASTE

Touch lower lip with middle finger

TAX

Thumb of T strikes straight down across palm

(see "cost")

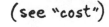

TAXI

C moves back from behind left X

(See "car")

TEA

Circle 9 above O as if swishing a tea bag

TEACH

Flat O's, pointing to temples, move forward slightly; repeat

Taught = teach + -ed

Teacher = teach + -er

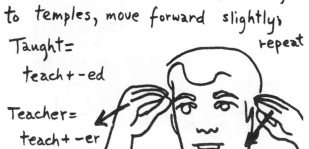

TEAM

Palm-out T's circle horizontally to palm-in

(See "class")

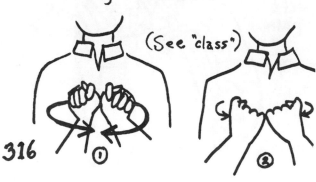

① ②

316

TEAR
(cry)

Drag 2 T's down cheeks

(See "cry")

TEAR (RIP)
Thumb-in X-hands in front of you, together, then pull right back and left forward as if tearing something

Tore = tear + -ed, Torn = tear + -en

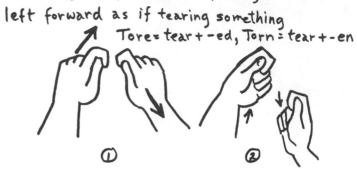

① ②

TEASE
Right X on left, right brushes forward on hand several times quickly

TEEN
T touches first at temple and then at cheek

teenager = teen + age + -er

(See "parent")

TEETH
X-hand crosses right to left in front of teeth

TELEGRAM
Palm-down X fingertip taps along index 3 times

Telegraph = telegram + -h

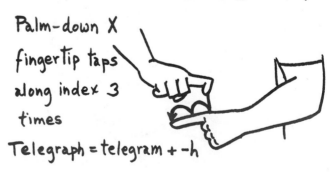

TELESCOPE
Right behind left at eye, twist O's to focus telescope

317

TELEVISION T+V

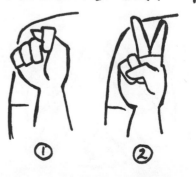

① ②

TELL

Palm-down index under chin flips out to palm-up

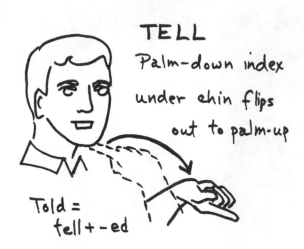

Told = tell + -ed

TEMPER   T slides up and down index

Temperature = temper + -ure

(See "thermometer")

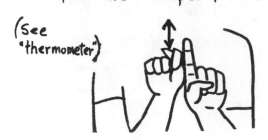

TEMPLE   Tap heel of T on back of S twice

(See "church")

TEMPORARY

Side of T slides back and forth a bit on side of H

(See "short")

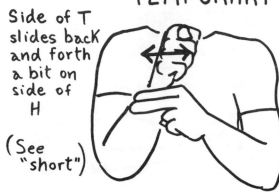

TEMPT

Tap elbow with X-index

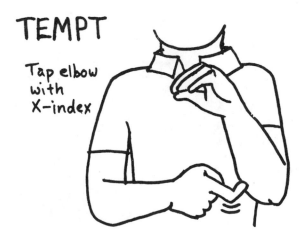

TENNIS

Swing racket with right A-hand

TENT   V-fingertips touch, separate sideways and down   (See "tepee")

TEPEE

T's together separate and fall in a tall inverted V

(See "tent")

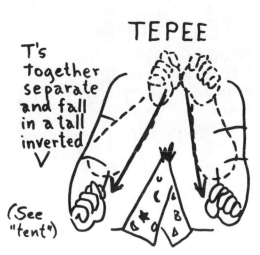

318

TERM

T on palm-right hand; circles and touches left palm again

(See "hour")

TERMITE

Right T rides forward on left claw

(See "ant")

TERRIFIC
Palm-out T's make small outward circles, then flat palm-out hands push forward slightly
(See "fabulous")

① ②

TERROR

Palm-out

T-hands shake down from left toward body

Terrible= terror + -ible
(See "afraid")

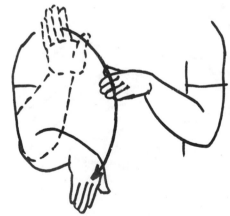

TEST

Indexes from 1 to X, moving downward

THAN

Slap down across left fingertips

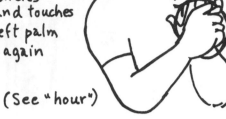

THANK

From chin down to palm-up

Thanksgiving= thank + S + give + -ing

THAT

L-and-i hand placed on left palm

319

THE

Palm-down Y drops slightly

THEATER

T's brush alternately down chest

(See "act")

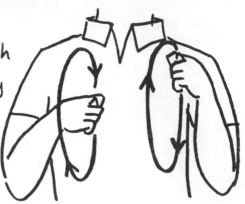

THEIR

Palm-up hand at left of body sweeps right to palm-out R

Theirs = their + -s

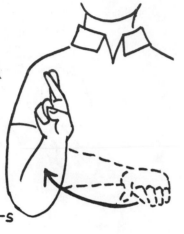

THEM

Palm-up hand at left of body sweeps right to palm-out M

THEME

T circles beneath left hand

(See "base")

THEN

1-hand from off thumb to off finger

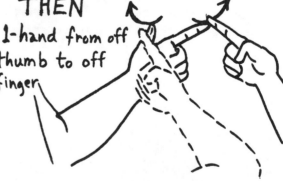

THEORY

T circles from forehead upward to right

(See "fantasy")

THERAPY

Left palm lifts right T

Therapist = therapy + -ist

320 (See "help")

THERE
Palm-up hand arcs forward

THERMOMETER
Slide right index finger rapidly up and down side of left index finger

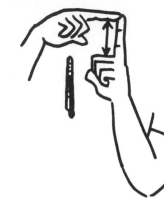

THESE
Palm-down Y on palm of left hand; twist or move Y across left fingers

THEY
Palm-up hand at left of body, sweep right to palm-out Y

THICK
Thumb moves right on back of hand

Thicken =
thick + -en

THIEF
Fingers of H slide from corner of nose

thieves= add -s

theft= add -t

THIGH
Pat thigh with T-hand

THIN
G-fingertips move down near face and body

321

THING, -THING ✗

Palm-up, arc right hand slightly up and down to right

THINK ✗

Finger above brow on head

THIRD Palm-down 3 twists to palm-up

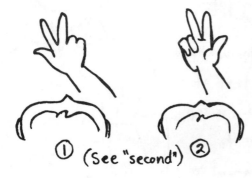

① (See "second") ②

THIRST

Stroke finger down throat

Thirsty = thirst + -y

(See "throat")

THIS

Palm-down Y drops on palm of left hand

THOROUGH Right hand slides through fingers of left; returns in opposite direction

① ②

THOSE

Palm-down L-and-i on palm of left hand; twist or move across left fingers

THOUGH

Slap hands against each other alternately

Although = al- + though

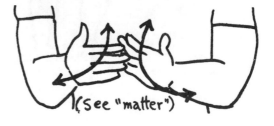

(See "matter")

322

THOUGHT
(noun)

T circles near temple

(See "reason")

THOUSAND

Fingertips of bent hand **strike** palm

THREAD

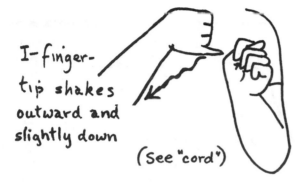

I-finger-tip shakes outward and slightly down

(See "cord")

THREAT

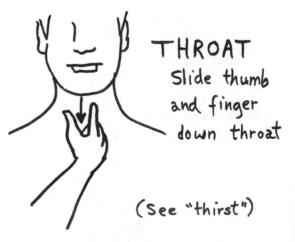

T arcs up, hitting back of left S; repeat

(See "danger")

THRILL

Middle fingers on chest flick to sides

THROAT

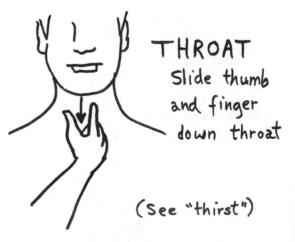

Slide thumb and finger down throat

(See "thirst")

THROW   Flat-O throws forward into 5-hand

Threw = throw + -ed

Thown = throw + -en

(See "pitch")

THROUGH

Hand slides between fingers

323

THUMB
Rub thumb with fingertip

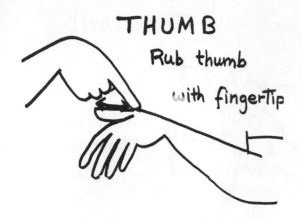

THUNDER
Index finger from ear to 2 S's jerking forward alternately

THURSDAY
T-hand to H-hand

(See "Friday")

TICKET
Bent-V fingers slide onto side of palm-up left hand

(Punch ticket)

TICKLE
Tickle near side with bent index finger

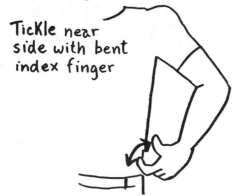

TIDE
Palm-down right T slides out and up onto back of left hand; back off

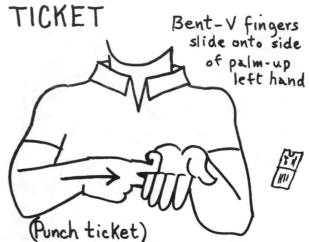

(See "shore")

TIE
Circle U-fingers around each other, then separate

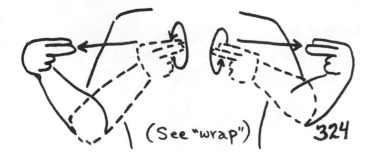

(See "wrap")   324

TIGER
Claw to side twice, drawing stripes
(See "cat")

TIGHT Claw on S, twist slightly right, as if to tighten cap

TILL
Right palm-in L arcs over to touch tip of palm-in left L

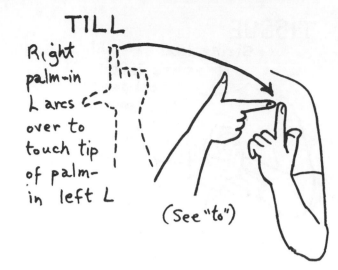

(See "to")

TIMBER

Shake T, with elbow resting on left hand

(See "tree")

TIME Tap wrist

TIN

T arcs right, hitting side of index

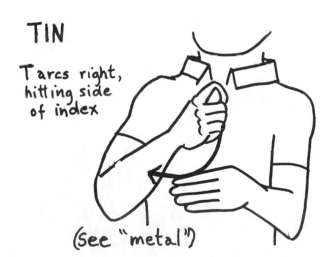

(See "metal")

TINY Palm-down right index bounces just above palm-up left index

TIP

Index taps tip of T-thumb

(See "cap")

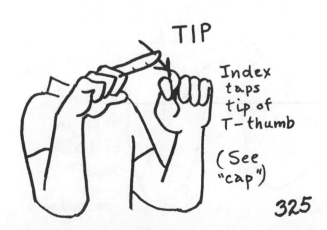

325

TIRE
Fingertips of bent hands touch waist and drop downward to palm-up

Tired = tire + -ed

(See "weary")

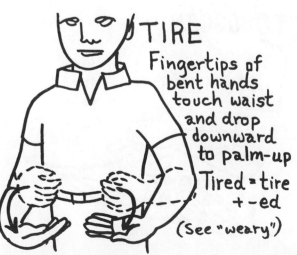

TISSUE
Strike heel of right T across left heel several times

(See "paper")

TITLE
Palm-out T's twist to face each other

(See "quote")

① ②

TO
Horizontal index finger approaches and touches vertical index finger

TOAD
Flick out V when jumping; land with S; flick V again

TOAST
Stab V on palm and then on back of hand

① ②

TOBACCO
Straight-M fingertips twist on cheek

TOBOGGAN
T rides forward on palm (See "sled")

TOE
Pass T-hand around margin of flat hand

(See "edge")

326

TOGETHER

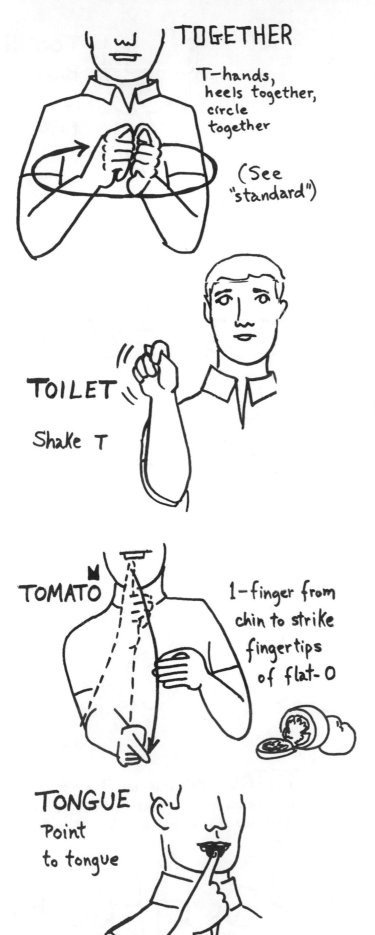

T-hands,
heels together,
circle
together

(See
"standard")

TOIL

T bounces
back and
forth on
S

(See
"work")

TOILET

Shake T

TOLERATE

Draw T downward
over mouth and
chin

tolerant =
tolerate + -ant

(See "lonesome")

TOMATO

1-finger from
chin to strike
fingertips
of flat-O

TON

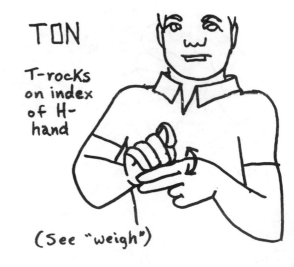

T-rocks
on index
of H-
hand

(See "weigh")

TONGUE
Point
to tongue

TOO

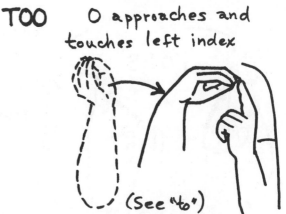

O approaches and
touches left index

(See "to")

327

TOOL

Arc palm-up T twice right

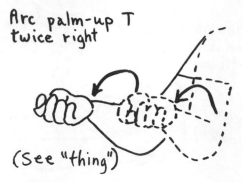

(See "thing")

TOP

Pat top of left T

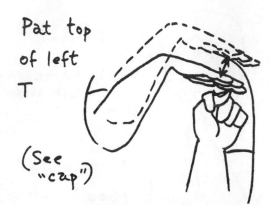

(See "cap")

TORNADO

T's rotate around each other, rising to right

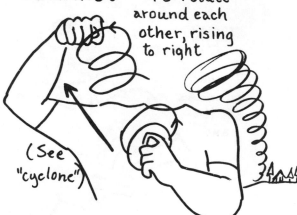

(See "cyclone")

TOOTH

Point to a tooth

TORCH

O opens to 5, and with fingers fluttering, rises above left T-hand

(See "flare")

TORTOISE

Hands point forward, right on left; move forward, wiggling thumbs

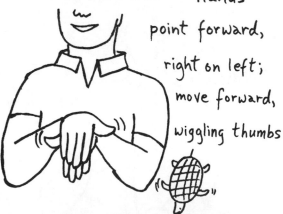

TOSS

Snap T-thumbs out to sides

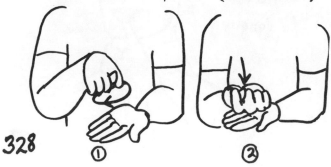

TOTAL   Palm-down T over left palm, circles and inverts to palm-up T on palm   (See "whole")

① ②

TOUCH
Touch hand with right middle finger

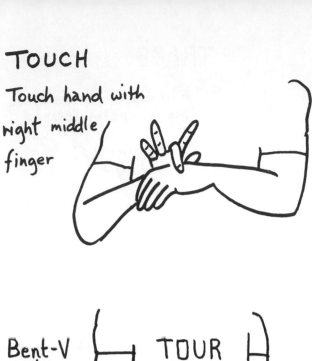

TOUGH
Bent-V hits side of left S in arc down to the right

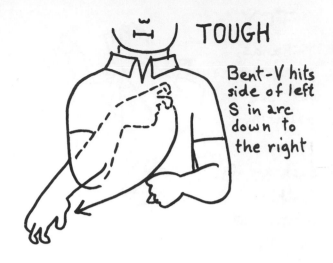

TOUR
Bent-V circles jerkily counter-clockwise

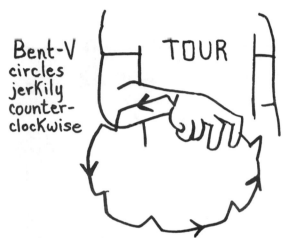

TOURNAMENT
Bent V's face each other move up and down alternately

TOW
Right X pulls left X to the right

TOWEL
Wipe near cheeks twice

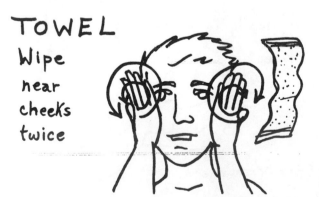

TOWER
Palm-out T's swing in and then up

(See "chimney")

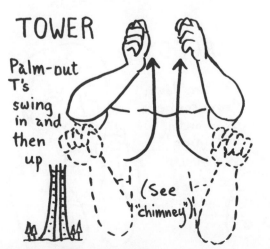

329

TOWN
Fingertips touch at left, separate, touch at right

TOY

T-hands, one palm-out, one palm-in, swing back and forth, pivoting at wrists

① ②

(See "play")

TRACE

Palm-down T draws wavy line on palm toward you

TRACK
Palm-down V at side of palm-out T; V moves forward

TRACTOR

Steer large wheel with T's

(See "drive")

TRADE
T-hands, right in front of left vertically to change places

(See "exchange")

TRADITION

Right T on left near right shoulder, move forward and down

TRAFFIC

5-palms brush each other, moving rapidly forward and back

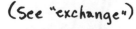
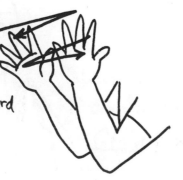

TRAGEDY

T's arc down from corners of mouth, outlining sad mouth

(See "grim")

330

TRAIL

Palm-down T weaves
side-to-side
towards body

Trailer = trail + -er

TRAIN Palms down, rub right H on back of left H

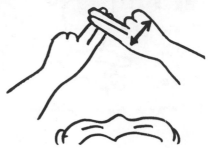

TRANSFER

Palm-down V
lifts to bent-V
and shoots to
right to V
again

TRANSFORM T-hands face each other, right above left; reverse

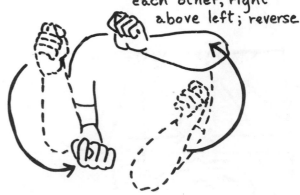

TRANSLATE Palms of T-hands touch, twist to reverse position

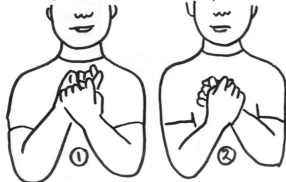

TRANSPARENT

V from eye, points
between first and
second fingers
of left.

TRANSPORT

Palm-up T's at
left arc
toward
body
right
(see
"bring")

TRAP

Bent-V
fingers
drop
to
trap
index

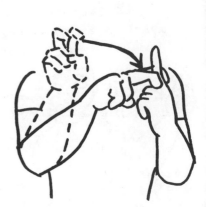

331

TRASH

Back of T on left palm, slide forward and off to 5

(See "waste")

TRAVEL

Index fingers circle each other, alternately, moving out and around

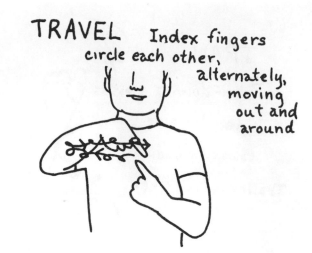

TRAY

T's draw square tray

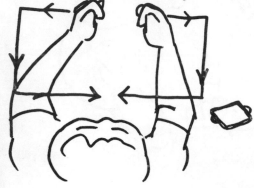

TREAT

Palm-up T's push forward twice

(See "urge")

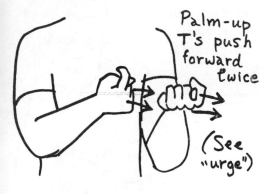

TREASURE

Palm-up T on palm rises to palm-down T over palm

(See "rich")

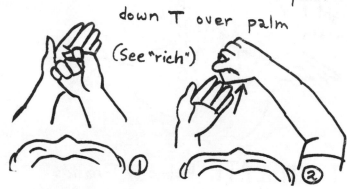

TREE

Elbow on back of hand; shake 5

TREMENDOUS

X's face each other pull apart in an exaggerated gesture

(See "big")

TRIANGLE

Indexes draw a triangle

332

TRIBE
Palm-out T's circle out to palm-in B's, touching

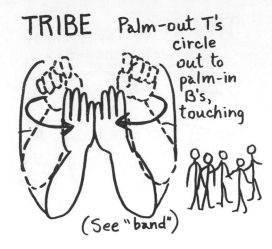

(See "band")

TRICK
Right index on nose, quickly twists sideways under left hand, both palms inward

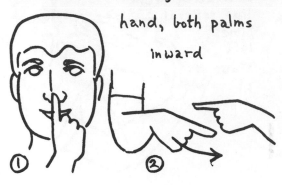

① ②

TRIKE
Circle T-hands up and out alternately

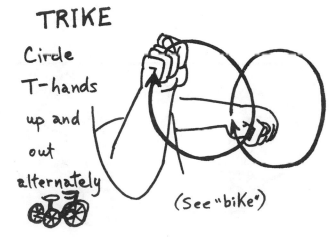

(See "bike")

TRILLION
Palm-down T arcs forward from heel to hit fingertips

(See "billion")

TRIM
V-fingers scissor across tip of T

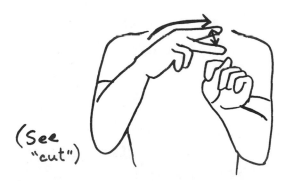

(See "cut")

TRIP
Middle fingertip trips over index

TRIPLE
Middle finger of 3 brushes up left palm

(See "once")

333

TRIUMPH
T spirals up off left S

(See "win")

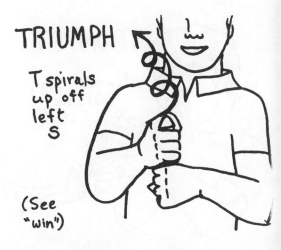

TROMBONE

Right A moves out and back from lips several times; left A stays at lips

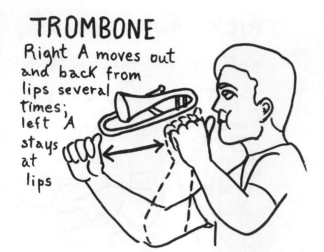

TROPHY

Tap palm of claw on index

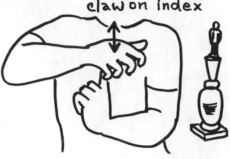

TROUBLE

Flat hands circle alternately before face

(See "worry")

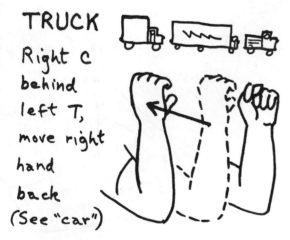

TROUSER

Tap waist with T-hands

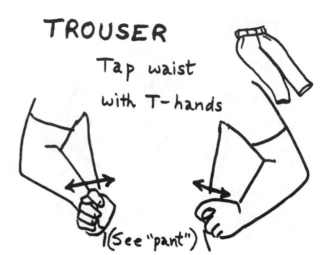

(See "pant")

TRUCK

Right C behind left T, move right hand back

(See "car")

TRUE

Side of T on left palm, slide forward across palm and fingers

Truth = true + -th

(See "honest")

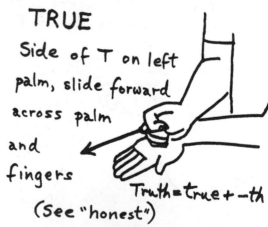

TRUMPET

Fingers play outside T at lips

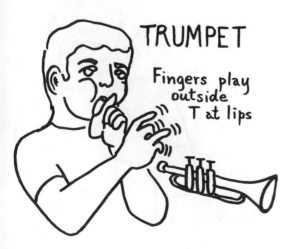

TRUNK

Draw down, on chest, T-hands

334

TRUST

5-hands pull out and close to S's near shoulder

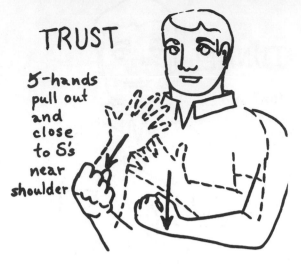

TRY

T-hands, palms facing each other, move forward with slight arc

Tried = try + -ed

(See "attempt")

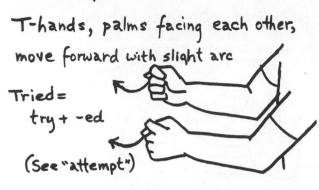

TUB

Swing T's upward to outline tub-bottom

(See "jar")

TUBA

Right T against left T at lips, right moves out and rises to 5

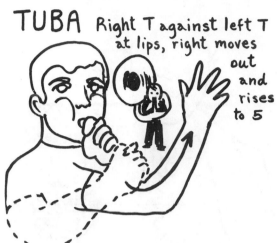

TUESDAY

Palm-out T circles slightly

(See "Friday")

TUG

Pull T's diagonally inward

(See "pull")

TUMBLE

Roll V twice off palm forward

(See "somersault")

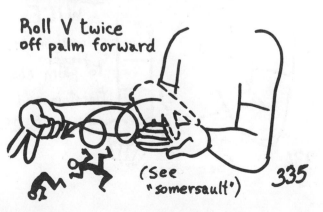

335

TUNA

T swims forward
(See "fish")

TUNE
Right T arcs from side to side behind left palm

(See "music")

TUNNEL
Right index spirals through left palm-down C

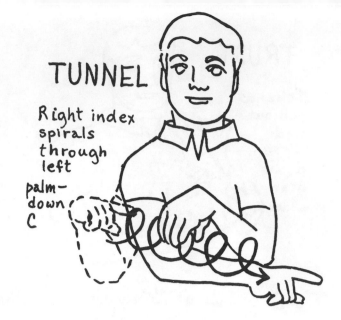

TURKEY
G shakes down and out a little

TURN
Right palm curves around left index

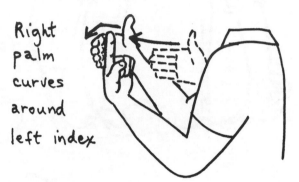

TURNIP
Slice side of T with finger twice

(See "tomato")

TURTLE
Wiggle right thumb for turtle's head, move hands forward

TUTOR
T's at temples move slightly forward twice

(See "teach")

TWICE
Touch middle finger to palm and twist in and up to 2

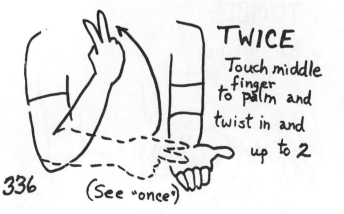

336

(See "once")

TWIN

Index of V touches left, then right corner of mouth

(See "bachelor")

TWIST

Palm-down right V above palm-up left V; reverse positions

① ②

TYPE

Type with palms down

Typist = type + -ist

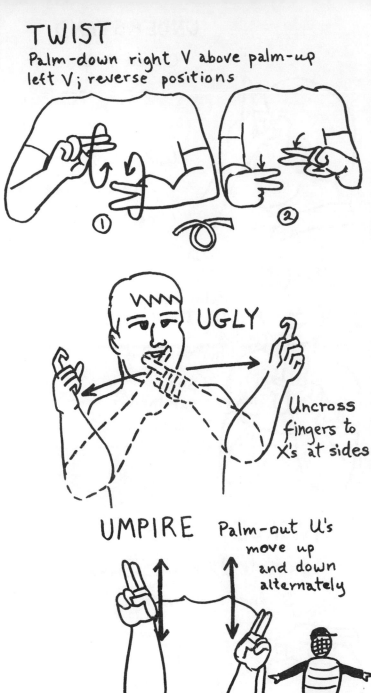

UGLY

Uncross fingers to X's at sides

UMBRELLA

Right S moves up once from left S

UMPIRE

Palm-out U's move up and down alternately

(See "balance")

UNCLE

Shake U near temple

(See "aunt")

UNDER

Right A slides under left palm

UNDERSTAND

Closed-X at temple snaps open to 1

Understood= understand+-ed
(See "realize")

UNIFORM

Palm-out U's move down body

(See "coat")

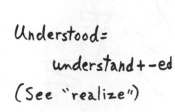

UNION

Palm-out U's together; circle horizontally

(See "standard")

UNITE

Right 9 grasps left U; both circle horizontally

(See "standard")

UNIVERSE

H on S, circle H forward around S and rest on top

(See "world")

UNIVERSITY

Horizontal, palm on palm, right circles up, changing to U

(See "college")

UNLESS

Right U, palm-down under left palm, drops slightly

(See "less")

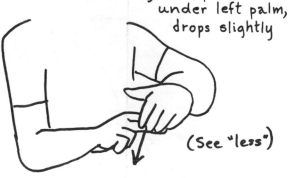

UNTIL

Palm-in right U arcs over to touch tip of palm-in left L

(See "to")

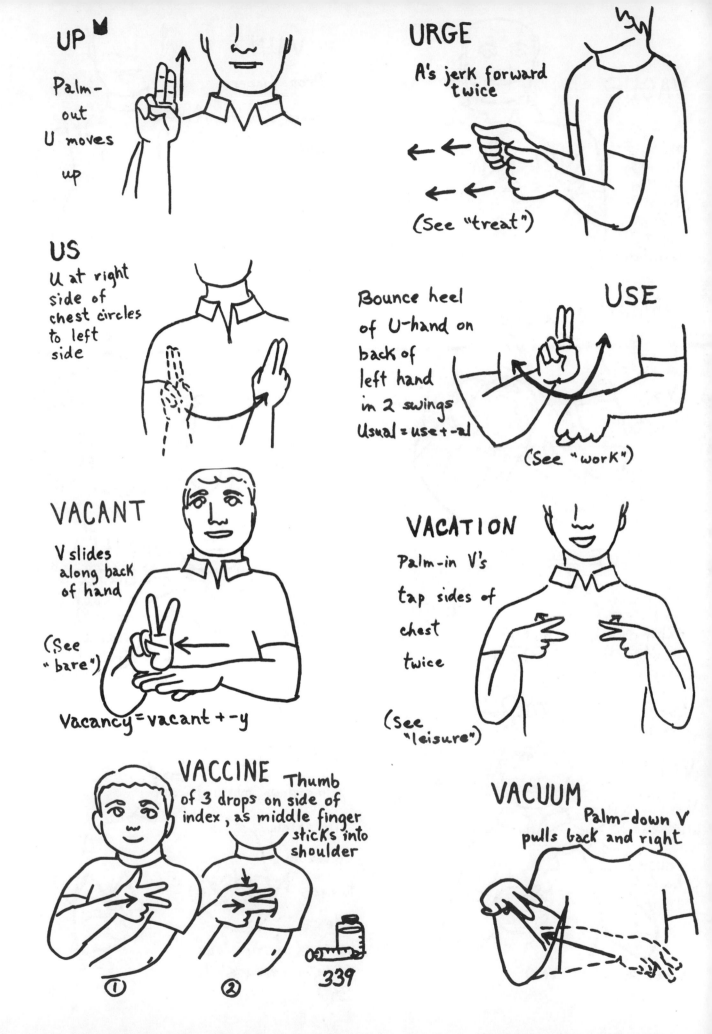

UP

Palm-out
U moves
up

URGE

A's jerk forward twice

← ←
← ←

(See "treat")

US

U at right side of chest circles to left side

USE

Bounce heel of U-hand on back of left hand in 2 swings
Usual = use + -al

(See "work")

VACANT

V slides along back of hand

(See "bare")

Vacancy = vacant + -y

VACATION

Palm-in V's tap sides of chest twice

(See "leisure")

VACCINE

Thumb of 3 drops on side of index, as middle finger sticks into shoulder

① ② 339

VACUUM

Palm-down V pulls back and right

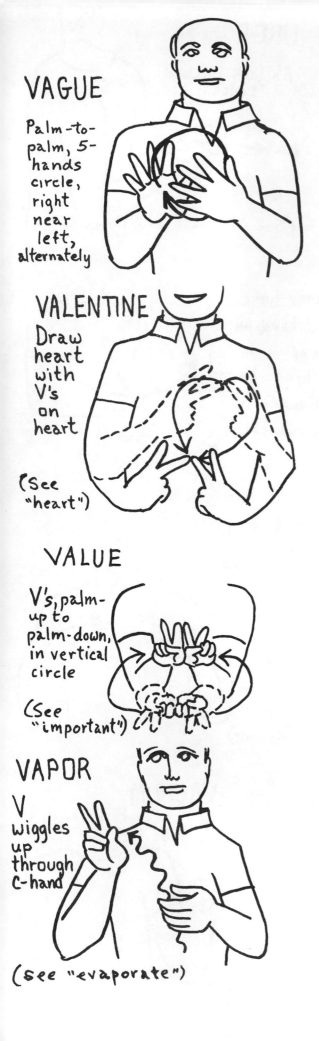

VAGUE

Palm-to-palm, 5-hands circle, right near left, alternately

VALENTINE

Draw heart with V's on heart

(See "heart")

VALUE

V's, palm-up to palm-down, in vertical circle

(See "important")

VAPOR

V wiggles up through C-hand

(see "evaporate")

VAIN

Drop fingers toward shoulders, hands remain stationary; repeat

VALLEY

Beginning at sides, palms-down, draw valley

(See "canyon")

VANILLA

V circles on back of left hand (See "chocolate")

VARY

1's, palms-down, move alternately up and down to each side

Various = vary + -ous
Variety = vary + -ity

340

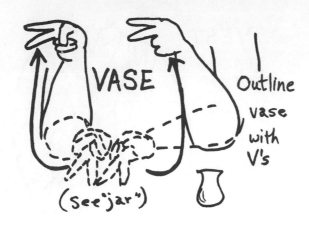

VASE

Outline vase with V's

(See "jar")

(See "jar")

VASELINE

Rub V on palm

(See "medicine")

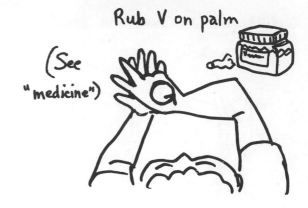

VEAL

Pinch tip of index finger of V and shake

(See "meat")

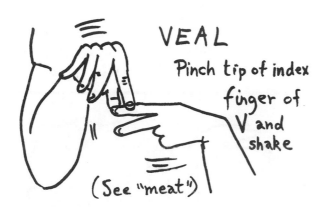

VEGETABLE

Index fingertip of V on cheek; twist

(See "apple")

VEHICLE   Palm-left C moves back from palm-right V

(See "car")

VEIN   Draw fingertips of palm-down V up back of wrist

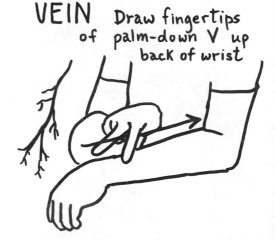

VERB

Side of palm-in V slides across chin below mouth

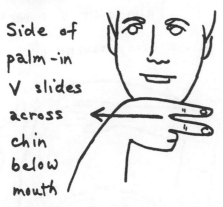

VERTICAL

Pull palm-in V downward

(See "down")

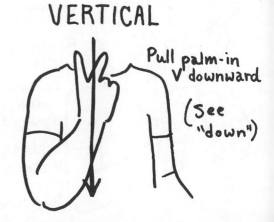

341

VERY
Middle finger-tips of V's touch and then arc apart

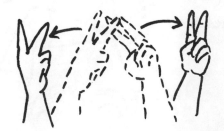

VEST
Palm-in V-hands arcs inward on chest (See "coat")

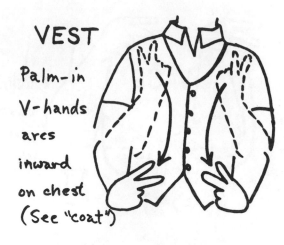

VETERINARIAN
Tap heel of V on left pulse

veterinary = veterinarian + -y
(See "doctor")

VIBRATE
Palm-down 5-hands jerk forward and back alternately quickly

VICE, VICE- (Prefix)
Tap temple twice with V

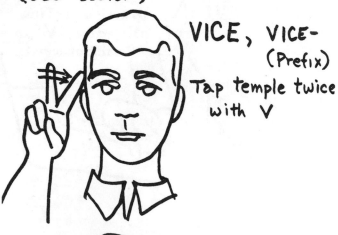

VICTIM
Knuckles of A hit side of palm-out V

(See "bump")

VICTOR
Right V on left S spirals quickly upward
Victory = victor + -y
(See "win")

VIEW
Palm-down V sweeps left above arm, "scanning"

Review = re- + view

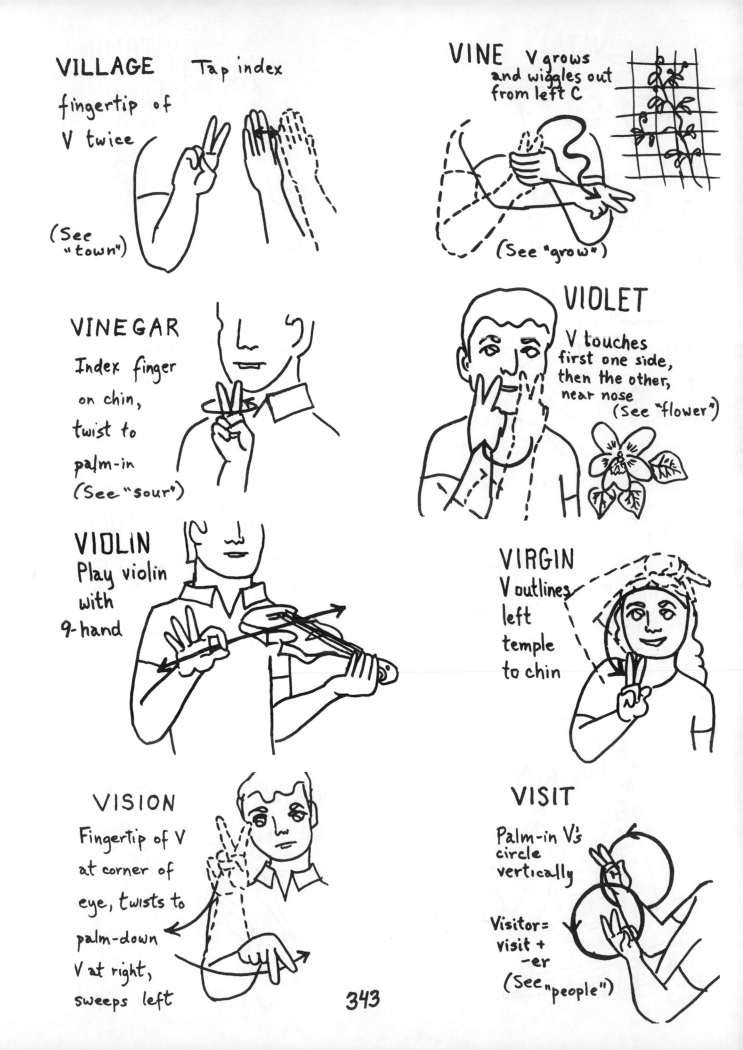

VILLAGE

fingertip of V twice — Tap index

(See "town")

VINE

V grows and wiggles out from left C

(See "grow")

VINEGAR

Index finger on chin, twist to palm-in (See "sour")

VIOLET

V touches first one side, then the other, near nose

(See "flower")

VIOLIN

Play violin with 9-hand

VIRGIN

V outlines left temple to chin

VISION

Fingertip of V at corner of eye, twists to palm-down V at right, sweeps left

VISIT

Palm-in V's circle vertically

Visitor= visit + -er

(See "people")

343

VITAL

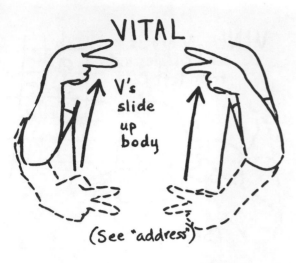

V's slide up body

(See "address")

VITAMIN

Throw side of V toward mouth

(See "pill")

VOCABULARY

Tap fingertips of V on side of index twice

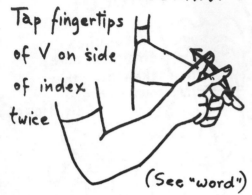

(See "word")

VOCATION

Palm-out V arcs side-to-side, hitting back of left S
(See "work")

VOICE

Fingertips of palm-in V move up throat and out under chin

VOLCANO

From flat O to 5 repeatedly, arm rises out of C

VOLLEYBALL

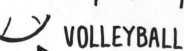

Push up ball several times

VOLUNTEER

Right F-hand pulls material forward

344

VOMIT
5-hand arcs from throat diagonally to left

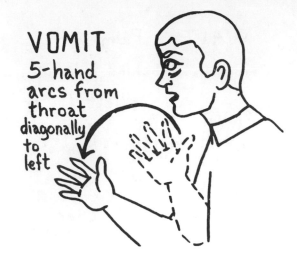

VOTE
Thumb and finger of 9 into O twice

VOW
Index on chin to heel of V on back of S

①   (See "promise") ②

VOWEL
Palm-out V brushes across fingers of palm-in 5

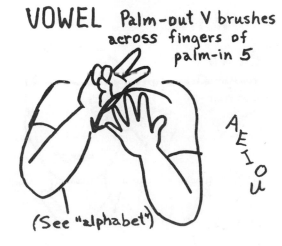

AEIOU

(See "alphabet")

WADDLE
Inverted right Y rocks (waddles) forward on left horizontal palm

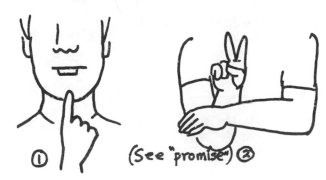

WAFFLE
Stab back of W with palm-down V

WAG
Wag inverted W hanging over index

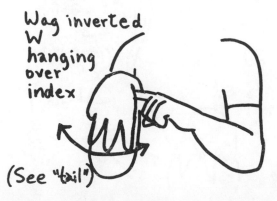

(See "tail")

WAGON
Right-C behind left W; right moves back

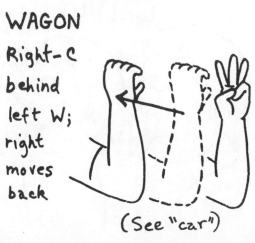

(See "car")

345

WAIST
Drag W-hand
across waistline

WAIT   Palm-up
right hand behind palm-up
left, flutter
fingers

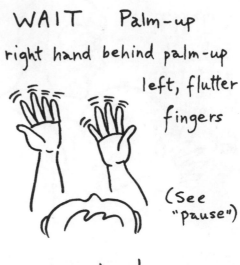

(See
"pause")

WAKE

Closed G-
hand at
corner of
eye
opens to
L

Awake=
a + wake

Woke=
wake + ed

WALK
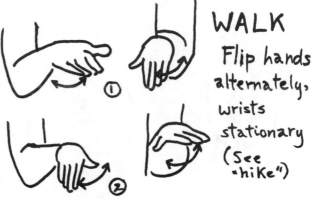
Flip hands
alternately,
wrists
stationary
(See
"hike")

WALL

Palm-in
W hands
together,
separate,
turn to
face each
other and
move towards body

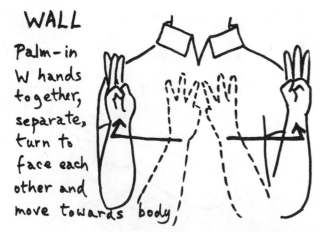

WALLET

Slide inverted
W down hip
as if into pocket

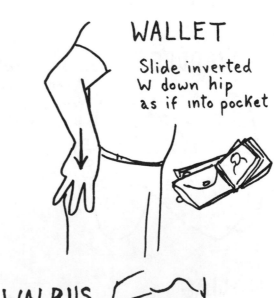

WALNUT   Index of
W and then
thumb of A
jerk from
under
teeth

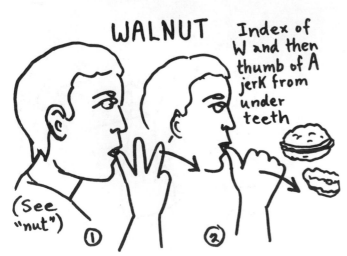

(See
"nut")
① ②

WALRUS
Curve C's
out and down
to S's

346

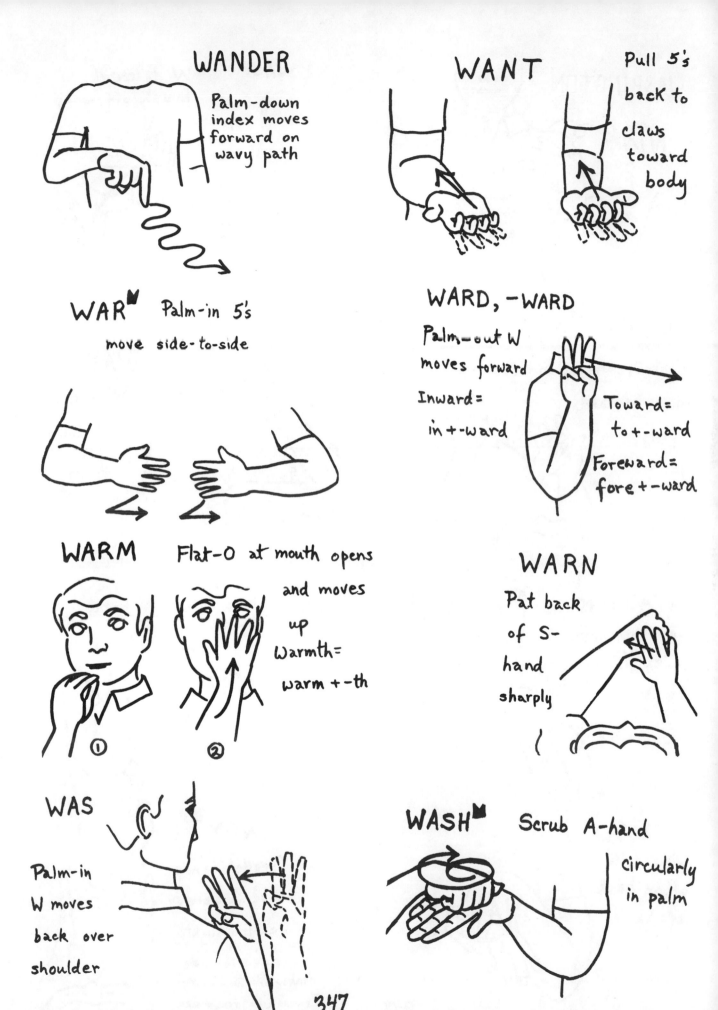

WANDER
Palm-down index moves forward on wavy path

WANT
Pull 5's back to claws toward body

WAR Palm-in 5's move side-to-side

WARD, -WARD
Palm-out W moves forward
Inward = in + -ward
Toward = to + -ward
Foreward = fore + -ward

WARM Flat-O at mouth opens and moves up
Warmth = warm + -th
① ②

WARN
Pat back of S-hand sharply

WAS
Palm-in W moves back over shoulder

WASH Scrub A-hand circularly in palm

347

WASHINGTON

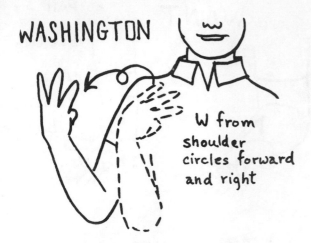

W from shoulder circles forward and right

WASP

W to cheek, brush off wasp

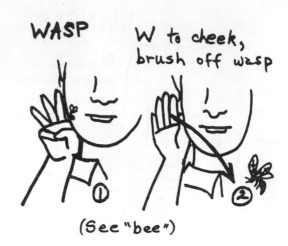

(See "bee")

WASTE

Flat-O, palm-up on left palm, slides off and opens to 5

WATCH

V at eye, twist down and tap on wrist

WATER

Tap chin with index finger of W

WAVE

Wave with right hand twice

WAX

Wax with W on back of hand

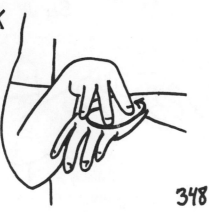

WAY

Parallel hands move forward, weaving slightly side-to-side

Highway = high + way

Freeway = free + way

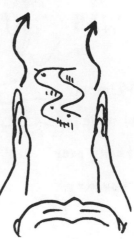

WE

W on right side of chest circles to left side

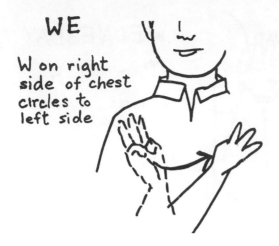

WEAK   At right angle, fingertips on palm, bend fingers, repeat

(See "fragile")   ①   ②

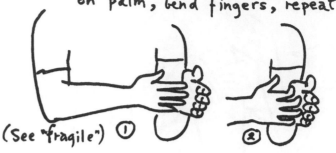

WEALTH

Back of W on palm-up left hand, outline a pile of money on palm
(See "rich")

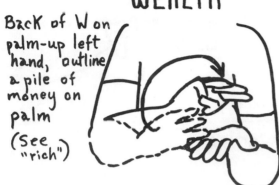

WEAR   Palm-out W arcs side-to-side hitting back of S

Wore= wear + -ed

Worn= wear + -en

(See "work")

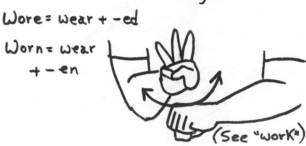

WEARY

Fingertips of W's touch waist and drop downward to palm-up

(See "tire")

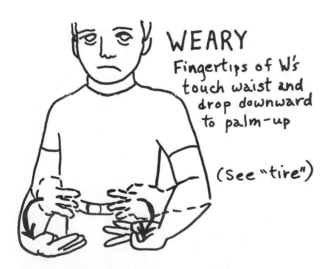

WEATHER

Palm-out W shakes downward

(See "season")

WEAVE

Right 5-hand makes weaving motion across back of palm down 5-hand

349

WEB   Right W lies on left W

WED
Hands swing together and left clasps right

Wedding = wed + -ing

WEDNESDAY
Palm-out W circles slightly

(See "Friday")

WEE
W's, close together, move slightly toward and away from each other

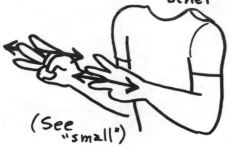

(See "small")

WEED
Flat-O grows rapidly through C to W, twisting

(See "grow")

WEEK
Brush 1-hand across palm

WEEP
Drag 2 palm-in W's down cheeks

Wept = weep + -ed

(See "cry")

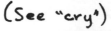

WEIGH
Rock middle finger of right H on side of left H index

Weight = weigh + -t

WEINER
Pull out of W alternately S's and C's

C ← S

(See "baloney")

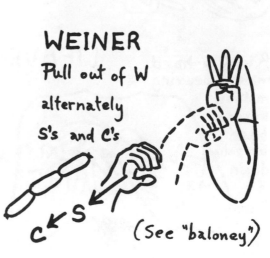

350

WEIRD

Fluttering
Wares
past
eyes

(See "strange")

WELCOME

Palm-up W
curves horizontally
towards body

(See "invite")

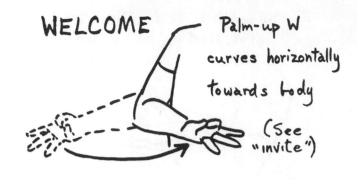

WELD

Thumb extended,
point at left palm,
move back and
forth

welding=
weld +-ing

(See "solder")

WELL

W-hands face
each other, drop straight down

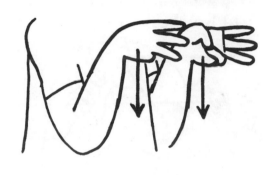

WERE

Palm-in
R moves
back over
shoulder

WEST

Palm-out
W moves
left

WET

Drop palm-in
flat hand off
chin, then
open and
close
flat-O

WHALE

W makes 2 curves
to the left,
outside arm

(See "dolphin")

351

WHARF
W outlines left palm-down arm, starting on outside

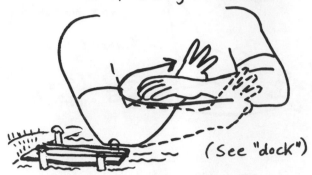

(See "dock")

WHAT
Index fingertip brushes down across left fingers

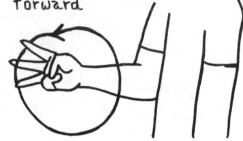

WHEAT
W brushes up G twice

(See "grain")

WHEEL
Rotate palm-left W vertically forward

WHEN
Touch fingertips, make a circle with right fingertip; return tip to tip

WHERE
Palm-out index shakes sideways

WHETHER
Palm-out W off thumb, then off fingertip of L

(See "then")

WHICH
Alternately, A's pump up and down

(See "balance")

352

WHILE

W-hands face each other near right shoulder, arc down and forward

(See "during")

WHIP

Fingers of W whip past left index; repeat

(see "beat")

WHISKEY

Strike side of W on side of 1+I-hand

(See "liquor")

WHISPER

Whisper behind hand while fingers flutter

WHISTLE

Bent V-fingers near mouth

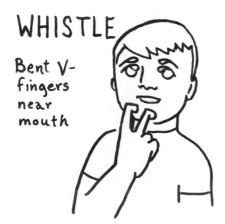

WHITE

5 on chest moves outward, closing to a flat O

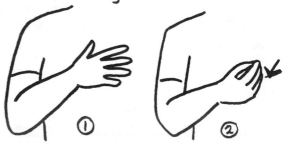

① ②

WHO

Thumb of L on chin; wiggle index finger

353

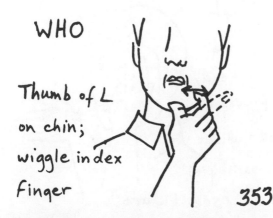

WHOLE

Right flat hand circles and turns over, resting on left hand

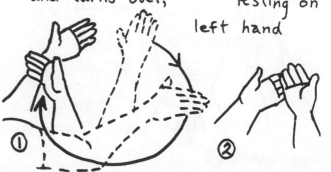

① ②

WHY

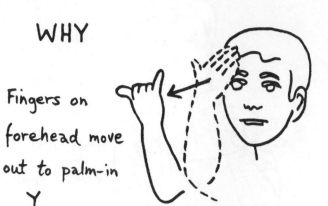

Fingers on forehead move out to palm-in Y

WICKED

Palm-in W on chin; twist to palm-out and throw down

(See "bad")

WIDE

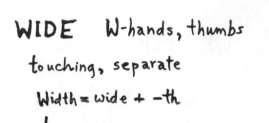

W-hands, thumbs touching, separate

Width = wide + -th

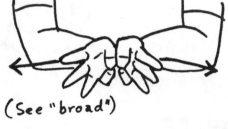

(See "broad")

WIFE

A at jaw to clasped C's

Wives = wife + -s

WIG

Pull wig on with W-hands

WIGGLE

W wiggles forward

(See "fish")

WILD

Twirl W off temple

(See "fantasy")

WILL

Palm facing side of head, arc forward

Would = will + -en (past participle)

(See "future")

WIN

Right S
on left,
spirals
quickly
upward
Won = win + -ed

WIND (verb)

Fingertips of W on wrist,
circle
horizontally
forward

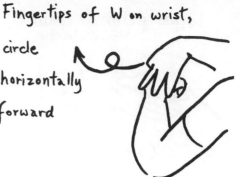

WIND

Hands swing back and
forth, twisting at wrists (as wind
"blows" them)

① ②

WINDOW

Open
and
close,
hitting
sides
of
hands

WINE

W circles
on cheek,
palm in

(See "beer")

WING

Left hand on right
shoulder flap right hand at the side

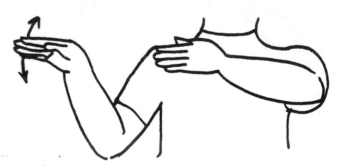

WINK

Wink with L
hand stationary;
shut and open
thumb and
finger

WINTER

Vertical
W's face
each
other,
shake
slightly

(shivering) (See "cold")

355

WIPE

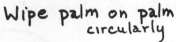

Wipe palm on palm circularly

(See "wash")

WIRE

I-finger-tip shakes outward from left W and slightly down

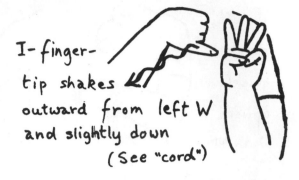

(See "cord")

WISE

Palm-down X nods near center of forehead several times

Wisdom = wise + -dom

(See "philosophy")

WISH

Palm-in W slides down chest

(See "hunger")

WIT

Index of W on temple; W swings outward from wrist

WITCH

Right X moves from nose to rest on left X, heels together

WITH

Closed hands together

Within = with + in

With out = with + out

WITHOUT

Knuckles together, A's move apart to 5's

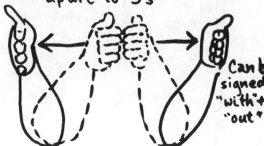

Can be signed "with" + "out"

356

WOLF

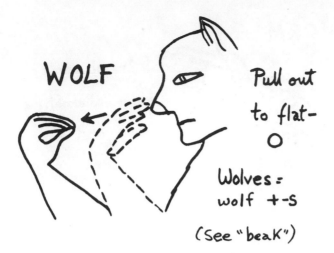

Pull out to flat-O

Wolves = wolf +-s

(See "beak")

WOMAN

A at jaw moves up to show height with bent hand

WOMEN

A at jaw, measure 2 heights with bent hand

WONDER

W, palm-in, circles near temple

(See "reason")

WOOD

Elbow of W on back of left hand; twist W slightly side-to-side

(see "tree")

WOOL

W slides up left upper arm

(See "fur")

WORD
Right G-fingers rest against left index

WORK
Palm-out S arcs from side-to-side, hitting back of S

WORLD 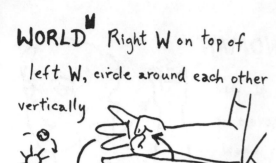 Right W on top of left W, circle around each other vertically

WORM 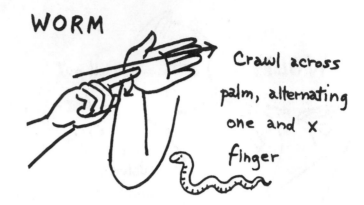 Crawl across palm, alternating one and x finger

WORRY

W-hands circle alternately before face

(see "trouble")

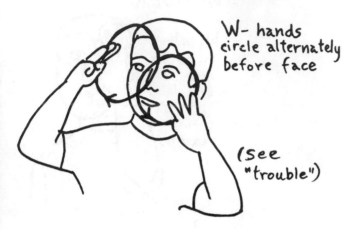

WORSE 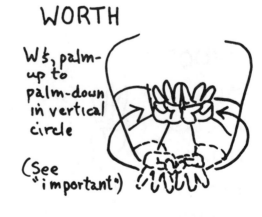 Cross wrists

Worst = worse + -est

WORSHIP Left hand closed over right, move in very slight vertical circle

WORTH

W's, palm-up to palm-down in vertical circle

(See "important")

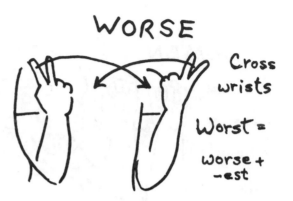

WOW Place W's on each side of O-mouth

WRAP W's circle each other, separate

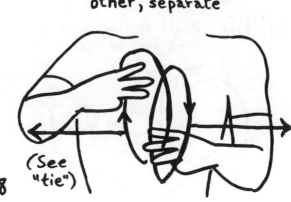

(See "tie")

358

WREATH
Palm-out W's touch, circle vertically, and touch again (See "bulb")

WRECK
Hit side of W with S

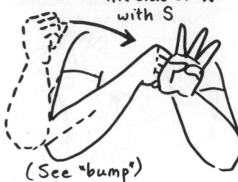

(See "bump")

WRENCH
With W-hand, "tighten" left index once

(See "mechanic")

WRESTLE
Mesh 5-hands, fingers straight move forward and back slightly

WRING
C's close to S's in a wringing motion

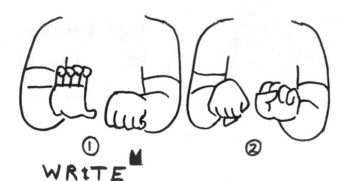

① ②

WRIST
Draw W across wrist

WRITE

Thumb and finger of closed X write on palm

Wrote = write + -ed
Written = write + -en

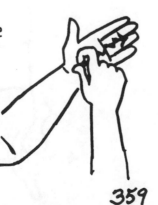

WRONG
Palm-in Y on chin

XEROX
5, palm-down, rises to X under left palm, drops to 5 again

XYLOPHONE
Alternately play side to side on xylophone with A's

YARD
Y on back of hand up to inside of elbow

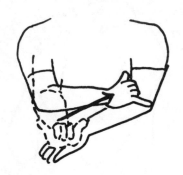

YARN
Wiggle i-hand from Y, out and slightly down

(See "cord")

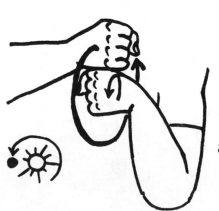

YAWN
Under chin Y rises from palm-down to palm-out, drops again

YEAR
Right S rests on left S; circle S's around each other and return to start

YELL
Palm-in Y moves up and out from chin

(See "scream")

YELLOW
Palm-left Y shakes

(See "blue")

YES

Nod
Y-hand

YET

Palm
slaps
gently
backwards
near
waist

YOGURT

Y ladles from
palm to mouth

Yoghu

(See
"soup")

YON
-YOND- (Affix)

Y against Y;
right Y moves
forward

(See "far")

YOU

Index points
at person
addressed

YOUNG

Brush tips of
hands upward
twice off chest

Youth = young
+ -th

(See "juvenile")

YOUR

Palm moves
toward
person
addressed

Yours = your + -s

ZEBRA

4-hands mark stripes
on body

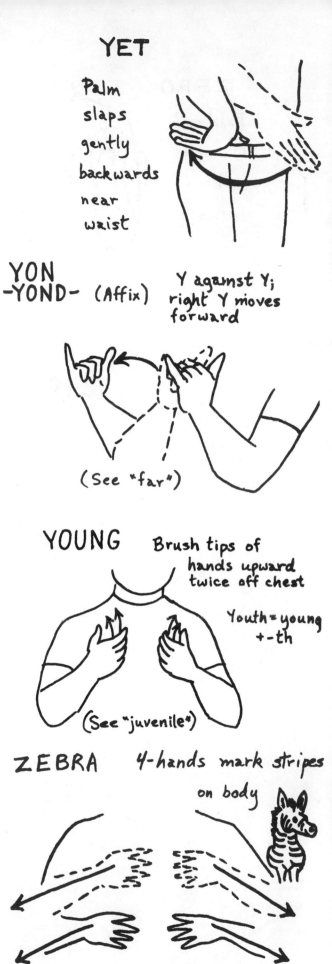

ZERO

Palm-out
O circles
once
vertically

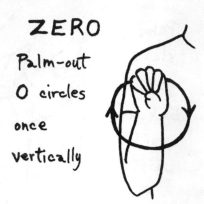

ZIP

Zip thumb
and index
knuckle
up palm

ZOO

Draw
Z on
5-hand
with index
finger

SIGNS GROUPED BY FAMILIES

The following groups of signs are those which are similar in movement and belong together conceptually. We have found doing this has helped people to remember signs with greater ease. If a group of words originated from a traditional sign, we used that sign as the head of the family. If all the words are new, we merely alphabetize the list.

- The head of the family is shown with a ▲ after the word in the text.

- An asterisk (*) means look for a slight variation.

- Where we say see "_____", the "_____" will be the head of the family.
  When there are only 2 words in a family, we cross referenced them.

ACT	ADDRESS	ADVICE	AFRAID
drama	exist	advise	fear
perform	life	affect	horror
theater	live	counsel	terror
	reside	effect	
	survive	influence*	
	vital		

AGAINST	AIM	ALGAE	ALLOW
con	goal	bacteria	let
prejudice	object	cell	opportune*
	target	fungus	permit

ALPHABET	ANGEL	ANGER	ANT
consonant	elf	fury	beetle
vowel	fairy	irritate	cricket
	gremlin	rage	insect
	leprechaun		pest
	pixie		roach
			scorpion
			termite

APPLE	APRICOT	ARITHMETIC	ART
fruit	fig	algebra	architect
pineapple	nectarine	calculus	draw
vegetable	plum	figure	
	tangerine	geometry	
		math	

363

ASPARAGUS	ATTEMPT	AUNT	AX
broccoli	effort	cousin*	chop
celery	try	nephew*	hatchet
rhubarb		niece	
		uncle*	

BACHELOR	BAD	BALANCE	BALONEY
spinster	evil	court	frankfurter*
twin	naughty	doubt	sausage
	rude	evaluate	wiener
	wicked	judge	
		may	
		probable	
		umpire	
		which	

BAND	BANQUET	BAR	BARE
club	dine	line	abort
tribe	feast	row	empty
	picnic		naked*
			nude*
			vacant

BASE	BASKET	BAY	BEAN
denominator	April	cove	carrot
element	purse	harbor	pea
fundamental			
inferior			
kindergarten			
-neath			
primary			
sub			
theme			

BEAT	BED	BEGIN	BIG
hit	dorm	commence	grand*
punch	hotel	initiate	great
strike	motel	origin	large
whip	nap*	start	tremendous
	pillow*		

BIKE	BILLION	BIRD	BLUE
cycle	million	crow	green
tricycle	trillion	duck	purple
		pigeon	yellow
		robin	

BODY

health
physical

BONNET

kerchief
scarf

BORROW

credit
rent

BOX

apartment
case
den
garden
kitchen
room

BROAD

general
public
wide

BROOK

river
stream

BULB

globe
wreath

BUMP

bang
crash
damage*
victim
wreck

BUTTER

grease
lard
margarine
mayonnaise
oleo

BUY

cash
purchase
shop

CABBAGE

cauliflower
lettuce

CALIFORNIA

gold
silver

CAP

lid
tip*
top

CAR

bus
taxi
truck
vehicle
wagon

CARPET

linoleum
mat
rug

CAT

kitten
leopard
panther
tiger

CATERPILLAR

creep
slug
snail

CENT

dime
nickel
penny
quarter

CERTAIN

fact
serious
sure*

CHANGE

adapt
adjust
alter
amend
convert
distort
evolve
modify*
reverse
translate

CHARACTER

attitude
detect
noble
personality

CHICAGO

Detroit
Philadelphia

CHILD

dwarf
midget

CHINA

Asia
Japan
Korea

CHIP	CHOCOLATE	CHRIST	CIRCLE
flake	cocoa	king	ever
piece	vanilla	lord	round
		prince	
		queen	

CLASS	CLOTH	COAT	COLD
district	fabric	blouse	chill
family	rag	jacket	refrigerate
group		robe	winter
herd		shirt	
league		uniform	
organize		vest	
team			

COLLEGE	COMPLAIN	CONTINUE	CORD
graduate	fuss	constant	cable*
university	gripe	permanent	ribbon
	object	remain	string
			thread
			wire
			yarn

COST	COUNTRY	CRAB	CRY
charge	county	lobster	tear
fee	foreign	shrimp	weep
price			
tax			

CULTURE	CUT	CYCLONE	DANGER
environment	snip	hurricane	harm
local	trim	storm	threat
social		tornado	

DARK	DEER	DEMONSTRATE	DENMARK
dim	elk*	example	Finland
fog	moose*	sample	Norway
shade	reindeer*		Swede

DIAMOND	DO	DOCK	DOCTOR
jewel	behave	pier	medic
ring	manner	wharf	nurse
			psychiatry
			pulse
			veterinary

DOLL	DOLPHIN	DOWN	DRESS
cartoon	porpoise	low	attire
fun	whale	vertical	costume
		south	gown
			pajama

DRIFT	EAT	EDGE	ELECTRIC
float	breakfast	hoof	battery
glide	dinner	toe	physics
	lunch		
	supper		

EQUATOR	EVAPORATE	EXACT	EXPERT
latitude	gas	perfect	excel*
solar	vapor	specific	skill

FABULOUS	FACE	FALSE	FANTASY
amaze*	beauty*	fake	abstract
marvel	handsome	pretend	concept
terrific	pretty		fiction
			myth
			theory
			wild

FAR	FEEL	FINE	FINISH
distant	emotion	courtesy	complete
yon	mood	polite	end
	pride		
	proud		

FIRST	FLAG	FLOWER	FORBID
January	banner	rose	prohibit
prior	pennant	violet	flunk
			minus
			negative

FORM	FREE	FRESHMAN	FRIDAY
image	liberty	Junior	Monday
shape	rescue	Sophmore	Saturday
			Thursday*
			Tuesday
			Wednesday

FRIEND	GENERATE	GHOST	GIFT
acquaint	heredity	goblin	award
mate	inherit	haunt	prize
neighbor	legend	spirit	reward
partner		spook	
relate			

GIRL	GOD	GOVERN	GRAIN
female	admire	capitol	alfalfa
her	honor	federal	barley
Miss	respect	mayor	hay
Mrs*		politic	oat
she	**GRIM**		rye
			straw
	pout		wheat
	tragedy		

GROUND	GROW	GUARD	HALL
continent	plant	defend	lane
-dom	spring*	protect	parallel
ecology	vine*		
field	weed		
land			
meadow			
plain			
range			

HAPPEN	HAPPY	HE	HEART
chance	enjoy	fellow	February
event	glad	guy	valentine
fate	joy	him	
incident	merry	his	
luck		mister*	
occur		sir*	
result			

HELP	HIDE	HOLY	HONEST
aid*	conceal	divine	frank
assist*	intrigue	pure	real
rehabilitate	mystery	saint	true
therapy			

HORSE	HOSPITAL	HOUR	HOUSE
colt	ambulance	age	barn
mule*	infirmary	period	cabin
pony		semester	factory
stubborn*		term	garage
			hut
			museum
			station

HUNGER	HURT	ICE CREAM	IMPORTANT
appetite	ache	lollipop	main
desire	injure	popsicle	value
wish	pain		worth
			essence

INSPECT	INVITE	JAIL	JAR
explore*		cage	nest*
investigate	hire	prison	net
pioneer*	welcome		pot
research			tub
			vase

KILL	LAW	LECTURE	LEISURE
assassin	constitute	minister	holiday
murder	curriculum*	preach	idle*
	doctrine		vacation
	formula		
	principle		
	rule		
	state		

LESSON	LONESOME	LOVE	LUTHERAN
course	patient	dear	Presbyterian
subject	tolerate	fond	Protestant

MAKE	MANAGE	MASK	MEAN
create	control	Halloween	define
produce	handle	October	purpose
	reign		

MEASLES	MEAT	MEDICINE	MELON
freckle*	beef	alcohol	cantaloupe
pimple*	ham	drug	jack-o-latern
pox	pork	prescription	pumpkin
rubella	steak	vaseline	
	veal*		

MEMBER	METAL	MIDDLE	MINUTE
committee	aluminum	center	instant
congress	brass	intermediate	late
faculty	copper	nucleus	moment
legislate	iron		soon
parliament	lead		tardy
senate	steel		
	tin		

MONEY	MONKEY	MOUSE	MOUTH
economy	ape	gerbil	oral
finance	gorilla	hamster	speech
		rat	

MUCH	MUSIC	NEW	NOT
quite	chorus	fresh	dis-
such	hymn	modern	il-
	lyric	raw	im-
	poem*		in-
	poetry*		ir-
	rhythm		mis-
	song		un-
	tune		

NUT	OFFICE	ONCE	OPEN
peanut	boss	double	expose
walnut	capital	triple	hatch
	captain	twice	reveal

OPPOSE	OVEN	PANT	PAPER
enemy	broil	slack	kleenex
foe	grill	trouser	tissue

PARENT	PEOPLE	PERSON	PICTURE
adult	folk	human	illustrate
gender	visit	-ist	photo
neuter			
orphan			
sex			
teen			

PIG	PLACE	PLAY	PRACTICE
dirt*	area	game	coach
mud	island	party	drill
	lot	recess	rehearse
	situate	sport	
		toy	

PROMISE	PUSH	QUIET	QUOTE
guarantee	buggy*	calm	idiom
oath	cart*	gentle	slang
pledge		peace	title
vow		silence	

REASON	REQUIRE	RICH	SAVE
logic	condition	fortune	safe
opinion	demand	wealth	reserve
thought	impress	treasure	
wonder	insist		

SCIENCE	SCREAM	SENTENCE	SHINE
biology	call	grammer	glow
chemistry	shout*	language	polish
experiment	yell		

SHOE	SHORT	SHOW	SIT
boot	abbreviate	indicate	bench
galoshes	brief	represent	chair
	temporary	symbol	couch*
			perch
			roost
			seat
			sofa

SMALL	SMELL	SMILE	SOME
little	fragrant	comic	factor
wee	odor	grin	part
		laugh*	

SOUND	SOUP	SOUR	SPAGHETTI
hear	broth	bitter	bacon
listen	cereal	vinegar	macaroni
noise*	dessert		noodle
radio*	meal		
	pudding		
	rice		
	yogurt		

STANDARD	STONE	STORE	STRAIGHT
common	brick	bank	career
company*	concrete	grocer	direct
together	gravel	market	major
union	pebble		profess
unite*	rock		

STRANGE	STRONG	SUCCESS	SUGGEST
fool	authority	accomplish	offer
odd	energy	achieve	present (v)
queer	intense	succeed*	recommend
weird*	might		
	power		

SUMMER	TALK	TEACH	THEN
desert	communicate	educate	either
humid	converse	instruct	neither
July	dialogue	tutor	nor
	interview		or
			rather
			whether

THERMOMETER	THING	THINK	TO
degree	equip	familiar	til
fever	furnish	know	too
meter	item	mind	until
temper	material	remind	
	tool		

TOMATO	TOWN	TREE	UP
beet	city	forest	elevate
cucumber	village	jungle	high
parsnip		lumber	north
turnip		orchard	rise
		timber	
		wood	

WAR	WASH	WASTE	WAY
battle	launder	eliminate	path
quarrel	wipe	garbage	road
struggle		junk	
		remove	
		trash	

WEIGH	WHOLE	WIN	WIND
ounce	entire	truimph	air
pound	total	victor	breeze
ton			

W ORD	WORK	WRITE	WORLD
noun	busy	author	geography
vocabulary	commerce	chalk	planet*
	employ		universe*
	function	manuscript	
	industry	pen	
	job*	pencil*	
	labor	record	
	operate	secretary*	
	toil		
	use		
	vocation		
	wear		

372

Selected References

Babbidge, H. D. Education of the deaf: A report to the Secretary of Health, Education and Welfare by his Advisory Committee on Education of the Deaf. U. S. Dept. of Health, Education, and Welfare, 1965.

Bellugi, U. and E. Klima, "The roots of language in the sign of the deaf," Psychology Today, June 1972, p. 61-64, 76.

Bergman, E., "Autonomous and Unique Features of American Sign Language," American Annals of the Deaf, 117:20-24, Feb. 1972.

Bishop, H. M. "The testing of deaf and hard-of-hearing children in St. Paul schools with the Arthur Performance Scale," Natl. Educ. Assn. Proc. 74:393-394, 1936.

Boatner, E. B. The need of a realistic approach to the education of the deaf. Paper given to the joint convention of California Association of Parents of Deaf and Hard of Hearing Children, California Association of Teachers of Deaf and Hard of Hearing Children, and the California Association of the Deaf, Nov. 6, 1965.

Bornstein, H. "Some Current Sign Systems," American Annals of the Deaf, 118:454-463, June 1973.

Bragg, B., "Ameslish—Our American Heritage," American Annals of the Deaf, 118:672-674, Dec. 1973.

Braine, M. D. S. "The otogeny of English phrase structure: the first phrase," Language ,39:1-13, Jan-Mar 1963.

Brown, R. and U. Bellugi. "Three processes in the child's acquisition of syntax," Harvard Educational Review, 39:133-152, Spring, 1964.

Caccamise, F., and C. Norris. Animals in Signs, Home in Signs, Food in Signs; Community in Signs. (Box 553, Eureka, CA; Alinda Press) 1973-74.

Cazden, C. B. "The acquisition of noun and verb inflections," Child Development, 39:433-448, June, 1968.

Cokely, D. and R. Gawlik. "Options: A Position Paper on the Relationship Between Manual English and Sign," The Deaf American, May 1973, p. 7-11.

_____"Options II: Childrenese as Pidgin," The Deaf American, April 1974, p. 5-6.

Communication, Gallaudet Today, winter 1974-75 , Wash D.C.: Gallaudet College Office of Alumni & Public Relations, 1975.

Cooper, R. L. "The ability of deaf and hearing children to apply morphological rules." Unpublished doctoral dissertation, Columbia, 1965.

Fant, L., "Enough of imitations," The Deaf American, Jan. 1971, p. 14–15.

-----Letter to the editor, American Annals of the Deaf, 119:299-301, June 1974

-----"On Idols and Ideals," The Washingtonian, v. 77 #4, Dec. 1972, p. 1-3.

-----"Why Ameslan?" California News, June 1974.

Fast, J. Body Language. New York: M. Evans and Company, Inc., 1970.

Goetzinger, C. P. and C. L. Rousey. "A study of the Wechsler Perform-ance Scale (Form II) and the Knox Cube Test with deaf adolescents," American Annals of the Deaf, 102:388-398, 1957.

Goetzinger, C. P. and C. L. Rousey. "Educational achievement of deaf children," American Annals of the Deaf, 1959, 104: 221-231.

Graham, E. E. and E. Shapiro. "Use of the performance scale of the WISC with the deaf child, "Journal of Consulting Psychology, 17:396-398, 1953.

Gustason, G. "Signing Exact English," Gallaudet Today, vol. 5, #2, 11-12, winter 1974-75.

Gustason, G., D. Pfetzing and E. Zawolkow. "The Rationale of Signing Exact English," The Deaf American, September 1974, 5-6.

Hart, B. O. and J. Rosenstein. "Examining the language behavior of deaf children," The Volta Review, 66:679-682, 1964.

Heider, F. and G. Heider. "Comparison of sentence structure of deaf and hearing children," Psychological Monographs, 1940, 52:42-103.

Hockett, C. F. "Age-grading and linguistic continuity," Language, 26:449-457, 1950.

Labov, W. "Linguistic reserach on the nonstandard English of Negro children," 1965 Yearbook, New York Society for the Experimental Study of Education, pp. 110-117.

Lowell, E. L. John Tracy Clinic Research Papers III, V, VI, and VII. Los Angeles, Calif.: John Tracy Clinic, 1957-58.

Lowell, E. L. "Research in speechreading: some relationships to language development and implications for the classroom teacher," Report of the Proceedings of the 39th Meeting of the Convention of American Instructors of the Deaf, 1969, 68-73.

McClure, W. J. "Current problems and trends in the education of the deaf," The Deaf American, 1966, 8-14.

MacPherson, J. and H. S. Lane "A comparison of deaf and hearing on the Hiskey test and in performance scales," American Annals of the Deaf, 77:292-304, 1932.

Meadow, K. "The effect of early manual communication and family climate on the deaf child's development." Unpublished doctoral dissertation, University of California, Berkeley, 1967.

Montgomery, G. W. "Relationship of oral skills to manual communication in profoundly deaf students," American Annals of the Deaf, 111:557-565, 1966.

Morkovin, B. V. "Helping the deaf child toward adequate language and speech," Journal of Rehabilitation, May-June 1963.

Mussen, P. H. The Psychological Development of the Child. Englewood Cliffs, N. J.: Prentice-Hall, Inc., 1963.

Myklebust, H. R. "Clinical psychology and children with impaired hearing," The Volta Review, 50:55-60, 90, 1948.

Myklebust, H. R. Development and Disorders of Written Language: Volume One. Picture Story Language Test. New York: Grune and Stratton, 1965.

Newman, L. "Bilingual Education," The Deaf American, May 1973

Newman, L. "A Total Communication Family," The Deaf American, April 1973, p. 21-22.

Office of Demographic Studies. Academic Achievement Test Performance of Hearing Impaired Students. Series D, No. 1. Washington, D.C.: Gallaudet College, Sept. 1969.

Office of Demographic Studies. Summary of Selected Characteristics of Hearing Impaired Students, United States; 1969-70. Series D, No. 5. Washington, D.C.: Gallaudet College, June 1971.

O'Rourke, T. J. (ed.) Psycholinguistics and Total Communication: The State of the Art. Washington, D. C.: American Annals of the Deaf, 1972

Peterson, E. G. "Testing deaf children with Kohs Block Design," American Annals of the Deaf, 81:55-60, 90, 1948.

Penfield, W. "The uncommitted cortex: the child's changing brain," The Atlantic Monthly, 77-81, July 1964.

Pintner, R. "The measurement of language ability and language process of deaf children," The Volta Review, 20:755-766, 1918.

Pugh, G. S. "Summaries from appraisal of the silent reading abilities of acoustically handicapped children," American Annals of the Deaf, 1946, 91, 331-349

Quigley, S. P. and D. Frisina. Institutionalization and Psychoeducational Development of Deaf Children. Council of Exceptional Children Research Monographs, Series A, #3, 1961.

Ross, G. "Testing intelligence and maturity of deaf children," Exceptional Children, 20:23-24, 42, 1953.

Schlesinger, H. and K. Meadow. Sound and Sign: Childhood Deafness and Mental Health. Berkeley, Calif.: University of California Press, 1972.

Scyster, M. "Summary of four years' experiment with preschool children at the Illinois School for the Deaf," American Annals of the Deaf, 81:212-230, 1936.

Shirley, M. and F. Goodenough. "Intelligence of deaf children in Minnesota," American Annals of the Deaf, 77:238-247, 1932.

Simmons, A. A. "A comparison of the type-token ratio of spoken and written language of deaf and hearing children," The Volta Review, 64:417-421, 1962.

Slobin, D. "Grammatical development in Russian speaking children," The Development of Language Functions, ed. Klaus F. Riegel. Report #8, pp. 93-102. Ann Arbor: University of Michigan Center for Human Growth & Development, 1965.

Springer, N.N. "A comparative study of the intelligence of a group of deaf and hard of hearing children," American Annals of the Deaf, 83:138-152, 1938.

Stevenson, E. A. A study of the educational achievement of deaf children of deaf parents. Berkeley: California School for the Deaf, 1964.

Stokoe, W. C. "CAL Conference on Sign Languages," The Linguistic Reporter, 12:5-8, April 1970.

-----"Sign Language Diglossia," Studies in Linguistics, 1970.

----"Sign Language Structure: An Outline of the Visual Communication Systems of the American Deaf," Studies in Linguistics, #3, 1960.

-----The Study of Sign Language. Silver Spring, Md.: National Association of the Deaf, 1971.

Stuckless, E. R. and J. W. Birch. "The influence of early manual communication on the linguistic development of deaf children," American Annals of the Deaf, 111:452-462, 1966.

Thompson, W. H. "An analysis of errors in written compositions of deaf children," American Annals of the Deaf, 81:95-99, 1936.

Velten, H. V. "The growth of phonemic and lexical patterns in infant language," Language, 19:281-292, 1943.

Vernon, M. "Fifty years of research on the intelligence of the deaf and hard of hearing: a survey of the literature and discussion of implications," Journal of Rehabilitation of the Deaf, 1:1-11, 1968.

Vernon, M. "Sociological and psychological factors associated with hearing loss," Journal of Speech and Hearing Research, 12:541-563, 1969.

Weir, R. Language in the Crib. The Hague: Mouton and Company, 1962.

Wrightstone, J.W.,M.S. Aranow, and S. Muskowitz, "Developing Test Norms for the Deaf Child," American Annals of the Deaf, 108:311-316, 1963.

Zeckel, A. and J. J. Kalb. "A comparative test of groups of children born deaf and of good hearing by means of the Porteous Maze Test," American Annals of the Deaf, 84:114-123, 1939.

RESOURCES

In new sign development, there is often a great deal of overlap among signs used by various groups due to the use of
traditional signs as a base and the borrowing of signs among
groups. Some of those working on new signs include:

1. Gallaudet College, Kendall Green, Washington, D.C. 20002.
   (Preschool Signed English Storybooks)

2. Seeing Essential English, Laboratory School, University of
   Northern Colorado, Greeley, Colorado. (D. Anthony)

3. David Watson, Winnecone, Wisconsin, 54986

A complete list of publications available from the National
Association of the Deaf may be obtained by writing the NAD,
814 Thayer, Silver Spring, Maryland, 20910. Some of the sign
books available there include:

Ameslan

1. Fant, L. Ameslan.

2. Madsen, W. Conversational Sign Language II.

Traditional signs

1. Fant, L. Say It With Hands.

2. O'Rourke, T.J. A Basic Course in Manual Communication.

3. Riekehoff, L. Talk to the Deaf.

4. Watson, D. Talk with your Hands.

A book of Manual English is available from:

Washington State School for the Deaf
P.O. Box 2036
Vancouver, Washington 98661

NOTES

NOTES

NOTES

REFERENCE
ONLY

The Annual of Annuals

Project developed and
co-ordinated by ADC*E

PROJECT MANAGER
Mercè Segú

ADC*E ANNUAL COLLABORATORS
Elisa Huguet, Laura Kaliebe, Ramon Sorribes

ART DIRECTION & DESIGN
Mucho

LAYOUT
Carla Bahna

DVD DESIGN & PRODUCTION
ESIETE

JURY PHOTOGRAPHS
Xavier Padrós

COVER AND CHAPTER PAGE
PHOTOGRAPHS
Nacho Alegre

PRE-PRESS & PRINTING
Nova Era

Printed in Spain

Copyright©2006

Art Directors Club of Europe
ISBN – 13: 978-84-611-3759-6
ISBN – 10: 84-611-3759-0
D.L. B-50917-2006

THE ADC*E IS SUPPORTED BY
Miami Ad School Europe
Hewlett Packard
Eulda
Arctic Paper
Jelgavas Tipografija
Vilks Studija
Gloss Postproduction
Bombay Sapphire
Brandia Central
Glòria de Pallejà

The
Annual
of
Annuals

Best of
European
Design
and
Advertising

ADC*E
The Art Directors
Club of Europe

Manifesto

To those who chase a dream in life - the obstinate, the tenacious, the committed, the sincere, the open-minded.

To those who strive for excellence, work to a higher standard and never give up.

To those with passion for crafting detail.

To those who place integrity before profit and believe in the triumph of enthusiasm over scepticism.

To those committed to honour excellence beyond prejudice, cultural borders and national differences.

To those with the vision and ability to challenge what is accepted.

To those who never stop dreaming.

Contents

24 Grand Prix

30 Film

Welcome

ADC*E unites the leading advertising and design Clubs/Associations and creatives across Europe.

On Saturday 8th July, 2006, a jury of over 60 top European creatives chaired by the ADC*E President Johannes Newrkla met at the FAD building, the centre of creativity in Barcelona, and judged over 900 Gold, Silver and other awarded pieces of work in 19 categories from 28 countries across Europe. After a long and rewarding day the jury nominated 80 pieces of work. From these 18 Golds were awarded across the different categories and the overall Grand Prix Award, Europe's top creative honour, went to Poland.

The ADC*E aims to unite, excite and inspire European creativity and act as a gateway to its respective community. ADC*E 2006 brings you "the best of the best" in advertising and design.

The following pages are a testimony of the great diversity in creativity that is being done across Europe.
We hope you enjoy reading this book on European creativity as much as we did compiling it.

Board of Directors

My reasons to be a member

I am Member of the ADC*E Board because of you.

Michael Conrad

Great ideas can come from anywhere — the more places you have visited, the more chances you have to recognize them.

Eda Kauba
Czech Republic

I am on the ADC*E Board because I am European.

Sebastian Turner
Germany

The ADC*E is the only non-profit organization that awards, celebrates, and promotes the creative diversity of Europe.

Martin Spillmann
Switzerland

I deliver the best in Russian creative work to a versatile and highly professional European community. Like a sponge, I absorb ideas that I can bring back home to help develop even better Russian creative work.

Alexander Alexeev
Russia

As a member of the Portuguese creative community, I'm honoured to be an active part of a truly representative European creative organization: Contributing some ideas, discussing many others, and adding value and diversity from the West Coast of Europe.

Mário Mandacaru
Portugal

I am a Board Member because I believe that by collecting and showing all of Europe's best work, we can raise the quality of design and advertising to an even higher standard.

Haukur Már Hauksson
Iceland

My involvement with the ADC*E is an opportunity to meet people and share ideas, which is difficult to do on a daily basis. It is a chance not only to follow what's going on in the advertising world, but also to help define the trends that will lead tomorrow's industry.

J. Margus Klaar
Estonia

I am a Member of ADC*E Board because good work should go global.

Helena Rosa-Trias
Spain

To be or not to be? There is no question: to be is the verb!

Franco Moretti
Italy

If you meet the people of ADC*E Board, you will instantly recognize why being a part of it is so special. Brilliant brains, great hearts and inspiration for everybody.

Johannes Newrkla
Austria

I am a Board Member because I am the President of the Creative Club of Poland, but also because the idea of comparing works from local shows is appealing to me. Unlike most international shows, you get a slightly different take on what counts as good work – you're trying to look at ideas with local eyes in the local context.

Kot Przybora
Poland

I am a Board Member of ADC*E because in this world of global communications where one answer is designed to fit all, the ADC*E still champions and rewards true creativity, individuality and relevance.

Ian Doherty
Ireland

Most terrible things in the world happen simply because people don't communicate enough. Parents with kids, wealthy with poor, state with its people, Christians with Muslims… It's true in your family, in politics and in advertising too. That's what ADCE is for – to help people to convey their ideas to other people.

Eriks Stendzenieks
Latvia

President's Statement

You may call it "Art Directors Club of Europe Annual 2006", we call it "The Book of Books".

It took Art Directors Clubs around the world many years of work, but today there is a common understanding not only in the advertising industry: creativity is better for business.

For professional evaluation of most creative ads and design, each country's local Art Directors Clubs are the most trusted authorities. Every year a competition of ads submitted in each country are judged and afterwards published in Annuals. They show only the best of them – the Gold, Silver, Bronze winners - as well as some of the more exceptional works. The Art Directors Club of Europe starts here: this year more than 60 creatives from 16 countries sat down together in Barcelona to judge the award-winning work - and whittled it down to 1 Grand Prix and 18 Gold winners. This Annual contains all the Gold and Silver work from these countries, plus the ADC*E Gold winners.

Too many awards shows are tarnished as self-serving. The ADC*E is the only European awards scheme which you cannot enter, unless you have won Gold, Silver, or a nomination in your respective country. That's why we may call our award "the best of the best".

Thus, the ADC*E has consolidated its position in 2006 as the most respected 'Awards of Awards' show to focus on European creativity. This is reflected by their prestige in the industry and inclusion in the most important industry rankings.

Since the Art Directors Club of Europe was founded in 1991 the advertising world has changed with the world. But it is still ideas that drive us towards our interminable quest for inspiration.

The Art Directors Club of Europe is currently owned and managed by its 16 members – leading creative Clubs/Associations from across Europe. It is the only international Awards scheme to bring all of the European Award-winning work together in one competition. Now, the "Best of European Design and Advertising Awards " is no longer the exclusive domain of ADC*E member countries. Gold and Silver winners from all national premier Awards scheme are now eligible for entry, as ADC*E has opened its doors to more Award winning advertising and design work from Europe to take part in these Awards.

This is why 28 countries have submitted their award-winning work to the competition, which took place in the beautiful city of Barcelona on July 8th, at the seat of ADG-FAD.

I wish to extend my gratitude to wonderful Mercè Segú, ADC*E manager and her staff. Thanks also go to the fantastic members of the Board, who are the heart of our organization.

This year the Jury awarded 18 Gold Stars and a Grand Prix that goes to Poland for an amazing campaign against censorship in Belarus. The 20,000 Euro Miami-Ad School sponsorship goes to the European student of the year, Austrian designer Anna Oberascher (Black-Braille), while the "European Juniors of the year" is Felix Fenz, another Austrian, for a banner design for "Rich, Poor World" a EU-platform of NGOs.

Lastly, I would like to express my appreciation for our jurors from all over Europe for coming to Barcelona and making this award so European. Take a closer look at what work they selected as the best of the best.

JOHANNES NEWRKLA
ADCE President

The Annual of Annuals

Members of ADC*E

AUSTRIA
Creativ Club Austria
Kochgasse 34/16,
A-1080 Wien
T +43 1 408 53 51
F +43 1 408 53 52
office@creativclub.at
www.creativclub.at

CZECH REPUBLIC
Art Directors Club C R
V Jircharich 8
110 00 - Praha 1
Czech Republic
T +420 296 334 850-2
F +420 296 334 853
info@adc-czech.cz
www.adc-czech.cz

FRANCE
Le Club des Directeurs Artistiques
40 Boulevard Malesherbes
F-75008 Paris
T +33 1 47 42 29 12
F +33 1 47 42 59 90
nroland@aacc.fr
www.leclubdesad.org

ICELAND
FIT Association of Icelandic
Graphic Designers
Félag Íslenskra teiknara
P.O. Box 8766
128 Reykjavik
T +354 552 9900
fit@loremipsum.is
www.loremipsum.is

BOSNIA & HERZEGOVINA
Art Directors Club B-H
Velika Avlija 14
BH - 71000 Sarajevo
T +387 33 272 630
F +387 33 272 660
dupanovic@futuramedia.ba
www.media-marketing.ba

ESTONIA
Art Directors Club Eesti
Pärnu mnt. 20A
10141 Tallinn
T +372 6691 950
F +372 6691 951
tiia@korpus.ee

GERMANY
Art Directors Club für
Deutschland
Leibnizstraße 65
D-10629 Berlin
T +49 (0) 30 59 00 310–0
F +49 (0) 30 59 00 310–11
adc@adc.de
www.adc.de

IRELAND
Institute of Creative Advertising
& Design
26 Upper Baggot Street
Dublin 4
T +353 1 6609768
F +353 1 6630026
icadadmin@icad.ie
www.icad.ie

ITALY
Art Directors Club Italiano
Via Moscova 46/3
20121 Milan
T +39 02 655 5943
F +39 02 659 0736
info@adci.it
www.adci.it

POLAND
The Polish Association
of Advertising Agencies (SAR)
ul. Łowicka 25 lok. P4
02 - 502 Warszawa
T +48 22 898 84 25
F +48 22 898 26 23
office@sar.org.pl
www.sar.org.pl

RUSSIA
Art Directors Club of Russia
11, Bolshoi Karetnyi Pereulok
Moscow, 127051
T +7 495 9330500
F +7 495 9330501
mail@adcrussia.ru
www.adcrussia.ru

SPAIN
Art Directors & Graphic Designers
Association / ADG-FAD
Convent dels Àngels
Plaça dels Àngels, 5-6
08001 Barcelona
T +34 93 443 75 20
F +34 93 329 60 79
hola@adg-fad.org
www.adg-fad.org

LATVIA
Latvian Art Directors Club
13 Janvära iela 33,
Riga, LV 1050,
T +371 72 28 21 8
F +371 75 03 61 6
info@adclub.lv
www.adclub.lv

PORTUGAL
Clube de Criativos de Portugal
Rua Carlos Testa 1, 1˚A
1050-046 Lisbon
T +351 21 312 15 65/6
F +351 21 312 15 69
clubedecriativos@apap.co.pt
www.clubecriativos.com

SLOVENIA
Art Directors Club of Slovenia
StudioMarketing JWT
Vojkova 50
1000 Ljubljana
T +386 1 58 968 10
Jernej.Repovs@smjwt.com

SWITZERLAND
Art Directors Club Schweiz
Oberdorfstr. 15
CH-8001 Zürich
T +41 44 262 00 33
F +41 44 262 02 74
info@adc.ch
www.adc.ch

Forum Laus Europe

BEYOND OUR OWN FRONTIERS

During the same week that the ADC*E Awards were held, from July 5th to July 8th the Forum Laus Europe 06 took place. This lively event, organised by the ADC*E and the Spanish association of designers, the ADG-FAD, consisted of a four day gathering and was attended by more than 400 people — mostly graphic designers and art directors from Europe and beyond.

Under the motto of "Frontiers. Freedom calls", the Forum attracted heterogeneous creative minds from a wide range of countries and professions. In accordance with its main objective, the event provided a meeting point for interdisciplinary nomads — for anyone working within various disciplines and redefining the limits of his or her own field.

Forum Laus Europe 06 comprised 12 conferences and 6 workshops. Freelancers, design studios, and teams had the opportunity to learn from each other's works and points of view.

The participants included: Åbäke, Spin, A2/SW/HK, Alexandre Bettler, Oliviero Toscani, Tony Hertz, Red Spider and Wieden&Kennedy. The Forum also included Spanish lecturers such as the philosopher David Casacuberta, geographer Francesc Muñoz, professor Ana Hidalgo, and artist Francesc Ruiz.

The audience was able to share their wealth of experiences, learn innovative approaches, and debate great ideas. It was as eclectic as the group of speakers: senior designers and young designers, students and teachers, art directors and their clients, copywriters and typographers, illustrators and photographers. Regardless of their personal profile, all participants in the Forum were aware of their role in the driving the future of art direction and graphic design.

George Shepherd

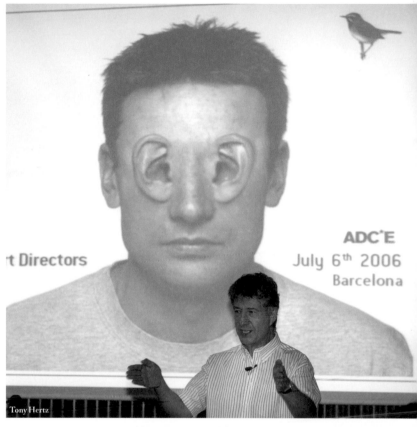
Tony Hertz

From the Chairmen

Today's creative people are increasingly more influenced by experiences of crossing borders and cultures seamlessly.

The ADC*E is the place to celebrate all cross-cultural creative work and the people who craft it.

The 2006 Annual of Annuals encompasses the very best in this brave new thriving cross-cultural creative community.

On behalf of the board and the ADC*E, I extend appreciation and thanks to our committed team of judges from 14 European countries.

So thanks to Karim, Radouane, J. Margus, Kai, Stefan, John, Andrea, Zane, Maciek, Nuno, Kirill, Carlitos, Martin, and Mark, for your contribution, passion and integrity.

At the end of the day what is really important is to feel good about what has been nominated to represent this confrontation between cultural diversities. And, out of the 5 audiovisual categories, for the 29 nominations and the 6 gold medals that made these pages, for my part, I do feel good.

Franco Moretti
Film Jury

Although it was not the first time I have chaired a jury at ADC*E awards, I always feel apprehensive when I am faced with the responsibility of such a task. Not that any of my previous experiences were bad — on the contrary. But that feeling of apprehension only lasts until I meet the members of the jury in person. Once again I was lucky to share a day's work with responsible, competent, and humorous professionals, all focused on the tough task of judging pre-judged pieces of work. The different and sometimes opposing opinions about the submissions generated lively debate, but we managed to reach a consensus on all the issues that arose. Different opinions from different backgrounds, different experiences, different references, and different cultures worked together to achieve one goal: to elect the best of the best. It was a pleasure!

Mário Mandacaru
Advertising Print Jury

This must have been one of the most fascinating juries I have worked on. Not only was the work a snapshot of the very best of what is happening in these disciplines across Europe, but also in many cases, it is where the real innovation in communications is taking place. A true touch point where creativity pushes the boundaries of technology.

I must thank all the judges who worked so hard in debating the merits of each and every piece of work, a job made all the harder by the incredibly high standard of the entries.

There was some truly outstanding work, which I believe is highlighted by the fact that this year's Grand Prix winner came from this section.

Ian Doherty
New / Mixed Media Jury

The jury met in Barcelona on a very hot Saturday.

Twelve judges from all over Europe, and our special guest from the UK, got involved straight away in sifting through all the entries, considering each piece carefully.

There were many innovative and complex ideas that took the jury a long time to go through. Finally we narrowed them down to a shortlist. By early afternoon the works were nominated. The judging process got a little rough at one point, but after a heated and stimulating debate we settled on three gold awards.

Graphic Design had a huge number of entries. Curiously, the jury settled easily for the gold award: a magnificent piece that links contemporary work with the best in graphic design tradition.

Corporate Identity was a clear winner, and beautifully crafted.

Packaging was finally awarded, after a close tie, to a very much needed modern version of a butane gas cylinder.

Finally allow me to praise all the creatives who entered the ADC*E Awards: aiming to score in the European league of awards is no small feat.

Helena Rosa-Trias
Design Jury

Film

Advertising Print

New/Mixed
Media

Design

Film Jury

Chairman
FRANCO MORETTI
Chief Creative Officer, Leo Burnett
Italy

MARTIN SPILLMANN,
Executive Creative Director,
Spillmann/Felser/Leo Burnett
Switzerland

ZANE BĒRZINA
ADC Latvia
Latvia

ANDREA CONCATO
Creative Director, Andrea Concato Ag.
Italy

KAI RÖFFEN
Executive Creative Director, TBWA
Germany

KARIN KAMMLANDER
Creative Director, Freelance
Austria

J. MARGUS KLAAR
Managing Director, Indigo Bates
Estonia

KIRILL SMIRNOV
Executive Director, ADCR
Russia

NUNO JERÓNIMO
Creative Director, BBDO
Portugal

MARK TUTSSEL
Deputy Chief Creative Officer,
Leo Burnett Worldwide
United Kingdom

RADOUANE HADJ MOUSSA
Art Director, McCann-Erickson
Czech Republic

CARLITOS
Creative Director, SCPF
Spain

JOHN FLYNN
Creative Director, Leo Burnett
Ireland

STEFAN EINARSSON
Creative Director, The White House
Iceland

MACIEK KOWALCZUK
TV ads Director
Poland

Advertising Print Jury

Chairman
MÁRIO MANDACARU
Design Director. Brand Design
Brandia Central
Portugal

PIUS WALKER
Creative Director, Walker Werbeagentur
Switzerland

RONAN NULTY
Senior Copywriter, QMP Publicis
Ireland

JAN KONSTANTY PRZYBORA
President, PZL
Poland

MICHELE MARIANI
Creative Director, Armando Testa Spa
Italy

DAN MIKKIN
Art Director, McCann-Erickson
Estonia

HAUKUR MÁR HAUKSSON
Art Director, Mixa Advertising
Iceland

ALEXANDER ZELMANOVICS
Lowe GGK
Austria

JOAO ROQUE
Art Director, Leo Burnett
Portugal

MICHAEL PREISWERK
Managing Partner, GPP
Germany

MARTIN PASECKY
Art Director, Leo Burnett
Czech Republic

New/Mixed Media Jury

Chairman
IAN DOHERTY
Managing Partner, Bonfire
Ireland

ALEXANDER ALEXEEV
Executive Creative Director, McCann-Erickson
Russia

MIRO MINAROVYCH
Art Director, Kaspen
Czech Republic

MARK STAHEL
Creative Director, Stahelpartner W. Ag.
Switzerland

MARC WIRBELEIT
Executive Creative Director, Tequila
Germany

....

ANDRIS RUBINS
DDB
Latvia

VICKY GITTO
Group Executive Creative Director, DDB
Italy

PEDRO NEVES
Proximity
Portugal

GRETA GUDMUNDSDOTTIR
Art Director, Fabrikan Adv.
Iceland

HENDRIK ALLA
Copywriter, Korpus
Estonia

....

NICK MERRIGAN
Senior Designer, New Media
Ireland

EDUARD BÖHLER
Creative Director, Wien Nord Pilz
Austria

MAREK PIOTROWSKI
CEO & Partner, FFCreation.com
Poland

Design Jury

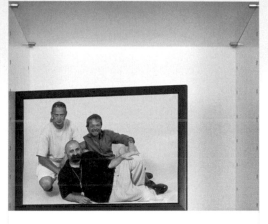

Chairman
HELENA ROSA-TRIAS
Art & Design Director,
Book division/Grupo Planeta
Spain

JAANUS TAMME
Art Director, Tank
Estonia

MICHAEL FANTACCI
Creative Director, Model T
Italy

WOJCIECH MIEROWSKI
Creative Director, Brand Nature Access Sp.
Poland

....

DAVID HANOUSEK
Creativ Director, Masina
Czech Republic

ANDREAS PUTZ
Creative Director, Jung Von Matt/Donau
Austria

JOCHEN RÄDEKER
Managing Partner, Strichpunkt
Germany

RUI SAMPAIO DE FARIA
Ind. Design, Team Dir., Brandiacentral
Portugal

LAURA MESSEGUER
Graphic Design & Typography,
Spain

LUKE GIFFORD
Senior Graphic Designer, Wolff Olins
UK

HALLA GUDRUN
Art Director, Mixa
Iceland

....

LUKAS FREI
Art Director, Jung von Matt/Limmat
Switzerland

CORA CRISHAM
Senior Designer, Design Works
Ireland

SANDIJS LUSENS
Euro RSCG
Latvia

Grand
Prix

★ GP
Freedom of speech *Poland*

●

National Award....Bronze	*Copywriter*.........Jakub Korolczuk,
Agency................Saatchi & Saatchi	Ryszard Sroka
Poland	*Photographer*.......Andrzej Georgiew
Client................Amnesty International	
Creative Director...Jacek Szulecki	
Art Director........Ryszard Sroka,	
Jakub Korolczuk	

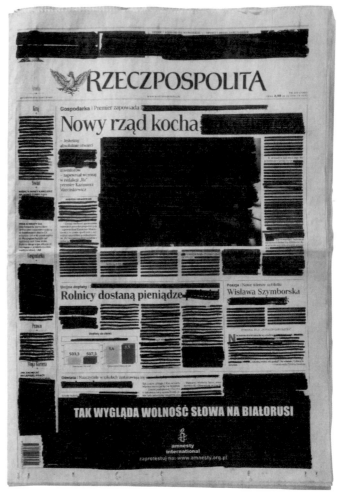

The Brief
The brief was to encourage people to support Amnesty International to fight for freedom of speech in Belorus.

The Solution
Europe's 6th largest newspaper and the largest Polish daily, Gazeta Wyborcza, were censored along with the most popular Polish website (www.gazeta.pl). Silver tape, the type usually used for gagging, was attached to 15,000 posters representing the Belorussian opposition activists.

The result
With the combined circulation of Poland's two largest newspapers, the event touched a captive audience of over 700,000 readers. There were over 300,000 visits to the www.amnesty.org.pl website and over 100,000 protests emailed to president Lukashenko within one day.

01
Film

01.1
TV COMMERCIALS

Italy: 1 gold ★ 2 nominations ☆
Austria: 1 nomination ☆
Czech Republic: 1 nomination ☆
Germany: 4 nominations ☆
Poland: 1 nomination ☆
Switzerland: 1 nomination ☆
United Kingdom: 2 nominations ☆

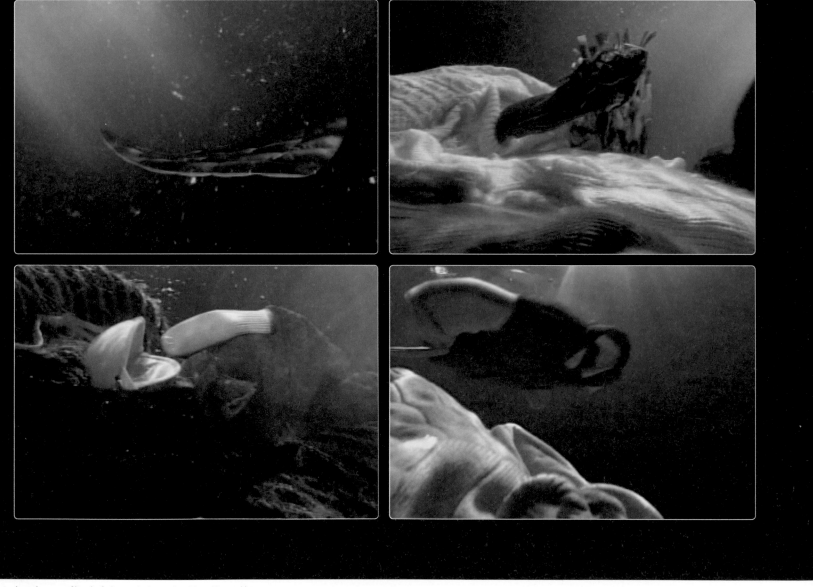

An entire ocean of laundry finds space in the new Aqualtis washing machine.

★

Underwater World *Italy*

●

National Award	Gold	*Film Director*	Dario Piana
Agency	Leo Burnett Italy (Milan)	*Production Comp*	Filmmaster
Client	Indesit Company		
Creative Director	Enrico Dorizza		
Art Director	Antonio Cortesi		
Copywriter	Francesco Simonetti		

Big inside.

AQUALTIS

Two men are zig-zagging down a street in a car. Only when a fly smashes against the windshield does the audience realize the men are dodging flies.

☆
Let's Mini - Zig Zag *Italy*   ●

National Award	Bronze	*Copywriter*	Nicola Lampugnani, Lorenzo Crespi
Agency	D'Adda, Lorenzini, Vigorelli, BBDO	*Film Director*	John Dolan
Client	Mini	*Dir. of Photography*	Tobias Schissler
Creative Director	Giuseppe Mastromatteo, Luca Scotto di Carlo	*Agency Producer*	Isabella Guazzone
		Production Comp.	The Family
Art Director	Anselmo Tumpic, Pier Giuseppe Gonni	*Postproduction*	You Are

The safest cars are French.

RENAULT

CRÉATEUR D'AUTOMOBILES

To demonstrate Renault's success at the Euro NCAP, this commercial shows how different car brands, represented by various types of food, performed in the crash test.

☆
Crashtest *Germany*   ●

National Award	Gold	*Designer* .... C. Bielefeldt,
Agency	Nordpol Hamburg	P. Dörner,
Client	Renault Germany	B. Kirschenhofer
Creative Director	Lars Rühmann	*Film Director* ...... Silvio Helbig
Art Director	Gunther Schreiber	*Dir. of Photography* Silvio Helbig
Copywriter	Ingmar Bartels	*Production Comp.* Element e
		Dir. Marketing ..... Jörg Ellhof

Relax. It's the new Polo.

☆

Black Cat *Germany*

●

National Award	Shortlist	*Copywriter*	Ludwig Berndl
Agency	DDB Germany/ Berlin	*Film Director*	Sebastian Strasser
Client	Volkswagen AG	*Dir. of Photography*	Julian Hohndorf
Creative Director	Amir Kassaei,	*Agency Producer*	Marion Lange
	Wolfgang Schneider,	*Production Comp.*	@radical.media
	Mathias Stiller		GmbH, Berlin
Art Director	Kristoffer Heilemann	*Producer*	Christiane Lochte
		Editor	Nils Landmark

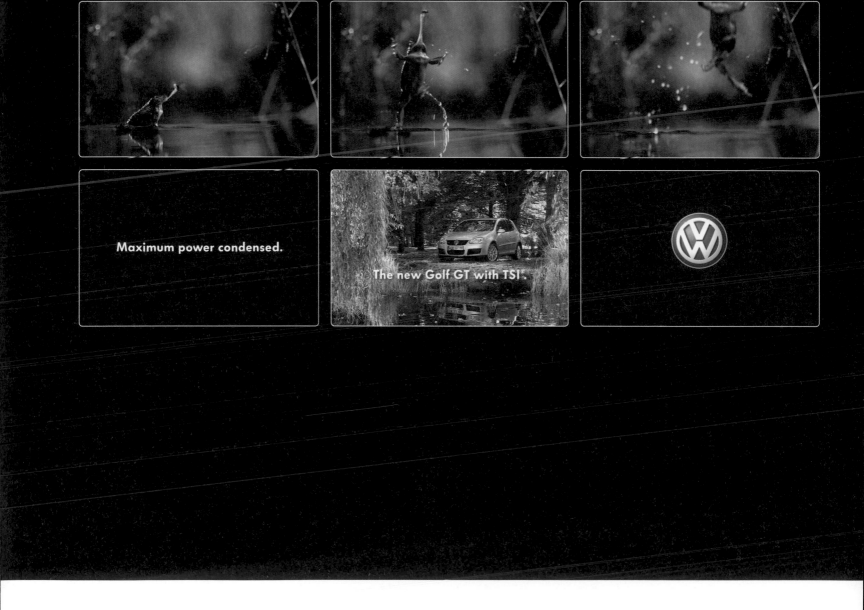

Maximum power condensed.

The new Golf GT with TSI.

☆
Fly *Germany*   ●

National Award	Bronze	*Copywriter*	Ludwig Berndl
Agency	DDB Germany/ Berlin	*Film Director*	Henry Littlechild
Client	Volkswagen AG	*Dir. of Photography*	David Luther
Creative Director	Amir Kassaei, Wolfgang Schneider, Mathias Stiller	*Agency Producer*	Marion Lange
		Production Comp.	Markenfilm GmbH & Co KG, Hamburg
Art Director	Kristoffer Heilemann	*Producer*	Simona Daniel, Nele Schilling

NOTHING'S FASTER.

DHL is the fastest courier service in the world.

☆
Hummingbird *Germany*   ●

National Award	Silver	
Agency	Jung von Matt AG	
Client	DPWN	
Creative Director	Oliver Handlos, Michael Pfeiffer-Belli	

Film Director	Nicolai Niemann
Agency Producer	Nadja Catana
Production Comp.	Entspannt Film
Audio production	Studio Funk Berlin

Italian houses can talk to each other like never before, thanks to Telecomony's promotion. In the film, houses sing the famous Rigoletto opera tune "La figlia dell'amore" by G. Verdi.

☆
Home to Home *Italy*   ⬤

National Award	Bronze	*Copywriter*	Andrea Rosagni
Agency	Leo Burnett Italia	*Film Director*	Matteo Pellegrini
Client	Telecom Italia	*Dir. of Photography*	Manfredo Archinto
Creative Director	Enrico Dorizza, Sergio Rodríguez	*Agency Producer*	Antonello Filosa
		Production Comp.	The Family
Art Director	Corrado Cardoni	*Postproduction*	You Are

The National Geographic Channel is more than entertainment, it engages viewers intellectually. The brief was to devise a spot that would engage, entertain, and stimulate the audience. The strap-line was "Think again."

☆
Manhattan *United Kingdom* ●

National Award	Silver	*Film Director*	Brendan Gibbons
Agency	Devilfish	*Dir. of Photography*	Barry Markowits
Client	National Geographic Channel	*Agency Producer*	Anna Grund
		Production Comp.	Hungry Man
Creative Director	Richard Holman		
Copywriter	Barry Kimber, Andy Poyiadgi, Claire Lambert		

The National Geographic Channel is more than entertainment, it engages viewers intellectually. The brief was to devise a spot that would engage, entertain, and stimulate the audience. The strap-line was "Think again."

Words *United Kingdom*

National Award	Bronze	*Designer*	Samuel Christopher
Agency	Devilfish	*Film Director*	Samuel Christopher
Client	National Geographic Channel	*Agency Producer*	Anna Grund
		Production Comp.	Devilfish
Creative Director	Richard Holman	*Sound Design*	750mph
Copywriter	Alan & Sandy Cinnamond		

FIAT

Najwyższy czas na twój własny samochód

Sharing a car with your parents can lead to inconvenient and embarrassing situations. This ad encourages young people to think about buying a Fiat Panda, the car that can solve their problems.

☆

Feet *Poland*   ●

National Award	Silver	*Film Director*	Nice and Sune
Agency	Leo Burnett	*Production Comp.*	Opus Film
Client	Fiat Auto Poland	*Editing*	Chimney Pot Jarek
Creative Director	Martin Winther		Kaminski
Art Director	Leszek Ziniewicz		
Copywriter	Lukasz Witkiewicz		

Der neue Audi RS4 mit 420 PS.
Von 0 - 100 in 4,8 Sekunden.

Vorsprung durch Technik

A man gently opens his dustbin, afraid of pushing the pedal too hard. He knows the same feeling from his powerful Audi RS4.

☆

Audi Pedal *Austria*   ●

National Award	Bronze	*Copywriter*	Karlheinz Wasserbacher
Agency	Saatchi & Saatchi Vienna	*Film Director*	George Moringer
		Dir. of Photography	Michi Kaufmann
Client	Porsche Austria	*Agency Producer*	Daniela Rager
Creative Director	Hubert Goldnagl	*Production Comp.*	Jerk Films
Art Director	Marcus Hartmann		

NICHTS IST SICHER.

NATIONAL VERSICHERUNG

Accidents can always happen, even in the most perfect of worlds - in advertising. To underline this we changed well-known ads.

☆
Cliff *Switzerland*

National Award	Shortlist	*Film Director*	Marcel Langenegger
Agency	Spillmann/Felser/ Leo Burnett	*Agency Producer*	Sebahat Derdiyok
Client	National Versicherung	*Production Comp.*	Chocolate Films
Creative Director	Martin Spillmann	*Producer*	Michela Trümpi
Art Director	Dana Wirz		
Copywriter	Stefan Ehrler		

We all need some care

Everyone needs some care. Women care a great deal about their face, but often neglect their hands. How unfair.

☆

Hands *Czech Republic*   ●

National Award	Silver		*Copywriter*	Pavel Sobek,
Agency	Mark BBDO			Leon Sverdlin
Client	Zentiva		*Film Director*	Jaromir Maly
Creative Director	Leon Sverdlin,		*Dir. of Photography*	Martin Douba
	Martin Charvat		*Agency Producer*	Lenka Da Costa
Art Director	Tereza Zitkova		*Production Comp.*	Filmservice Productions

Tough guys do their dirty deeds and talk their dirty talk. They do all this in diminutive form because with Heyah, everything is very, very little—especially the prices.

Diminuitions *Poland* ⦿

National Award	Gold	*Copywriter*	Tomasz Kapuscinski
Agency	G7	*Film Director*	Tomasz Kapuscinski
Client	PTC Heyah	*Dir. of Photography*	Bartek Kaczmarek
Creative Director	Dariusz Rzontkowski	*Production Comp.*	ITI
Art Director	Karolina Lewicka		

First intelligent email: Centrum.cz.

Keyboard: This shows a dialogue between a decorator and salesman in a mobile phone outlet. The decorator becomes irritated with the salesman's sophisticated language and smashes the salesman's keyboard with his paintbrushes. But the word he accidentally writes on the screen leaves both men totally awestruck.

Centrum.cz - Blondes *Czech Republic* ⬤

National Award....Silver
Agency..............Leo Burnett
                     Advertising, spol. s.r.o.
Client..............NetCentrum
Creative Director...Jiri Pleskot
Art Director........Martin Pasecky
Copywriter.........Jiri Pleskot

Film Director......Jan Kalvoda
*Dir. of Photography*Tomas Sysel
Agency Producer...Lubo Prochazka
Production Comp...Stillking Films
Account Team......Jiri Tosovsky,
                     Andrea Vavrova

Keyboard, Car wash, Knitwear, Billboard *Poland* ⬤

National Award....Silver
Agency..............PZL Warsaw
                     (Leo Burnett Group)
Client..............Polkomtel S.A.
Creative Director...Iwo Zaniewski,
                     Kot Przybora
Art Director........Iwo Zaniewski

Copywriter.........Iwo Zaniewski,
                     M.Goll, D.Basinski,
                     J.Borusinski
Film Director......Iwo Zaniewski
Production Comp...Easy Hell

OVIP LOKOS means war against TV propaganda.

An ad created by Publicis for the nationwide supermarket chain.

Gold'n'Trash *Russia*   ●

National Award	Gold	*Copywriter*	Valentine Vlassov
Agency	Mother's Tongue	*Film Director*	Ilya Hotinenko
Client	Efes Moscow Brewery	*Production Comp.*	Fibr-Film
Creative Director	Ilya Olenev	*Cameraman*	Jonathan Bloom
Art Director	Julia Chernisheva		

Leniwe *Poland*   ●

National Award	Gold	*Film Director*	Sebastian Panczyk
Agency	Publicis Sp. z o.o.	*Dir. of Photography*	Marek Sanak
Client	JMD	*Agency Producer*	Publicis Sp. z o.o.
Creative Director	Michal Nowosielski	*Production Comp.*	OTO
Art Director	Danuta Nierada	*Editing*	Platige Image
Copywriter	Kasia Kowalska		

Cobbler Twine: Dratewka is a cunning Polish shoemaker who defeated a Cracow dragon by giving him a lamb stuffed with sulphur. The thirsty dragon drank water from the river and burst. This is the original version of a fairy tale. Heyah's version is a little different simply because Heyah does not know how to tell fairy tales.

Little Red Ridinghood: In a cruel sea of mobile telecoms, Heyah is something of a virgin island. No promotions, no time offers, no behind-the-curtains costs. Heyah is unable to tell a lie. In other words, Heyah cannot tell a fairy tale.

Cobbler Twine, Little Red Ridinghood *Poland* ●

National Award	Silver	*Copywriter*	Tomasz Kapuscinski
Agency	G7	*Film Director*	Sebastian Panczyk
Client	PTC Heyah	*Agency Producer*	G7
Creative Director	Dariusz Rzontkowski	*Production Comp.*	Opus Film
Art Director	Karolina Lewicka	*Music*	Piotr Skorupa

Sokol Izolda *Russia* ●

National Award	Silver	*Copywriter*	Alexander Salangin
Agency	Mother's Tongue	*Film Director*	Alex Rozenberg
Client	Efes Moscow Brewery	*Production Comp.*	Park Production
Creative Director	Ilya Olenev	*Cameraman*	Vlad Opelyants
Art Director	Dmitry Lunev		

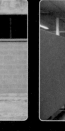

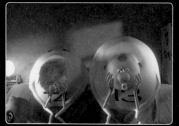

"The Kid Lotto" is the translation for "Loterìa del Niño". This is the 2nd most popular Spanish lotto from the National Lottery. Its name is due to the fact that it takes place on January 6th, Epiphany, when the Three Wise Men visited the Baby Jesus to.

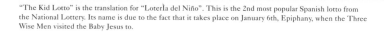

Swiss Lotto *Switzerland* ⦿

National Award	Gold
Agency	RiveGauche TBWA
Client	Loterie Romande (Swiss Lotto)
Creative Director	Alphonse Garcia
Film Director	Pierre Coffin
Production Comp.	Le Studio, Thierry Bourdeille

Office *Spain* ⦿

National Award	Gold
Agency	Vitruvio Leo Burnett
Client	National Lottery
Creative Director	Rafa Antón, Fernando Martín, Javier Álvarez
Art Director	Laura Buencuerpo
Copywriter	Laura Buencuerpo
Film Director	Pep Bosch
Agency Producer	Dionisio Naranjo, Guzmán Molín Pradel
Production Comp.	Lee Films, Missing Sparky

The intentionally low-tech launch campaign of the discount mobile phone operator: As good as self-made.

Can Manuel, a male home help hired for spreading butter on sandwiches, be useful for any other activities?

Discount Operator Diil in Action *Estonia* ●

National Award	Silver	*Copywriter*	Leslie Laasner, Alvar Jaakson, Promoline
Agency	Division McCann-Erickson	*Film Director*	Alvar Jaakson
Client	Diil	*Dir. of Photography*	Alvar Jaakson
Creative Director	Leslie Laasner, Alvar Jaakson, Promoline	*Agency Producer*	Katri Gailit
Art Director	Leslie Laasner, Alvar Jaakson	*Production Comp.*	Division McCann-Erickson

Curtains *Poland* ●

National Award	Silver	*Art Director*	Iwo Zaniewski
Agency	PZL Warsaw (Leo Burnett Group)	*Copywriter*	Iwo Zaniewski
Client	ZT Kruszwica S.A.	*Film Director*	Iwo Zaniewski
Creative Director	Iwo Zaniewski, Kot Przybora	*Dir. of Photography*	Witold Sobocinski
		Production Comp.	Graffiti

The idea of the TVC - to inform customers that on the opening day they will receive presents for their purchases

Presents *Russia* ●

National Award	Silver	*Copywriter*	Alexey Meshkov
Agency	Instinct	*Film Director*	Tom Geens
Client	Merlion Marketing Tecnologi	*Production Comp.*	Bazelevs Production
Creative Director	Roman Firainer , Yaroslav Orlov	*Cameraman*	Ilya Ovsenev
Art Director	Victor Emelyanov		

Suva bfu Horror *Switzerland* ●

National Award	Silver	*Copywriter*	Markus Ruf, Patrick Suter
Agency	Ruf Lanz Werbeagentur AG	*Designer*	Dani Bittel
Client	Suva Accident Insurance	*Film Director*	Martin A. Fueter
Creative Director	Danielle Lanz, Markus Ruf	*Production Comp.*	Condor Films
Art Director	Danielle Lanz	*Sound*	Space Train, Dave Kohler, Dean Montenegro

Euskaltel wanted to inform customers of a big opportunity. This campaign marked the start of a new Euskaltel venture involving the socialization of digital TV.

The commercials devoted to the new IKEA store opening. We show how the two existing IKEA stores are jealousy over of the new one. They don't want people to know that new the IKEA store is opening or has already opened.

Battle, Final *Spain* ⦿

National Award	Silver	*Copywriter*	Santi Hernández, Javi Sánchez
Agency	Dimension	*Film Director*	Marco Aguilar
Client	Euskaltel	*Agency Producer*	Laura Aristeguieta
Creative Director	Guille Viglione, Santi Hernández	*Production Comp.*	The Family
Art Director	Iñaki Huegun		

New IKEA store (Belaya Dacha) opening *Russia* ⦿

National Award	Gold	*Copywriter*	Nina Mashinskaya
Agency	Instinct	*Film Director*	Gleb Orlov
Client	IKEA	*Production Comp.*	Okey-Dokey Production
Creative Director	Ludmila Bausheva	*Cameraman*	Marat Adelshin
Art Director	Andrey Lukiyanov		

With a mix of curiosity and anxiety, a young man follows his presumed double around the city.
Only at a parking lot is their difference revealed: The double doesn't have a Series 1.

Scary gas prices *Austria* ⊙

National Award	Gold	*Copywriter*	Alexander Lauber, Thomas Troppmann
Agency	JWT Vienna	*Film Director*	Kai Sehr
Client	Austrian Railway Federation Passanger Transport	*Production Comp.*	TALE Filmproduktion
Creative Director	Alexander Lauber, Markus Zauner	*Camera*	Marco Zwitter
Art Director	Markus Zauner, James Teal	*Edit*	Cordula Werner

Doppelganger - Man *Italy* ⊙

National Award	Silver	*Film Director*	Giuseppe Capotondi
Agency	D'Adda, Lorenzini, Vigorelli, BBDO	*Dir. of Photography*	Simon Chadoir
Client	BMW Italia	*Agency Producer*	Francesca Nussio
Creative Director	Gianpietro Vigorelli	*Production Comp.*	Mercurio Cinematografica
Art Director	Gianpietro Vigorelli	*Post Production*	You Are\Green Movie (audio)
Copywriter	Luca Scotto di Carlo		

Why wait for such a long time?

People with Stendhal's syndrome suffer from anxiety attacks when they are confronted with an excess of beauty and perfection. This is what happens to those who get in an Audi A8.

Mercedes Benz C- and E-Class *Austria* ◉

National Award	Silver	*Art Director*	Simon Schwaighofer, Hakim Berbour
Agency	Springer & Jacoby Austria	*Copywriter*	Farbrice Basil, Gilbert Konrad
Client	Mercedes Benz Österreich	*Film Director*	Sebastian Strasser
Creative Director	Paul Holcmann, Franck Rey, Alexander Schill	*Dir. of Photography*	Peter Meyer
		Production Comp.	Cobblestone (Hamburg) Close Up (Vienna)

Stendhal *Spain* ◉

National Award	Silver	*Art Director*	Jaume Badia
Agency	DDB España	*Copywriter*	Alfredo Binefa
Client	V.A.E.S.A	*Film Director*	Nacho Gayán
Creative Director	Alberto Astorga, Turi Tollesson, Mireia Roda	*Agency Producer*	Vicky Moñino
		Production Comp.	Pirámide

If you decide to go to a real estate agency to tour a house, be careful of the scale models—they can conceal big surprises.

Scale model *Spain* ●

National Award	Silver	*Art Director*	Quito Leal
Agency	DDB España	*Copywriter*	Oscar Vidal-Larsson
Client	V.A.E.S.A	*Film Director*	Pep Bosch
Creative Director	Josep Maria Roca de Vinyals	*Agency Producer*	Vicky Moñino
		Production Comp.	Missing Sparky

Ham *Austria* ●

National Award	Silver	*Copywriter*	Helena Giokas, Alexander Rabl
Agency	Jung von Matt/Donau		
Client	Bank Austria Creditanstalt	*Film Director*	Christian Aeby
Creative Director	Andreas Putz, Gerd Schulte-Doeinghaus	*Production Comp.*	Glassfilm Hamburg
Art Director	Christian Hummer-Koppendorfer		

Grandma bores her grandson with endless talk. But don't worry—clients are not charged anything after the 10th minute.

Grandma's Advice *Estonia* ●

National Award	Gold
Agency	Division McCann-Erickson
Client	Elion
Creative Director	Tınu Sikk
Art Director	Tınu Sikk
Copywriter	Tınu Sikk, Veiko Õunpuu
Film Director	Veiko Õunpuu
Agency Producer	Klarika Lepamets
Production Comp.	Kuukulgur

AMIGO X-mas *Latvia* ●

National Award	Silver
Agency	TBWA/Latvija
Client	ZetCom
Creative Director	Martins Kibilds
Art Director	Mareks Hofmanis
Copywriter	Zane Asare
Film Director	Edmunds Jansons
Production Comp.	Style Master Studio

New scooters for a new prize!!!!

The goal of this advertisement was to make the population aware of the need to separate organic waste in order to convert it into reusable resources.

Kentoya *Czech Republic* ●

National Award	Gold	*Copywriter*	Petr Stancik, Adam Svatos
Agency	Young and Rubicam Prague	*Film Director*	Premysl Ponahly, Hynek Bernard
Client	Kentoya	*Agency Producer*	GPS Production
Creative Director	Frantisek Bumbalek, Miroslav Pomikal		
Art Director	Premysl Ponahly, Hynek Bernard		

Apple *Spain* ●

National Award	Silver	*Art Director*	Fernando Planelles
Agency	SMÄLL	*Copywriter*	Xavier Hidalgo
Client	Generalitat de Catalunya	*Film Director*	Ramsès Albiñana
Creative Director	Xavier Hidalgo, Fernando Planelles	*Production Comp*	Albiñana Films

People who mull over cheap prices when they look at their own Do It Yourself (DIY) project just don't under-stand what DIY is all about. The tiled pool created with elbow grease is brimming with the passion of DIYers.

A circus family has to face several unforeseen and incredible events. But they are not anxious: The Reale Mutua agent is always with them to suggest the best way to prevent problems.

Heartbeats *Germany*   ●

National Award	Gold	*Copywriter*	Till Eckel, Guido Heffels, Carl Erik Rinsch
Agency	Heimat, Berlin		
Client	Hornbach Baumarkt AG	*Designer*	Eva Bajer
		Film Director	Carl Erik Rinsch (RSA)
Creative Director	Guido Heffels, Jürgen Vossen	*Agency Producer*	Kerstin Breuer
Art Director	Tim Schneider, Carl Erik Rinsch	*Production Comp.*	Markenfilm, Berlin

Circus *Italy*   ●

National Award	Silver	*Art Director*	Daniele Ricci
Agency	Saffirio Tortelli Vigoriti	*Copywriter*	Michela Grasso
Client	Reale Mutua Assicurazioni	*Film Director*	Carl Erik Rinsch
		Dir. of Photography	Philippe Le Sourde
Creative Director	Aurelio Tortelli	*Production Comp.*	The Family

It takes the happiest cows to make Kerrymaid.

It is a good idea to produce chocolate in a triangular shape. After all, it made Toblerone a world-famous brand. This is why the form of the triangle is the focus of the campaign.

Pampered Cows *Ireland* ●

National Award	Silver	*Copywriter*	Ted Barry
Agency	Chemistry	*Film Director*	Des Mullan
Client	Kerry Foods	*Dir. of Photography*	Gerry Floyd
Creative Director	Mike Garner	*Agency Producer*	Fiona McGarry
Art Director	Adrian Fitz-Simon, Mike Garner	*Production Comp.*	Rocket Productions

Toblerone *Austria* ●

National Award	Silver	*Copywriter*	Werner Buehringer
Agency	Ogilvy & Mather Austria	*Film Director*	Mr. J.
Client	Kraft Foods Austria	*Production Comp.*	PPM Filmproductions, MG Sound
Creative Director	Alexander Zelmanovics, Mag. Dieter Pivrnec		
Art Director	Hannes Boeker		

A B-Movie producer turns down some of the biggest grossing movies over four decades, he just can't see the big picture. He tells the young scriptwriter that this movie is never getting made , but where there's a will...

The people famous for the black stuff give the people of Ireland a Christmas present of a white Christmas.

The Producer *Ireland*   ●

National Award	Silver	*Copywriter*	Mark Tuthill
Agency	McCann Erickson Advertising	*Film Director*	John O'Driscoll
		Dir. of Photography	James Mather
Client	Heineken Ireland	*Agency Producer*	Genie Dorman
Creative Director	Shay Madden	*Production Comp.*	Toytown Films
Art Director	Michael Walsh		

Christmas Card *Ireland*   ●

National Award	Gold	*Copywriter*	Mark Nutley
Agency	Irish International BBDO	*Film Director*	Stuart Douglas
		Dir. of Photography	Tony Brown
Client	Diageo	*Agency Producer*	Margo Tracey
Creative Director	Mal Stevenson	*Production Comp.*	Nice Shirt
Art Director	Pat Hamill		

This commercial was created to add force to the tagline of Postimees, Estonia's most important newspaper.

Our first home is really small. And our last - even smaller. And maybe that's why we all long for space.

Fire *Estonia*   ●

National Award	Silver	*Art Director*	Marko Kekishev
Agency	Zavod BBDO	*Copywriter*	Marek Reinaas
Client	Postimees	*Film Director*	Kaido Veermäe
Creative Director	Marek Reinaas	*Production Comp.*	Rudolf Konimois Film

Vestabalt *Latvia*   ●

National Award	Silver	*Copywriter*	Zoom!
Agency	Zoom!	*Designer*	Zoom!
Client	Vestabalt	*Film Director*	Eriks Stendzenieks
Creative Director	Zoom!	*Production Comp.*	Arkogints
Art Director	Zoom!		

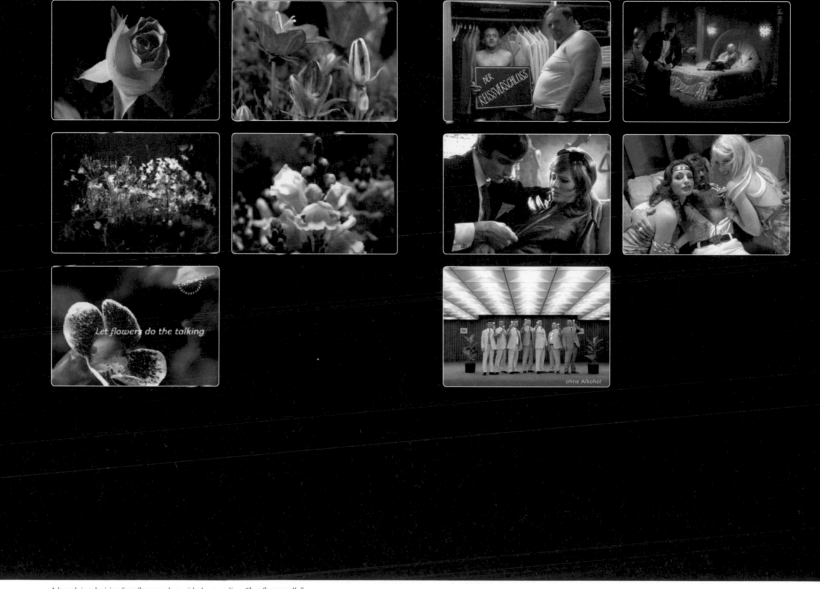

A launch in television for a flower e-shop with the strap-line: "Let flowers talk."

Euflorie *Czech Republic* ●

National Award	Silver
Agency	Cayenne communications s.r.o.
Client	Euflorie
Creative Director	Lester Tullet, Klemens Schuettken
Art Director	Lester Tullet
Copywriter	Klemens Schuettken
Film Director	Klemens Schuettken, Lester Tullet
Agency Producer	Radka Dolezalova
Production Comp.	Cobblestone Hamburg

Zipper *Switzerland* ●

National Award	Silver
Agency	Spillmann/Felser/ Leo Burnett
Client	Feldschlösschen Getränke AG
Creative Director	Martin Spillmann, Peter Brönnimann
Art Director	Patrik Rohner
Copywriter	Peter Brönnimann, Martin Spillmann
Film Director	Michael Fueter
Agency Producer	Sebahat Derdiyok
Production Comp.	Condor Films
Producer	Martin Fueter, Michèle Seligmann

Johnny 11 Fingers, a genius piano player with a 10% natural bonus, is a character that was created for the campaign of the mobile operator Heyah. With every reload in Heyah, customers were given 10% extra. Johnny 11 Fingers shows that as little as it might seem, 10% more can change your life.

The goal of the ad was to prove that Moskovskaya is a very special vodka. So special that it makes "special" people from circles of power forget their special routine and become normal again ... while the others are waiting.

Johnny 11 Fingers *Poland* ●

National Award	Gold	*Film Director*	Tomasz Kapuscinski
Agency	G7	*Dir. of Photography*	Marek Sanek
Client	PTC Heyah	*Agency Producer*	G7
Creative Director	Dariusz Rzontkowski	*Production Comp.*	ITI
Art Director	Karolina Lewicka	*Music*	Michal Urbaniak
Copywriter	Tomasz Kapuscinski		

Plane *Latvia* ●

National Award	Gold	*Copywriter*	Janis Jonevs
Agency	McCann-Erickson Riga	*Film Director*	Janis Kalejs
Client	Latvijas Balzams	*Dir. of Photography*	Gints Berzins
Creative Director	Armands Leitis	*Production Comp.*	Angel Studio
Art Director	Reinis Petersons, Janis Jurkans		

The ad helped to reposition the beer brand from a prestigious and lifestyle attribute to Latvian and traditional one. We see simple people - Latvians. Aldaris beer for them is a benchmark for testing different things in life.

Son *Latvia* ●

National Award	Gold	*Art Director*	Armands Leitis
Agency	McCann-Erickson Riga	*Copywriter*	Armands Leitis, Ainars Scipcinskis
Client	Aldaris	*Film Director*	Viktors Vilks
Creative Director	Armands Leitis, Ainars Scipcinskis	*Dir. of Photography*	Gints Berzins
		Production Comp.	Vilks Studio

01.2
CINEMA COMMERCIALS

Spain: 1 gold ★ 1 nomination☆
Germany: 3 nominations ☆

The organization celebrated the 30th anniversary of Jaws, a film that was translated as "Shark" in Spain. The agency created a 60 second spot, which aired on Catalonia's television channels and at movie theatres.

★

Jaws *Spain*   ●

National Award	Gold	*Copywriter*	Juan Carlos Martínez
Agency	Vitruvio Leo Burnett S.A. (Madrid)	*Film Director*	Igor Fioravanti
Client	Sitges Sci-Fi & Fantasy Film Festival	*Agency Producer*	Dionisio Naranjo, Guzmán Molin-Pradel
Creative Director	Fernando Martín	*Production Comp.*	Wind
Art Director	Anne		

30th ANNIVERSARY OF JAWS
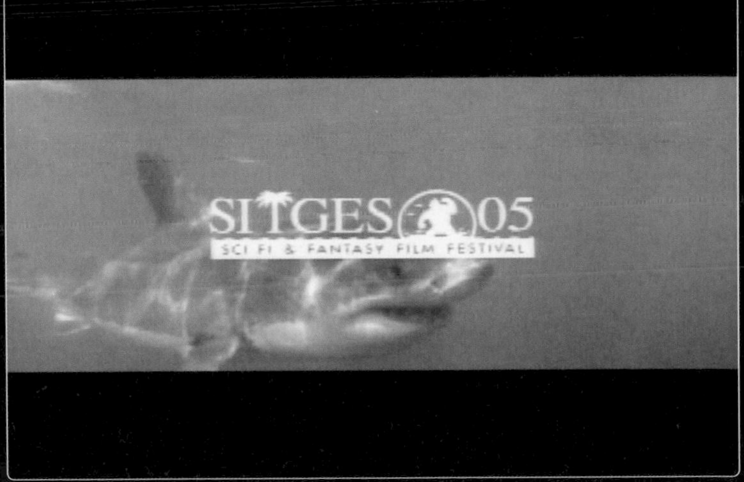
SITGES 05
SCI FI & FANTASY FILM FESTIVAL

The safest cars are French.

RENAULT

CRÉATEUR D'AUTOMOBILES

To demonstrate Renault's success at the Euro NCAP, this commercial shows how different car brands, represented by various types of food, performed in the crash test.

☆

Crashtest *Germany* ●

National Award	Gold
Agency	Nordpol Hamburg
Client	Renault Germany
Creative Director	Lars Rühmann
Art Director	Gunther Schreiber
Copywriter	Ingmar Bartels

Designer	C. Bielefeldt,
	P. Dörner,
	B. Kirschenhofer
Film Director	Silvio Helbig
Dir. of Photography	Silvio Helbig
Production Comp.	Element e
Dir. Marketing-Com	Jörg Ellhof

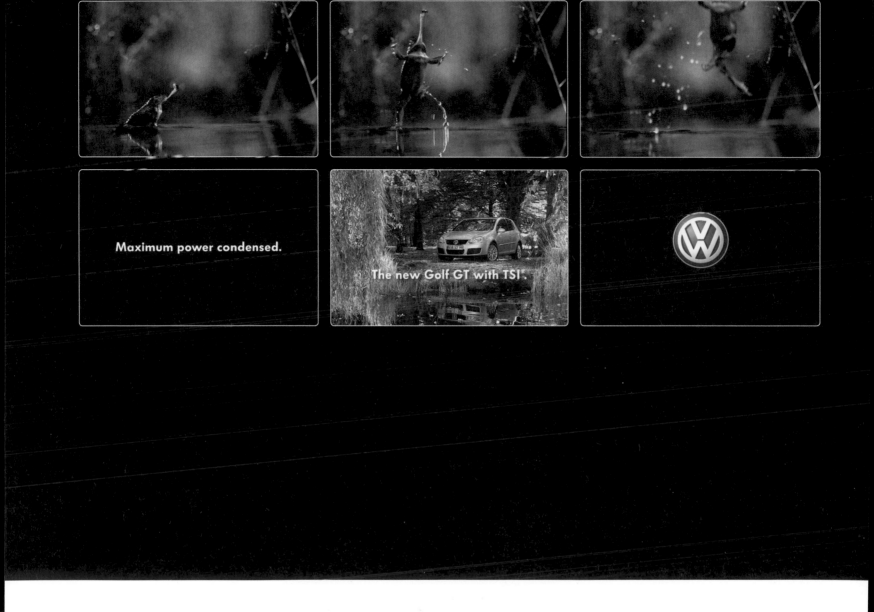

Maximum power condensed.

The new Golf GT with TSI.

☆
Fly *Germany*   ●

National Award	Silver	*Art Director*	Kristoffer Heilemann
Agency	DDB Germany/ Berlin	*Copywriter*	Ludwig Berndl
		Film Director	Henry Littlechild
Client	Volkswagen AG	*Dir. of Photography*	David Luther
Creative Director	Amir Kassaei, Wolfgang Schneider, Mathias Stiller	*Agency Producer*	Marion Lange
		Production Comp.	Markenfilm GmbH & Co KG, Hamburg
		Producer	Simona Daniel, Nele Schilling

NOTHING'S FASTER.

DHL is the fastest courier service in the world.

☆
Hummingbird *Germany*

●

National Award	Bronze	*Agency Producer*	Nadja Catana
Agency	Jung von Matt AG	*Production Comp*	Entspannt Film
Client	DPWN	*Audio Production*	Studio Funk Berlin
Creative Director	Oliver Handlos, Michael Pfeiffer-Belli		
Film Director	Nicolai Niemann		

This is a concept the agency developed in 4 different spots.

☆
If Fantasy never existed *Spain* ●

National Award	Silver	*Copywriter*	Santiago Saiegh
Agency	Vitruvio Leo Burnett	*Film Director*	Eric Morales
Client	Sitges Sci-Fi &	*Agency Producer*	Dionisio Naranjo,
	Fantasy Film Festival		Guzmán Molin Pradel
Creative Director	Rafa Antón,	*Production Comp.*	Got
	Fernando Martín	*Producer*	David de la Flor
Art Director	Julita Pequeño		

Suva bfu Horror *Switzerland* ●

National Award	Silver	*Copywriter*	Markus Ruf,
Agency	Ruf Lanz		Patrick Suter
	Werbeagentur AG	*Designer*	Dani Bittel
Client	Suva Accident	*Film Director*	Martin A. Fueter
	Insurance	*Production Comp.*	Condor Films
Creative Director	Danielle Lanz,	*Sound*	Space Train,
	Markus Ruf		Dave Kohler,
Art Director	Danielle Lanz		Dean Montenegro

A short life story of two hedgehog producers.

People who mull over cheap prices when they look at their own Do It Yourself (DIY) project just don't understand what DIY is all about. The tiled pool created with elbow grease is brimming with the passion of DIYers.

Super8 Short Film Festival *Czech Republic* ⊙

National Award	Gold	*Copywriter*	Ondrej Hubl,
Agency	McCann Erickson		Jaroslav Schovanec
	Prague	*Film Director*	Daniel Ruzicka
Client	McCann Erickson	*Dir. of Photography*	Jakub Simunek
	Prague	*Agency Producer*	Roxana Pfeffermannova
Creative Director	Lars Killi	*Production Comp.*	AdWood
Art Director	Ondrej Hubl,		
	Jaroslav Schovanec		

Heartbeats *Germany* ⊙

National Award	Silver	*Copywriter*	Till Eckel,
Agency	Heimat, Berlin		Guido Heffels,
Client	Hornbach Baumarkt		Carl Erik Rinsch
	AG	*Designer*	Eva Bajer
Creative Director	Guido Heffels,	*Film Director*	Carl Erik Rinsch
	Jürgen Vossen	*Agency Producer*	Kerstin Breuer
Art Director	Tim Schneider,	*Production Comp.*	Markenfilm, Berlin
	Carl Erik Rinsch		

It is a good idea to produce chocolate in a triangular shape. After all, it made Toblerone a world-famous brand. This is why the shape of the triangle is the focus of the campaign.

Vodafone Safety Message *Ireland* ●

National Award	Gold	*Agency Producer*	Jenni O'Reilly
Agency	Screenscene	*Production Comp.*	ScreenScene
Client	Vodafone	*3D & Compositing*	Hubert Montage
Art Director	Tim Mudie		
Copywriter	Emma Feilding		

Toblerone *Austria* ●

National Award	Gold	*Art Director*	Hannes Boeker
Agency	Ogilvy & Mather Austria	*Copywriter*	Werner Buehringer
Client	Kraft Foods Austria	*Film Director*	Mr. J
Creative Director	A. Zelmanovics, Mag. Dieter Pivrnec	*Production Comp.*	PPM Filmproductions, MG Sound

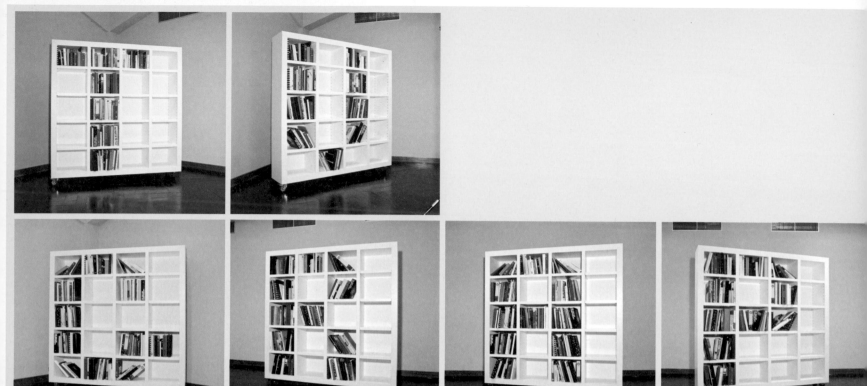

OI.3
TV GRAPHICS

Germany: 1 gold ★ 1 nomination☆

MTV shows its audience the parallel world of urban sticker culture. An artsy interpretation of the characters
is opposed to the reality of everyday life.

★

MTV Redesign 2005 *Germany*   ◉

National Award	Bronze	*Art Director*	Lacic, Brettschneider,
Agency	MTV Networks		Gotzoll, Biewer, Goode
	GmbH & Co OHG	*Designer*	Lacic, Brettschneider,
Client	MTV Networks		Gotzoll, Biewer, Goode
	GmbH & Co OHG	*Production Comp*	Die Drei Ausrufezeichen
Creative Director	Thomas Sabel		

The logo is the main character in this show packaging. The sound reflects various styles in music. The logo is sound and noise in one.

☆
MTV Noise Show Packaging *Germany* ⬤

National Award	Bronze	*Creative Director*	Thomas Sabel
Agency	MTV Networks GmbH & Co OHG	*Art Director*	Dinko Lacic
Client	MTV Networks GmbH & Co OHG	*Designer*	Dinko Lacic

T-Rex *Ireland* ⬤

National Award....Gold	*Film Director*.......Ruairi Robinson
Agency................ScreenScene	*Agency Producer*....DDB Canada-Sue Bell
Client ....BC Dairy Milk	
Art Director.........Dean Lee	
Copywriter ....James Lee	

Sabre Tooth *Ireland* ⬤

National Award....Gold	*Film Director*.......Ruairi Robinson
Agency................ScreenScene	*Agency Producer*....DDB Canada-Sue Bell
Client ....BC Dairy Milk	
Art Director.........Dean Lee	
Copywriter ....James Lee	

The Italian advertising superstar from the 60s comes back on TV with a trendy 12 episodes sit-com

In a sea of mobile telecoms, Heyah is something of a virgin island. No promotions, no behind-the-curtains costs, because Heyah is unable to tell a lie. In other words, Heyah cannot tell a fairy tale.

Carmencita - Sitcom in 12 episodes *Italy* ◉

National Award	Gold	*Film Director*	David Kelley, Peter List
Agency	Armando Testa SpA	*Dir. of Photography*	Massimo Hanozet
Client	Luigi Lavazza SpA	*Production Comp.*	Little Bull in cooperation with Curious Pictures
Creative Director	German Silva		
Art Director	German Silva, Andrea Lantelme		
Copywriter	Cristiano Nardò	*Post Production*	Augusto Storero; Green Movie (audio)

Little Red Ridinghood *Poland* ◉

National Award	Silver	*Copywriter*	Tomasz Kapuscinski
Agency	G7	*Film Director*	Sebastian Panczyk
Client	PTC Heyah	*Production Comp.*	Badi Badi
Creative Director	Dariusz Rzontkowski	*Animation*	Adam Wyrwas
Art Director	Karolina Lewicka, Tomasz Kapuscinski		

A fresh, bold, optimistic, and even provocative approach. The antidote to a low budget: Good ideas.

Four women do a stand-up act every night in a small pub. The mixture of 3-D collage and 2-D animation reflects the environment and the range of surreal characters they refer to in their act.

Third floor third door *Spain* ●

National Award	Silver	*Designer*	Sira Viñolas
Agency	TV3 Televisió de Catalunya	*Production Comp.*	TV3 Televisió de Catalunya
Client	TV3 Televisió de Catalunya		

4 Arreplegats *Spain* ●

National Award	Silver	*Agency Producer*	Ana Giménez (El Terrat), Marc Clotet (Antomic)
Agency	Antomic		
Client	TV3 & El Terrat		
Art Director	Frankie De Leonardis	*Production Comp.*	Antomic Event
Film Director	Frankie De Leonardis	*3D*	Joseph Winston
		2D	Linterna Mágica

How are frog legs related to mortgage loan interests? France's economy influences the economics of all Europe. The better the French live, the more frog legs they eat, which means that the consumption of goods is growing.

Opening title sequence for a leading irish childrens tv programme

Frogs *Latvia* ●

National Award	Gold	*Designer*	Gints Apsits
Agency	Apsits	*Film Director*	Gints Apsits
Client	Seb Vilnus	*Dir. of Photography*	Gints Apsits
Creative Director	Aleksandrs Betins	*Agency Producer*	Garage 4x4
Art Director	Gints Apsits	*Production Comp.*	Apsits & Film Angels
Copywriter	Aleksandrs Betins		

Dustins Daily News *Ireland* ●

National Award	Gold	*Designer*	Michael McKeon
Agency	RT... Graphic Design	*Agency Producer*	Mathew Talbot Kelly
Client	RT...	*Production Comp.*	Glimpse
Creative Director	Michael McKeon		

On-air branding for an independent, noncommercial cinema channel that was searching for a young and fresh image.

The magic of cinema: Improvement with time.

Cinemateka *Spain* ●

National Award Silver	*Art Director* Cómodo Screen
Agency Cómodo Screen	*Copywriter* Cómodo Screen
Client Cinemateka	*Designer* Cómodo Screen
Creative Director Cómodo Screen	*Agency Producer* Cómodo Screen

Music Box *Spain* ●

National Award Gold	*Creative Director* Agustín Cantero
Agency Sogecable S.A.	*Art Director* Pau Bosch
Client Cinemanía Clásico	

This television commercial compares the various tastes of Darbo Fruitsirups to the illustrious members of a family: Everyone has his own character.

This is the whole TV3 generic image restyling. The look of the former image had lost its original characteristics. They needed a modern logo to reconnect with a younger generation.

Family *Austria* ⊙

National Award	Silver	*Copywriter*	Gerda Schebesta, Arno Reisenbüchler
Agency	Demner, Merlicek & Bergmann	*Film Director*	Melanie Bridge
Client	Adolf Darbo AG	*Dir. of Photography*	Ginny Loane
Creative Director	Franz Merlicek, Gerda Schebesta	*Agency Producer*	Maresi McNab
Art Director	Franz Merlicek	*Production Comp.*	ffp (Vienna), The Sweet Shop (Auckland)

TV3 On-air *Spain* ⊙

National Award	Gold	*Executive Producer*	Teresa Guitart
Agency	Gédéon	*Designer*	Nicolas Thepot
Client	TV3 Televisió de Catalunya	*Production Comp.*	TV3 Televisió de Catalunya
Creative Director	François Dameron, Bernard Brechet	*Music composer*	Plush Monkey

With a mix of curiosity and anxiety, a young man follows his presumed double around the city. Only at a parking lot is their difference revealed: The double doesn't have a Series 1.

With Martin Scorsese's Goodfellas, Analyze This, and the recent TV series "The Sopranos," the Italian-American mafia are shown from a cinematographic point of view.

Doppelganger - Man *Italy* ●

National Award	Silver	*Film Director*	Giuseppe Capotondi
Agency	D'Adda, Lorenzini, Vigorelli, BBDO	*Dir. of Photography*	Simon Chadoir
Client	BMW Italia	*Agency Producer*	Francesca Nussio
Creative Director	Gianpietro Vigorelli	*Production Comp.*	Mercurio Cinematografica
Art Director	Gianpietro Vigorelli	*Post Production*	You Are\Green Movie (audio)
Copywriter	Luca Scotto di Carlo		

Family Reunion *Italy* ●

National Award	Silver	*Film Director*	Tom De Cerchio
Agency	Saatchi & Saatchi	*Dir. of Photography*	Dante Spinotti
Client	Renault Italia	*Agency Producer*	Emanuela Concato
Creative Director	Guido Cornara, Agostino Toscana	*Production Comp.*	Fred Films
Art Director	Agostino Toscana	*Editor*	Marco Perez
Copywriter	Guido Cornara	*Music*	Bad Boy-Buster Poindexter

The world of the circus in motion colours.

Rock Monster *Ireland* ●

National Award	Gold	*Film Director*	Ruairi Robinson
Agency	ScreenScene	*Agency Producer*	DDB Canada-Sue Bell
Client	BC Dairy Milk		
Art Director	Dean Lee		
Copywriter	James Lee		

Circ *Spain* ●

National Award	Silver	*Creative Director*	David Torrents
Agency	Pere Ginard,	*Film Director*	Pere Ginard,
	Laura Estragués,		Laura Estragués
	David Torrents	*Production Comp.*	Laboratorium
Client	KRTU		

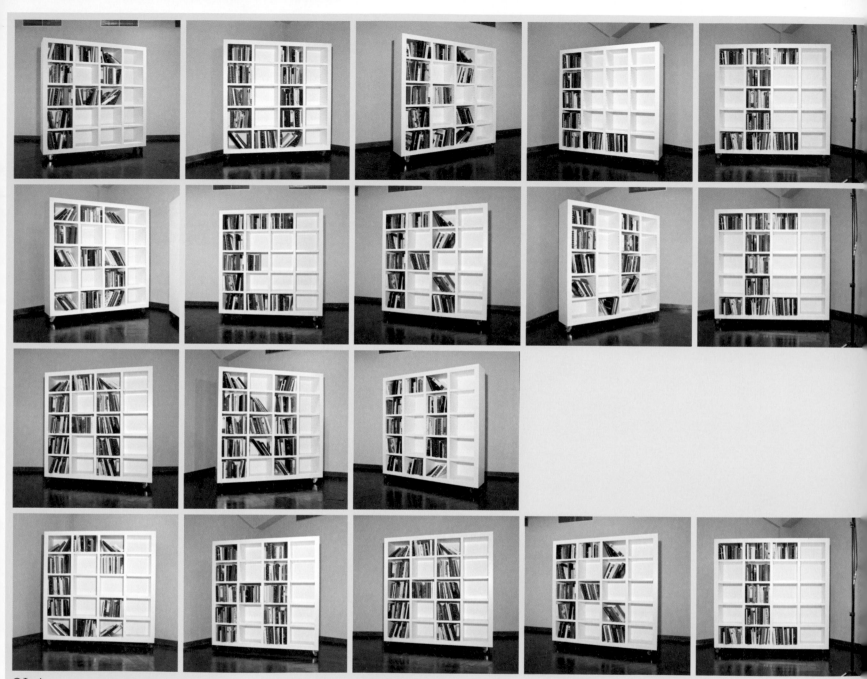

01.4
PUBLIC SERVICE AND CHARITY

Portugal: 1 gold ★ 1 nomination ☆
United Kingdom: 1 gold ★
Spain: 1 nomination ☆

A woman visits her mum at a nursing home. As they speak, the audience realizes that the elderly woman has Alzheimer's: She doesn't recognize her daughter and she thinks her nurse is her aunt.

★

Alzheimer *Portugal* ⬤

National Award	Silver	*Film Director*	Carlos Manga Jr.
Agency	Leo Burnett Lisboa	*Dir. of Photography*	Lito Mendes da Rocha
Client	IAC	*Agency Producer*	Cristina Almeida
Creative Director	Fernando Bellotti	*Production Comp.*	Republika Films
Art Director	Fernando Bellotti, Paulo Arias		
Copywriter	Fernando Bellotti, R. Corsaro		

AN ABUSED CHILD NEVER FORGETS.

Instituto
de Apoio
à Criança

Traffic accidents are the biggest killer of teenagers in the UK. The task was to put road safety back on their agenda. This road safety commercial was shot entirely on a mobile phone, dramatizing the distracted behaviour that causes many of the accidents.

★

Camera Phone *United Kingdom* ◉

National Award	Silver	*Copywriter*	Angus Macadam, Paul Jordan
Agency	Leo Burnett Limited, London	*Film Director*	Chris Palmer
Client	Department of Road Safety	*Agency Producer*	Emma Gooding
		Production Comp.	Gorgeous Enterprises
Creative Director	Jim Thronton		
Art Director	Angus Macadam, Paul Jordan		

55 teenagers a week wish they'd given the road their full attention.

This shows images of young couples having sex. The voiceover says, "Condoms come in different quantities.
The packs with 3 units are good for beginners: One condom for Friday, one for Saturday, one for Sunday...
The 6-pack is perfect for those who are in college."

☆
Condoms *Portugal*   ●

National Award	Best photo	*Art Director*	Fabio Seidl
Agency	McCann Erickson	*Copywriter*	Fabio Seidl
Client	Portuguese League	*Film Director*	Marco Martins
	Against Aids	*Production Comp.*	Ministério de Filmes
Creative Director	Diogo Anahory,		(Lisbon)
	José Bomtempo		

We are not asking for too much

☆

Inside *Spain*

●

National Award.... Gold
Agency................ Villarrosas, SCPF
Client .... Barcelona City
                        Council
Creative Director.... Oriol Villar

Copywriter .... Oriol Villar,
                        Toni Segarra,
                        Claudio Letelier

By showing their everyday lives, disabled people invite drunk drivers to join their club.

Drink.Drive.Join: First_Step, Sit_up *Latvia*   ●

National Award	Silver	*Art Director*	Zoom!
Agency	Zoom!	*Copywriter*	Zoom!
Client	Latvian Road Safety Council	*Film Director*	Zoom!
		Production Comp.	Zoom!
Creative Director	Zoom!		

Speeding gets you there faster.

Lilia Baeka - a professional sportswoman. 3 times Latvian champion in stepping on a rake. Attitude to EU... Strictly no! We kindly ask the rest of you to vote for Latvia in Europe.

Stripes *Czech Republic* ◉

National Award	Silver	*Copywriter*	Jiri Pleskot
Agency	Leo Burnett	*Film Director*	Jan Kalvoda
	Advertising, spol. s.r.o.	*Agency Producer*	Lubo Prochazka
Client	UAMK (Road Safety	*Production Comp.*	Stillking Films
	Council)	*Music*	Richard Kolbe
Creative Director	Jiri Pleskot		
Art Director	Lumir Kajnar		

EU Champion *Latvia* ◉

National Award	Silver	*Art Director*	Zoom!
Agency	Zoom!	*Film Director*	Zoom!
Client	Public Institution	*Production Comp.*	Zoom!
Creative Director	Zoom!		

The goal of the advertisement was to encourage people to donate blood. The campaign was so successful, it had to be discontinued for the summer because there wasn't a way to preserve the amounts of donated blood.

Suva bfu Horror *Switzerland* ●

National Award	Silver
Agency	Ruf Lanz Werbeagentur AG
Client	Suva Accident Insurance
Creative Director	Danielle Lanz, Markus Ruf
Art Director	Danielle Lanz
Copywriter	Markus Ruf, Patrick Suter
Designer	Dani Bittel
Film Director	Martin A. Fueter
Production Comp.	Condor Films
Sound	Space Train, Dave Kohler, Dean Montenegro

Blood cell *Estonia* ●

National Award	Silver
Agency	Imagine AD
Client	Estonian Blood Centre
Creative Director	Andri Luup
Art Director	Kalev Külaase
Copywriter	Andri Luup
Designer	Kalev Külaase
Film Director	Margo Kütt
Dir. of Photography	Aare Varik
Agency Producer	Imagine AD
Production Comp.	Imagine AD

If you buy stolen goods you become a companion in crime.

Family, Lovers *Russia* ●

National Award	Gold	*Creative Director*	Natalya Bogomolova
Agency	Mother's Tongue	*Art Director*	Konstantin Kornakov
Client	Federal Agency of Press and Production Communication	*Copywriter*	Natalya Polyanichko
		Film Director	Gleb Orlov

For this campaign, two television commercials were filmed. One shows that parents can't buy their children happiness by giving them money. The other commercial shows that parents force their children to participate in activities parents like, not the ones kids really want.

On a metaphorical visit to the Fredreich's Ataxia Corporation, the company's CEO guides us through the effects of this terrible desease.

Child is not a Doll *Estonia* ●

National Award	Gold	*Designer*	Kalev Külaase
Agency	Imagine AD	*Film Director*	Kalev Külaase,
Client	Estonian Ministry		Toomas Valsberg,
	of Social Affairs		Kädi Kaasikmäe
Creative Director	Kalev Külaase,	*Dir. of Photography*	Kalev Külaase
	Toomas Valsberg	*Agency Producer*	Imagine AD
Art Director	Kalev Külaase	*Production Comp*	Imagine AD
Copywriter	Toomas Valsberg		

CEO *Italy* ●

National Award	Silver	*Art Director*	Ricardo Pagani
Agency	Armando Testa SpA	*Film Director*	Federico Brugia
Client	Comitato Rudi-Gofar	*Dir. of Photography*	Manfredo Archinto
Creative Director	German Silva,	*Production Comp*	The Family
	Ekhi Mendibil,	*Postproduction*	You Are
	Haitz Mendibil	*Audio*	Green Movie

Special offer: Life is possible to buy, just place a bread roll in a supermarket.

"It's up to you. Either you defend the planet or it will defend itself." The purpose of the campaign was to represent this choice through images of serious environmental calamities.

Special offer *Czech Republic* ●

National Award	Gold	*Art Director*	Jiri Langpaul
Agency	Leo Burnett Advertising, spol. s.r.o.	*Copywriter*	Vera Cesenkova
		Film Director	Tomas Barina
Client	Bone Marrow Transplant Foundation	*Dir. of Photography*	Tomas Sysel
		Agency Producer	Andrea Tomankova
Creative Director	Vera Cesenkova	*Production Comp.*	Filmservice Productions

Defend the planet *Italy* ●

National Award	Gold	*Art Director*	Francesca Risolo
Agency	Saatchi & Saatchi	*Copywriter*	Stefano Massari
Client	Greenpeace	*Agency Producer*	Saveria Marcucci
Creative Director	Luca Albanese, Francesco Taddeucci	*Production Comp.*	Moving Pictures

01.5
ANY OTHER

United Kingdom: 1 gold★
Ireland: 1 nomination☆

The goal of this campaign was to promote the new online movie rental service fivedvd.com through sponsorship of the reality television show "The Farm."

Sponsorship for The Farm *United Kingdom*

National Award Gold	*Agency Producer* Audrey Hawkins
Agency Devilfish	*Production Comp.* Devilfish
Client Five	*Voice Over Artist* Chris Langham
Creative Director Richard Holman	
Copywriter Claire Lambert	
Film Director Claire Lambert	
Dir. of Photography Trevor Forrest	

sponsored by

FIVEDVD.COM

A series of sponsorship stings for a weekly football highlights programme.

☆

Football *Ireland*　　　　　　　　　●

National Award	Silver	*Film Director*	Rory Kelleher
Agency	Irish International BBDO	*Agency Producer*	Aileen Concannon
Client	Diageo	*Production Comp.*	Company Films
Creative Director	Eoghan Nolan		
Art Director	Bill Hollingsworth		
Copywriter	Adrian Cosgrove		

Wsciekle Pieski, Chinatown, Ostateczne Starcie Tough guys do their dirty deeds and talk their dirty talk. They do all this in diminutive form because with Heyah, everything is very, very little—especially the prices.

This is an audiovisual project, created by Miguel Marin and Onionlab, that mixes electronic and acoustic live music with a synchronized video. With this project, the music can be interpreted visually.

Diminuitions *Poland* ●

National Award	Silver	*Copywriter*	Tomasz Kapuscinski
Agency	G7	*Film Director*	Tomasz Kapuscinski
Client	PTC Heyah	*Dir of Photography*	Bartek Kaczmarek
Creative Director	Dariusz Rzontkowski	*Production Comp*	ITI
Art Director	Karolina Lewicka		

Imaginary Soundtracks *Spain* ●

National Award	Silver	*Designer*	Aleix Fernández, Eduard Hervás
Agency	Onionlab	*Film Director*	Aleix Fernández, Eduard Hervás
Client	Arbol	*Agency Producer*	Onionlab
Creative Director	Aleix Fernández, Eduard Hervás	*Production Comp*	Onionlab
Art Director	Aleix Fernández, Eduard Hervás	*Music*	Miguel Marín

An ad created by Publicis for the nationwide supermarket chain.

When there are elections in Germany, every official political party gets to broadcast a number of election campaign commercials on public television for free. In 2005 The Party sold its airtime to the low-cost airline HLX.

Leniwe *Poland* ⚫

National Award	Silver	*Dir. of Photography*	Marek Sanak
Agency	Publicis Sp. z.o.o.	*Agency Producer*	Publicis Sp. z.o.o.
Client	JMD	*Production Comp.*	OTO
Creative Director	Michal Nowosielski	*Editing*	Platige Image
Art Director	Danuta Nierada		
Copywriter	Kasia Kowalska		
Film Director	Sebastian Panczyk		

The HLX election campaign *Germany* ⚫

National Award	Silver	*Art Director*	Johannes Hicks
Agency	Scholz & Friends / Titanic Verlag GmbH & Co. KG	*Copywriter*	M. Sonneborn, R.A. Coertlen, S. Kummer, L. Baldermann
Client	Hapag-Lloyd Express GmbH	*Film Director*	Matthias Spaetgens
Creative Director	M. Spaetgens, J. Leube, M. Pross, S. Turner	*Production Comp.*	Cine plus Media Service GmbH & Co. KG
		Account Executive	K. Seegers, W. Schlutter, V. Hofmann

Regardless of the heavy rain and wind in an English town, two men struggle to walk down the street.

Great brewers of Oak (Debowe) Beer salute great masters of carpentry.

Gale *Poland* ⦿

National Award	Silver	*Art Director*	Robert Rosol
Agency	PZL Warsaw (Leo Burnett Group)	*Copywriter*	Kot Przybora, Magdalena Goll
Client	Kompania Piwowarska S.A.	*Film Director*	Kot Przybora
		Dir. of Photography	Slawomir Idziak
Creative Director	Kot Przybora, Iwo Zaniewski	*Production Comp.*	Opus Film Sp. z o.o.
		Post Production	Platige Image

Carpenter's Orchestra *Poland* ⦿

National Award	Gold	*Art Director*	Iwo Zaniewski
Agency	PZL Warsaw (Leo Burnett Group)	*Copywriter*	Cezary Filew
		Film Director	Iwo Zaniewski
Client	Kompania Piwowarska S.A.	*Production Comp.*	Opus Film Sp. z o.o.
Creative Director	Iwo Zaniewski, Kot Przybora	*Set Designer*	Jeremi Brodnicki

Ministry Messiah is part of Diesel Dream project. The film speculates on the surreal world of dreams.

For a Women Secret brand presentation, four real women talk about themselves. Four women with names and surnames, hopes, weaknesses, passions, and doubts: Magali, Amandine, Natalia, and Paola tell women secret things they were not asked.

Ministry Messiah *Latvia* ●

National Award....Gold	*Designer* ....Gints Apsits	
Agency.................Apsits	*Film Director*.......Gints Apsits	
Client ....Diesel	*Dir. of Photography*..Gints Apsits	
Creative Director...Dave Bell	*Agency Producer*.... KesselsKramer	
Art Director.........Gints Apsits	*Production Comp*...Apsits	

Three Inside Portraits *Spain* ●

National Award....Silver	*Designer* ....Daniel Ayuso	
Agency.................Cla-se	*Film Director*.......Isabel Coixet	
Client ....Women Secret	*Production Comp*..Miss Wasabi	
Creative Director...Cla-se		
Art Director.........Daniel Ayuso, Isabel Coixet		

02
Advertising
Print

02.1
POSTER ADVERTISING

Austria: 1 nomination ☆
Germany: 4 nominations ☆
Poland: 1 nomination ☆
Portugal: 1 nomination ☆

Netter Versuch, Mama…

i'm lovin' it

Mother is trying to cheat by wrapping a normal sandwich.

☆
Butterbrot (Sandwich) *Germany*

National Award	Bronze		*Art Director*	Zeljko Pezely
Agency	GBK, Heye Werbeagentur		*Copywriter*	Marcel Koop
Client	McDonald's Werbeges. m.b.H.		*Photographer*	Thomas Hannich
Creative Director	Alexander Bartel, Martin Kiessling			

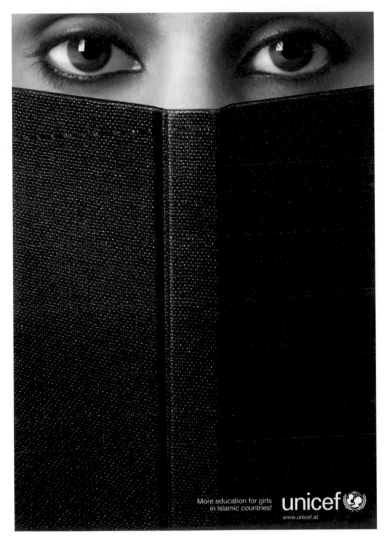

More than education for girls in Islamic countries.

☆
Unicef Islam *Austria*

National Award Gold	*Copywriter* Patrik Partl,
Agency FCB Kobza	Joachim Glawion
Client Unicef Austria	*Designer* Tolga Büyükdoganay
Creative Director Joachim Glawion,	*Photographer* Joe Fish
Patrik Partl	*Graphics* Tolga Büyükdoganay
Art Director Tolga Büyükdoganay	

"No cage is big enough. Pity won't help. Donations do." The goal of the campaign was to create public awareness of the unnatural and brutal living conditions of animals in captivity.

☆
Kein Käfig ist gross genug (No cage is big enough) *Germany*

National Award	Bronze	*Copywriter*	Jens Petter Waernes, Erik Dagnell
Agency	Jung von Matt AG		
Client	NOAH Menschen für Tiere e.V.	*Account Supervisor*	Turan Tehrani, Dennis Schneider
Creative Director	Jan Rexhausen, Doerte Spengler-Ahrens		
Art Director	Erik Dagnell, Jens Petter Waernes		

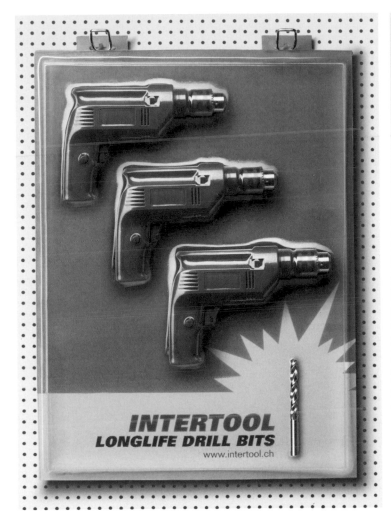

Tools from Intertool live longer than the machines.

☆
Intertool Longlife tools Campaign *Germany*

National Award	Bronze	*Art Director*	Philipp Boettcher, Marco Weber
Agency	Ogilvy & Mather Frankfurt	*Copywriter*	Philipp Boettcher
Client	Intertool AG, Switzerland	*Photographer*	Heinz Wuchner
		Graphics	Marc Wuchner, Kapka Dotcheva
Creative Director	Christian Mommertz, Dr. Stephan Vogel	*Art Buying*	Christina Hufgard

☆
The wrong working environment campaign *Germany*

National Award	Silver	*Agency Producer*	Soeren Gessat
Agency	Scholz & Friends	*Photographer*	Hans Starck
Client	Jobsintown.de	*Graphics*	Inga Schulze, Sara dos Santos Vieira
Creative Director	Matthias Spaetgens, Jan Leube	*Account Executive*	Katrin Seegers, Katrin Ploska
Art Director	David Fischer		
Copywriter	Axel Tischer		

This is what Freedom of Speech looks like in Belarus. 15.000 posters presenting the Belorussian opposition activists were attached with a silver tape, the one usually used for gagging.

☆

Freedom of speech *Poland*

National Award	Gold	*Copywriter*	Jakub Korolczuk,
Agency	Saatchi & Saatchi		Ryszard Sroka
	Poland	*Photographer*	Andrzej Georgiew
Client	Amnesty International		
Creative Director	Jacek Szulecki		
Art Director	Ryszard Sroka,		
	Jakub Korolczuk		

Huge packages of Friskies were placed on billboards in the main squares of cities. The billboards had hidden deposits of bird food to attract pigeons to literally eat from the Friskies packages.

☆

Birds *Potugal*

National Award	Gold	*Art Director*	João Roque
Agency	Leo Burnett Lisbon	*Copywriter*	Miguel Brito
Client	Nestlé Purina Petcare	*Agency Producer*	Antonio Junior
Creative Director	Fernando Bellotti		

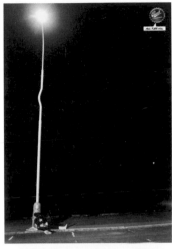

Coors Light - a taste born high in the Rocky Mountains

Superheroes *Czech Republic*

National Award	Gold	*Art Director*	Miro Minarovych
Agency	KASPEN Prague	*Copywriter*	Tomas Otradovec
Client	Budweiser Budvar	*Photographer*	Roman Dietrich
Creative Director	Tomas Otradovec		

Coors Light *Ireland*

National Award	Gold	*Art Director*	Mike Garner
Agency	Chemistry	*Copywriter*	Emmet Wright
Client	Heineken Ireland	*Photographer*	Kevin Griffin
Creative Director	Mike Garner	*Retouching*	Taylor James

Accidents can happen, even in the perfect world of advertising. To emphasize this, well-known ads were altered.

Nothing is certain *Switzerland*

National Award	Silver	*Copywriter*	Stefan Ehrler
Agency	Spillmann, Felser, Leo Burnett	*Agency Producer*	Sebahat Derdiyok
Client	National Versicherung	*Photographer*	Julien Vonier
Creative Director	Martin Spillmann		
Art Director	Dana Wirz		

Scary gas prices *Austria*

National Award	Silver	*Art Director*	Markus Zauner, James Teal
Agency	JWT Vienna	*Copywriter*	Alexander Lauber, Thomas Troppmann
Client	Austrian Railway Federation	*Photographer*	Günther Parth
Creative Director	Alexander Lauber, Markus Zauner	*Postproduction*	Rotfilter

Abolish the differences wage between men and women.

Fresh Meat *Finland*

National Award....Gold	*Art Director*.........Minna Lavola
Agency................TBWA PHS Helsinki	*Copywriter*..........Tommy Makinen
Client.................Union of Finnish	*Photographer*.......Ofer Amir,
Feminists	Asko Roine

Don't let appearances fool you *Iceland*

National Award....Silver	*Art Director*.........Dora Isleifsdottir
Agency................Fiton	*Designer*.............Arni Thor Arnason
Client.................VR	*Photographer*.......Ari Magg
Creative Director....Ulfur Eldjarn	

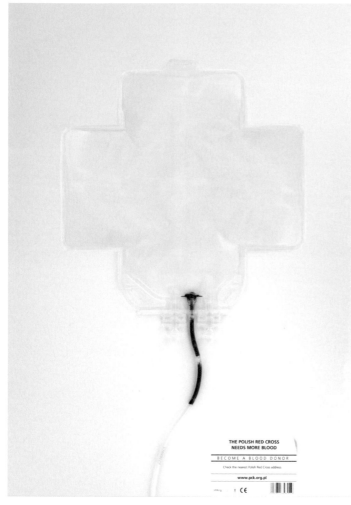

The Polish Red Cross needs more blood.

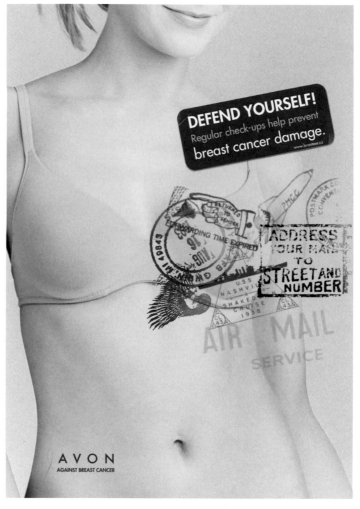

Defend yourself. Regular check-ups help to prevent breast cancer damage.

Red Cross *Poland*

National Award	Silver	*Art Director*	Filip Berendt,
Agency	Saatchi & Saatchi		Maciej Waligora
	Poland	*Copywriter*	Filip Berendt,
Client	Polish Red Cross		Maciej Waligora
Creative Director	Jacek Szulecki	*Photographer*	Adam Wlazly

Defend Yourself *Czech Republic*

National Award	Silver	*Art Director*	Ondrej Karasek
Agency	Mark BBDO	*Copywriter*	Pavel Sobek
Client	Avon	*Designer*	Martin Kubac
Creative Director	Martin Charvat	*Photographer*	Roman Dietrich

"Anybody out there?"

Teresa Maxova Foundation for abandoned kids *Czech Republic*

National Award....Silver
Agency.................McCann Erickson
                Prague
Client.................Tereza Maxova
                Foundation

Creative Director...Lars Killi
Art Director.........Zdenek Hejda
Copywriter...........Lucia Eggenhofferova
Photographer........Goran Tacevski

Non-smoking trains *Switzerland*

National Award....Silver
Agency.................Jung von Matt,
                Zürich AG
Client.................Schweizerische
                Bundesbahnen SBB
Creative Director...Alexander Jaggy

Art Director.........Lukas Frei
Copywriter...........Michael Kathe
Agency Producer....Ilonka Galliard
Photographer........Mats Cordt
Graphics.............Yves Gerteis

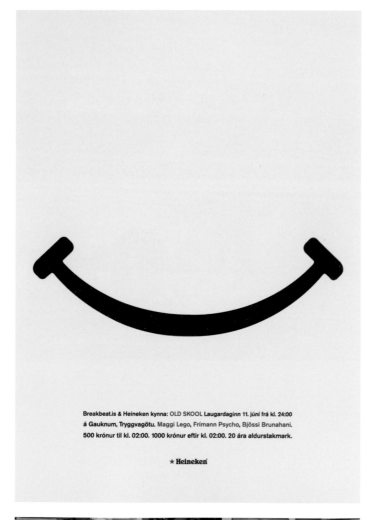

Poster for a musical event.

Poster for Og Vodafone.

Old school *Iceland*

National Award	Gold	*Art Director*	Ragnar Freyr Palsson
Agency	Front	*Designer*	Ragnar Freyr Palsson
Client	Breakbeat.is		

Lost *Iceland*

National Award	Silver	*Art Director*	Dora Isleifsdottir,
Agency	Fiton		Armann Agnarsson
Client	Og Vodafone	*Designer*	Armann Agnarsson
Creative Director	Ulfur Eldjarn		

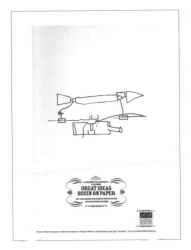

This was an interactive installation at bus stops

ESB Energy Awareness Week *Ireland*

National Award	Silver	*Creative Director*	Laurence Keogh
Agency	McConnells Advertising	*Art Director*	Emma Hogan
Client	ESB	*Copywriter*	Laurence Keogh
		Designer	Emma Hogan

Day Watch *Russia*

National Award	Gold	*Art Director*	Matvei Evstigneev, Dmitry Likin
Agency	ORT-Design (Channel One Russia)	*Designer*	Evgeny Raytses, Matvei Evstigneev, Alexei Torohov
Client	ORT-Design (Channel One Russia)	*Agency Producer*	SHIP
Creative Director	Konstantin Ernst, Evgeny Raytses		

The "Art of Shopping" campaign emphasized the uniqueness of Viru Keskus shopping center: It has its own modern art gallery.

To reinforce the claim "Looks better, doesn't it?" used by mömax furniture stores chain, special City light displays were developed featuring an ugly naked man in the shower that could be covered with a mömax curtain that carried the "Looks better, doesn't it?" claim.

Shower Curtain *Austria*

National Award	Silver	*Art Director*	Bernhard Grafl
Agency	Demner, Merlicek & Bergmann	*Copywriter*	Alistair Thompson
		Designer	Roman Steiner
Client	Mömax Furniture Stores	*Agency Producer*	Norbert Rabenseifner, Karl Murnberger
Creative Director	Gerda Reichl-Schebesta	*Photographer*	Georg Schlosser
		Graphics	Aron Cserveny-Mizner

Art of shopping *Estonia*

National Award	Silver	*Designer*	Jaanus Veerberk
Agency	Agency	*Agency Producer*	Marget Haug
Client	Viru Keskus	*Photographer*	Toomas Tikenberg
Creative Director	Madis Ots		
Art Director	Jaanus Veerberk		
Copywriter	Madis Ots		

Jewellery & timepieces.

Look at the boots, you pervert!

Desire *Austria*

National Award	Gold	*Designer*	Birgit Schuster
Agency	FCB Kobza	*Concept*	Doris Kaser,
Client	Jeweller Haban		Tobias Federsel
Creative Director	Tobias Federsel		
Art Director	Matthias van Baaren		
Copywriter	Doris Kaser,		
	Matthias Wernicke		

Pervert *Latvia*

National Award	Silver	*Art Director*	Janis Lauznis
Agency	Euro RSCG Riga	*Copywriter*	Sandijs Lusens
Client	Carre	*Designer*	Janis Lauznis
Creative Director	Sandijs Lusens	*Photographer*	Valts Kleins

This was a campaign to challenge the runners of Lisbon to take part in a 10 kilometre fun run along the mouth of the River Tajo. The river itself, in the form of sea creatures, was the main competitor.

The things you wear reflect your personality and shoes are an important part of what you wear

Corrida do Tejo *Spain*

National Award....Silver	*Art Director*.........Frank Hahn,
Agency................Villarrosas, SCPF	Cristina Martín
Client ....American Nike	*Copywriter* ....Oriol Villar,
Creative Director...Oriol Villar	Mauricio Alarcón
	Designer ....Destroy Rock City

Converse Portraits *Poland*

National Award....Gold	*Art Director*.........Katarzyna Macharz
Agency................J.W.T. Warsaw	*Copywriter*..........Kamil Nazarewicz
Client ....AmerSport	*Photographer* ....Andrzej Dragan
Creative Director...Darek Zatorski	*Stylist*................Agnieszka Hodowana

Make your hotel laundry shine with whiteness with Tide Professional.

TIENI VIVA LA FORZA DEL NERO.

Keeps black power alive. This ad shows a scowling black sweater.

Lamp (Tide Professional) *Czech Republic*

National Award	Silver	*Art Director*	Roman Baigouzov
Agency	Saatchi & Saatchi Prague	*Copywriter*	Daniel Prokes
Client	Procter & Gamble	*Agency Producer*	David Kopal
Creative Director	Petr Vlasak, Richard Stiebitz	*Photographer*	Nikola Tacevski

Panther *Italy*

National Award	Silver	*Art Director*	Serena Di Bruno
Agency	D'Adda, Lorenzini, Vigorelli, BBDO	*Copywriter*	Giovanni Chiarelli
Client	Henkel	*Photographer*	Fulvio Bonavia
Creative Director	Giuseppe Mastromatteo, Luca Scotto di Carlo		

Официальный сервис Mercedes-Benz

Only original service. Only original spare parts.

ŠkodaAuto - official partner of The Tour de France

ŠkodaAuto - official partner of The Tour de France

Skoda Auto is an official partner of the Tour de France.

Dag *Russia*

National Award	Silver	*Creative Director*	Maria Zaharova
Agency	Advertising Group NFQ	*Art Director*	Andrew Klimov
		Designer	Andrew Klimov
Client	Daimler Chrysler Automotive Russia SAO	*Illustrator*	Neuron studio

Tour de France *Czech Republic*

National Award	Silver	*Art Director*	Ales Kolaja
Agency	Cayenne Communications s.r.o.	*Copywriter*	Christian Anhut
		Agency Producer	Eva Kubelikova
Client	Skoda Auto	*Photographer*	Pavel Aschemann
Creative Director	Lester Tullett, Klemens Schuettken	*Prod. Company*	2 pm production

Mud *Germany*

National Award	Silver	*Art Director*	Hanadi Chawaf, Oliver Fermer
Agency	KNSK Werbeagentur GmbH	*Copywriter*	Berend Brüdgam
Client	Daimler Chrysler AG	*Agency Producer*	Heinz-Rudi Junge
Creative Director	Tim Krink, Niels Holle	*Graphics*	Hanadi Chawaf, Boris Schatte

French culture in film.

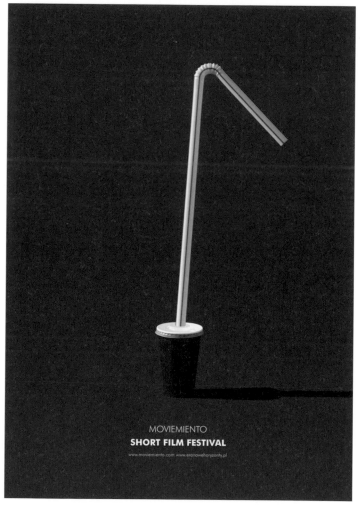

All you need during short movie is a small mug with drink.

Snail Popcorn *Czech Republic*

National Award Silver	*Creative Director* Dejan Stajnberger
Agency Euro Rscg Prague	*Designer* Jakub Mraz
Client French Film Festival	

Cup *Poland*

National Award Gold	*Art Director* Bartek Grala
Agency Saatchi & Saatchi Poland	*Copywriter* Daniel Piecka
Client Stowarzyszenie Nowe Horyzonty	*Agency Producer* Saatchi & Saatchi Poland
Creative Director Jacek Szulecki	*Photographer* Slawomir Smolarek

The world of the circus is full of colors.

The Serralves Museum showed its contemporary art collection at the Parliament, an important centre of political power. Symbols of parties represented in the Parliament were used for the outdoor campaign.

Circ *Spain*

National Award	Gold	*Creative Director*	David Torrents
Agency	David Torrents	*Designer*	David Torrents
Client	KRTU		

Parties *Portugal*

National Award	Gold	*Art Director*	José Bomtempo
Agency	McCann Erickson	*Copywriter*	Diogo Anahory
Client	Serralves Foundation		
Creative Director	Diogo Anahory, José Bomtempo		

In order to stage a good play you need: actors (photographs of them), a text (typographies that change based on the audience), a curtain (a colourful form that hides and shows the work), and a backdrop (paper that supports).

Teatre Cal Bolet *Spain*

National Award	Gold	*Art Director*	Martí Ferré, Agnès Simon
Agency	Bildi Grafiks		
Client	Patronat del Teatre Municipal Cal Bolet	*Photographer*	Various
		Print	Imprèsràpid
Creative Director	Martí Ferré, Agnès Simon		

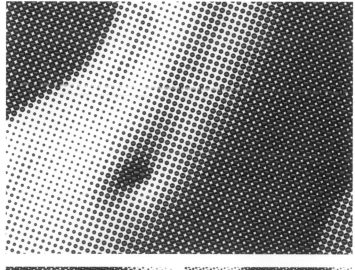

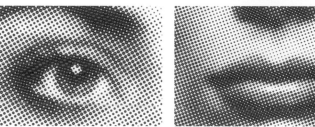

Young Director Award *Finland*

National Award	Gold	*Copywriter*	Markku Ronkko,
Agency	TBWA PHS Helsinki		Jyrki Reinikka
Client	Commercial Film	*Agency Producer*	Kirsi Parni
	Producers of Europe	*Photographer*	Elina Moriya
	& Shots	*Graphics*	Pia Pitkanen
Art Director	Minna Lavola,	*Ilustrator*	Pia Pitkanen,
	Zoubida Benkhellat		Tommi Rapeli

Dots *Germany*

National Award	Silver	*Copywriter*	Regine Becker
Agency	TBWA Germany	*Agency Producer*	Alexander Heldt
Client	Beiersdorf AG	*Retouching*	Helmut Gass
Creative Director	Dietrich Zastrow		Reprotechnik
Art Director	Sandra Birkemeyer,		
	Katja Krüger		

The campaign introduced the new brand identity of Hanzas Maiznicas.

Titty Twister *Austria*

National Award	Silver	*Art Director*	Elli Hummer, Robert Wohlgemuth	
Agency	TBWA Wien			
Client	Sony Computer Entertainment Austria	*Copywriter*	Gerd Turetschek	
		Photographer	Gerhard Merzeder	
Creative Director	Elli Hummer, Gerd Turetschek, Robert Wohlgemuth	*Graphics*	Louis Funke	
		Other	Johannes Krammer (CEO, Creative Director)	

The favourite bread of Latvia *Latvia*

National Award	Gold	*Art Director*	Laila Apšeniece
Agency	DDB Worldwide Latvia	*Copywriter*	Edgars Ubrovskis
Client	Hanzas Maiznicas	*Designer*	Laila Apšeniece
Creative Director	Kriss Salmanis	*Account Director*	Reins Grants

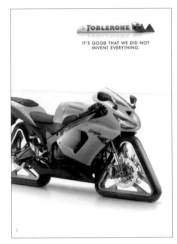 

It's good that we did not invent everything!

Toblerone *Austria*

National Award	Silver	*Art Director*	Hannes Boeker
Agency	Ogilvy & Mather Austria	*Copywriter*	Werner Buehringer
Client	Kraft Foods Austria	*Photographer*	Staudinger & Franke
Creative Director	Alexander Zelmanovics, Mag. Dieter Pivrnec		

O**2.2**
NEWSPAPER ADVERTISING
Germany: 1 gold ★
Spain: 1 gold ★
Ireland: 1 nomination ☆

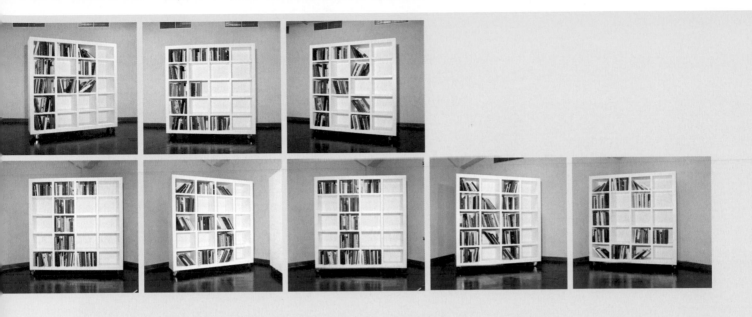

What happens when people are moved from their place.

★

Roots *Spain*

National Award	Bronze	*Art Director*	Vaneza Sanz
Agency	Publicis Comunicación España, S.A.	*Copywriter*	Natalia Vaquero
		Agency Producer	José Ramón Uceda
Client	Survival International	*Photographer*	Joan Garrigosa
Creative Director	Nicolás Hollander		

stern supports "Exit", a programme that helps people get out of the right-wing extremist scene.

★

Labyrinth *Germany*

National Award	Bronze	*Art Director*	Tomas Tulinius
Agency	Grabarz & Partner	*Copywriter*	Teja Fischer
Client	Stern Gruner + Jahr AG & Co.	*Graphics*	Florian Pack
Creative Director	Ralf Nolting, Patricia Patzold, CCO: Ralf Heuel		

Full Page Yo, baby! Stand waaay back. I am a *full page ad*. Printers are scared of me - they call me the 'great white'. There ain't no ad like me. You want hard sell? I'll give you hard sell. I'll sell your whole shop. I'll carry ten washing machines, ten tumble driers, fifty cameras and then ask, "Hey, what about those widescreen TVs you wanna shift?" But I'm more than all that. You launching a product? I'll launch your product - I'll launch it into space. You got a picture? Blow it up, I ain't afraid. You got words? Bring 'em on. Big or small, when they're on me, they look important. Because I *announce*. I got the *dimensions*. I am the undisputed heavyweight king of press advertising and I will make your product my queen. Hear me roar. **The Power of Press**

L-shape I'm the new guy. The weird one. Attention-seeking. A bit... crazy. I'm L for long, L for lovely, L for L-Diablo. You know who loves me? Technology companies, mobile phones, anyone who thinks, like, different. Because I own the whole page without needing one of those, you know, ads from the 'square' community. You're reading down, dum-di-dum, thinking I'm only on one side of the paper, then BAM! I'm over the other side. I'm everywhere. Isn't that amazing? Look, look, what am I now? I'm a golf club. Now I'm the tail of an airplane. I'm a palm tree and a long sandy beach. I'm a new apartment block. Try me - I'm just so comfortable with my shape. **The Power of Press**

35 x 6 (the page killer) Some may think I didn't get enough attention when I was smaller. You know, "His father always worked late; his mother was a drunk" - textbook psycho stuff. Not true. I was *born* to kill. Killing is my job. I'm a paid professional - a contract killer, if you will. I have no mercy and I don't discriminate. I kill whatever's around me. *Kill. Kill. Kill.* All kinds of people have used me to clean up for them: fast food chains, carpet showrooms, manufacturers of hi-fi equipment. Once you hire me, your competitors' days are numbered. I never miss my target. I'm cool and calculating, quick and clean. In and out - job done. Next please. **The Power of Press**

Promoting the power of Press Advertising

☆
Various Sizes *Ireland*

National Award....Gold
Agency...............Chemistry
Client ....National Newspapers of Ireland
Creative Director...Mike Garner

Art Director.........Adrian Fitz-Simon, Emmet Wright
Copywriter ....Adrian Fitz-Simon, Emmet Wright

Long-term Clients: "We treat all our clients as if they were long-term clients. Even if they have been with us for only 10 years. Julius Bär. True to you."
Backbone: "There's a difference between having a spinal column and having a backbone. Julius Bär. True to you."

True to you *Switzerland*

National Award	Silver	*Copywriter*	A. Jaggy, T. Seinige,
Agency	Jung von Matt, Zürich AG		A. Eckstein, M. Rottmann
Client	Julius Bär	*Graphics*	Inken Rohweder
Creative Director	Alexander Jaggy, Tom Seinige		
Art Director	Axel Eckstein		

This is what Freedom of Speech looks like in Belarus. The biggest Polish daily and Europe's 6th largest newspaper were censored to represent what freedom of speech looks like in Belarus.

Freedom of speech *Poland*

How it is not nice to drink? With black-outs (without picture)!
Let's drink with pleasure! SAAREMAA Vodka

The text begins with a question: How to interpret history? The idea behind the advertisement was to depict national history through the people who live on the small island of Saaremaa.

How to interpret history? *Estonia*

National Award	Gold	*Art Director*	Marge Nuggis
Agency	Kontuur Leo Burnett	*Copywriter*	Anti Naulainen
Client	Altia Eesti AS	*Photographer*	Toomas Tikenberg
Creative Director	Urmas Villmann	*Illustrator*	Toomas Tikenberg

Without picture *Estonia*

National Award	Silver	*Art Director*	Marge Nuggis
Agency	Kontuur Leo Burnett	*Copywriter*	Andrus Niit
Client	Altia Eesti AS	*Photographer*	Toomas Tikenberg
Creative Director	Urmas Villmann		

This graphic suggests the perils of a water shortage and promotes awareness of water consumption habits.

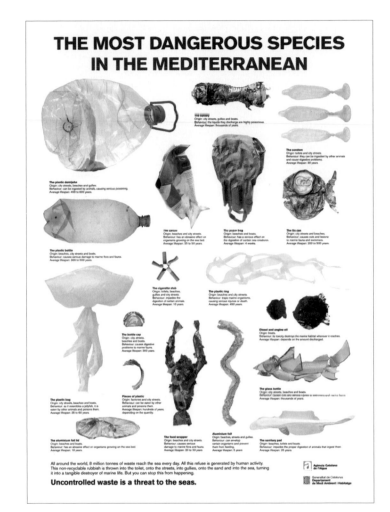

This advertisement promotes awareness of the threat that solid waste poses to marine life.

Or (Gold) *Spain*

National Award	Silver	*Art Director*	Fernando Planelles
Agency	SMÄLL	*Copywriter*	Xavier Hidalgo
Client	Generalitat de Catalunya	*Photographer*	Joan Garrigosa
Creative Director	Xavier Hidalgo, Fernando Planelles		

Dangerous Species *Spain*

National Award	Gold	*Art Director*	Klas Ernflo, Fernando Planelles
Agency	SMÄLL	*Copywriter*	Xavier Hidalgo, Fran Segarra
Client	Generalitat de Catalunya	*Photographer*	Ramón Serrano
Creative Director	Xavier Hidalgo, Fernando Planelles		

Keep black power alive. Scowling black sweater

Panther *Italy*

National Award	Silver	*Art Director*	Serena Di Bruno
Agency	D'Adda, Lorenzini, Vigorelli, BBDO	*Copywriter*	Giovanni Chiarelli
Client	Henkel	*Photographer*	Fulvio Bonavia
Creative Director	Giuseppe Mastromatteo, Luca Scotto di Carlo		

Diena-Astrological/Logical forecast *Latvia*

National Award	Gold	*Art Director*	Zoom!
Agency	Zoom!	*Copywriter*	Zoom!
Client	Newspaper Diena	*Photographer*	Zoom!
Creative Director	Zoom!		

For the Panasonic print and billboard

Liberty Zoom *Switzerland*

National Award	Silver	*Agency Producer*	Ilonka Galliard
Agency	Jung von Matt, Zürich AG	*Photographer*	David Kempinski
Client	John Lay Electronics		
Creative Director	Alexander Jaggy		
Art Director	Lukas Frei		
Copywriter	Johannes Raggio		

Suva Accident Insurance Ski Jump *Switzerland*

National Award	Silver	*Art Director*	Sascha Fanetti, Katja Puccio
Agency	Ruf Lanz Werbeagentur AG	*Copywriter*	Patrick Suter
Client	Suva Accident Insurance	*Designer*	Marcel Jäger
Creative Director	Danielle Lanz, Markus Ruf	*Photographer*	Stefan Minder
		Postproduction	Felix Schregenberger

The Fantasporto Film Festival at home.

It's an old cliché that people count sheep while trying to fall asleep.

Baby *Portugal*

National Award	Silver	*Art Director*	André Moreira,
Agency	BBDO Portugal, S.A		Ivo Purvis
Client	Público	*Copywriter*	Nuno Leal
Creative Director	Nuno Jerónimo	*Account Supervisor*	Filipa Robalo,
			Lizete Oliveira

Sheep *Finland*

National Award	Silver	*Agency Producer*	Karolina Mattsson
Agency	TBWA PHS Helsinki	*Photographer*	Jari Riihimaki
Client	Unikulma	*Graphics*	Hugo d'Alte
Art Director	Jyrki Reinikka	*Account Director*	Antti Karava,
Copywriter	Jussi Turhala		Planner Tommi Laiho

When you drive too fast, too often you find a policeman hiding behind a bush. Thanks to Volkswagen Touareg, they have expanded their hiding area to the deepest forests.

This graphic was published the same day as the largest draw for the national lottery, "El Gordo" ("The Fat One"). The tradition is for the pupils of Sant Ildefonso College to display the winning numbers to the press.

Police *Estonia*

National Award	Silver	*Art Director*	Peeter Pullerits
Agency	Tank	*Agency Producer*	Terje Pihl
Client	Saksa Auto	*Photographer*	Jyri Seljamaa
Creative Director	Joel Volkov		

Maybe next time *Spain*

National Award	Gold	*Art Director*	Xavi Sitjar
Agency	DDB España	*Copywriter*	Isahac Oliver
Client	V.A.E.S.A	*Photographer*	Fergus Stothart
Creative Director	Josep Maria Roca de Vinyals		

The dialogues of Woody Allen's films are filled with so many creative, odd, and unforgettable one-liners, it is safe to claim that the subtitles alone make it worth it.

The subtitles alone make it worth it *Portugal*

National Award Gold	*Art Director* André Moreira,
Agency BBDO Portugal, S.A.	Juliano Bertoldi
Client Público	*Copywriter* Hellington Vieira
Creative Director Nuno Jerónimo	*Account Supervisor* Lizete Oliveira

Accidents can happen, even in the perfect world of advertising. To emphasize this, well-known ads were altered.

Diena-The mind is also an erogenous zone *Latvia*

National Award	Gold	*Art Director*	Zoom!
Agency	Zoom!	*Copywriter*	Zoom!
Client	Newspaper Diena	*Photographer*	Zoom!
Creative Director	Zoom!		

Nothing is certain *Switzerland*

National Award	Silver	*Copywriter*	Stefan Ehrler
Agency	Spillmann, Felser, Leo Burnett	*Agency Producer*	Sebahat Derdiyok
Client	National Versicherung	*Photographer*	Julien Vonier
Creative Director	Martin Spillmann		
Art Director	Dana Wirz		

DACH
MAUT
BUCH
BERG

Holocaust: memory lost?   AKTION MENSCH

Holocaust *Austria*

National Award....Silver	*Art Director*........René Pichler
Agency................Lowe GGK	*Copywriter*..........Walther Salvenmoser
Client ....Aktion Mensch	*Graphic*..............Helmut Kansky
Creative Director...Walther Salvenmoser	

Good Friday *Austria*

National Award....Gold	*Art Director*........Walther Salvenmoser
Agency................Lowe GGK	*Photographer*.......Dieter Brasch
Client ....CS Hospiz Rennweg	*Graphics*............Vienna Paint
Creative Director...Walther Salvenmoser	

Comic *Austria*

National Award....Silver	*Art Director*........René Pichler
Agency.............Lowe GGK	*Copywriter*.........Alexander Hofmann
Client.............CS Hospiz Rennweg	*Graphics*...........René Pichler
Creative Director..Walther Salvenmoser	*Illustrator*..........René Pichler

Alzheimer's Day *Finland*

National Award....Silver	*Copywriter*.........Erkko Mannila
Agency.............TBWA PHS Helsinki	*Agency Producer*...Karolina Mattsson
Client.............Pfizer	*Graphics*...........Sasu Haanpaa
Art Director........Mikko Torvinen	*Account Director*...Jere Teutari

O2.3
MAGAZINE ADVERTISING
United Kingdom: 1 gold ★
Austria: 1 nomination ☆
Germany: 5 nominations ☆
Netherlands: 1 nomination ☆

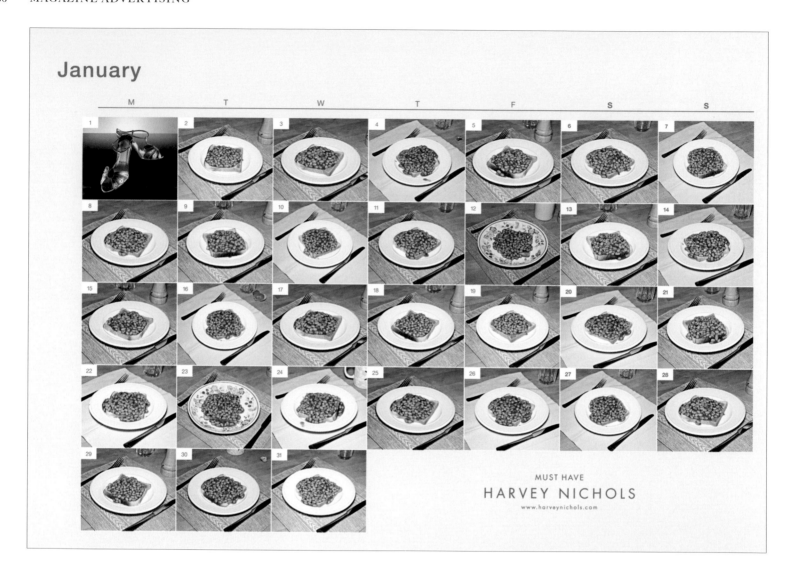

★

Beans / Cat / Jigsaw / Toilet Paper *United Kingdom*

National Award Silver		*Art Director* Justin Tindall	
Agency DDB London		*Copywriter* Adam Tucker	
Client Harvey Nichols		*Designer* Peter Mould	
Creative Director Justin Tindall, Adam Tucker		*Photographer* James Day	

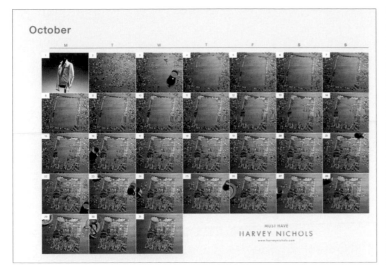

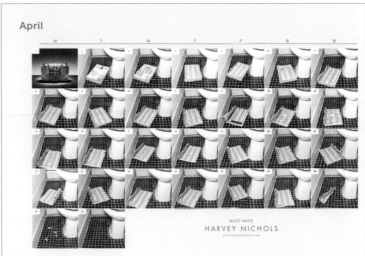

It would be great if compassion could help. But we need your money.

☆
World Vision Campaign *Germany*

National Award	Bronze	*Art Director*	Kristoffer Heilemann
Agency	DDB Germany, Berlin	*Copywriter*	Ludwig Berndl
Client	World Vision Deutschland e.V.	*Agency Producer*	Sandra Markus
		Graphics	Dorus Brekelmans
Creative Director	Amir Kassaei, Wolfgang Schneider, Mathias Stiller	*Account*	Michael Lamm, Louisa Ibing

More education for girls in Islamic countries!

☆
Unicef Islam *Austria*

National Award	Silver	*Copywriter*	Joachim Glawion, Patrick Partl
Agency	FCB Kobza		
Client	Unicef Austria	*Designer*	Tolga Büyükdoganay
Creative Director	Joachim Glawion, Patrick Partl	*Photographer*	Joe Fish
Art Director	Tolga Büyükdoganay		

stern supports "Exit", a programme that helps people get out of the right-wing extremist scene.

☆
Labyrinth *Germany*

National Award	Silver	*Art Director*	Tomas Tulinius
Agency	Grabarz & Partner	*Copywriter*	Teja Fischer
Client	Stern Gruner + Jahr AG & Co.	*Graphics*	Florian Pack
Creative Director	Ralf Nolting, Patricia Patzold, CCO: Ralf Heuel		

☆
German Foundation for Monument Protection *Germany*

National Award	Bronze	*Creative Director*	Simon Oppmann, Peter Roemmelt
Agency	Ogilvy & Mather Frankfurt	*Art Director*	Simon Oppmann
Client	German Foundation for Monument Protection	*Copywriter*	Peter Roemmelt
		Photographer	Hana Kostreba
		Graphics	Hana Kostreba
		Art Buying	Christina Hufgard

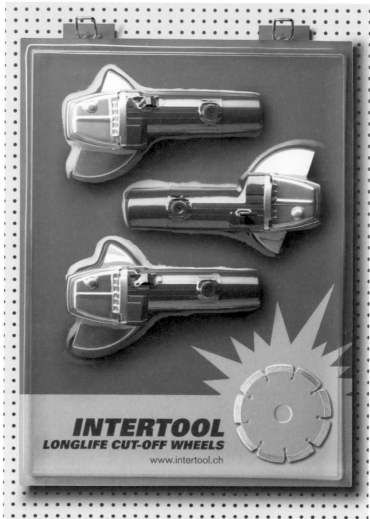

Tools from INTERTOOL live longer than the machines

☆

Intertool Longlife Tools Campaing *Germany*

National Award	Shortlist	*Art Director*	Philipp Boettcher, Marco Weber
Agency	Ogilvy & Mather Frankfurt	*Copywriter*	Philipp Boettcher
Client	Intertool AG, Switzerland	*Photographer*	Heinz Wuchner
		Graphics	Marc Wuchner, Kapka Dotcheva
Creative Director	Christian Mommertz, Dr. Stephan Vogel	*Art Buying*	Christina Hufgard

☆
The Cleaning Ladies Campaign *Germany*

National Award	Bronze	*Art Director*	Axel Schilling, Marc Ebenwaldner
Agency	Scholz & Friends	*Copywriter*	Johan H. Ohlson, Alexander Schierl
Client	BSH Bosch und Siemens Hausgeraete GmbH	*Photography*	hiepler, brunier
		Graphics	Pia Schneider
Creative Director	Stefan Setzkorn, Silke Schneider, Gunnar Loeser	*Postproduction*	Metagate GmbH, Hamburg

☆

Peugeot 1007. With handy sliding doors *Netherlands*

National Award	Silver	*Art Director*	Stan Severin
Agency	Euro RSCG Amsterdam	*Copywriter*	Marijn Peters
Client	Peugeot Nederlands b.v.	*Agency Producer*	Loes Plekker
Creative Director	Edward Bardoul	*Photographer*	Paul Ruigrok

It's sugar free

The Salt and Pepper Hug from Vinçon.

Ants *Spain*

National Award	Silver	*Art Director*	Bernat Sanromà
Agency	DDB España	*Copywriter*	David Pérez Barrachina
Client	Chupa Chups	*Photographer*	Ramón Serrano
Creative Director	Mario Gascón		

Salt and Pepper Hug *Spain*

National Award	Gold
Agency	Vitruvio Leo Burnett S.A. (Madrid)
Client	Vinçon Design Shop

Sharp Knives *Germany*

National Award	Silver	*Art Director*	Thomas Thiele
Agency	KNSK Werbeagentur GmbH	*Copywriter*	Steffen Steffens
		Agency Producer	Heinz-Rudi Junge
Client	WMF AG	*Photographer*	Arte & Immagini srl/ CORBIS, Araldo de Luca/CORBIS
Creative Director	Tim Krink, Niels Holle		
		Graphics	Hanadi Chawaf, Boris Schatte

Opening soon *Austria*

National Award	Silver	*Art Director*	Sandra Jakovcic, Max Jurasch
Agency	Publicis		
Client	Miracle's Wax Museum GmbH	*Photographer*	Gregor Ecker
		Graphics	Sandra Jakovcic
Creative Director	Max Jurasch		

Ariel colour won't let your memories fade.

Keep black power alive.

Ariel *Poland*

National Award	Silver	*Creative Director*	Jacek Szulecki
Agency	Saatchi & Saatchi Poland	*Art Director*	Bartek Grala
		Copywriter	Daniel Piecka
Client	Procter & Gamble Poland	*Photographer*	Andrzej Ratajczyk

Animals *Italy*

National Award	Gold	*Creative Director*	Giuseppe Mastromatteo, Luca Scotto di Carlo
Agency	D'Adda, Lorenzini, Vigorelli, BBDO	*Art Director*	Serena Di Bruno
		Copywriter	Giovanni Chiarelli
Client	Henkel	*Photographer*	Fulvio Bonavia

Massage, Trampoline, Cow-dog *Russia*

National Award	Silver	*Creative Director*	Mikhail Kudashkin
Agency	Leo Burnett Moscow	*Art Director*	Alexander Porshnev
Client	Ehrmann	*Copywriter*	Viktor Lander

for family

for health

for celebration

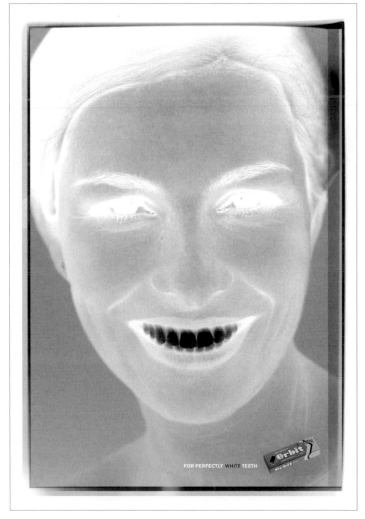

Perfectly white teeth - it's black and white.

Druva *Latvia*

National Award	Silver	*Creative Director*	Armands Leitis
Agency	McCann-Erickson Riga	*Art Director*	Armands Leitis
Client	Druva	*Copywriter*	Armands Leitis

Orbit Smile *Czech Republic*

National Award	Silver	*Art Director*	Michal Kotulek
Agency	Mark BBDO	*Copywriter*	Leon Sverdlin
Client	Wrigley	*Photographer*	Sundayphoto
Creative Director	Leon Sverdlin, Martin Charv·t		

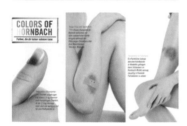

HORNBACH is a chain of D.I.Y. stores.

Silence hurts. Call 707200077.

Women at work *Germany*

National Award	Silver	*Copywriter*	J. Bosse, A. Ardelean, G. Heffels, S. Kainz, T. Eckel
Agency	Heimat, Berlin		
Client	Hornbach Baumarkt AG		
Creative Director	Guido Heffels, Jürgen Vossen	*Designer*	Joachim Zeh, Eva Bajer, Oliver Schneider
Art Director	Marc Wientzek, Tim Schneider	*Photographer*	Sven Schrader

Shut Up! *Portugal*

National Award	Gold	*Creative Director*	João Espírito Santo
Agency	JWT Lisbon	*Art Director*	José Carlos Fonseca
Client	APAV (Portuguese Association for Victim Support)	*Copywriter*	Líber Matteucci
		Photographer	Filipe Rebelo
		Graphics	Irene Bandeira

Scary gas prices

Marine monsters and the gods of the ocean are forced to surrender their supremacy and fame as terrors of the deep to the unchallenged authority of the new king of the seas—Yamaha Marine.

Scary gas prices *Austria*

National Award	Gold	*Art Director*	Markus Zauner, James Teal
Agency	JWT Vienna	*Copywriter*	Alexander Lauber, Thomas Troppmann
Client	Austrian Railway Federation	*Photographer*	Günther Parth
Creative Director	Alexander Lauber, Markus Zauner	*Postproduction*	Rotfilter

Monsters *Italy*

National Award	Silver	*Art Director*	Giorgio Cignoni
Agency	1861 United	*Copywriter*	Laura Cattaneo
Client	Yamaha Marine	*Illustrator*	Alessandro Bavari, Direct 2 Brain
Creative Director	Pino Rozzi, Roberto Battaglia		

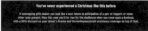

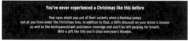

The nice present - a new scooter!!! At a new price.

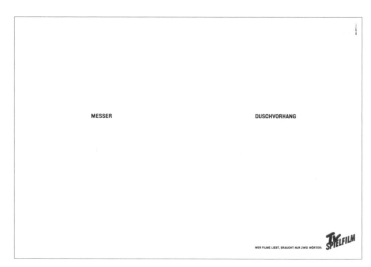
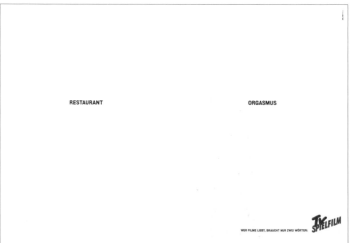

A print campaign for the TV Guide "TV Spielfilm".

Christmas - Apple, Candels, Carps *Czech Republic*

National Award	Silver	*Art Director*	Premysl Ponahly
Agency	Young and Rubicam Prague	*Copywriter*	Stanislav Becka
		Designer	Premysl Ponahly
Client	Kentoya		
Creative Director	Frantisek Bumbalek, Miroslav Pomikal		

Two Words *Germany*

National Award	Silver	*Art Director*	Till Monshausen
Agency	Jung von Matt AG	*Copywriter*	Dennis May, Fabian Frese
Client	TV Spielfilm	*Agency Producer*	Ulrich Grimm
Creative Director	Goetz Ulmer, Daniel Frericks, Oliver Voss	*Graphics*	Javier Suárez Argueta
		Account Supervisor	Turan Tehrani

Indicate the books you've read.

Books *Portugal*

National Award	Silver	*Art Director*	Paulo Arias
Agency	Leo Burnett Lisbon	*Copywriter*	Marilu Rodrigues
Client	Cafes Heredia	*Agency Producer*	Cristina Almeida
Creative Director	Fernando Bellotti		

More Intense Music *Germany*

National Award	Silver	*Art Director*	Till Monshausen, Martin Terhart
Agency	Jung von Matt AG	*Copywriter*	Dennis May, Fabian Frese
Client	Beyerdynamic GmbH & Co. KG	*Agency Producer*	Carsten Koeslag
Creative Director	Goetz Ulmer, Daniel Frericks, Oliver Voss	*Account Supervisor*	Philipp Schnitzler

The Sprinter James Cook.

Mercedes-Benz

☆
The Globetrotter Ad *Germany*

National Award	Shortlist	
Agency	Scholz & Friends	
Client	DaimlerChrysler AG, DCVD	
Creative Director	Constantin Kaloff, Julia Schmidt	
Art Director	Gregory French	
Copywriter	Peter Quester	
Photographer	Map Resources	
Account Executive	S. Wurst, T. Caprano, J. Rahaus	

Schallschutz (Sound Insulation) *Austria*

National Award	Silver	*Copywriter*	Patrik Partl,
Agency	FCB Kobza		Eva Sommeregger
Client	Fachverband der	*Designer*	Heike Weiss
	Stein-und keramisch-	*Photographer*	Wolfgang Zajk
	en Industrie	*Concept*	Patrick Partl,
Art Director	Goran Golik		Goran Golik

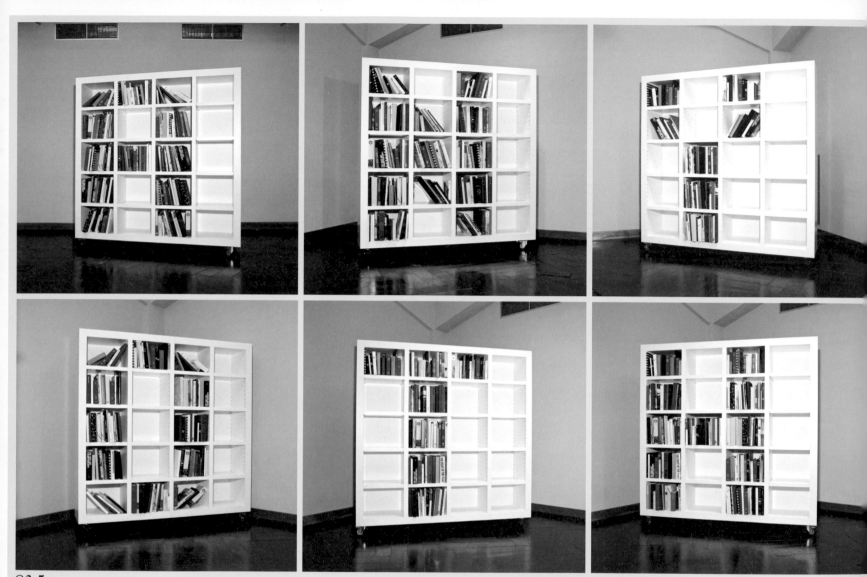

02.5
ANY OTHER

Children can discover the fun of cooking with the culinary academy for kids. Every month you can find a new recipe in your cooking magazine, Annemarie Wildeisen's Kochen (Cooking). "Enjoy Every Day."

Jewellery & timepieces.

Cooking School for Kids *Austria*

National Award	Gold	*Creative Director*	Reinhold Weber,
Agency	Bicher/Rabl/Mark-		Christian Bircher
	steiner	*Copywriter*	Alexander Rabl
Client	Aargauer Medien	*Photographer*	Robert Marksteiner
	Gruppe		

Desire *Austria*

National Award	Silver	*Copywriter*	Doris Kaser,
Agency	FCB Kobza		Matthias Wernicke
Client	Jeweller Haban	*Designer*	Birgit Schuster
Creative Director	Tobias Federsel	*Concept*	Doris Kaser,
Art Director	Matthias van Baaren		Tobias Federsel

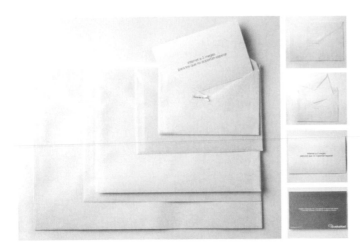

"Not to be opened until 22.00 h." The primary envelope contained 4 smaller envelopes with this message. The last envelope had a card with subscription information that read: "3 megas of Internet for those who can't bear to wait."

This sunscreen lotion kit was used as advertising media for a festival. The city where the festival takes place is a tourist destination because of its beaches. The kit was both advertising and a practical item.

Despega 3m *Spain*

National Award	Silver	*Art Director*	Joseba Zabalo
Agency	Dimension	*Copywriter*	Gerardo López
Client	Euskaltel	*Agency Producer*	Marta Parra
Creative Director	Guille Viglione, Santi Hernández		

Flavoured Sunscreen Lotion *Spain*

National Award	Silver	*Art Director*	Pablo Burgués, Roberto de la Cruz
Agency	Vitruvio Leo Burnett	*Copywriter*	Pablo Burgués, Roberto de la Cruz
Client	Sitges Sci-Fi & Fantasy Film Festival	*Agency Producer*	Rodrigo Roco
Creative Director	Rafa Antón		

Outdoor - bus shelter

Converse masks *Poland*

National Award ... Silver
Agency .... J.W.T. Warsaw
Client .... AmerSport
Creative Director ... Darek Zatorski

Art Director .... Lukasz Kotlinski
Copywriter .... Iza Przepiorska
Photographer .... Szymon Swietochowski

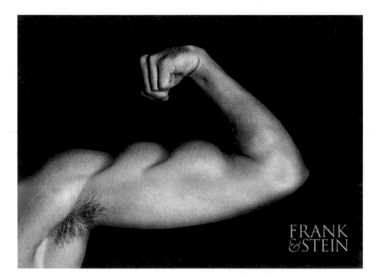

Frank & Stein - Two times stronger advertising.

Egg *Poland*

National Award....Silver	*Art Director*.........Pawel Borowski
Agency.................TBWA Warsaw	*Copywriter*..........Pawel Borowski
Client ....BE Store	*Agency Producer*....Pawel Borowski
Creative Director....Pawel Borowski	

Two times stronger advertising *Latvia*

National Award....Silver	*Creative Director*...Ingus Josts,
Agency.................Frank & Stein	Kriss Salmanis
Client ....Frank & Stein	*Art Director*.........Kriss Salmanis
	Copywriter..........Ingus Josts

Decide: Either you defend the planet, or it defends itself.

Defend the planet *Italy*

National Award	Gold	*Art Director*	Francesca Risolo
Agency	Saatchi & Saatchi	*Copywriter*	Stefano Massari
Client	Greenpeace	*Photographer*	Stock
Creative Director	Luca Albanese, Francesco Taddeucci		

When a shop is being remodelled or is simply empty, Bulevard Rosa covers the windows with one of these giant posters to make the wait more fun.

Easter card

Tiendas vacías *Spain*

National Award	Silver	*Art Director*	Juan Mingarro
Agency	Villarrosas, SCPF	*Copywriter*	Oriol Villar
Client	Bulevard Rosa	*Designer*	Juan Mingarro
Creative Director	Oriol Villar, Fernando Codina	*Agency Producer*	Inés Vilaseca

Jesus Christ! *Poland*

National Award	Gold	*Art Director*	Jozef Dudtkiewicz
Agency	TBWA Warsaw	*Copywriter*	Mariusz Pitura, Weronika Zarebska
Client	TBWA Warsaw		
Creative Director	Pawel Borowski		

03 New/Mixed Media

03.1
INTERACTIVE MEDIA
Sweden: 1 gold ★
Germany: 3 nominations☆
Switzerland: 1 nomination☆

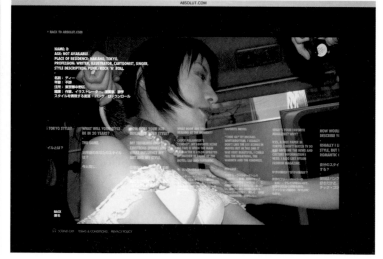

ABSOLUT VODKA has, with its heritage in art, fashion and music always been looking for new creative forms to reach the right people. ABSOLUT METROPOLIS invites the visitor on a journey around Tokyo's underground scene.

★

Absolut Metropolis *Sweden* ◉

National Award	Gold	*Designer*	F. Karlsson, O. Sundberg, J. Wissing
Agency	Great Works		
Client	V&S Spirits AB	*Photographer*	N. Kander
Creative Director	Ted Persson, Sebastien Vacherot	*Illustrator*	F. Karlsson
		Programmer	F. Karlsson, O. Sundberg, J. Wissing
Art Director	Max Larsson von Reybekiel		
Copywriter	D. Sundin, K. Triumf	*Url*	www.absolut.com/metropolis

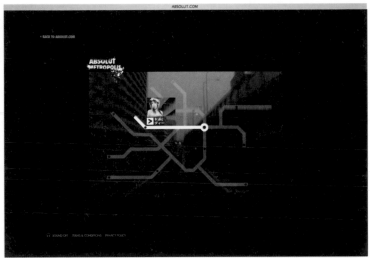

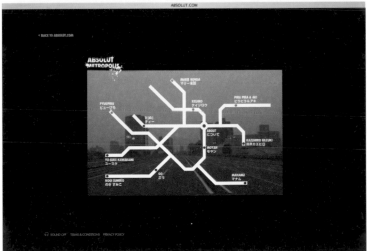

A holographic projection in the shop window of C&A's flagship store in Berlin shows a model in Seite*1Girl underwear. A live webcam streams the reaction of the passers-by to www.seite1*Girl.de. There, the website users are able to control the projected model and thus initiate a dialogue with the passers-by.

☆

Bild Seite* 1 Girl *Germany*   ●

National Award Bronze	*Programmer* Benjamin Herholz,
Agency Jung von Matt AG	Jan M. Studt
Client Axel Springer AG	*Url* http://award.jvm.
Creative Director Bernd Kramer	de/en/seite1girl
Art Director Sven Loskill	
Copywriter Robert Ehlers	

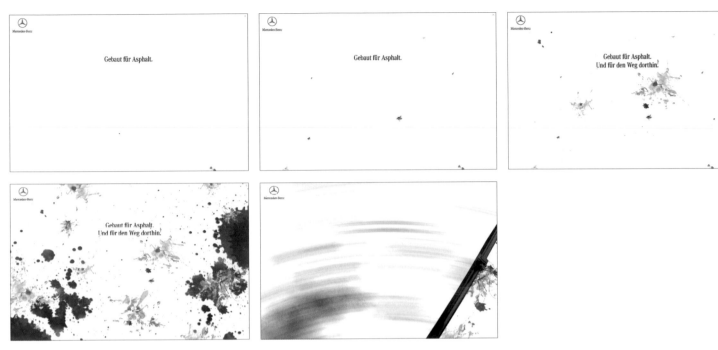

The campaign for the market launch of the new M-Class bears the strap-line "Built for the road. And for getting that far." This is a radically different approach to car advertising.

☆
Mercedes-Benz M-Class, Splatter *Germany*   ●

National Award	Shortlist		*Production Comp.*	Rainer Sax
Agency	Elephant Seven AG		*Graphics*	Till Hinrichs
Client	DaimlerChrysler VD		*Programmer*	Rouven Laurien (Flash)
Creative Director	Dirk Ollmann, Daniel Richau		*Url*	http://bannertool.e-7.com/awards/2006/en/mb_screensaver_splatter/
Art Director	Kai Becker			
Copywriter	Benjamin Bruno			

Digital photography means the end of memory as we know it. You now have the power to select, edit, manipulate, delete or send photos at the touch of a button. Remember the whole story or just your version of the story. Remember with sound or video. Remember on memory card, CD or hard disk. Remember what you choose to remember.

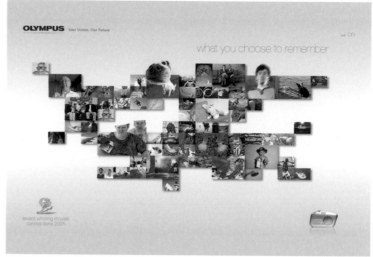

The idiosyncratic viral films work especially well on the internet. The disturbingly amusing effects of the films are effectively communicated and expanded via the microsite. They are an interpretation of the digital photography campaign "What you choose to remember."

☆

What you choose to remember *Germany*   ●

National Award	Nomination	*Designer*	André Bourguignon
Agency	Neue Digitale GmbH	*Programmer*	Heiko Schweickhardt
Client	Olympus Europe	*Url*	www.neue-digitale.de
Creative Director	Olaf Czeschner		/projects/olympus_
Art Director	Rolf Borcherding		brand

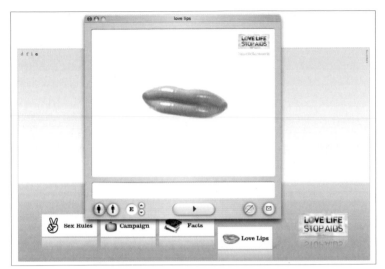

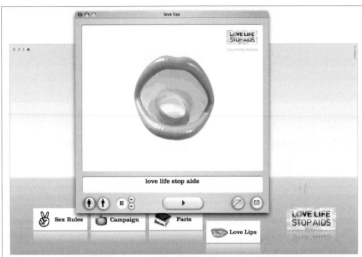

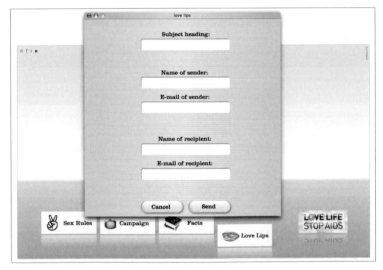

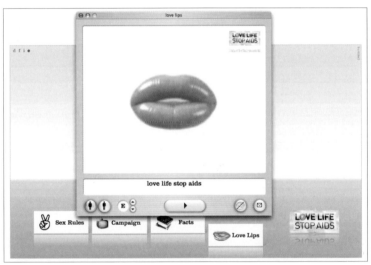

Love Lips is a tongue-in-cheek version of the round condom redesigned to resemble a mouth. Love Lips speaks with an erotic voice and makes sensuous movements

☆

Love Lips *Switzerland*   ●

National Award	Silver	*Copywriter*	Serge Deville
Agency	Euro RSCG Switzerland	*Programmer*	Station AG, Zürich
Client	BAG/Stop AIDS	*Url*	http://www.lovelife.ch
Creative Director	Petra Bottignole	*CEO*	Frank Bodin
Art Director	Patrick Beeli		

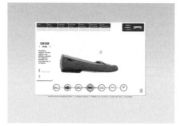

Have you tried travelling without a destination or simply going where your footsteps take you? A travel diary in collage form shows all the stages of a journey through India marked by Camper shoes.

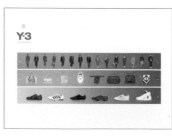

The current Y-3 autumn and winter collection for 2005-2006 is presented in a new multimedia space dimension, which breaks away from the norm. The effect is bizarre and out of the ordinary.

I go where my shoes take me *Spain*

National Award	Silver
Agency	Wysiwyg Comunicacion Interactiva
Client	Camper
Url	www.camper.com /web/en/basica. asp?flsid=162&

Adidas Sport Style Y-3 *Germany*

National Award	Gold
Agency	Neue Digitale GmbH
Client	Adidas
Creative Director	Olaf Czeschner
Art Director	Joerg Waldschuetz
Designer	Peter Kirsch, André Bourguignon, Stefan Schuster
Programmer	Jens Steffen
Url	www.neue-digitale.de /projects/y-3_fw2005

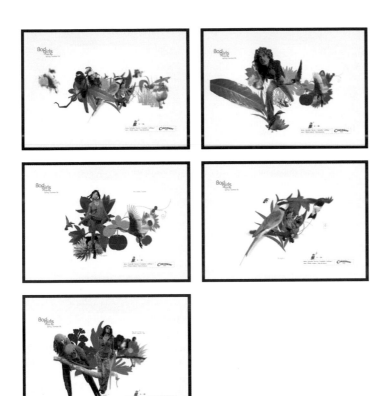

Bad girls can charm you with vivid colours, they can camouflage themselves among print works, they know how to make you look: They use their Cimarron clothing as a weapon.

The agency's new website showcases not only their ideas, but also emphasizes interactivity. The site has interactive videos to show the agency's clients, their recent work, and how to contact them.

Bad girls can fly *Spain*

National Award	Silver
Agency	Wysiwyg Comunicacion Interactiva
Client	Sáez Merino-Cimarrón
Url	www.cimarronjeans.com/

Wysiwyg *Spain*

National Award	Silver
Agency	Wysiwyg Comunicacion Interactiva
Client	Wysiwyg
Creative Director	Adolfo González, Nuria Martínez
Art Director	Marga Castaño
Copywriter	Daniel Molinillo, Esther de la Rosa
Programmer	Filippo de la Casa
Url	www.wysiwyg.net
Digital Arts	Charly Rodríguez

Your girlfriend is calling you! This Flash email contained an interactive video to promote the convenience of calling via a VoIP service (Voice over IP).

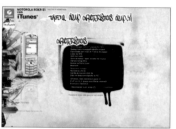

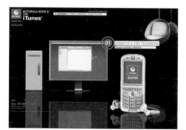

This mini-website was developed with the purpose of demonstrating and selling the Motorola ROKR mobile phone. Focusing on its major feature, the Apple iTunes software integration, the website revolves around a musical concept.

Girlfriend *Italy*

National Award	Silver
Agency	Version 4
Client	Parla.it (Gruppo France Telecom)
Creative Director	Carlo Maria Fasoli, Raffaella Bertini
Art Director	Carlo Maria Fasoli, Raffaella Bertini
Copywriter	Carlo Maria Fasoli
Url	www.effects.it/parlait
Postproduction	Borsani.com

Optimus Motorola ROKR *Portugal*

National Award	Gold
Agency	By
Client	Optimus
Creative Director	Rui Vieira
Art Director	Rui Vieira
Designer	Rui Vieira, Luis Silva, Filipe Mesquita
Illustrator	Raul Castro (3D)
Programmer	Sérgio Garcez
Url	www.bycom.com.pt/rokr

Relax your sight, stimulate your hearing, feel the touch: The new Nokia 8800 has been designed so that you can enjoy your senses. You can also do it on the Internet with the launch of Club Nokia's virtual spa.

This is a viral email project.

Spa Virtual *Spain*

National Award	Silver	*Client*	Nokia
Agency	Wysiwyg Comunicacion Interactiva	*Url*	www.nokia.es/club-nokia/evento8800/

Ego *Italy*

National Award	Gold	*Programmer*	Omar Odino, Alessandro Bider, Paolo Villani
Agency	Nurun Italia Srl		
Client	ADCI		
Creative Director	Carlo Maria Fasoli, Raffaella Bertini	*Url*	www.nurun.it /awards06/adci-ego
Art Director	Carlo Maria Fasoli, Raffaella Bertini	*Audio Postprod.*	MusicProduction
Copywriter	Joseph Menda (Arnold Worldwide)		

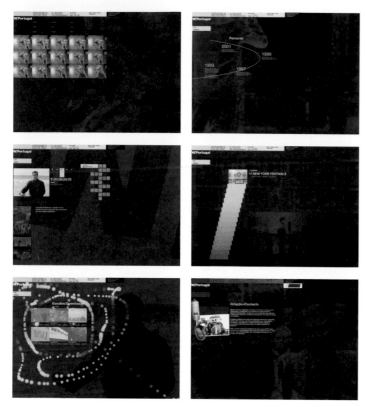

This is an institutional website for the Portuguese advertising agency W/Portugal with 100% Flash Action-script 2.0., and video and original soundtrack integration. Each area of the site has its own personality and secret details for the visitor to discover.

This is a fashion wear website.

W/Portugal *Portugal*

National Award	Gold	*Art Director*	Spirituc
Agency	Spirituc	*Designer*	Spirituc
Client	W/Portugal	*Programmer*	Spirituc
Creative Director	Spirituc	*Url*	www.wportugal.com

Raid Gauloises *Italy*

National Award	Gold	*Designer*	Alessandro Orlandi, Matteo Giuricin
Agency	Fishouse.net		
Client	Raid Gauloises	*Graphics*	Alessandro Orlandi, Matteo Giuricin
Creative Director	Alessandro Orlandi		
Art Director	Alessandro Orlandi	*Programmer*	Logicweb
Copywriter	Katia Marin, Vincent Spaccapeli	*Url*	www.raidgauloises.com

The objectives for the website were to be visually impacting and to showcase the designs made by Hiroshi Tsunoda. The site needed to be simple to use and the content easy to find.

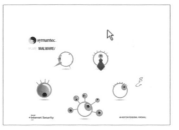
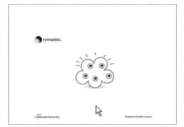

This is an Internet alert guide.

HiroshiTsunoda.com *Spain*

National Award	Silver
Agency	Aer-comunicación visual
Client	Hiroshi Tsunoda Design Studio
Creative Director	Aer-comunicación visual
Art Director	Aer-comunicación visual
Designer	Aer-comunicación visual
Programmer	Aer-comunicación visual
Url	www.hiroshitsunoda.com

Malware *Italy*

National Award	Silver
Agency	Nurun Italia Srl
Client	Symantec Italia
Creative Director	Carlo Maria Fasoli, Raffaella Bertini
Art Director	Carlo Maria Fasoli, Luca Daminelli
Copywriter	Carlo Maria Fasoli, Raffaella Bertini
Designer	Luca Daminelli
Illustrator	Carlo Maria Fasoli, Luca Daminelli
Programmer	Francesco Cinollo, Alessandro Bider
Url	www.nurun.it /awards06/guidasymantec

RMAC
BRAND DESIGN™

Member of BBDO Worldwide Network

These are not sofas made only for decoration. They function. They ensure comfort and style. They have personality. They define a living room, a home, and the people who own them.

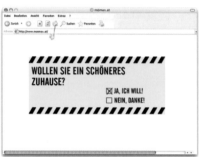

As a challenger brand, Mömax has to draw attention to itself in the intense clutter of the "big players" with their extensive budgets.

Website Zerodois *Portugal*

National Award	Silver
Agency	RMAC Brand Design
Client	Zerodois
Creative Director	Ricardo Mealha, Ana Cunha
Art Director	Ricardo Mealha, Ana Cunha
Designer	Patrick Goor
Programmer	Patrick Goor
Url	www.zerodois.com

Houseblasting-Banner *Austria*

National Award	Silver
Agency	Demner, Merlicek & Bergmann
Client	Mömax Furniture Stores
Creative Director	Gerda Reichl-Schebesta
Art Director	Bernhard Grafl
Copywriter	Alistair Thompson
Designer	Roman Steiner
Programmer	Men on the moon
Url	www.menonthemoon. com/clients/moemax/
Concept	Gerda Reichl-Schebesta, Philipp Ennemoser

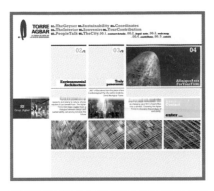

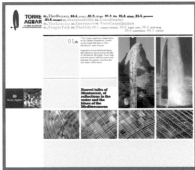

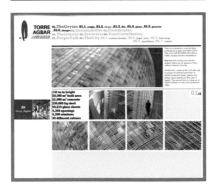

The goal was to develop an innovative and educational website for the emblematic tower in Barcelona.

This site was made for an artist-led expedition of the famous mountain Nanga Parbat. It lets you experience the difficulty of climbing Nanga Parbat. Website visitors can actually watch the expedition making their way up the mountain in real time.

Torre Agbar *Spain*

National Award	Silver
Agency	VIS-TEK
Client	Torre Agbar
Url	www.torreagbar.com

http://www.nanga-parbat.org *Germany*

National Award	Silver	*Designer*	Fabian Roser, Fabian Buergy
Agency	Jung von Matt AG		
Client	Artist Group Mangan	*Photographer*	Thorsten Eichhorst
Creative Director	Stefan Walz	*Programmer*	Marko Ritter, Fabian Roser
Art Director	Stefan Walz		
Copywriter	Matthias Kubitz	*Url*	www.nanga-parbat.org
		Account Executive	Brigitte Dingler

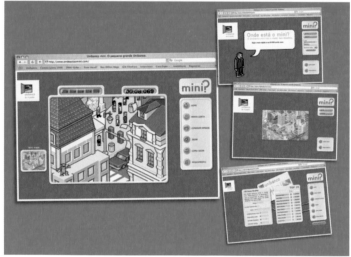

This was a viral marketing solution to publicize the launch of the Unibanco Mini, the first reduced size Visa card in Portugal. A small credit card is easier to carry, but harder to find.

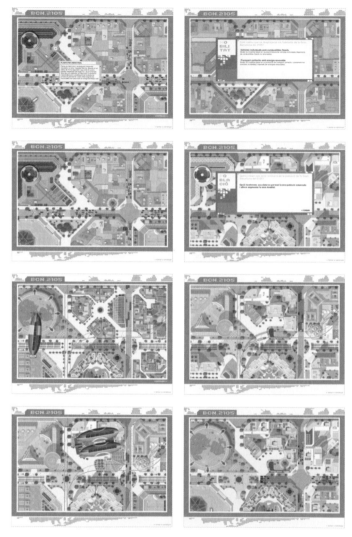

This is an interactive interface and image editor for the exhibition Torres i Temps. The exhibition centres on the history and impact of Barcelona's two towers and what the cityscape will be like in 2105.

Where's Mini? *Portugal*

National Award	Silver	*Copywriter*	André Freitas, João Magalhães
Agency	Touch_Me Wunderman	*Illustrator*	PANC
Client	Unibanco	*Programmer*	Djomba
Creative Director	Miguel Paté	*Url*	www.ondeestaomini.com
Art Director	Rui Saraiva, Alexandra Silva		

Barcelona 2105 *Spain*

National Award	Silver	*Designer*	D. Garitonandia
Agency	Trigital, S.L.	*Production Comp.*	Trigital, S.L.
Client	Museu Agbar-Fundació Agbar	*Graphics*	D. Garitonandia
Creative Director	M. Caparrós de Olmedo	*Illustrator*	M. Caparrós de Olmedo, David Garitonandia
Art Director	D. Garitonandia, M. Caparrós de Olmedo	*Programmer*	I. Caño, R. Romero
Copywriter	S. Arnauda, J. Serra	*Url*	www.museuagbar.com
		Coordinator	Oriol Ramírez

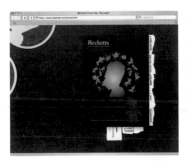

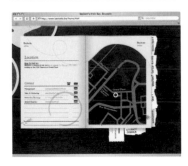

The Americanos website is characterized by its unique graphics, design, innovative animations, and intriguing author's soundtrack. Additionally, original navigation and copy, a number of electronic gadgets, and interactive tools are the features that make the new Americanos website different from typical product sites.

Website for an Irish bar based in Belgium, named after the Irish writer Samuel Beckett. The identity was based on two characters, Vladmir and Estragon, from his famous play, "Waiting for Godot".

Becketts Irish Bar *Ireland*

National Award	Silver
Agency	Red&Grey Design
Client	EVG Eventures Group
Creative Director	Richard Weld Moore
Art Director	Bob Gray
Copywriter	Red&Grey Design

Designer	Richard Weld Moore
Production Comp.	Red&Grey Design
Photographer	Eoghan Kavavnagh
Graphics	Keith McGuinness
Illustrator	Dave Muyllaert
Programmer	Ger Lawlor
	www.beckets.be

Americanos website *Poland*

National Award	Silver
Agency	Engine sp. z.o.o.
Client	Americanos

Art Director	Adam Szulc
Production Comp.	Engine
Url	www.americanos.pl

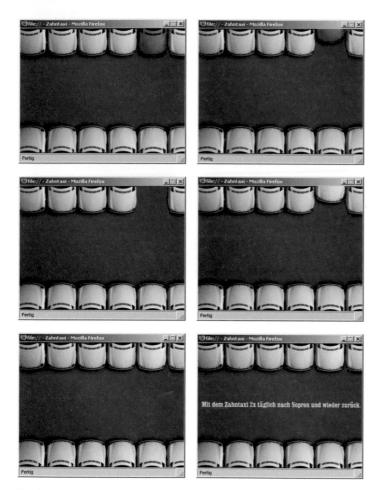

Tooth Taxi: Twice a day to Sopron and back.

The concept was to use World Book Day to communicate Bertrand's positioning as "Master Booksellers" and to emphasize the importance of reading as a source of cultural awareness and knowledge.

Tooth Taxi *Austria*

National Award	Gold	*Copywriter*	Florian Schwab, Eva Sommeregger
Agency	FCB Kobza	*Designer*	Birgit Schuster
Client	Top-Dent Dental Surgery	*Programmer*	Markus Winkler, Florian Deichstetter
Creative Director	Patrik Partl	*Concept*	Florian Schwab, Patrick Partl, Matthias van Baaren
Art Director	Matthias van Baaren, Markus Winkler		

Small Mouth *Portugal*

National Award	Gold	*Programmer*	Nelson Pimenta
Agency	Ogilvy One	*Url*	www.leitorbertrand.pt /dia_do_livro/index. html
Client	Bertrand		
Creative Director	Jorge Coelho		
Art Director	Hernani Dias		
Copywriter	Frederico Nunes, Jorge Coelho		

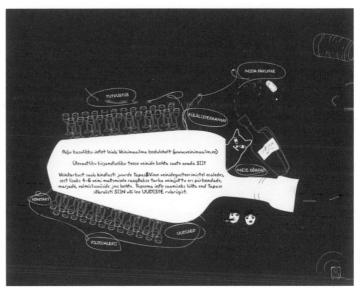

A rich and lively website for Tapas & Vino winebar.

The main goal was to raise awareness for the Raiffeisen Youth Club and to involve the target group in communication with the company.

Make it better *Austria*

National Award	Gold	*Copywriter*	Alexander Zelmanovics, Jan Hosa
Agency	Ogilvy Interactive Vienna	*Production Comp.*	Atticus
Client	Raiffeisen Bausparkasse	*Graphics*	Teresa Menzel
Creative Director	Alexander Zelmanovics, Georg Warga, Jan Hosa	*Programmer*	Andreas Heissenberger
		Url	awards.interactive.at /zrw_machsbesser_en
Art Director	Romain Berthet	*Account Manager*	Jürgen Jägersberger

Tapas & Vino Website *Estonia*

National Award	Gold	*Illustrator*	Marju Tammik, Hannes Unt
Agency	Loovvool		
Client	Tapas & Vino	*Programmer*	Martin Leppik
Creative Director	Hannes Unt	*Url*	www.tapas.ee
Art Director	Hannes Unt		

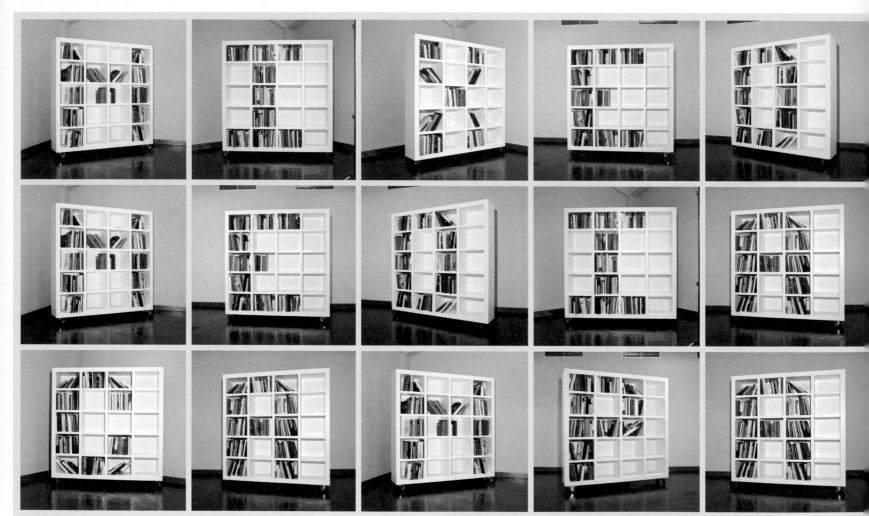

03.2
MIXED MEDIA CAMPAIGNS
Poland: 1 gold GP ★
Czech Republic: 1 nomination ☆

15.000 posters presenting the Belorussian opposition activists were attached with a silver tape, the one usually used for gagging. The biggest Polish daily and Europe's 6th largest newspaper were censored to represent what freedom of speech looks like in Belarus.

★ GP
Freedom of speech *Poland*

National Award	Bronze	*Copywriter*	Jakub Korolczuk, Ryszard Sroka
Agency	Saatchi & Saatchi Poland	*Photographer*	Andrzej Georgiew
Client	Amnesty International		
Creative Director	Jacek Szulecki		
Art Director	Ryszard Sroka, Jakub Korolczuk		

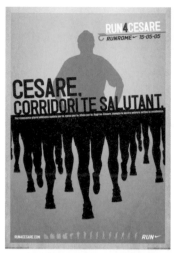

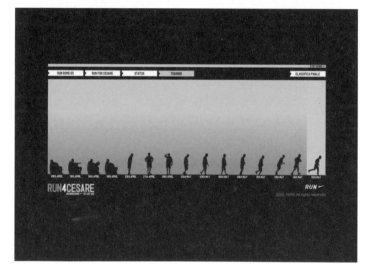

"Defend yourself. Regular check-ups help to prevent breast cancer damage."

See Cesare and run.

☆

Defend Yourself *Czech Republic*   ●

National Award....Shortlist	*Production Comp*...Mimofilm, Prague
Agency..............Mark BBDO	*Photographer*.......Roman Dietrich
Client................Avon	
Creative Director...Martin Charvat	
Art Director.......Ondrej Karasek	
Copywriter..........Pavel Sobek	

Run4Cesare *Italy*

National Award....Gold	*Art Director*........Patrizio Marini
Agency..............frdb Srl	*Copywriter*........Emanuele Madeddu
Client ....Nike Italy	*Illustrator*.........Patrizio Marini

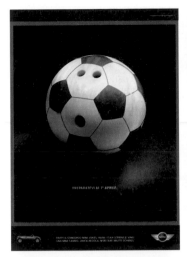

April Fool's: Objects that surprise at second glance.

Announcing the new Getz, a small vehicle that is big on the inside, for young people. This campaign emphasizes its interior space and promotes test-drives at car retailers. Cars are sometimes used as motels. But Getz is much more: It is a spacious room to discover.

Jokes *Italy*

National Award	Silver	*Art Director*	Anselmo Tumpic, Giuseppe Valerio
Agency	D'Adda, Lorenzini, Vigorelli, BBDO	*Copywriter*	Nicola Lampugnani
Client	MINI	*Photographer*	Andrea Melcangi, Luca Perazzoli
Creative Director	Giuseppe Mastromatteo, Luca Scotto di Carlo		

KarSutra *Portugal*

National Award	Silver	*Creative Director*	Miguel Pate
Agency	Touch_Me Wunderman	*Art Director*	Leonor Rasteiro
Client	Hyundai	*Copywriter*	Pedro Dias

This was an extensive guerrilla campaign that utilized posters, graffiti, stickers, banners, free T-shirts, and rat noses to direct people to a revolutionary website of alternative squatters.

For the Model-Makers Fair posters, advertisements and a radio spot were created.Sandwich-board people: Model-makers Fair 2005. A promotion using sandwich-boards was created for the opening of the model-makers fair.

NPNK *Estonia*

National Award	Gold	*Copywriter*	Juhan Ulfsak
Agency	Tank	*Illustrator*	Jan Tomson
Client	Hansabank	*Project Manager*	Rein Ott
Creative Director	Joel Volkov		
Art Director	Jaanus Tamme		

Model–Makers Fair *Austria*

National Award	Silver	*Copywriter*	Bernd Wildinger,
Agency	Jung von Matt/Donau		Helena Giokas
Client	Reed Messe Vienna	*Graphics*	Georg Feichtinger
Creative Director	Andreas Putz, Gerd		
	Schulte-Doeinghaus		
Art Director	Georg Feichtinger		

For the launch of the new Seitenblicke magazine, billboards, radio spots, and banners were created. The labels on the items are wordplays: They are the names of celebrities as well as the German dialect for the names of the objects.

Has last night caused you to fall asleep while standing up? Until now, Guronsan was only a remedy for hangovers. This year, Guronsan is a drug that helps overcome morning fatigue—it is loaded with caffeine.

Sleeping Standing Up *Portugal*

National Award	Silver	*Creative Director*	Miguel Pate
Agency	Touch_Me Wunderman	*Art Director*	Leonor Rasteiro
Client	JABA Pharmaceuticals	*Copywriter*	Pedro Dias

Stars nonstop *Austria*

National Award	Silver	*Copywriter*	Christoph Gaunersdorfer, Bernd Wilfinger
Agency	Jung von Matt/Donau		
Client	Red Bulletin Verlag	*Graphics*	Georg Feichtinger
Creative Director	Andreas Putz, Peter Kaimer		
Art Director	Georg Feichtinger		

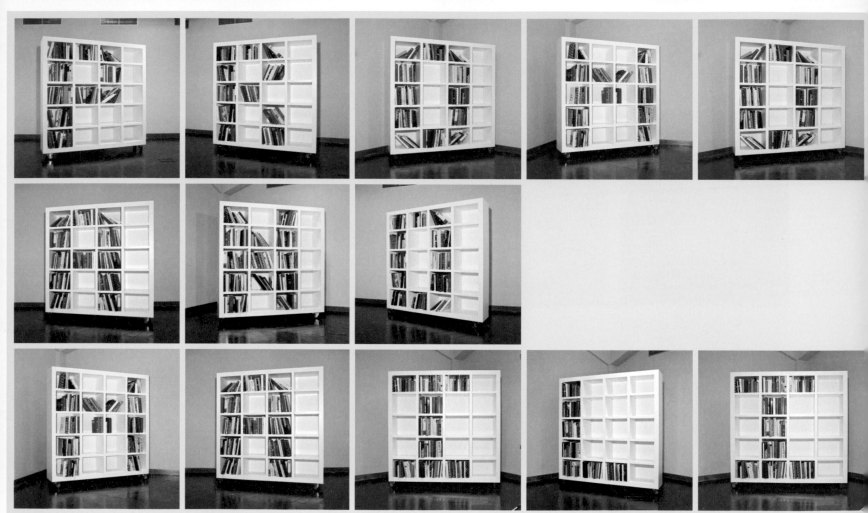

03.3
PROMOTIONS AND MAILINGS
Germany: 1 gold ★ 3 nominations ☆
Austria: 1 nomination ☆

For the TOYS "R" US Christmas promotion, real fire engines, garbage trucks, and diggers with oversized price tags drove through urban areas. Hopefully the children were not disappointed when they unwrapped smaller versions on Christmas Eve.

★

Real Toys. The TOYS *Germany*

National Award	Silver	*Copywriter*	Claudia Meimberg,
Agency	Grey Worldwide GmbH		Torsten Pollmann
Client	Toys	*Account Executive*	Sandra Friedrich
Creative Director	Florian Meimberg,		
	Torsten Pollmann		
Art Director	Florian Meimberg		

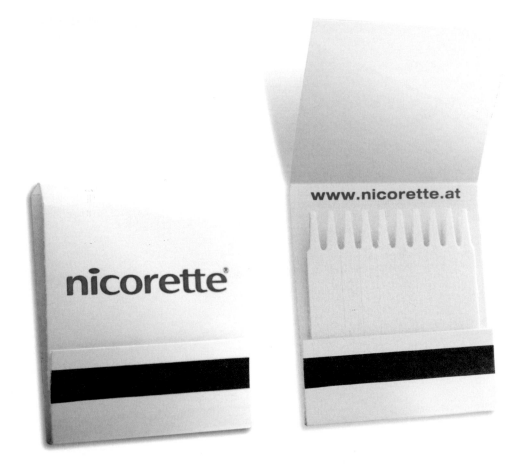

The match against smoking.

☆
Nicorette Match Box *Austria*

National Award	Gold	*Designer*	Daniel Senitschnig
Agency	FCB Retail	*Graphics*	Helga Hofbauer
Client	Pfizer Corporation Austria	*Concept*	Andreas Gesierich, Christoph Reicher, Daniel Senitschnig
Creative Director	Erich Falkner		
Art Director	Andreas Gesierich		
Copywriter	Christoph Reicher		

The goal of the promotion was to communicate that there is no better way to get music. For the promotion, Germany's street buskers (street musicians) did what they always do—but without making any noise.

No Music *Germany*

National Award	Shortlist	*Art Director*	Sebastian Oehme
Agency	Kolle Rebbe Werbeagentur GmbH	*Copywriter*	Sebastian Oehme
		Graphics	Kerstin Berk
Client	T-Online International AG		
Creative Director	Sven Klohk, Christoph Hildebrand		

The quarantine box protects potential readers from the deadly virus in Ken Follett's new novel Eisfieber.

☆
Quarantine box *Germany*

National Award	Shortlist	*Art Director*	Ekkehard Frenkler,
Agency	Serviceplan Zweite		Michaela Gressbach,
	Werbeagentur GmbH		Sybille Stempel
Client	Verlagsgruppe Luebbe	*Copywriter*	Christine Deinhart
	GmbH & Co. KG	*Designer*	Hayo Ross
Creative Director	Ekkehard Frenkler	*Account Executive*	Melanie Stagg

We let the tongue travel with a postal stamp booklet that includes postcards. Sounds boring? It's not: Licking the stamps releases the original Häagen-Dazs flavour.

☆
Tasty Stamps *Germany*

National Award	Silver	*Art Director*	Kirsten Frenz
Agency	TBWA Germany	*Copywriter*	Susanne Thomé
Client	General Mills	*Agency Producer*	Alexander Heldt
Creative Director	Dietrich Zastrow		

Before Latvia joined the European Union in spring 2004, the new EU member states were omnipresent in the European press. But of course, most articles were about economic development, population and employment statistics, and occasionally about tourism.

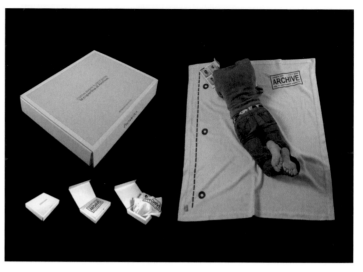

How to have the archive cover all year long.

Citizens of Europe *Latvia*

National Award	Silver	*Copywriter*	Rene Fischer,
Agency	Bates / RC		Janis Grivins,
Client	Bates / RC		Karlis Streips
Creative Director	Rene Fischer,	*Photographer*	V. P. Upeniece,
	Janis Grivins		S. Lusens, V. Svetlov
Art Director	Edgars Makens	*Graphics*	Edgars Makens

Cover *Italy*

National Award	Silver	*Art Director*	Francesco Guerrera,
Agency	Arnold Worldwide		Williams Tattoli
	Italy	*Copywriter*	Paolo Troilo,
Client	Arnold Worldwide		Alessandro Sabini
	Italy		
Creative Director	Maurizio Maresca		

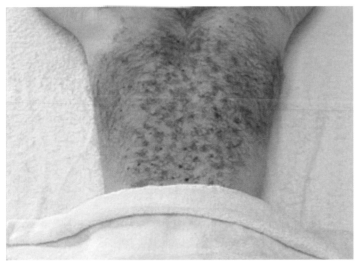

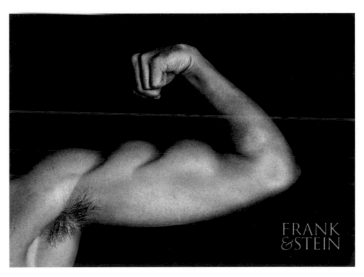

Frank & Stein - Two times stronger advertising. A postcard promoting the new creative team consisting of I.Josts and K.Salmanis.

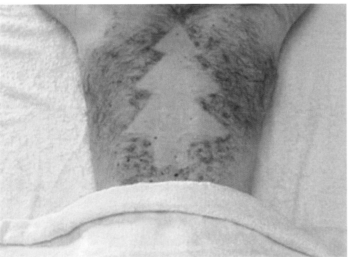

Every Christmas, Jung von Matt/Donau holds a party for the company's employees and clients. The invitation to the 2005 Christmas party was an email which included all the relevant details about the party plus two films.

Hairy Christmas *Austria*

National Award	Gold	*Art Director*	Volkmar Weiss
Agency	Jung von Matt/Donau	*Copywriter*	Christoph Gaunersdorfer
Client	Jung von Matt/Donau	*Production Comp*	Close up
Creative Director	Andreas Putz, Christoph Gaunersdorfer		

Two times stronger advertising *Latvia*

National Award	Silver	*Art Director*	Kriss Salmanis
Agency	Frank & Stein	*Copywriter*	Ingus Josts
Client	Frank & Stein		
Creative Director	Ingus Josts, Kriss Salmanis		

This is a promotional DVD with Christmas greetings that was mailed to friends and clients for the past three years.

The mailing reminds medical doctors to encourage parents to diagnose deafness early in their children's lives.

Jurguen Sorensen *Spain*

National Award....Silver	*Client* ....Porcuatro
Agency................Porcuatro	*Creative Director*...Porcuatro Team

Silent Rattle *Austria*

National Award....Silver	*Art Director*........Andreas Lierzer
Agency................Wien Nord Pilz	*Copywriter*.........Felix Fenz
Client ....Neuroth	*Graphics*...........Martin Faiss
Creative Director...Eduard Böhler, Edmund Hochleitner	

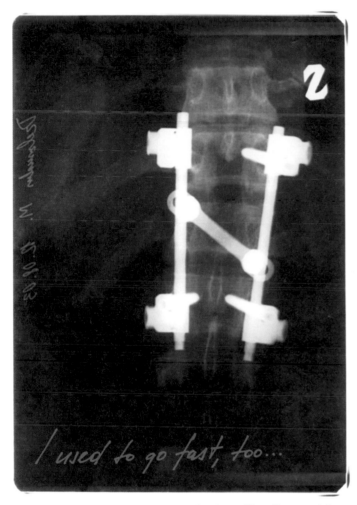

Disabled people patrolled on the highways along with traffic policemen. When a driver was caught for speeding, they wheeled to the car and handed over an x-ray copy of their own broken backbone with a handwritten text.

For the launch of the new Seitenblicke magazine, billboards, radio spots, and banners were created. The labels on the items are wordplays: They are the names of celebrities as well as the German dialect for the names of the objects.

I used to go fast, too *Latvia*

National Award	Gold	*Creative Director*	Zoom!
Agency	Zoom!	*Art Director*	Zoom!
Client	Latvian Road Safety Council		

Stars nonstop *Austria*

National Award	Silver	*Art Director*	Georg Feichtinger, Volkmar Weifl
Agency	Jung von Matt/Donau		
Client	Red Bulletin Verlag	*Copywriter*	Christoph Gaunersdorfer, Bernd Wilfinger
Creative Director	Andreas Putz, Peter Kaimer, Christoph Gaunersdorfer	*Graphics*	Georg Feichtinger

Ford has a loyalty program for independent garages that rewards the use of original parts. The aim of this brief was to publicize the prizes catalogue. The target audience received a box, similar to the ones that carry fine tableware.

Dishware *Portugal*

National Award	Silver	*Creative Director*	Nuno Duarte
Agency	Touch_Me Wunderman	*Art Director*	Rui Domingos
Client	Ford	*Copywriter*	José Castelo

Naps Mix *Austria*

National Award	Silver	*Copywriter*	Werner Buehringer
Agency	Ogilvy & Mather Austria	*Photographer*	Staudinger & Franke
		Graphics	Justin Nickerl
Client	Kraft Foods Austria		
Creative Director	Alexander Zelmanovics, Mag. Dieter Pivrnec		
Art Director	Hannes Boeker		

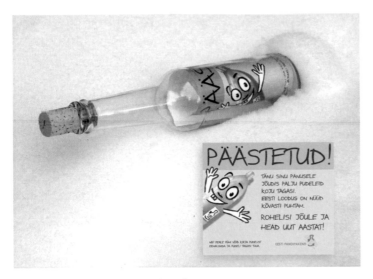

A Christmas message in a bottle from the bottle recycling company.

One of the best known Portuguese companies, "Bom Petisco," donated 50.000 to Ajuda de BerÂo (Cradle Aid). They also developed a special pack offering the institution's mascot to each client who purchases the product

Bottle Mail *Estonia*

National Award	Gold		*Art Director*	Andi Stumer
Agency	Division McCann-Erickson		*Copywriter*	Alvar Jaakson
Client	Pandipakend		*Illustrator*	Alvar Jaakson
Creative Director	Alvar Jaakson			

Joyful Can *Portugal*

National Award	Silver		*Creative Director*	Jorge Coelho
Agency	Ogilvy One		*Art Director*	Hernani Dias
Client	Ajuda de Berço/ Bom Petisco		*Copywriter*	Frederico Nunes, Jorge Coelho

Big IT solutions don't fit the budgets of small companies. What's the solution?

Torn Envelope *Portugal*

National Award	Silver	*Creative Director*	Nuno Duarte
Agency	Touch_Me Wunderman	*Art Director*	Nuno Duarte
Client	Microsoft	*Copywriter*	José Castelo

Trinity *Poland*

National Award	Gold	*Art Director*	Grzegorz Badzio, Karolek Prussak
Agency	Ogilvy One		
Client	IBM Polska	*Copywriter*	Piotr Alchimowicz
Creative Director	Piotr Alchimowicz	*Production Comp.*	Ogilvy One

This was created to notify Mastercard holders that they will not receive any more mailings from the company, but can easily check their monthly statement on the Internet.

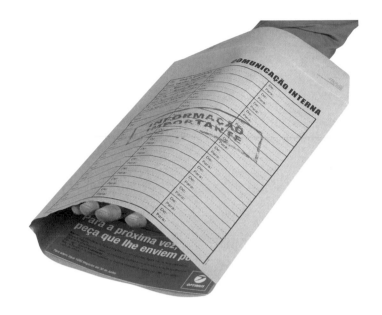

This mailing consisted of an empty internal mail envelope, which had been opened at both ends. It was developed with the Portugese saying "cair em saco roto" ("to store in a ripped bag") in mind.

Empty Envelope *Austria*

National Award	Gold	*Designer*	Roman Steiner
Agency	Demner, Merlicek & Bergmann	*Production Comp.*	Sandra Fauster
Client	Mastercard		
Creative Director	Gerda Reichl-Schebesta		
Art Director	Bernhard Grafl		
Copywriter	Alistair Thompson		

Lost Memo *Portugal*

National Award	Gold	*Creative Director*	Nuno Duarte, João Geada
Agency	Proximity Portugal	*Art Director*	Luís Gonçalves
Client	Optimus Telecomu-nicações	*Copywriter*	Pedro Neves

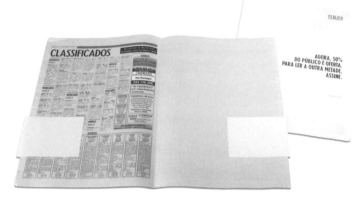

The teaser mailing was a card torn in half, that told people not to read only half of the news. The following DM was a real newspaper with only half of the text. The goal was to let readers know that 50% of the newspaper was free—they Just have to subscribe.

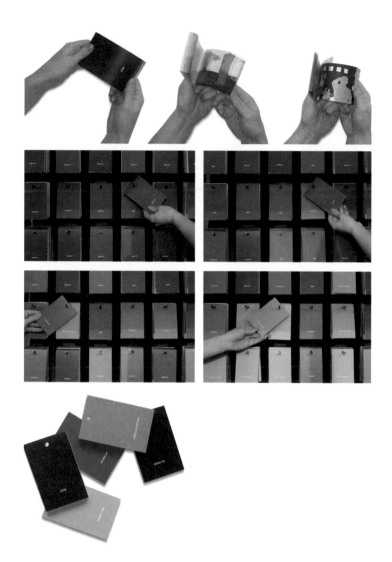

This project was a response to an unusual briefing: To attract the public but to avoid the sector's habituallures like big slogans and photos of the product. The goal was to create an empty communicative space.

Publico 50% *Portugal*

National Award	Gold
Agency	Proximity Portugal
Client	Publico Newspaper
Creative Director	João Geada, Nuno Duarte
Art Director	Nuno Duarte
Copywriter	Pedro Neves
Production Comp	Publico

Layetana Flipbook *Spain*

National Award	Silver
Agency	BAG.Disseny
Client	Layetana Real Estate
Creative Director	Xavier Mora
Art Director	Sandra Compte

This is a promotion that explains in an amusing and fresh way the services that Work & Fun offers.
The objective was to entertain the potential client while they read the content.

Work & Fun *Spain*

National Award	Gold	*Art Director*	Martí Ferré, Agnès Simon
Agency	Bildi Grafiks	*Copywriter*	Neli Caldentey
Client	El Color de los Proyectos SL	*Print*	Arts Gràfiques Orient
Creative Director	Martí Ferré, Agnès Simon		

O3.4
ANY OTHER
Switzerland: 1 gold ★
Austria: 1 nomination ☆
Germany: 1 nomination ☆

This shows five fictitious announcements made by a park attendant over a public address system. In the announcements, individuals who do not recycle their PET bottles are reprimanded.

★
Announcements *Switzerland* ◉

National Award ....Bronze	*Creative Director* ...Martin Spillmann
Agency ....Spillmann/Felser/	*Art Director* ....Dana Wirz
Leo Burnett	*Copywriter* ....Stefan Ehrler
Client ....PET Recycling Schweiz	*Production Comp.* ...Hastings

...should immediately go an get the empty Sinalco bottle...

...take it to the blue PET container.

...that he just threw on the grass and...

It's easy to find, even if you're stoned.

In addition to classical advertising, the agency used model figurines to develop a low budget, high impact advertising medium for the Model-Makers Fair: The world's smallest sandwich board men were placed in public areas.

☆
The wrong working environment *Germany*

National Award	Bronze	*Photographer*	Hans Starck
Agency	Scholz & Friends	*Graphics*	Inga Schulze,
Client	Jobsintown.de		Sara dos Santos Vieira
Creative Director	Matthias Spaetgens,	*Account Executive*	Katrin Seegers,
	Jan Leube		Katrin Ploska
Art Director	David Fischer		
Copywriter	Axel Tischer		

☆
Sandwich people *Austria*

National Award	Silver	*Copywriter*	Helena Giokas
Agency	Jung von Matt / Donau	*Photographer*	Jork Weismann
Client	Reed Messe Vienna		
Creative Director	Andreas Putz, Gerd		
	Schulte-Doeinghaus		

Car proposed as yo-yo.

Post code boundaries *Germany*

National Award	Silver	*Creative Director*	Carsten Bolk
Agency	BBDO Campaign GmbH Duesseldorf	*Art Director*	Jacques Pense
		Copywriter	Andreas Walter
Client	Deutsche Post AG	*Graphics*	Marco Becker

Yo-yo *Italy*

National Award	Gold	*Art Director*	Dario Agnello
Agency	D'Adda, Lorenzini, Vigorelli, BBDO	*Copywriter*	Cristino Battista
		Photographer	Armando Rebatto
Client	Mini		
Creative Director	Giuseppe Mastromatteo, Luca Scotto di Carlo		

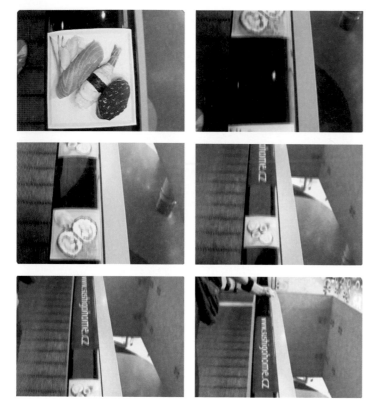

Sushi goes with you into your house. Stickers placed on handrails in the subway and shopping malls for a sushi delivery service remind us of the back conveyor belt found at sushi bars.

We let the tongue travel with a postal stamp booklet that includes postcards. Sounds boring? It's not: Licking the stamps releases the original Häagen-Dazs flavour.

Sushi Go Home *Czech Republic*

National Award	Silver	*Art Director*	Anna Barton
Agency	Euro RSCG Prague	*Copywriter*	Filip Kukla,
Client	Sushi Go Home		Stepan Zalesak
Creative Director	Filip Kukla,		
	Dejan Stajnberger		

Tasty Stamps *Germany*

National Award	Silver	*Art Director*	Kirsten Frenz
Agency	TBWA Germany	*Copywriter*	Susanne Thomé
Client	General Mills	*Agency Producer*	Alexander Heldt
Creative Director	Dietrich Zastrow		

ART+COM created an interactive room where exhibition visitors could get in touch directly with aliens.

Evangelie from... *Russia*

National Award	Gold
Agency	Antimultmsk
Producer	Maxim Kuderov, Andrey Saimakov
Scenario	Maxim Kuderov, Andrey Saimakov
Graphics	I. Malkin, P. Sudakov, R. Kolesnikov, E. Kuznetsov
Animation	I. Nikitin
Voices	I. Nikitin, I. Malkin, P. Sudakov
Sound	Roman Kolesnikov

Alien Worlds *Germany*

National Award	Silver
Agency	ART+COM AG
Client	Science + Media LLP, The Science Museum, London
Creative Director	Prof. Joachim Sauter
Designer	Jussi Ängeslevä, Dennis Paul, Patrick Kochlik
Production Comp.	ART+COM AG
Graphics	Big Wave Production, Channel 4

Announcing the new Getz, a small vehicle that is big on the inside, for young people. This campaign emphasizes its interior space and promotes test-drives at car retailers. Cars are sometimes used as motels. But Getz
is much more: It is a spacious room to discover.

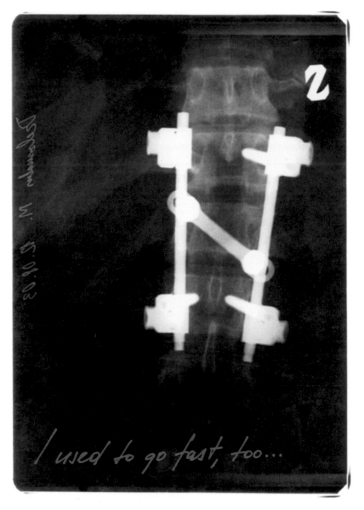

Disabled people patrolled on the highways along with traffic policemen. When a driver was caught for
speeding, they wheeled to the car and handed over an x-ray copy of their own broken backbone with a handwritten text.

Hyundai Getz Dimmed *Portugal*

National Award	Silver	*Creative Director*	Miguel Paté
Agency	Touch_Me Wunderman	*Art Director*	Leonor Rasteiro
Client	Hyundai	*Copywriter*	Pedro Dias

I used to go fast, too *Latvia*

National Award	Gold	*Creative Director*	Zoom!
Agency	Zoom!	*Art Director*	Zoom!
Client	Latvian Road Safety Council		

"Warning! Extremely reduced prices."

When Germany holds elections, every official political party can broadcast a number of election campaign commercials on public television for free. In 2005, The Party sold its airtime to the low-cost airline HLX.

Precios muy pequeños *Spain*

National Award	Silver
Agency	Villarrosas, SCPF
Client	Bulevard Rosa
Creative Director	Oriol Villar
Art Director	Frank Hahn, Cristina Martín
Copywriter	Oriol Villar
Photographer	Katseys (Simsan)

The HLX election spots *Germany*

National Award	Gold
Agency	Scholz & Friends, Titanic Verlag GmbH & Co. KG
Client	Hapag-Lloyd Express GmbH
Creative Director	M. Spaetgens, J. Leube, M. Pross, S. Turner
Art Director	Johannes Hicks
Copywriter	M. Sonneborn, R. A. Coertlen, S. Kummer, L. Baldermann
Production Comp.	cine plus Media Service GmbH & Co. KG

04 Design

04.1
GRAPHIC DESIGN
Spain: 1 gold ★
Austria: 2 nominations ☆

A series of 7 notepads that recreate the grids that changed design history: Le Modulor (Le Corbusier), Twen magazine (Willy Fleckhaus), Die neue Typographie (Jan Tschichold), Raster Systeme (Josef Muller-Brockmann), The Guardian (David Hillman) ...

★

Grid-it! Notepads *Spain*

National Award	Silver	*Designer*	Birgit Pfisterer, Astrid Stavro
Agency	Astrid Stavro		
Client	The Royal College of Art	*Graphics*	Birgit Pfisterer, Astrid Stavro
Creative Director	Astrid Stavro		
Art Director	Astrid Stavro		

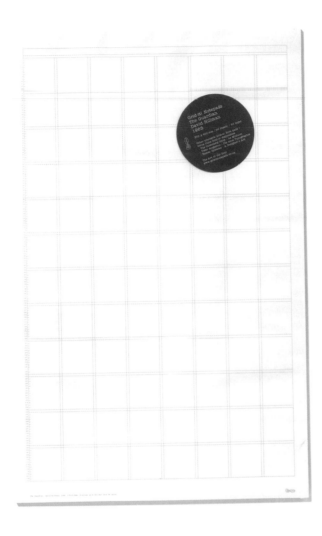

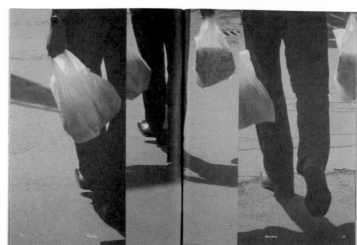

The relief organization Jugend am Werk creates livable conditions for people who are disadvantaged. Five unique people told their stories to illustrate the role Jugend am Werk played in their lives. Each of these accounts could be a title story in its own right, so this annual report was published with five different covers.

☆

Jugend am Werk Annual Report 2005 *Austria*

National Award	Silver	*Art Director*	Ralf Herms, Fritz T. Magistris
Agency	Rosebud, Inc.		
Client	Jugend am Werk Steiermark	*Copywriter*	Franziskus Kerssenbrock
		Production Comp.	Rosebud, Inc.
Creative Director	Ralf Herms, Fritz T. Magistris	*Photographer*	Klaus Vyhnalek

  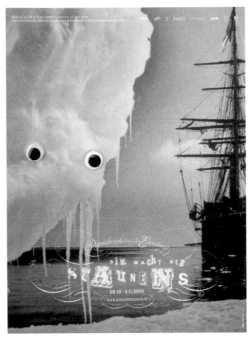

Puppet theatre festival. Eyes can bring anything to life—even lifeless material. Small bags filled with adhesive wobbly eyes were sent so that the receiver could create a puppet out of everything.

☆
The Power of Amazement *Austria*

National Award	Shortlist	*Art Director*	Caroline Bruckner
Agency	Jung von Matt/Donau	*Designer*	Caroline Bruckner
Client	Theater ohne Grenzen	*Graphics*	Caroline Bruckner
Creative Director	Caroline Bruckner, Andreas Putz	*Illustrator*	Caroline Bruckner

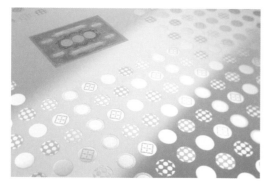

For its 2006 calendar, Strichpunkt used 150-year-old chromolithographies from the Kurt Weidemann collection to tremendous effect. They are complemented by contemporary designs in white on white in various finishes.

Gallery concept for new free notists. Titles of works must only contain the letters "H" and "P."

Non plus ultra *Germany*

National Award	Silver	*Art Director*	Kirsten Dietz
Agency	Strichpunkt	*Designer*	Susanne Hörner,
Client	Papierfabrik Scheufel-en GmbH+Co. KG		Felix Widmaier
		Production Comp.	Grafisches Zentrum
Creative Director	Kirsten Dietz, Jochen Rädeker		Drucktechnik, Ditzingen
		Illustrator	Susanne Hörner

Creative sphere *Italy*

National Award	Gold	*Art Director*	Giuba Vescovi,
Agency	Publicis Srl		Marco Maccagni,
Client	HP		Marco Cantalamessa
Creative Director	Alasdhair Macgregor, Stefano Colombo	*Copywriter*	Ugo Cesare Tonelli, Marco Venturelli
		Graphics	Garonzi, Seniga, Luongo&Plank, Luzo Lazzara

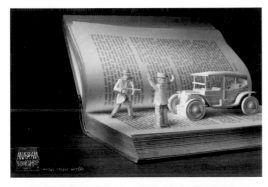

Words create Worlds.

Against the backdrop of the prestigious La Scala Milan, photographed by Satoshi Saikusa, Federico Pepe, the official sponsor of the corps de ballet, illustrated an uncontainable explosion of movement.

Words Create Worlds *Czech Republic*

National Award	Silver	*Copywriter*	Jaime Mandelbaum, Christian Liu
Agency	KASPEN Prague		
Client	Anagram Bookstore	*Photographer*	Ondrej Hosek, Marcelo Ribero
Creative Director	Tomas Otradovec		
Art Director	Jaime Mandelbaum, Christian Liu	*Graphics*	Claudio Ishii

The Scala Theatre *Italy*

National Award	Gold	*Art Director*	Federico Pepe
Agency	1861 United	*Copywriter*	Stefania Siani
Client	Freddy	*Photographer*	Satoshi Saikusa
Creative Director	Pino Rozzi, Roberto Battaglia		

Each of the tales is dedicated to the concrete paper. Ready calendar was the Christmas present for cooperation partners but at the same time it's an example book to see how different types of printing implemented on different paper look.

I am driving. When I drive, I live. When I am still, I just speed. I free myself from the unnecessary and All men know it. Because all men behave the same. them? Who understands what they actually want? not an evil guy but whoever wants to get along with have gotten out of the way damn it. She must know not. When I get full of it I just go silent. Just turn If you want to be like this… I do not look back, I do not reply to calls. I go to her. She is waiting. She is faithful, does not argue, does not nag when I come a little late, doesn't make a fuss when I have a few drinks. She is always ready, washed and smelling nice, ready to have me. And I come. I open the gates and geta sense of her shapes in the darkness. I get the feeling she is smiling at me. When I turn the light on she reveals all her beauty. She is smooth and shiny. It is simply the love every man must know. I enter. Her velvety skin welcomes me back and the sedative scent goes up my nose. I go in likea notched key into an ignition barrel one tooth at a time. She is alive, control lights greet me one by one, the tank is full. My hands slide across the steering wheel, I tweak the mirrors, play the music. For a tiny moment my head leans on the headrest and I savour the moment. I take a deep breath and then I let the air out slowly again. I open my eyes. The courtship is over, it is time to go. I need to get in touch with me again. I turn the key all the way. The engine starts churning, it wakes up from a dream and replies with a growl as my foot touches the pedal. Handbrake, clutch, gear shift, gas. Seat belts are for the girls. The tyre's song of war rips the blanket of the night. Let everybody know! You Bellysleeper, can only dream of this. Off we go into the night. Just like two tireless hunters in chase of a demon. A Demon that I have inside me, that keeps me going and that can be fed by only one thing—speed. I drive. I just drive and nothing else matters. Speed is my middle name, I am the speed, the speed defines me. For a tiny moment my head of motion, a guided missile. I am a man. You know it: slow for a while, lost forever. I am not naive, I want to fight for my rights in life and I know what it takes. I am the chief of Testosterone. The speed is my advantage. I have always played it straight and I am not gonna change it here and now—on the road. I love roads. Black veins, tarmac tentacles spread into the devoted country creating new arenas in which we face each other daily. We—the new knights with our shiny machines with horses under the hood. Honour is a piece of shit and we ride only to win. This is my territory I set the rules and I will arrive sooner. I am the winner. No question about it. Loosing isn't my style, not mine. Why can't women understand this? Especially, this one of mine. Why does she make my hell with all her neuroses and nagging. What is she always worried about? I have been driving for so many years. Of course, there were some minor accidents but every one of them makes a man more experienced with a firm hand, only cowards try to "learn a lesson". She drove me mad the other day—by "do not go fast, be careful". I am not a child any more, and I do not have to put up with this, not me… I drive. The engine sings in the ritual ceremony of strength. I bring sacrifices to the altar of power. Petrol and oil instead of myrrh and incense, windscreen washer rather then holy scented oils. Wheels tear the tarmac at an insane tempo, high beams bite into the night. When I brake the dragon, his power passes into me, I feel his rage. I rage a bit, only what is necessary. White line like a strobe light always faster and faster disappearing under the belly of the terror of night seeking compassion, safety, who knows. And then leaving it again they disappear somewhere at the back just as quickly. Why worry what's behind us? I don't, not my style, I run forward to the finish no matter where it is. Speed, speed, speed. Drugged with speed, tickling ends of fingers, something stretching in the belly and legs getting heavier. My eyes squint. Rev max, heartbeat max. I fly, I pulse, I live. Imperception. I'm driving. All of a sudden the whole universe gets concentrated into one spot and I become its centre. Blinding light and unbearable noise fill me up completely. I fall into a motionless tank of timelessness, saturated by echoing tattoo of the tarmac—the white line of pain. Pain so excruciating, that it cannot be perceived. The surface closes above my head and I keep falling deeper towards the darkness. I hear the characteristic whispers. Valkyries of the night. Magic chorales echoing in thousands hit me, interlace and disappear again. Gloomy loneliness. Who am I? A body without a soul or soul without a body? Who am I and mainly where am I? How did I get here and why do not I feel anything? There must be a body somewhere around me, I do not sense it, though. I'm driving. Fluorescent light burns into my eyes. On the move, I keep moving. Pain? For a short moment I feel that unbearable torment of self-awareness. A Tiny man huddling in the middle of nothingness. I am on my back and burning fluorescent light perform a maccabre dance mimicking the colours of the road. One by one shortening my voyage disappearing somewhere in the remoteness. Speed, flashing through my head. It is speed again accompanying me on my way. Where is it actually heading this hasty and sinister entourage? Who are those white figures above me? Kaleidoscopic, faceless figures, talking to each other, but I do not understand. Blinding white with dark red. Those hear their colours. Colours. God, is that blood? Whose blood? I am cold. Possibly for the first time in my life I am starting to be scared. Fear. Mind clamped in cramps. I want to go away. Right now. I am starting to understand, something must have happened, that crimson is surely mine. So as it seems you were right. Oh, where are you? I want you near me, I am so sorry. Humble conscience making its way through the white veil, I know, who I am. I am a defeated knight. Defeated with his own weapon, humiliated by himself. You were right. Where are you now? Do not leave me here. I am small. Damn I should have told her, I should have told her that she is the most important thing to me. Much more important then a stupid machine, a pile of junk. Oh my god, if you exist then this must be the right moment for a talk. I know I've always said that I do not need anyone, no crutch, no god. Not me. My god is the speed and I am the Pontifex maximus in its temple. Now I do not know. God I do not know. Now I am a child again, helpless, bereft of motion. I am leaving the familiar territories, something keeps pulling me away. From above I watch the bustle above a hospital stretcher. White figures dancing. Birth, childhood, adolescence—life. I see running scenes on the background of non-being. Rivers of memories one by one, each fade sinking like firelight in the dead ends of oblivion. The darkness is closing and on comes the tunnel. So it exists. I always laughed at the stories of the other side and now I am the main hero of one. My story is at the end. Unnecessarily soon and stupid. The demon has been fed and is leaving me with that smirky grin. Arrived sooner once again, sooner then everyone else. There is light in the distance. I have to go to it. www.uamk-cr.cz

Speeding gets you there faster.

Calendar of tales *Latvia*

National Award	Silver	*Art Director*	Sandro Chaidze
Agency	LARSONI advertising agency	*Production Comp.*	Printing hause Rigas Parugtipografija
Client	Map Latvia	*Graphics*	Sandro Chaidze
Creative Director	Normunds Bakis		

Stripes *Czech Republic*

National Award	Silver	*Creative Director*	Jiri Pleskot
Agency	Leo Burnett Advertising, spol. s.r.o.	*Art Director*	Lumir Kajnar
Client	UAMK (Road Safety Council)	*Copywriter*	Richard Kolbe

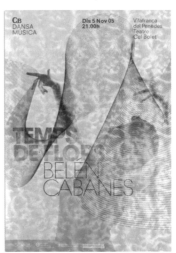

A calendar is nothing more than a trivial communications piece for most brands. But for M2 it represents the maximum climax of production potential in terms of technological innovative printing solutions: It is an exclusive object to be enjoyed calmly.

In order to make a good play you need: actors (photographs of them), a text (typographies that change based on the audience), a curtain (a colourful form that hides and shows the work), and a backdrop (paper or support).

M2 *Portugal*

National Award	Silver	*Creative Director*	Miguel Reis
Agency	Brandia Central	*Art Director*	José Carlos Mendes
Client	M2 Artes Gráficas	*Designer*	Carlos Vieira

Teatre Cal Bolet *Spain*

National Award	Gold	*Art Director*	Martí Ferré, Agnès Simon
Agency	Bildi Grafiks		
Client	Patronat del Teatre Municipal Cal Bolet	*Copywriter*	Dani Sáez
		Photographer	Various
Creative Director	Martí Ferré, Agnès Simon	*Illustrator*	Martí Ferré
		Print	Imprèsgràfic

The world of circus.

Logo for Askja - a car dealership.

Circ *Spain*

National Award	Gold	*Creative Director*	David Torrents
Agency	David Torrents	*Designer*	David Torrents
Client	KRTU		

Askja *Iceland*

National Award	Silver	*Art Director*	Einar Gylfason
Agency	Ó!	*Designer*	Einar Gylfason
Client	Askja		

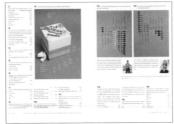

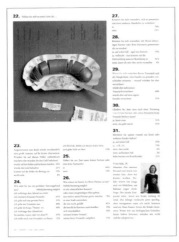

"How are we doing?"

Annual report for the holding company Baugur Group.

Wie geht es uns denn so? *Germany*

National Award....Silver
Agency................Neon
Client ....Verlag Neon Magazin
                      GmbH
Art Director........Gunter Schwarzmaier

Production Comp...Verlag Neon Magazin
                  GmbH
Photographer.......Sarah Illenberger

Annual report *Iceland*

National Award....Gold
Agency................Hzeta
Client ....Baugur Group

Art Director.........Hildur Helgadottir
                     Zoega
Designer...............Hildur Helgadottir
                       Zoega

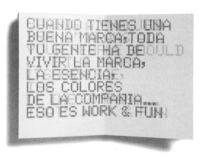

Egoista is a trimonthly theme magazine which contains regular contributions from some of the great names in photography, journalism, arts, and literature in Portugal.

This promotion explains the services that Work & Fun offers in an amusing and fresh way. The objective was to entertain the potential client while they read the content.

Egoista *Portugal*

National Award	Silver	*Art Director*	Henrique Cayatte
Agency	Atelier 004	*Designer*	Filipa G., Hugo N.,
Client	Estoril-Sol		Rita S., Rodrigo S.
Creative Director	Patrícia Reis	*Production Comp.*	Atelier 004
		Producers	Francisco Ponciano,
			Cláudio Garrudo

Work & Fun *Spain*

National Award	Gold	*Art Director*	Martí Ferré,
Agency	Bildi Grafiks		Agnès Simon
Client	El Color de los	*Copywriter*	Neli Caldentey
	Proyectos	*Print*	Arts Gràfiques Orient
Creative Director	Martí Ferré,		
	Agnès Simon		

This is an art, fashion, and photography fanzine. The limited edition of 1,137 issues was distributed worldwide.

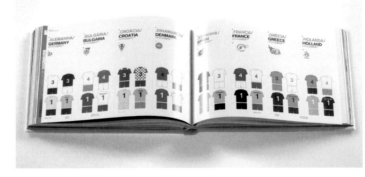

With Euro 2004, Portugal became the centre of this popular game organized by UEFA. The Portugal Society 2004 S.A. was the public and private organization that commissioned the construction of the stadiums.

Fanzine 137 *Spain*

National Award	Silver
Agency	Albert Folch Studio
Client	Luis Venegas
Creative Director	Albert Folch
Art Director	Albert Folch

Portugal 2004: Much more than football *Portugal*

National Award	Silver
Agency	RMAC Brand Design
Client	Sociedade Portugal 2004, SA
Creative Director	Ricardo Mealha, Ana Cunha
Art Director	Ricardo Mealha, Ana Cunha
Designer	Ana Cunha

Book for the artist Brynhildur.

This was a campaign for the Mercat de les Flors theatre. This season, all materials were conceived as covers for tabloids: The shows and their contents were detailed as if they were daily news.

Mercat de les Flors *Spain*

National Award	Silver	*Creative Director*	Toormix
Agency	Toormix	*Art Director*	Toormix
Client	ICUB-Ajuntament de Barcelona, Mercat de les Flors	*Designer*	Toormix
		Graphics	Toormix

Brynhildur 2005-1955 *Iceland*

National Award	Silver	*Art Director*	Amundi Sigurdsson
Agency	Gott fólk	*Designer*	Amundi Sigurdsson
Client	Brynhildur Thorgeirs	*Photographer*	Various

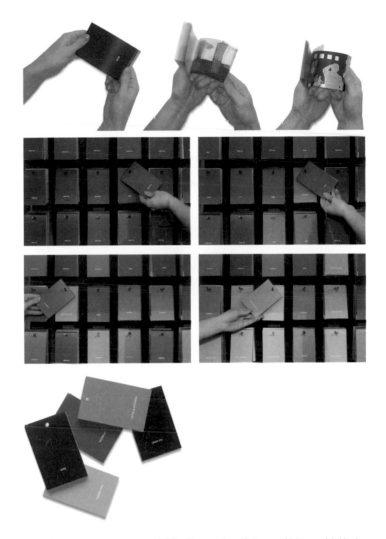

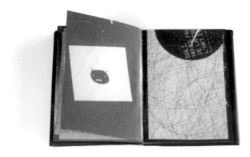

This booklet explains the nature of the studio. It goes beyond a mere description of the design work to reveal the visual environment of Cla-se.

This project was a response to an unusual briefing: To attract the public but to avoid the sector's habitual lures like big slogans and photos of the product. The goal was to create an empty communicative space.

Cla-se Cuts *Spain*

National Award	Silver	*Art Director*	Enrique Hernández, Claret Serrahima
Agency	Cla-se	*Copywriter*	Raquel Pelta
Client	Cla-se	*Designer*	Enrique Hernández
Creative Director	Cla-se	*Photographer*	Manel Capell

Layetana Flipbook *Spain*

National Award	Silver	*Creative Director*	Xavier Mora
Agency	BAG.Disseny	*Art Director*	Sandra Compte
Client	Layetana Real Estate		

This is an invitation book for the 50th birthday of Albert Ferré.

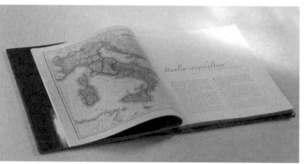

This is a cookbook by the renowned Italian chef—his trade secrets are revealed.

L'Albert *Spain*

National Award....Silver	*Creative Director*..Wladimir Marnich
Agency................Marnich Design	*Designer* ....Hanna Martus
Client ....Albert Ferré	

Bocca cookbook *Estonia*

National Award....Silver	*Art Director*........Dan Mikkin
Agency ....Division McCann-Erickson	*Designer* ....Martin Mileiko
Client ....Bocca Restaurant	*Production Comp*...Ajakirjade Kirjastus
Creative Director...Dan Mikkin	*Photographer*.......Jaan Heinmaa

This is the 2004 annual report for Wienerberger AG.

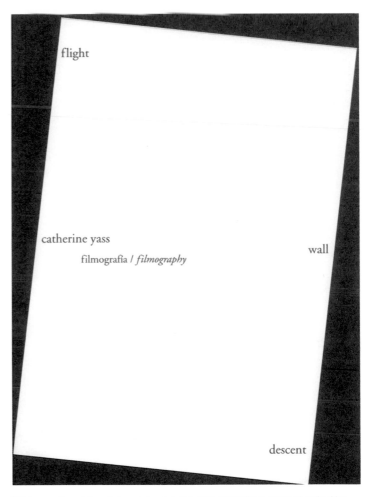

This is a cover for a catalogue that summarizes three films with unconventional camerawork by the video artist Catherine Yass. The concept of the screen is emphasized by the tilted white rectangle.

Annual Report *Austria*

National Award	Silver	*Copywriter*	Wolfgang Schreiner, Christian Pott
Agency	Büro X Design	*Photographer*	Maria Ziegelboeck, Wolfgang Zajc, Robert Marksteiner
Client	Wienerberger AG		
Creative Director	Andreas Miedaner		
Art Director	Andreas Miedaner	*Graphics*	Sonja Handl
		Illustrator	Heri Irawan

Flight, Wall, Descent *Spain*

National Award	Silver	*Designer*	Ena Cardenal de la Nuez
Agency	Ena Cardenal de la Nuez	*Production Comp.*	T.F. editores
Client	Centro Atlántico de Arte Moderno, CAAM		

This book details a selection of the works of architect Josep Lluís Mateo. The book evokes the materials commonly found in an architect's studio: The edges are painted in metal and the words on the cover are in relief.

Book design

José Luis Mateo *Spain*

National Award	Silver	*Client*	Editorial Polígrafa
Agency	Cosmic	*Creative Director*	Juan Dávila

Material time, work time, life time *Iceland*

National Award	Gold	*Designer*	Borkur Arnarsson,
Agency	Borkur and Gunnar		Gunnar Thor
Client	Eidastoll		Vilhjalmsson
Creative Director	Borkur Arnarsson,		
	Gunnar Thor		
	Vilhjalmsson		

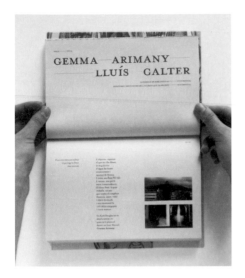

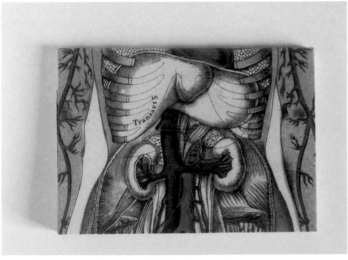

This was a collective exposition where each artist gave a name to a part of the human body. The illustration of the book jacket, which turns into the exhibition poster, comes from a nineteenth century book of anatomy.

The Assignment: To create an unconventional promotion book for 2pm Model Management using 16 portraits of the most famous models represented by the agency.

Transart5 *Spain*

National Award	Gold	*Creative Director*	Alex Gifreu
Agency	Alex Gifreu. bis	*Art Director*	Alex Gifreu
Client	Museu de l'Empordà, Ajuntament de Girona	*Designer*	Alex Gifreu, Ana Domínguez

Who am I? *Denmark*

National Award	Gold	*Production Comp.*	Scanprint
Agency	Scandinavian DesignLab	*Photographer*	Andreas Sjödin
Client	2pm Model Management	*Graphics*	Per Madsen
Art Director	Per Madsen	*Account Executive*	Jesper von Wieding, Anne-Mette Hojland
Designer	Per Madsen		

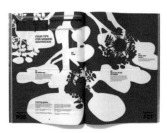

The Assignment: To create an in-house Trend book published twice a year that both in shape and content can be used as source of inspiration on trends in music, fashion, retail, art and sociology.

Black &White

Patrick Thomas

This is a compilation of the artist's recent work for the Spanish press, including various examples of cover images for Dinero, the financial supplement of La Vanguardia.

Tomorrow 03 *Denmark*

National Award	Gold	*Designer*	Per Madsen
Agency	Scandinavian Designlab	*Production Comp.*	Scanprint
Client	Style Counsel/Bestseller	*Graphics*	Per Madsen
Creative Director	Per Madsen	*Account Executive*	Jesper von Wieding, Anne-Mette Hojland
Art Director	Per Madsen	*Project Manager*	Christina Orth
		Produc. Manager	Christian Braender

Black & White *Spain*

National Award	Silver	*Creative Director*	Patrick Thomas
Agency	Studio laVista	*Designer*	Patrick Thomas
Client	Studio laVista		

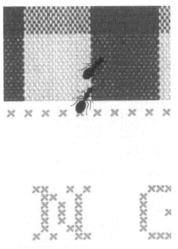

After a successful journey to a mature stage, the Portugal's Creatives Festival surged into quality with its seventh edition. It left the original format to become an event of a larger weight. The theme was the Orient.

This Lookbook is for the picnic-themed 2006 autumn collection.

Seventh Portugal's Creatives Festival *Portugal*

National Award	Silver	*Creative Director*	Rita Baltazar
Agency	By	*Art Director*	Ana Melo, Luís Castro
Client	Portugalís Creatives Club. CCP	*Copywriter*	José António Baço

Camper lookbook 2006 *Spain*

National Award	Silver	*Creative Director*	Pablo Martín
Agency	Grafica	*Art Director*	Pablo Martín
Client	Camper	*Designer*	Bárbara Castro

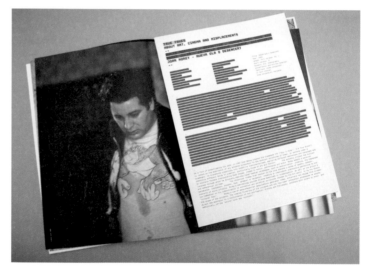

This is a poster and fold-inside of a bag for the promotion of an exhibition project.

Sí, yes, oui *Spain*

National Award	Silver	*Creative Director*	Alex Gifreu
Agency	Alex Gifreu. bis	*Art Director*	Alex Gifreu
Client	Dora García, Musac León	*Designer*	Alex Gifreu

True fakes. About art, cinema and misplacements *Spain*

National Award	Silver	*Art Director*	Albert Folch
Agency	Albert Folch Studio	*Copywriter*	Amanda Cuesta, Eva Soria
Client	Generalitat de Catalunya	*Designer*	Omar Sosa
Creative Director	Albert Folch		

"The Players" is an imaginary band formed not by musicians, but by models. The goal was to give more realism to the characters that have a made-up name and curriculum.

This is an exhibition catalogue.

Wearplay catalogues *Portugal*

National Award	Silver	*Creative Director*	Pedro Pires
Agency	Brandia Central	*Designer*	Antonio Neu
Client	Wearplay		

Dallibres *Spain*

National Award	Gold	*Art Director*	Alex Gifreu
Agency	Alex Gifreu. bis	*Designer*	Alex Gifreu
Client	Fundació Gala-Salvador Dalí	*Photographer*	Martí Gasull
Creative Director	Alex Gifreu		

This is a catalogue for an exhibition of contemporary art. Three book jackets were made with details of works by various artists to explain eroticism from different points of view.

For this edition, Fashion Show, the subject is "Fast-Forward: Speed Cars and Technology." The picture base of this edition is a composite illustration for the elusive elements of speed, modernity, and roads.

El Somni Eròtic *Spain*

National Award	Gold
Agency	Eumografic
Client	Centre d'Art La Panera

ModaLisboa 24th Edition *Portugal*

National Award	Gold	*Art Director*	Ricardo Mealha, Ana Cunha
Agency	RMAC Brand Design		
Client	Associação ModaLisboa	*Designer*	Ana Cunha
Creative Director	Ricardo Mealha, Ana Cunha		

A poster that, for budget constraints, converts into a catalogue with the help of printed instructions. The exhibition speaks about the philosophy of D.I.Y. (Do It Yourself), which is reflected in the format of the catalogue.

Salir a la calle y disparar al azar *Spain*

National Award	Silver	*Creative Director*	Alex Gifreu
Agency	Alex Gifreu. bis	*Art Director*	Alex Gifreu
Client	David G. Torres	*Designer*	Alex Gifreu

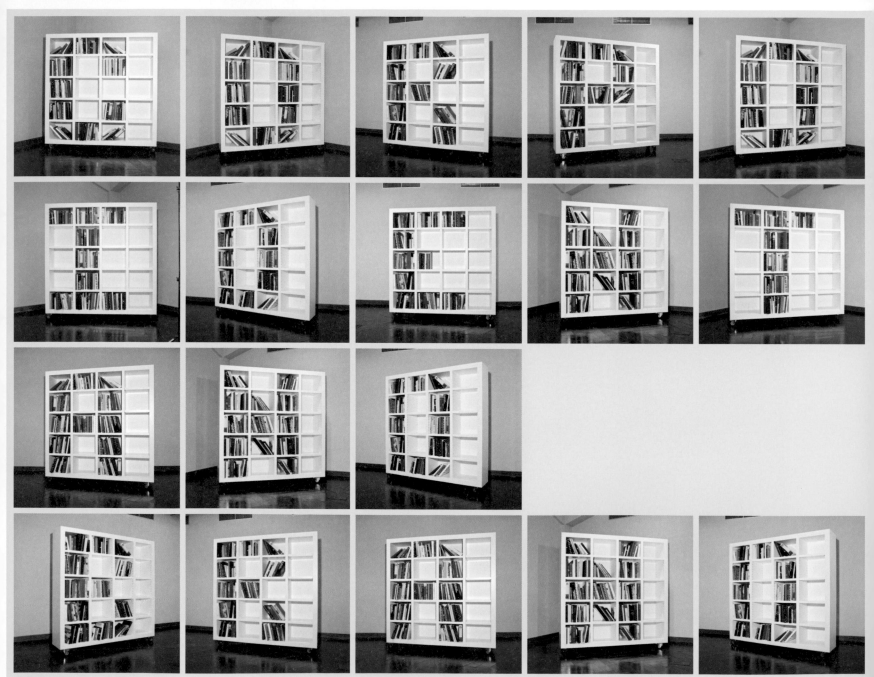

04.2
CORPORATE IDENTITY
AND BRANDING
Austria: 1 gold ★

Stationary for the bookbinder Hubert Lang. The miniature books are actually business cards.

★

The Bookbinders Stationary *Austria*

National Award	Gold	*Art Director*	Andreas Lierzer
Agency	Wien Nord Pilz	*Copywriter*	Felix Fenz
Client	Buchbinderei Lang	*Designer*	Martin Faiss
Creative Director	Eduard Böhler, Edmund Hochleitner		

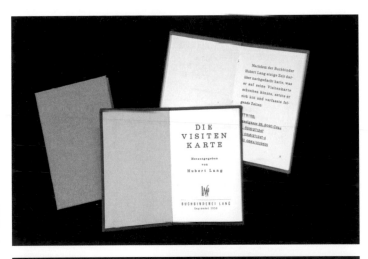

Stationery for a producer of dairy products.

Logo for Mjolka - a producer of dairy products

Stationery for Mjolka *Iceland*

National Award	Gold	*Art Director*	Einar Gylfason
Agency	Ó!	*Designer*	Einar Gylfason
Client	Mjolka		

Mjolka *Iceland*

National Award	Gold	*Art Director*	Orn Smari Gislason
Agency	Ó!	*Illustrator*	Orn Smari Gislason
Client	Mjolka		

Logo for the company Basis.

A family of logotypes and identity for different museums—from medieval art to artist's homes—under the Estonian Art Museum umbrella.

Estonian Art Museum *Estonia*

National Award	Gold	*Art Director*	Dan Mikkin, Andrus Lember
Agency	Division McCann-Erickson	*Designer*	Dan Mikkin, Andrus Lember
Client	Estonian Art Museum		
Creative Director	Dan Mikkin, Andrus Lember		

Basis *Iceland*

National Award	Silver	*Art Director*	Jón Ari Helgason
Agency	Jón Ari Helgason	*Designer*	Jón Ari Helgason
Client	Basis		

The brief was to create a corporate identity that combines the different parts of the three Riusech brothers' family business: architecture, real estate, and construction.

Riusech *Spain*

National Award	Gold	*Creative Director*	Pablo Martín
Agency	Grafica	*Designer*	Ellen Diedrich
Client	Riusech		

ADIVI_A

"Adivina" means "guess" in English. The main concept was to emphasize information exchange, open process, and participation with the client in the naming and the creation of the logo.

During the project we elaborated the concept of the design of BOSCO SPORT TM promo-materials for the Russian Olympic team and their fans during winter Olympics in Turin 2006.

Logotype Adivina *Spain*

National Award	Silver	*Art Director*	Sònia Rodríguez Grau
Agency	Oxigen, comunicació gràfica	*Designer*	Sònia Rodríguez Grau, Carol Rodríguez
Client	Adivina		

Complex works for TM Bosco Sport *Russia*

National Award	Gold	*Designer*	Tatyana Suhova, Aleksandra Zaharova
Agency	Direct Design		
Client	Bosco Di Chiliegi	*Illustrator*	Marina Novikova
Creative Director	Dmitry Peryshkov, Leonid Feigin		
Art Director	Dmitry Peryshkov, Leonid Feigin		

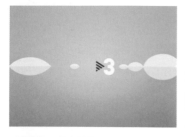

This is the whole TV3 generic image restyling. The look of the former image was old fashioned and had lost its original characteristics. They needed a modern logo to reconnect with younger generations.

Maintaining the naming and colour patrimony, a unique total brand experience was created. Under the motto "A Lifetime Experience," the brand was built on the diversity of the union of experiences.

TV3 Image *Spain*

National Award....Gold
Agency................Gédéon
Client................TV3 Televisió de
                        Catalunya
Creative Director...François Dameron,
                        Bernard Brechet

Executive producer
TV3: Teresa Guitart
Production Comp....TV3 Televisió
                        de Catalunya
Graphics...........Nicolas Thepot
Music composer....Plush Monkey

A Vida é Bela *Portugal*

National Award....Silver
Agency................Brandia Central
Client................A Vida é Bela

Creative Director...Miguel Reis
Designer...........José Carlos Mendes

Sita Murt's new identity reflects its approach to fashion: Simplicity, timelessness, and creativity. With this in mind, an identity in black and white was created with an element of versatile application: A disorderly line that suggests a restless spine.

Far more than a simple interior design store, Area is a home supply department store. The infinity symbol represents the endless solutions for all areas, either big or small.

Sita Murt *Spain*

National Award	Silver	*Art Director*	Daniel Ayuso, Claret Serrahima
Agency	Cla-se		
Client	Esteve Aguilera S.A.	*Designer*	Daniel Ayuso, Susana Frau
Creative Director	Cla-se		

Area_Corporate Identity *Portugal*

National Award	Gold	*Designer*	Ricardo Mealha, Ana Cunha
Agency	RMAC Brand Design		
Client	Area (store)	*Graphics*	Ricardo Mealha, Ana Cunha
Creative Director	Ricardo Mealha, Ana Cunha		
Art Director	Ricardo Mealha, Ana Cunha		

The board of directors of a small, well-respected Austrian investment bank sets the agenda for the company.

The record label Royal Plastic needed inexpensive stationery. To make this possible, only a poster and business cards were printed.

Stationery *Austria*

National Award	Silver	*Art Director*	Albert Handler
Agency	ArgeCC	*Copywriter*	Christian Halmdienst
Client	Capital Bank - GRAWE Gruppe AG	*Graphics*	Julia Klinger
		Costumer consult.	Ekkehard Schitter
Creative Director	Albert Handler		

One Poster fits all! *Austria*

National Award	Silver	*Art Director*	Susanne Vostrel
Agency	Dasuno Werbeagentur	*Illustrator*	Nora Sri Jascha,
Client	Royal Plastic Record Label		Susanne Vostrel, Verena Pöschl,
Creative Director	Nora Sri Jascha, Susanne Vostrel		Helga Schildböck

This annual report tells the stories of how wealthy people made their money—whether by chance or through hard work.

Corporate Identity (corporate style book) QUADRAT is made for a Real Estate company located in Riga.

The last year is History *Austria*

National Award	Gold	*Copywriter*	Christian Halmdienst, Detlef Gürtler
Agency	ArgeCC	*Graphics*	Michael Stenitzer, Julia Klinger
Client	Capital Bank - GRAWE Gruppe AG		
Creative Director	Albert Handler		
Art Director	Albert Handler		

Quadrat *Latvia*

National Award	Silver	*Production Comp.*	Design Agency DEPO
Agency	Design Agency DEPO	*Photographer*	Kristaps Epners
Client	Quadrat	*Graphics*	Kristaps Epners
Creative Director	Kristaps Epners	*Illustrator*	Kristaps Epners
Art Director	Kristaps Epners		
Copywriter	Kristaps Epners		
Designer	Kristaps Epners		

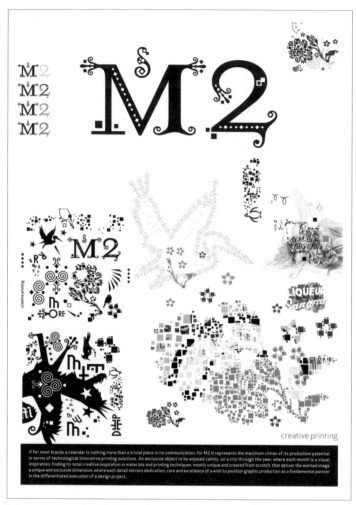

In the creation of a new brand for M2 it was important to find more than a symbol or a shape.

The graphic language of the Youth Bank of Hansabank is clearly defined, but it is also full of different possibilities. Organic is the key word.

M2 *Portugal*

National Award	Silver	*Art Director*	José Carlos Mendes
Agency	Brandia Central	*Designer*	Carlos Vieira
Client	M2 Artes Gráficas		
Creative Director	Miguel Reis		

NPNK *Estonia*

National Award	Gold	*Art Director*	Jaanus Tamme
Agency	Tank	*Copywriter*	Juhan Ulfsak
Client	Hansabank	*Illustrator*	Jan Tomson
Creative Director	Joel Volkov	*Project Manager*	Rein Ott

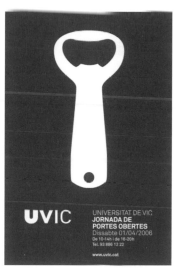

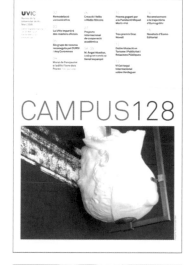

Corporate identity of the University of Vic.

A small, imaginary place to have fun while playing with tangible objects like stationery. Jaume & Miguel transport themselves and display the representation of their surrealistic world.

UVIC *Spain*

National Award	Silver
Agency	Eumografic
Client	Universitat de Vic

Un lloc, un món (one place, one world) *Spain*

National Award	Silver	*Designer*	David Resplandí Valiente
Agency	00.00.01		
Client	Un lloc, un món	*Illustrator*	Jordi Lafebre, Miguel Bosch
Creative Director	David Resplandí Valiente		
Art Director	David Resplandí Valiente	*Print*	Gràfiques Orient

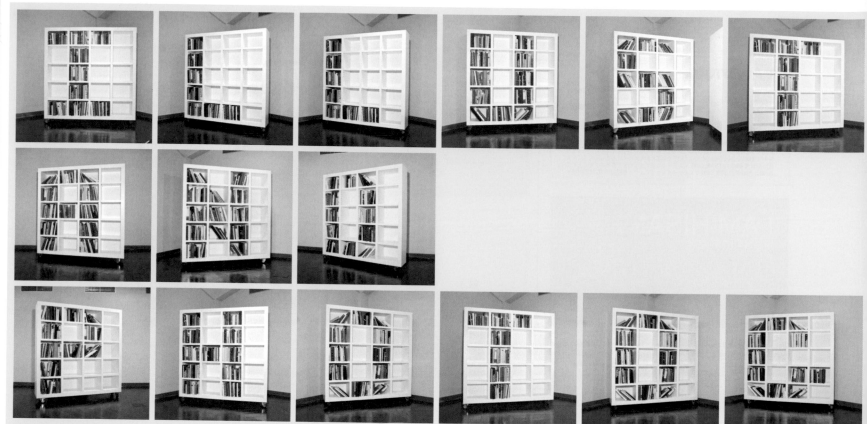

04.3
ILLUSTRATION
AND PHOTOGRAPHY
Germany: 3 nominations ☆
Poland: 1 nomination ☆

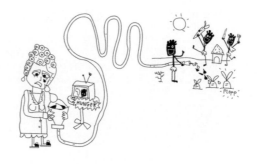

"It would be great if compassion could help. But we need your money."

☆
World Vision Campaign *Germany*

National Award	Shortlist	*Art Director*	Kristoffer Heilemann
Agency	DDB Germany/ Berlin	*Copywriter*	Ludwig Berndl
Client	World Vision Deutschland e.V.	*Production Comp.*	Art Box, Amsterdam
		Illustrator	Dorus Brekelmans
Creative Director	Amir Kassaei, Wolfgang Schneider, Mathias Stiller	*Account*	Michael Lamm, Louisa Ibing

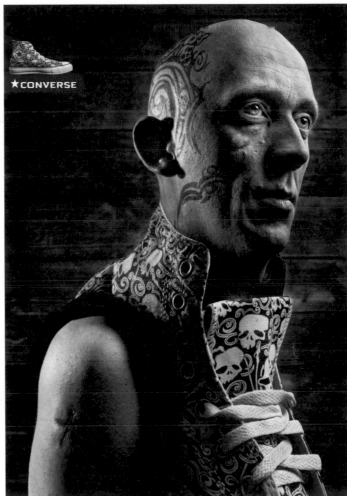

The Converse campaign presents four portraits of individuals possessed by their passion for Converse shoes. Each person represents a different lifestyle: The shoes they wear determine their characters and attitudes.

☆
Converse People *Poland*

National Award	Silver	*Art Director*	Lukasz Kotlinski
Agency	Photoby	*Copywriter*	Iza Przepiorska
Client	J.W.T. Warsaw	*Photographer*	Andrzej Dragan
Creative Director	Darek Zatorski		

A series of images of architecture in Hong Kong, one of the most densely populated places on earth.

☆
Architecture of density *Germany*

National Award....Silver	*Photographer*........Michael Wolf
Agency.................Laif Fotoreportagen	
Client ....qvest magazine	

☆
Massai *Germany*

National Award	Bronze	*Creative Director*	Armin Jochum,
Agency	BBDO Campaign		Andreas Rell
	GmbH Stuttgart	*Art Director*	Stefan Nagel,
Client	Aernout Overbeeke		Melanie Sonnenschein
	for Kamitei Foundation	*Photographer*	Aernout Overbeeke

Illustration for a children's book.

Meissen porcelain for adults only *Germany*

National Award	Gold	*Art Director*	Anje Jager
Agency	Scholz & Friends	*Copywriter*	Stephan Deisenhofer
Client	Staatliche Porzellan-Manufaktur Meissen GmbH	*Photographer*	Attila Hartwig c/o Nerger MaO
		Graphics	Melanie Fischbach
Creative Director	Martin Pross, Raphael Puettmann, Mario Gamper	*Account Executive*	Joerg Mayer, Michael Schulze

The bats *Iceland*

National Award	Gold	*Creative Director*	Halldór Baldursson
Agency	Halldór Baldursson	*Illustrator*	Halldór Baldursson
Client	Edda publishing		

The foreground shows women and men wearing Freddy clothing. Behind them, a majestic New York turns into an immense dance floor: Everywhere you look, graphic footprints indicate the dance steps.

Make a move *Italy*

National Award	Silver	*Art Director*	Federico Pepe
Agency	1861 United	*Copywriter*	Stefania Siani
Client	Freddy	*Photographer*	Pier Paolo Ferrari
Creative Director	Pino Rozzi,	*Graphics*	Federico Pepe
	Roberto Battaglia	*Post Production*	Martin Rainone

Nissan *Latvia*

National Award	Silver	*Art Director*	Inguss Krumins
Agency	f64	*Production Comp.*	f64
Client	Mcann Ericson Latvia	*Photographer*	Gatis Rozenfelds
Creative Director	Inguss Krumins		

The allegory of rabies is a modern Cerberus at the gate to Hell. This shows the heads of three animal species transmitting rabies in Central Europe.

The Mexican that never sleeps.

Mexicans *Czech Republic*

National Award ....Silver	*Art Director* ....Jaime Mandelbaum
Agency ....Kaspen Prague	*Copywriter* ....Jaime Mandelbaum
Client ....Picante	*Illustrator* ....Nina Broen
Creative Director ...Tomas Otradovec	

Rabies vaccination *Austria*

National Award ....Silver	*Creative Director* ...Toman Rom
Agency ....MedNews	*Illustrator* ....Stuart Matthews
Client ....Novartis	

Marine monsters and the gods of the ocean are forced to surrender their supremacy and fame as terrors of the deep to the unchallenged authority of the new king of the seas—Yamaha Marine.

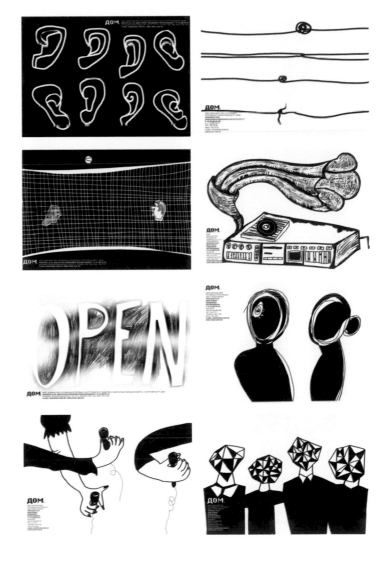

Monsters *Italy*

National Award	Gold	*Art Director*	Giorgio Cignoni
Agency	1861 United	*Copywriter*	Laura Cattaneo
Client	Yamaha Marine	*Illustrator*	Alessandro Bavari,
Creative Director	Pino Rozzi,		Direct 2 Brain
	Roberto Battaglia		

Flyers *Russia*

National Award	Gold	*Copywriter*	Cultural center DOM
Agency	Ostengruppe	*Designer*	Anna Naumova
Client	Cultural center DOM	*Illustrator*	Lisa Olshanskaya
Art Director	Anna Naumova		

International Dancing Theatre Festival.

Bloodbuster campaign: This print campaign is for a video shop in Milan that sells horror, splatter, and pulp films. The headline is "It's impossible to please everybody." The visual also suggests that not everyone will enjoy these films.

International Theatre Festival *Austria*

National Award	Silver	*Art Director*	Robert Uranitsch
Agency	Robert Uranitsch	*Photographer*	Robert Uranitsch
Client	International Dancing Theatre Festival		

Disgust *Italy*

National Award	Gold	*Art Director*	Stefano Rosselli
Agency	Leagas Delaney Italia Srl	*Copywriter*	Stefano Campora
Client	Bloodbuster	*Photographer*	LSD
Creative Director	Stefano Campora, Stefano Rosselli	*Post Production*	LSD

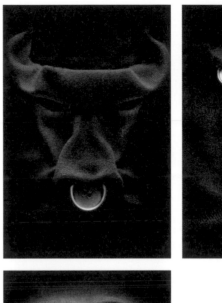

These photographs are an experimental attempt to smuggle more important ideas inside a fashion editorial. This is the author's personal comment on the world of fashion and on the economic laws governing it.

Keeps black power alive.

Stupidy *Poland*

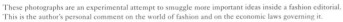

National Award	Silver	*Art Director*	Pawel Fabjanski
Agency	Photoby	*Photographer*	Pawel Fabjanski

Animals *Italy*

National Award	Gold	*Art Director*	Serena Di Bruno
Agency	D'Adda, Lorenzini, Vigorelli, BBDO	*Copywriter*	Giovanni Chiarelli
Client	Henkel	*Photographer*	Fulvio Bonavia
Creative Director	Giuseppe Mastromatteo, Luca Scotto di Carlo		

Wall mounted calendar.

This is a photo to illustrate a café located in the middle of the women's section in a department store. When you start seeing food on the shelves, you know it is time to go to Aura Cafe to have a bite to eat.

Shoes and Purses *Estonia*

National Award	Gold	*Art Director*	Kärt Villmann
Agency	Angels Advertising	*Designer*	Kärt Villmann
Client	Aura Cafe	*Photographer*	Jüri Seljamaa
Creative Director	Kärt Villmann		

Calendar *Iceland*

National Award	Silver	*Art Director*	Hildigunnur Gunnarsdottir
Agency	Hildigunnur & Snefrid	*Designer*	Hildigunnur Gunnarsdottir
Client	Hildigunnur		

This image was used inside the shops and on the advertising materials.

Photograph for advertising materials.

Monton Image Photo Summer 2005 *Estonia*

National Award	Silver	*Creative Director*	Jaanus Vahtra
Agency	Baltika AS	*Art Director*	Aet Alev
Client	Baltika AS	*Photographer*	Herkki-Erich Merila

Nora *Latvia*

National Award	Gold	*Photographer*	Oleg Zernov
Agency	Target Studio		
Client	Latvian National Theatre		

Floral stamps.

These illustrations from Hypegallery Milan are works by a group of select young artists to promote the Italian event.

Creative sphere *Italy*

National Award	Silver	*Copywriter*	Ugo Cesare Tonelli, Marco Venturelli
Agency	Publicis Srl	*Illustrator*	Federico Lorenzo Galvani
Client	HP		
Creative Director	Alasdhair Macgregor, Stefano Colombo		
Art Director	Giuba Vescovi, Marco Maccagni, Marco Cantalamessa		

Floral stamps *Iceland*

National Award	Silver	*Art Director*	Orn Smari Gislason
Agency	Nonni og Manni	*Illustrator*	Orn Smari Gislason
Client	Iceland Post		

Magazine for those who are interested in finance.

Popular Finance *Russia*

National Award....Silver   *Illustrator*..........Alexandra Bobkova
Agency................Popular Finance
Client................Popular Finance
                       magazine

O4.4
PACKAGING
Portugal: 1 gold ★
Spain: 1 nomination ☆

In a market devoid of innovative products, Pluma is born: A 100% Portuguese brand, a 100% innovative product, with sophistication and seduction.

★

Pluma *Portugal*

National Award	Gold	*Creative Director*	Rui Sampaio de Faria
Agency	Brandia Central	*Designer*	Rui Sampaio de Faria
Client	Galp	*Graphics*	José Carlos Mendes

The glass bottle labels of Sant Aniol spring water have been redesigned in order to convey a more sophisticated look. The bottles are only sold to restaurants.

☆
Glass bottles labels of Sant Aniol *Spain*

National Award	Gold	*Art Director*	Tema
Agency	Tema	*Designer*	Tema
Client	Sant Aniol	*Production Comp.*	Tema
Creative Director	Tema		

Collection of globes.

Dog in the fog label *Poland*

National Award	Silver	*Creative Director*	Iwo Zaniewski,
Agency	PZL Warsaw		Kot Przybora
	(Leo Burnett Group)	*Art Director*	Robert Rosol
Client	Kompania Piwowarska	*Designer*	Robert Rosol
	S.A.		

Geo Collection *Russia*

National Award	Silver	*Creative idea*	Alexey Yakushik,
Agency	UNIQA C.E.		Konstantin Kirillov
Client	Darcil	*Art Director*	Dmitry Valdt
		Illustrator	Dmitry Valdt

Line of packaging for various health food products.

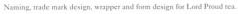

Naming, trade mark design, wrapper and form design for Lord Proud tea.

Lord Proud tea *Russia*

National Award	Silver	*Creative Director*	Grigory V. Matushin
Agency	Clëver Creative Group	*Art Director*	Larisa A. Avdoshina
Client	Dushes & Co		

Himnesk hollusta *Iceland*

National Award	Silver	*Art Director*	Orn Smari Gislason
Agency	Ó!	*Designer*	Orn Smari Gislason
Client	Himnesk hollusta		

The glossies- cover as a role model. Modern woman wants to be beautiful and healthy. The first lot was released in January 2006. According to client's information, the demand of wholesale partners for producer rose up greatly.

This is a corporate identity for a company that is dedicated to creating jewels for children. It is a logo, packaging, and general communication accomplishment.

Mermelada de lentejas (Lentil marmelade) *Spain*

National Award	Gold	*Designer*	Regina Puig
Agency	Estudi Regina Puig	*Production Comp.*	Graphic
Client	Yocary	*Photographer*	Xavi Valls
Creative Director	Regina Puig	*Illustrator*	Marta Petit

Muesli WOM *Russia*

National Award	Silver	*Art Director*	Anton Samsonov
Agency	Optima DMG	*Copywriter*	Anton Samsonov
Client	Fiesta Service	*Designer*	Dimitry Ershov
Creative Director	Anton Samsonov	*Photographer*	Alexey Petrov

Material-efficient sales packaging with an original glueless closing system for Klar, the brand of Tallinn Ceramics Factory.

Packaging for a line of Feta cheese.

Packages for series of ceramic tableware *Estonia*

National Award	Gold	*Creative Director*	Markko Karu
Agency	Velvet Design Bureau	*Art Director*	Markko Karu
Client	Tallinn Ceramics Factory	*Designer*	Markko Karu
		Photographer	Aivo Kallas

Feta cheese *Iceland*

National Award	Silver	*Art Director*	Orn Smari Gislason
Agency	Ó!	*Designer*	Orn Smari Gislason
Client	Mjolka	*Photographer*	Various

Glass bottles for promotional purpose.

"Hell" in Estonian means gentle. The ambigrammatic logo design is readable upside-down. The name can be interpreted in different ways: gentle (in Estonian), hell (in English), and light (in German).

Camper bottles *Spain*

National Award....Silver	*Art Director*.........Pablo Martín
Agency................Grafica	*Designer*.............Bárbara Castro
Client ....Camper	*Graphics*............Bárbara Castro
Creative Director....Pablo Martín	

Hell *Estonia*

National Award....Silver	*Creative Director*....Indrek Viiderfeld
Agency................Indigo Bates	*Art Director*.........Veiko Tammjärv
Client ....Puls Brewery	

Traditional and innovative; young, but with all the wisdom earned by effort. Nita expresses the personality of Priorat, an ancient land reborn with the growth of a modern vine.

Nita *Spain*

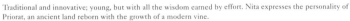

National Award	Silver	*Creative Director*	Xavier Bas
Agency	Xavier Bas Disseny	*Designer*	Gaelle Alemany
Client	Meritxell Pallejà	*Production Comp.*	Vidal Armadans

Lacplesis *Latvia*

National Award	Gold	*Art Director*	Eriks Sulcs
Agency	Brandbox	*Designer*	Eriks Sulcs,
Client	CIDO grupa		Dace Abola
Creative Director	Eriks Sulcs	*Graphics*	Eriks Sulcs

The density of a 35 year old wine becomes the main character in a labelless bottle where simplicity is the maximum expression.

Packaging for chocolate sold at the National Museum of Iceland.

Corum *Spain*

National Award	Gold	*Art Director*	Ainhoa Nagore
Agency	Lourdes	*Copywriter*	Eva Conesa
Client	Terra de Verema	*Designer*	Ainhoa Nagore
Creative Director	Eva Conesa		

Chocolate *Iceland*

National Award	Gold	*Art Director*	Snaefrid Thorsteins
Agency	Snaefrid	*Designer*	Snaefrid Thorsteins
Client	National Museum of Iceland	*Photographer*	Various

CD packaging for the band Trabant.

Trabant - Emotional *Iceland*

National Award	Gold	*Designer*	Rosa Hrund
Agency	Rósa		Kristjansdottir
Client	Trabant / 12 tónar		
Art Director	Rosa Hrund		
	Kristjansdottir		

Cosmos *Latvia*

National Award	Silver	*Production Comp.*	Parks Reklamai, Latvia
Client	Cosmos	*Photographer*	Oleg Zernov
Designer	Viesturs Ozolins,		
	Lelde Ozolina, Cosmos		

O4.5
ANY OTHER
Germany: 1 gold ★ 4 nominations ☆

Between 1936 and 1945, Sachsenhausen was used to train SS soldiers as well as to experiment with the concentration camp system. Located just outside Berlin, Sachsenhausen is now an important place of remembrance.

★

Sachsenhausen Memorial "Station Z" *Germany*   ◉

National Award	Gold	*Art Director*	Sebastian Reinhardt, Michel Weber
Agency	HG Merz Architekten Museumsgestalter	*Production Comp.*	Ingenieurgruppe Bauen, Werner Sobek Ingenieure
Client	Stiftung Brandenburgische Gedenkstätten		
Creative Director	Prof. Merz	*Graphics*	L2M3 Kommunikations Design

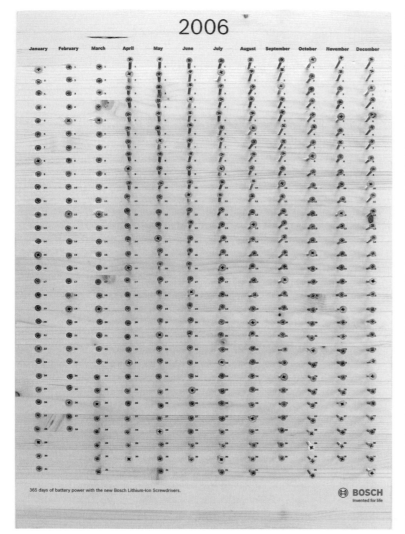

A calendar designed to celebrate the battery power of the Bosch Lithium-Ion Screwdriver 365 days a year.

☆
Bolts *Germany*

National Award	Silver	*Art Director*	Olaf Scheer
Agency	Jung von Matt AG	*Copywriter*	Sascha Hanke,
Client	Robert Bosch GmbH		Michael Okun
Creative Director	Wolf Heumann,	*Graphics*	Carolin Bastian
	Andreas Ottensmeier,		
	Ove Gley		

In Germany, Pilsner Urquell is not as well known as it should be. Due to a small media budget, they decided to create a new medium: An outdoor art exhibition.

☆
Pilsner Urquell Towel Exhibition 2005 *Germany*   ⊙

National Award	Bronze	*Creative Director*	Bert Peulecke
Agency	Oysterbay Advertising Agency	*Art Director*	Marc Isken
		Copywriter	Thomas Rendel
Client	Pilsner Urquell International Distributing GmbH	*Graphics*	Patrik Schittl, Do-Sun Robert Rhee
		Illustrator	Nicolai Heymann

This is a daily tear-off calendar developed for the FC Schalke 04 Supporters Club.
Every day on the calendar scoreboard stands for another goal against the archrival Dortmund.

☆
The Soccer Fan Calendar *Germany*

National Award	Shortlist	*Art Director*	Marcin Baba
Agency	Scholz & Friends	*Copywriter*	Dennis Lueck
Client	FC Schalke 04 Su-pporters Club e.V.	*Production Comp.*	Metagate GmbH, Hamburg
Creative Director	Suze Barrett, Tobias Holland		

Twin concept: Two almost identical issues published at the same time.

"We are the Pope." The day after Pope Benedict XVI was elected, Europe's biggest newspaper, BILD, printed these simple words on the front page.

☆
Zwillingsheft/Twins Issue *Germany*

National Award	Gold	*Art Director*	Mirko Borsche
Agency	Süddeutsche Zeitung Magazin Verlagsgesellschaft	*Copywriter*	Christian Gottwalt
		Graphics	Daniel Bognar,
Client	Süddeutsche Zeitung Magazin	*Illustrator*	Anne Blaschke, Marion Blomeyer

Wir sind Papst! *Germany*

National Award	Gold	*Art Director*	Patrick Markowski
Agency	Axel Springer AG	*Copywriter*	Georg Streiter
Client	Kai Diekmann	*Production Comp.*	BILD
Creative Director	Veronika Illmer, Markus Ackermann		

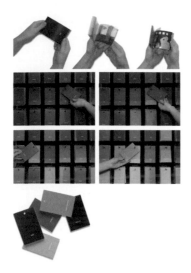

This project was a response to an unusual briefing: To attract the public but to avoid the sector's habitual lures like big slogans and photos of the product. The goal was to create an empty communicative space.

As one of the main sponsors for the 25th edition of Moda Lisboa, Nokia wanted to optimize its presence by promoting the new and sophisticated model 8800.

Layetana Flipbook *Spain*

National Award	Silver	*Creative Director*	Xavier Mora
Agency	BAG.Disseny	*Art Director*	Sandra Compte
Client	Layetana Real Estate		

Nokia Mirror Box *Portugal*

National Award	Gold	*Art Director*	Filipe Figueiredo
Agency	Brandia Central	*Copywriter*	André Freitas
Client	Nokia	*Designer*	Jorge Trindade
Creative Director	Gonçalo Cardoso		

Dynamic car presentation of the VW Fox

As one of the main sponsors for the 25th edition of Moda Lisboa, Nokia wanted to promote its new L'Amour collection and simultaneously be in touch with the year's theme—black.

VW Fox hotel remodelling *Germany*

National Award	Silver	*Production Comp.*	Eventlabs gmbh
Agency	Eventlabs gmbh	*Photographer*	Die Photodesigner
Client	Volkswagen AG	*Illustrator*	21 international groups of designers and artists

Nokia Secret Garden *Portugal*

National Award	Silver	*Art Director*	Sonia Azenha Henriques
Agency	Brandia Central	*Copywriter*	Nuno Moura
Client	Nokia	*Designer*	Jorge Trindade
Creative Director	Gonçalo Cardoso		

The central element of the exhibition was the Medienwolke (Media Cloud), a display screen which hovered above the heads of visitors. Connected interactively to a radio station, the Media Cloud allowed radio programmers to feed images and text into the sequences.

Pylons for mobile networks.

Medienwolke *Germany*

National Award	Gold	*Art Director*	Birgit Vogel, Christoph Rohrer, Kerstin Arleth
Agency	KMS Team / Schmidhuber+Partner		
Client	o2 Germany	*Designer*	Birgit Vogel, Julia Romeifl
Creative Director	Michael Keller, Susanne Schmidhuber	*Graphics*	Birgit Vogel, Julia Romeifl
		Tech. Director	Wahan Mechitarian

Baeumlein vom Amt/Pylons *Germany*

National Award	Gold	*Art Director*	Mirko Borsche
Agency	Süddeutsche Zeitung Magazin Verlagsgesellschaft	*Photographer*	Robert Voit
		Graphics	Daniel Bognar, Anne Blaschke, Marion Blomeyer
Client	Süddeutsche Zeitung Magazin		

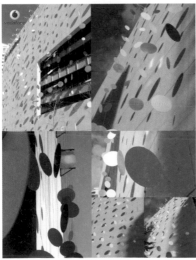

A drape that symbolized snow falling was placed in front. This drape, made up of circular mirrors, was sensitive to wind, creating dynamic and interesting movements.

Dynamic car presentation of the VW Fox.

Vodafone Christmas Decoration *Portugal*

National Award	Silver	*Creative Director*	Akis Konstantinidis
Agency	Brandia Central	*Designer*	Antonio Neu,
Client	Vodafone		Vasco Cotta,
			Paula Lopes

VW Fox Launch *Germany*

National Award	Gold	*Production Comp.*	Eventlabs gmbh
Agency	Eventlabs gmbh	*Photographer*	Die Photodesigner
Client	Volkswagen AG	*Illustrator*	21 international
			groups of designers
			and artists

Hotspot was intended to be a heater in Galp's portfolio to initiate a new generation of Galp Gas accessories. With this generation, innovation expresses itself in all the stages of development.

The idea was to create a typeface that in the Latin alphabet emulates Georgian script and its alphabet - Mkhedruli.

Hot Spot *Portugal*

National Award	Gold	*Creative Director*	Rui Sampaio de Faria
Agency	Brandia Central	*Designer*	Teresa Costa Reis
Client	Galp	*Graphics*	José Carlos Mendes

Pump *Latvia*

National Award	Silver	*Art Director*	Liene Drazniece
Agency	Lowe Age	*Designer*	Liene Drazniece

Mobile selling post.

Direct mail for the dairy producer Mjolka, announcing the opening of the company. NB - milk bottles are normally not used in Iceland.

Posto de Venda Móvel *Portugal*

National Award	Silver	*Designer*	Ricardo Silva,
Agency	N Design Integrado		Pedro Leal de Faria
Client	Unilever - Olá	*Production Comp*	Guliver
Creative Director	Ricardo Silva		

The milkman *Iceland*

National Award	Gold	*Creative Director*	Orn Smari Gislason
Agency	Ó!	*Designer*	Orn Smari Gislason
Client	Mjolka		

The installation of 30 oversized replicas of the Brockhaus Encyclopedia was a tribute to the knowledge they contain. In addition, the installation played a recorded performance from each of the different volumes.

Y is Publico's newspaper supplement with the themes of theatre, cinema, and music. With a very low budget and other kinds of weekly "problems," the company must innovate and use its creativity.

Knowledge of the World - Phonetic Opera *Germany*

National Award	Silver	*Designer*	Johannes Milla,
Agency	Milla und Partner		Stefan Morgenstern
	Agentur & Ateliers	*Construction*	Weimer Steinberg Vega
Client	Bibliographisches Institut	*Idea*	Milla und Partner,
	& F.A. Brockhaus AG		BBDO Campaign,
Creative Director	Johannes Milla		Stuttgart
Composer	Theo Bleckmann	*Director*	Martin Wagner
Project Manager	Marion Kerckhoff	*Production*	Marc Feigenspan

Y *Portugal*

National Award	Silver	*Art Director*	Hugo Pinto
Agency	Y	*Designer*	Hugo Pinto,
Client	Publico		Ana Carvalho
Creative Director	Hugo Pinto	*Illustrator*	Hugo Pinto

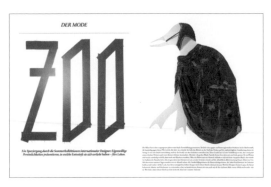

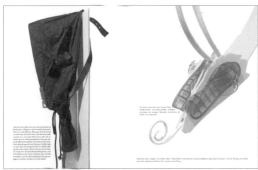

This limited-edition coffee table book is a new form of integrated communication. It is based on the TV spot "Linesmen" for Coca-Cola.

Unusual animals and people, made from styrofoam, were dressed with fashionable clothes and accessories.

Heimspiel *Germany*

National Award	Silver	*Art Director*	Nathanael Hamon
Agency	International Berlin	*Copywriter*	Bertram Job
Client	Coca-Cola GmbH	*Photographer*	Steffen Jagenburg
Creative Director	Todd Schulz	*Account director*	Gisela Widmer

Modezoo/Fashion zoo *Germany*

National Award	Gold	*Art Director*	Mirko Borsche
Agency	Süddeutsche Zeitung Magazin Verlagsgesellschaft	*Photographer*	Bela Borsodi, Paul Graves
Client	Süddeutsche Zeitung Magazin	*Graphics*	Daniel Bognar, Anne Blaschke, Marion Blomeyer

The client wanted not only every issue of the magazine to have a distinct design, but also copies of the same issue. Each copy includes original work from diverse artists. This issue contains: stickers from 28 artists, rubber seals from 17 artists, and engravings from 17 artists.

Concept, design and packaging of Euroset brand book. This brand book shows in an amusing way how managers are supposed to deal with clients.

Blank 06 - Trayectos *Spain*

National Award	Silver	*Art Director*	Pedro Moreno Tirapu
Agency	Dos click	*Copywriter*	Santiago Ortiz Herrera
Client	BLANKMGZ	*Designer*	Aurora Sánchez Pérez
Creative Director	Salvador Cuenca Fromesta	*Graphics*	Felipe Medrano Rubio

Useful thing *Russia*

National Award	Gold	*Creative Director*	Ruslana Kharitonova
Agency	Znamenka Creative Agency	*Art Director*	Anton Busygin
Client	Euroset	*Copywriter*	Yakov Krivitsky
		Designer	Alexey Fedonin

This annual business report for Switzerland's largest antique shop was printed on a dust cloth.

The Virgin Atlantic Upper Class Suite is a patented system, which provides passengers with an innovative piece of furniture for sitting and sleeping on, in the form of a chair and a separate bed. The aim of the design was to offer flight passengers similar comfort to that of a luxury lounge or a hotel.

Annual Report *Switzerland*

National Award	Silver	*Art Director*	Chantal Heimo
Agency	Wirz / BBDO	*Copywriter*	John Leuppi
Client	Zürcher Brockenhaus	*Graphics*	Britta Egger
Creative Director	Matthias Freuler		

Upper Class Suite *United Kingdom*

National Award	Silver	*Client*	VAA
Agency	Virgin Atlantic Airways, Agency used - PearsonLloyd's	*Creative Director*	Joe Ferry

Epilogue

EUROPEAN STUDENT OF THE YEAR

Austria: 1 gold ★

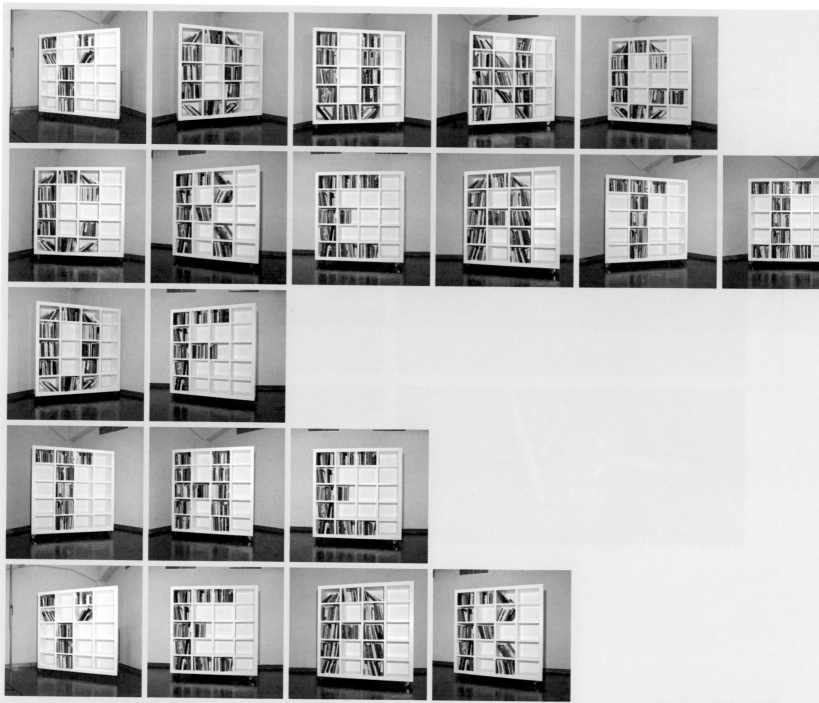

YOUNG CREATIVE OF THE YEAR

Austria: 1 gold ★

"Please don't! I know, you simply want to get rid of people like me as fast as possible. But as long as hunger, war and poverty exist in countries like mine, many of us leave their home and come here in the hope for a better life. Please don't turn away. Support the fight of the European Union against poverty in the world."

Please Don't *Austria*

National Award	Junior of the Year
Creative	Felix Fenz
Category	Interactive Media
Company	Wien Nord Pilz

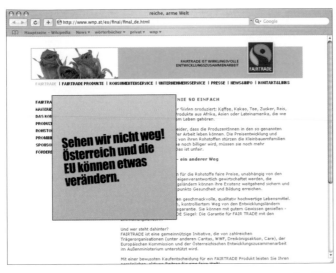

Eltipodromo (The Typodrom) *Spain*

National Award	Laus Estudiants 06
	Grand Laus
Creative	Carolina Montpart
	Algarte
Category	Graphic Design

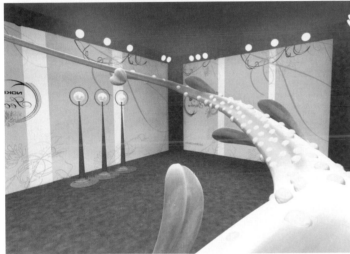

Nokia Collection *Portugal*

National Award....Young Creative
Creatives ....Gonçalo Cardoso,
　　　　　　　　Sónia Azehna,
　　　　　　　　Nuno Mura,
　　　　　　　　Jorge Trindade

Category ....New & Mixed Media
Company ....Brandia Central

"11 Freunde" Football-Poems *Germany*

National Award... Junior of the Year
Creative ....Dennis May
Category............Print: Magazine
College ....Jung von Matt

I'm lactose intolerant.

every intolerance is a disease

Lactose *Poland*

National Award	Young Creative Winner Poland
Creatives	Katarzyna Nowacka, Tomasz Zielinski
Category	Print
Company	TBWA/Warsaw

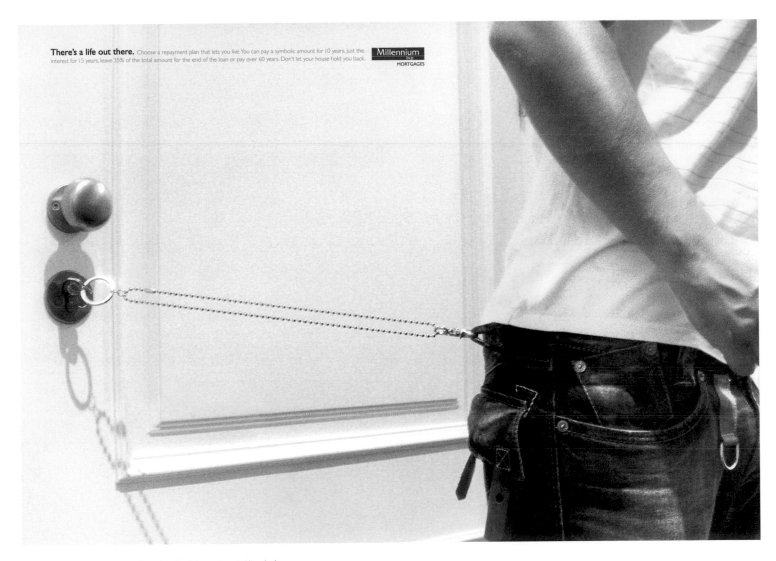

There's a life out there. Choose a repayment plan that lets you live. You can pay a symbolic amount for 10 years, just the interest for 15 years, leave 35% of the total amount for the end of the loan or pay over 60 years. Don't let your house hold you back.

Millennium bcp MORTGAGES

Millennium BCP Mortgages. There's a life out there. Don't let your house hold you back.

Chained *Portugal*

National Award ....Young Creative
Creatives ....Juliano Bertoldi,
                       Hellington Vieira
Category ....Newspaper Advertising
Company ....BBDO Portugal

Art Directors

Clients

Creative Directors

Designers

D.o.P. / Cinematographers

Film Directors

Various

Schools

Students

Young Creatives

THE FINESSE OF HP'S NEW PIGMENT INKS

MORGAN BY HP.

HP Photosmart Pro B9180

In Patrick Morgan's world work has to be printed quickly and correctly. Which is why he appreciates the accuracy and speed of HP's new pigmented ink technology. HP offer a range of dye and pigment-based ink printers led by the new HP Photosmart Pro B9180, each putting superb performance within reach of all artists and graphic designers.

BY PATRICK MORGAN. AND VICE VERSA.

"Speed and accuracy are crucial, especially in fashion work. The new HP printers' pigment-based ink technology prints faster yet still gives you precise colour control for vibrant, consistent colour. Every print turns out good enough for a gallery."

Patrick M

HP BY MORGAN.

Print sizes range from 13" to 24", with gallery-quality prints fade-resistant for up to 200 years.* And HP's vast range of durable Fine Art Medias from canvas to heavy Smooth Fine Art Papers guarantees even better results. To find out more and order your print sample go to www.hp.com/go/graphicprint

invent

Spa for You and Your Paper!

• r e l i e v e s   t h e   s t r e s s • b r i n g s   t o   h a r m o n y • e n c o d e s   f o r   s u c c e s s

Reliable print!   JELGAVAS TIPOGRĀFIJA

Printing house Jelgavas tipogrāfija • 27 Raiņa str. , Jelgava, LATVIA • phone: +371 3024501 • fax: +371 3022927 • jt@jt.lv • www.jt.lv

SHOOT BE SMASHING EXPERIENCE
www.vilks.com

The biggest production house in the Baltic with more than 10 years experience in commercials and music videos

• **hamburg**

• **new york**
spring 2007

• **barcelona**

www. **gloss** -postproduction.com

creative retouching | look development | cgi

"REIGN" martini glass design by EVA ZEISEL

BOMBAY ✦ SAPPHIRE
INSPIRED

UNA COMBINACIÓN DE 10 ELEMENTOS BOTÁNICOS Y UN PROCESO ÚNICO
DE ELABORACIÓN MEDIANTE "INFUSIÓN DE VAPOR" CONSIGUEN DAR A
BOMBAY SAPPHIRE SU CARACTERÍSTICO SABOR: SUAVE Y EQUILIBRADO.

The Annual
of Annuals
was typeset
with Book Book

Book Book is a font specifically
designed in 2006 by Mucho for
ADC*E, using more than 300 books.
Furniture design: Glòria de Pallejà
Photography: Nacho Alegre

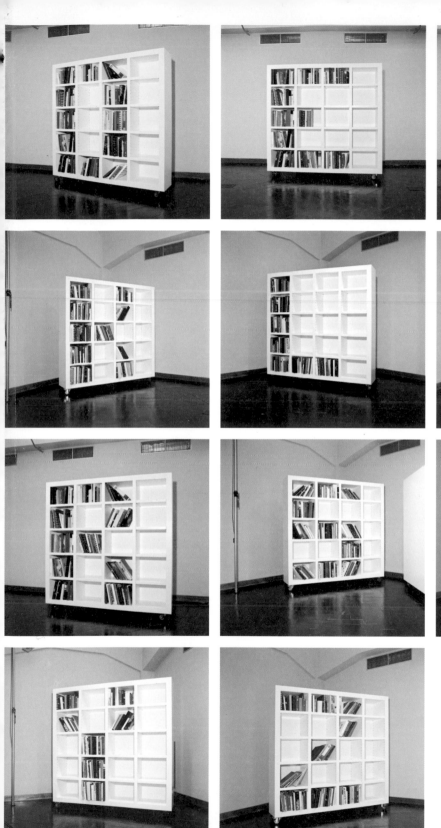